D1107175

DISCARD

Strangers and
Pilgrims

# NORWEGIAN UNIVERSITIES PRESS

Distribution offices

*NORWAY*

OSLO 3

*UNITED KINGDOM*

16, PALL MALL
LONDON S.W.1

# Strangers and Pilgrims

## AN ESSAY ON THE METAPHOR
## OF JOURNEY

BY

GEORG ROPPEN

AND

RICHARD SOMMER

NORWEGIAN UNIVERSITIES PRESS

# NORWEGIAN STUDIES IN ENGLISH
(formerly Oslo Studies in English)

## No. 11

*Editorial Board:*

© The Norwegian Research Council for Science and the Humanities 1964
(Norges almenvitenskapelige forskningsråd)
*Section: A. 603—8. T.*

Printed in Norway by John Grieg A.s., Bergen

These all died in faith, not having received the promises, but having seen them afar off, and were persuaded of them, and embraced them, and confessed that they were strangers and pilgrims on the earth.

*Hebrews* xi, 13

# CONTENTS

# ACKNOWLEDGMENTS

This book is a trans-Atlantic enterprise, and is dedicated to its chief mentors on either side of the ocean: Mrs. Eva S. Jerome of Minneapolis, U.S.A.; and Professor A. H. Winsnes of Oslo, Norway.

The idea for the book grew out of a conversation with Professor Paulus Svendsen of Oslo University.

The collaboration between the two authors was made possible, first by a Fulbright grant bringing the one to Harvard, then by an American-Scandinavian Fellowship bringing the other to Oslo. To both these institutions, and universities, the book owes its existence.

The authors wish to acknowledge the indispensable aid, in the preparation of the chapters on Homer and Virgil, of Mr. Charles Paul Segal of Harvard University, whose suggestions and scepticism were alike invaluable and based upon a high standard of scholarly integrity; germinal ideas for the section on Chaucer were drawn from lectures by Professor Samuel H. Monk of the University of Minnesota; and the authors are indebted to Professor E. A. Havelock and Mr. Michael Butler, both of Harvard University, for their lectures on Virgil.

The Norwegian author wishes to thank in particular Mrs. Peggy Quist-Hansen of Bergen for her kind help in reading Part Two of the manuscript and suggesting improvements in language.

For permission to quote copyright material, the authors wish to thank Mrs. W. B. Yeats for 'Sailing to Byzantium' and 'Byzantium' (from *Collected Poems of W. B. Yeats*) and for an extract from *A Vision*; and Mrs. J. W. Beach for a quotation from *The Concept of Nature in Nineteenth Century English Poetry* by Joseph Warren Beach.

G. R. R. S.

# PREFACE

It is the very complexity of the metaphor of the journey, as it appears in western literature, which determines its interest for the student of literary theory. Not only is it an image employed in the sense in which every metaphorical image functions, for the momentary exploration of a meaning or the relation of a group of interconnected meanings through the terms of an implied comparison; it is more: it ordinarily relates and subordinates a whole series of such images to the control of two organizing elements, space and time. It is, in other words, the metaphor of narration, of duration, extension, and purpose. Space and time operate in the metaphor under the control of a single element, a purpose or teleological focus. The traveller in his progress observes a sequence of images arranged along the spatial and temporal course of that progress. Sometimes, as we shall see in the *Odyssey*, the temporal arrangement is the more significant; sometimes, as in the *Aeneid*, it is the spatial, geographical sequence of the encountered images which carries the greater weight of the poet's intention; and both arrangements function simultaneously to organize the meaning of Dante's massive poem. Yet in every case these arrangements are subject to the nature of the poem's ultimate end, the traveller's destination. Within the terms of this metaphor, then, at least in its traditional form, imagery will ideally yield a three-fold indication of meaning: (1) In its static representation; allegorical pageants function mainly in this way —see, for example, *Purgatorio* XXXII. (2) In its dynamic relations, interactive or simply causal, with or upon other imagery; this is particularly evident in the *Faerie Queene*, where several heroes encounter allegorical enemies first as relatively static features of the landscape through which they pass, later as 'mobile units', so to speak, of evil. (3) In its purposive, hierarchical aspect, its character as sign-post, pointing the True Way or implying it by pointing in another manifestly false direction; the test question here is, why did the poet conceive that this image or metaphorical episode should have to *precede* the traveller's attainment of his ultimate destination?

This, in the ruthlessly compact fashion necessary to most prefatory remarks, is the character of the traditional metaphor, structurally perhaps the most complex and capacious in the history of the conventions of literature. Because of the way in which these three elements correspond to the three fundamental human concerns—(1) the intrinsic nature of man and inanimate substance; (2) society and ethical organization; and (3) the final purposes of existence and consciousness—it will be small occasion for wonder that the metaphor has lent itself well to great and comprehensive formulations of religious belief in literature; has, indeed, been almost exclusively employed to this end in pagan and Christian worlds alike. Depending upon the age and upon our own tolerance of vision, the Journey to Life, Empire, or God—as they are respectively viewed by Homer, Virgil, and Dante—is the projection of a single disposition of man: his adjustment to the unknown, the unrealized, and the untamed.

The first part of this book is concerned with the definition and the analysis of the traditional metaphor. It is consequently divided into two sections: the first of these presents, through examination of the *Odyssey* and the *Aeneid*, the two archetypal forms into which the poetic journey may be cast; the second section explores the central problem which the metaphor has posed throughout the history of its use: the tension existing between the experienced events of the journey and its controlling destination, the discrepancy between the concretely phenomenalistic and the ideational aspects of the journey. The separated concerns of these two sections are really one question, and we must ask the reader to pardon any abrupt or arbitrary moves we have made in the bewildering business of disentangling a unity from itself; we are already uncomfortably aware how many and how abrupt they are. We cannot claim, in any sense, to have written an exhaustive or continuous 'history' of the metaphor which more than any other has snared and conveyed the wondering restlessness of man. We can only claim to have suggested here, to have remarked there. It is only upon its germinal powers that such an account as this can hope to stand.

In Part Two our aim has been to examine the uses of the travel metaphor in some representative English poems of the nineteenth and twentieth centuries. While these will be seen to adhere to the basic types explored in Part One, they nevertheless depart widely from earlier conceptions, and we shall therefore be more concerned with their individual characteristics than with ties to tradition. For this reason a close reading of the texts will be necessary.

To offer, first, a broad general distinction, one may say that two things happened of great consequence to the modern poetic journey. On the one hand, there was the spiritual dissolution of the nineteenth century which shattered ancient beliefs and destinations and sent the poets on uneasy quests to rediscover these or to find new ones. On the other hand, there were the secular and materialistic systems of value gaining upon an increasingly philistine society uncongenial to the poet and yet making claims on him to sing its ideals or mend its ills. The alienation of the poet which found its culminating image in T. S. Eliot's *Waste Land* is already felt in Wordsworth, and we observe it grow more bitter and explicit with the generations. Exile, in its widest sense, is the basic theme common to the seven poems we have chosen. Common to all of them is also the idea of the journey as an inevitable and fruitful quest, and since the old landmarks as well as the traditional goals were now—to a large extent—denied the poets, it is the more important to examine, in detail, their efforts to solve their spiritual problems through the formal medium of the journey.

The formal problems which arose, partly from the loss of time-honoured teleological designs, partly from the loss of traditional iconography, had to be solved in terms of the unique poetic perception. But this hard necessity offered also a kind of freedom congenial to the metaphor. In the modern symbolic journey, like *The Rime of the Ancient Mariner* or *Sailing to Byzantium*, there is unlimited freedom in the treatment of the correlations between traveller, incidents and landscape, and consequently unlimited scope for symbolic representation.

All this bears, clearly, on the individual character of the modern poetic journey. Its lack of teleology deprives it of the completeness which gave the traditional journey such an aesthetically satisfactory and balanced structure. Yet the loss is made up by a greater imaginative freedom and a heightened poetic intensity derived in part from the poet's lonely struggle with despair, in part from his struggle with form. The seven poems chosen will show, we hope, that the struggle was not in vain.

# PART ONE

## *The Traditional Metaphor*

by

RICHARD SOMMER

# I

# THE JOURNEY

Poets have claimed many immediate motives for undertaking literary journeys for themselves or their heroes—escape, exile, the quest, the longing for home, a desire to explore the unknown. These are a few of the many categories into which we might divide our vast subject. But we may suspect the profundity of such classification; we may make endless additions to the list, indicating that it can be neither exhaustive nor descriptive of truly categorical differences in various poems of travel. Such a list is not useful to the reader as an analytic, probative instrument. At the risk of falling into new pitfalls, therefore, we shall approach the great body of poetry at our disposal through categories derived not from primary, but from teleological, causes. We shall consider the poetry less in terms of ostensible 'reasons' for embarking, and more in terms of the way in which the literary traveller regards the destination of his journey, the character of the sensibility with which he approaches his object. There appear to be two such archetypal sensibilities at work in the traditional metaphors of travel. One or the other may predominate, or both occur in combination.

The first of these stems from an impulse toward renewal, restoration, rejuvenation. When the metaphor is specifically and seriously religious in direction, this impulse tends to represent the *personal* expectations of belief, whether Christian or otherwise. The journey toward God is here regarded in terms of the renovation of self, life renewed, salvation and immortality granted. The journey away from God, in so far as it is undertaken for the expiation of guilt, is of this type, since what is sought is the renewal of a former state of innocence.

The great archetype of this regenerative impulse in Western literature is the *Odyssey*. As we shall see in the discussion following, it is ruled in its action by a cyclical concept of time, and its episodes are reminiscent of ancient rituals of a rejuvenative character, which were recurrent concomitants of certain critical points in the agricultural calendar. These rituals were intended to complete one cycle of time, and begin the cycle anew, whether it was a cycle of seasons or an initiatory ceremony in which the neophyte re-enacted birth in order to cross the boundary from one portion of his life to another.

From the *Odyssey* we may also derive the observation that often a destination which is rejuvenative or restorative in character is in a sense no actual destination at all; it is merely the beginning of things again. Odysseus' journey does not end in the poem: he leaves Penelope at once to greet his father, set up an expiatory altar to Poseidon, and then, according to extra-Homeric traditions, engage in a whole new series of adventures.

The second type of sensibility which seems to operate in forming a destination in the travel-metaphor, is concerned with a whole complex of closely related ideas. In part, it is an impulse after unity of knowledge, or understanding; in this respect it is, very simply, the product of man's desire to make sense out of his world, to make the disparate elements of spirit and experience cohere. (We shall find this the predominant feature of the Victorian poetic journeys.) Another related aspect is what we may call an impulse toward social, rather than intellectual, order. In its more salient forms, this impulse tends to equate with the ethical manifestations of society and religion. Both aspects take as the natural form of their object an image of the city or commonwealth, beginning perhaps with Plato's civic parable of the soul, or with the Biblical metaphors from which St. Augustine derived his *Civitas Dei*.

When the image of a city appears either as a metaphorical or a literal feature of the journey, it can be treated in either of two ways. Either the city represents a social and spiritual order conceived as adequate or as promising to be so, and the hero makes a journey into the society it localizes, or towards the creation of such a society; or, on the other hand, he makes a journey of transcendence and rejection, *out* of the city—which is conceived as an imperfect or inadequate order—toward a greater or more perfect or more comprehensive order. And yet both the society-builder and the exile, whether his flight is enforced or freely chosen, exhibit a personal relation to society. The same polarity of concern exists in them both: whether or not to view the society to which they are bound as the embodiment of the highest or most possible species of order.

We may take as the prototype of this impulse another great epic of the classical world, Virgil's *Aeneid*. Here the hero is a refugee dispossessed of a former order of life, embodied in the doomed city of Troy, who wanders in search of another social and spiritual order with which to supplant it. Troy is, to use Bunyan's phrase, a City of Destruction. It is presented to us from the first as a place overwhelmed by the treachery and unpredictable violence not only of the Greeks, but of the great gods themselves. The images in Book II of Troy's downfall portray almost without exception the disorders of mind and human relationships. It is because Troy is unfitted for the simple, quiet carrying-on of life so beautifully depicted in Virgil's *Georgics*, that Aeneas must set out to found another city where human life and labor can be fruitfully resumed and take its expected rewards under the aegis of order and peace.[1] The ashes of Troy are too deep to be built upon, but before Aeneas and his companions is the prospect of Rome, both an actual place and 'a spiritual city.'[2]

Before we pass on to discussions of the *Odyssey* and the *Aeneid* as representative of the two impulses, together with brief accounts of other works under each heading, we must warn the reader of one error to which he is liable. He may find that we say relatively little about travelling in itself, and that what might be regarded as an inordinate amount of time is spent upon wayside episodes, people, and human struggles apparently unrelated to the dreary process of plodding down a road or rowing a ship. Several good reasons for this mode of treatment will gradually become apparent, but one of them must be explained in advance: it is that the nineteenth-century attention to the journey for its own sake and in itself has few earlier counterparts. Odysseus, for example, is worn down and aged in his travels not by their duration or length, but by the episodes that befall him: the storm or shipwreck instigated by a god, the escape from a monster. This leap of attention from episode to episode occurs because ancient man, like the modern primitive, did not conceive of space or time as homogeneous or continuous;[3] he understood the space and time through which he travelled always in terms of destination-points and particular adventures which had emotional or religious importance for him.[4] What existed in the interstices between these 'points of interest' did not concern him; we may observe that although time between episodes is sometimes measured in the *Odyssey*, the measurements[5]—in nines and sevens—are numbers with shreds of mystic and cultic significance still clinging to them,[6] and are perhaps best interpreted as meaning 'many days' or 'few' or 'a while'. We will be dealing with important exceptions to this in the following pages, but the observation holds good in general application. Thus, to take another example, Aeneas' characterization of his fellow-travellers as 'socii ... passi graviora' (*Aen.* I. 198-9) is to be translated in as specific and concrete a way as possible, as 'companions ... having suffered heavier *things*' or experiences or evils; a plurality of discrete episodes is the meaning intended. The more recent examples of eighteenth-century picaresque and quixotic novels —Smollett's *Roderick Random* comes to mind—should be enough to indicate that, until close to the nineteenth century, most of the literature of travel retained this episodic character. Before that time, the journey was treated less as an experience in itself, and more as a formal arrangement of adventures in literature; we shall deal with it accordingly.

1.

> *Men die because they cannot join the beginning to the end.*
>
> —Alcmeon of Croton

Despite the great significance of Odysseus' achievement in visiting and returning from the Grove of Persephone as a mortal and yet-living man, and despite the fact that all the rest of his adventures group themselves with a startling symmetry around this central point in the epic,[1] the episode in Book XI remains curiously diffuse and non-climactic. Homer's Circe explains it as a necessary visit—which it is not[2]—to obtain Teiresias' prophecy, yet this office is fulfilled almost immediately, leaving three quarters of the book to trail behind as best they can. Yet one encounter takes up more lines than those with either Teiresias or Achilles: it is the meeting between Odysseus and Agamemnon which takes place after the so-called Catalogue of Heroines.[3] The appearance of Agamemnon climaxes a series of references in the early books of the *Odyssey* to his murder by Aegisthous and Clytemnestra, the former his usurper and member of a rival branch of the same family,[4] the latter his wife and first cousin to Penelope.[5] Athena, Nestor, and Menelaus all draw the parallels between Agamemnon and Odysseus, Orestes and Telemachus, and the implication is that the *fate* of Agamemnon is comparable to that of Odysseus, and that the poet has deliberately introduced the terms of the comparison.

Nor can there any longer be much serious question that the story of Agamemnon's death originally referred to a ritual event, probably repeated at regular intervals, or to a radical change in the character of that event worthy of being recorded in the mythological annals of an ancient people. Elements of the plot are familiar enough to the anthropologist who does not insist on looking the other way: the old king is disposed of by his queen and an outsider who takes the throne to rule by matrilinear right; the avenger, however, is the son of the old king, claiming patri-linear right to the crown. It is significant, however, that the *Odyssey* relates only this much of the story, and makes no mention of the punishment for matricide exacted from Orestes by the Erinnyes; the young rebel did not escape from the certainly older matrilinear order scot-free, though the *Eumenides* of Aeschylus makes it quite clear that his insurrection, approved (and this is worth remembering) by Athena, was to have been ultimately successful.

In this light the conversation between Odysseus and Aga-memnon takes on new meaning. The parallel existing between them is strengthened when Agamemnon, understandably vehe-ment, warns Odysseus: 'Never be too kind even to your wife. Never tell her all you have in your mind; you may tell something, but keep something to yourself. However, *you* will not be mur-dered by your wife, Odysseus. She is full of intelligence, and her heart is sound, your prudent and modest Penelopeia.'[6] Penelope is never in the *Odyssey* obtrusively other than this, yet Agamemnon has raised the question, and proceeds to deepen the shadow he has cast upon her integrity by advising Odysseus to bring his ship to the shore of his native land secretly, not openly, 'for there is no longer any faith in women.'[7]

Let us stop for a moment and see in exactly what terms the situations of Agamemnon and Odysseus are parallel. Both are kings. One has been murdered—clad in special robe, Aeschylus tells us, and killed by his wife and usurper-successor at the sacrificial altar he had approached on a crimson carpet designed, we are informed, for the tread of gods, not men.[8] The other is in danger of such a death at the hands, perhaps of his wife, and certainly of men who aspire to the kingship of Ithaca by marriage to her.[9] Agamemnon fought nine years at Troy and returned home in the tenth. Following this, Odysseus wandered for nine years and in the tenth year (the twentieth year all told) is returning to face the same crisis. This is the setting of his epic triumph. What remains for us to establish is the character of that triumph, for which we must turn to other quarters.

The forces that converge upon Odysseus' victory and dictate its nature have their beginnings so far back in the pre-history of Eurasian primitive culture that they will never be open to more than educated speculation. A few things we can be relatively sure of, the first being that in Eurasia generally, the first religions centered about a Goddess rather than a god,[10] and the reason of that worship was to promote the fertility, which the Goddess embodied, of fields and flocks and the tribe. Several writers have insisted that the eminence of the female deity in this early age reflects a similar state of affairs in the structure of the primitive societies, that, in short, matriarchy preceded patriarchy in the general development of man. We cannot be sure of this either way; whether women in ancient Eurasia were in positions of political, social, economic power over their men-folk or not, it cannot be disputed that they were numinal centers, with their strange discharges of blood, their mysterious creative powers, for the magical and religious attention of the tribe. Women were objects of veneration and fear, sources of life—and of death as well. In the early stages the Goddess, as a projection of this numinal power, seems to have reigned alone. Later, perhaps when the role of the male in producing children had been recognized and cultic practice had been adjusted to accommodate the fact, a consort God appears at the side of the Goddess and shares a portion of her prestige, suffering seasonal death and rebirth under the loving and deadly shadow of his powerful protectress.[11] The festivals of the religious pattern involved center about a 'mimic marriage of the powers of vegetation'[12]—the Goddess and God, emergent from a sacred tribal queen and her chosen king—designed to increase by imitating the fertility of flocks and crops. It has been suggested that Odysseus shows marks of having at one stage in the development of his story been one of these Dying Gods or, as Thomson suggests, a solar Year-

Spirit, an Eniautos-Daimon associated with Hermes or Poseidon Hippios or with Helios,[13] who is 'thought to die and come to life again, or to be obscured for a season only to reappear in renewed splendour.'[14] As Thomson explains, 'Eniautos means, not so much a measured space of time, as the completed cycle of the seasons, at the moment of its completion.'[15] This Daimon, then, is more in the nature of a regularly recurring 'momentary deity,' to use a phrase promulgated by Cassirer, a god who becomes real at certain critical junctures in the primitive calendar, who gains a sudden though regular importance in what we know as 'rituals of passage'. The adventures of Odysseus, occurring as they do in sudden episodic concentration with only the most perfunctory attention paid to interstitial time-lapses, show marked resemblance to this pattern. Aside from the obvious fact, however, that the Homeric Odysseus is not a god but a human being and emphatically says as much several times in the course of the epic,[16] his simple identification with the dying Eniautos-Daimon raises immediate difficulties: Odysseus does not die in the poem and is not absent for a single seasonal cycle but for twenty. Many traces of the pattern remain, it is true, and we contend that it remains one of the principle determinants of the form of this epic, yet the pattern by itself, distinct from the Homeric energy and cast of opinion exerted upon it, is not sufficient to explain the full scope of the story's final form.

The most curious and significant feature of the worship of the Goddess and her consort appears to have been a cultic practice parallel to the death of the God: in so far as he was considered a deity or embodied divine characteristics, the sacred king of the tribe was ritually murdered—whether in actuality or effigy may scarcely now be distinguished—or deposed when his powers began to fail.[17] Frazer himself, whose work on this savage rite remains the most exhaustive, should be allowed to explain the reasons for it:

> People feared that if they allowed the man-god to die of sickness or old age, his divine spirit might share the weakness of its bodily tabernacle, or perhaps perish altogether, thereby entailing the most serious dangers on the whole body of his worshippers who looked to him as their stay and support. Whereas, by putting him to death while he was yet in full vigour of body and mind, they hoped to catch his sacred spirit uncorrupted by decay and to transfer it in that state

to his successor. Hence it has been customary in some countries, first, to require that kings should be of unblemished body and unimpaired mind, and second, to kill them as soon as they begin to break up through age and infirmity. A more stringent application of these principles led in other places to a practice of allowing the divine king or human god to live and reign only for a fixed period, after which he was inexorably put to death. The time of grace granted to limited monarchs of this sort has varied from several years to one year or even less.[18]

Other incidents in the *Odyssey* likewise display a curiously disjointed resemblance to the dangerous reign of the sacred king. The boar, for instance, seems to have been seen as the Killer of the Dying God, such as Adonis or Tammuz, both in the Mediterranean region and to the east.[19] In the *Nekyia*, Agamemnon describes his and his comrades' murder as the slaughter of 'white-toothed swine' (Bk. XI. 413 ff.) at a marriage feast, thus reversing the situation; then, in Book XIX of the *Odyssey*, we are told how Odysseus happens to have a scar on his leg: he received it as a boy from the tusk of a wild boar while hunting with his maternal grandfather Autolycus. The importance of the incident lies not so much in the fact that it follows the ritual pattern,[20] but rather that Odysseus *escapes* the fury of what may well have been a holy killer.

We should keep this in mind as we explore the implications of another story about Odysseus' last years which Homer, whether intentionally or not, fails to mention at all. It is contained in the lost *Telegoneia* of Eugammon, a minor epic poem of which a short résumé by Proclus remains, as follows:

After the burial of the suitors Ulysses sacrifices to the nymphs and then goes to visit his herds in Elis, where he is entertained by Polyxenus. The stories of Trophonios, Agamede [*sic*], and Augeas are related. After returning to Ithaca to perform the sacrifices prescribed by Teiresias, Ulysses goes to the country of the Thesprotians, marries their queen Callidice, and leads them in a war against the Brygi, in which Ares takes part on behalf of the Brygi, and Athene for Ulysses, while Apollo intervenes as a mediator. On the death of Callidice, Polypoetes, son of Ulysses, becomes king, and Ulysses returns to Ithaca: then Telegonus son of Ulysses by Circe, who had been seeking for his father, makes a descent upon Ithaca. Ulysses comes to repel the attack and is killed by his own son. Telegonus finds too late what he has done, and takes his father's body, with Telemachus and Penelope, to his mother Circe, who makes them immortal. Finally, Telemachus marries Circe, and Telegonus Penelope.[21]

So much for Teiresias' prophecy in Homer, of a 'gentle' death from the sea.[22] Assuming for the *Telegoneia* story a genuinely ancient source, Homer's omission of any reference to it is perfectly understandable: he would not tolerate the murder of a hero by his son nor the placid matrimonial tangle which terminates the minor poem.[23] And he similarly disregards alternative and current traditions which claim that all or some of the suitors shared Penelope's affections with Odysseus,[24] and that she made love to Apollo or bore Arcadian Pan to Hermes.[25] The only remains of these anecdotes in Homer are an awkwardly explained incident in Book XVIII in which Penelope is prompted by Athena 'to show herself to the wooers, that she might make their heart all flutter with hope, and that she might win yet more worship from her lord and her son than heretofore,'[26] and the general situation of many men living in a house with one woman which is reminiscent of a polyandrical household.[27] Homer seems to have transferred the faithlessness attributed to Penelope to the twelve maids[28]—among them the most noticeable reversed image of Penelope herself, ungrateful Melantho, lover of Eurymachus, whom Telemachus hangs as penalty for having 'gone the way of shame.'[29]

A definite pattern to these Homeric omissions and modifications emerges, a pattern which becomes clearer if we accept, with certain qualifications, the thesis that the Homeric epics 'were composed for a race with patriarchal institutions out of materials derived from an older matrilinear society.'[30] Once again, we cannot emphasize strongly enough that what is meant is exactly a 'matrilinear' organization, for which evidence is plentiful enough through Greece and surrounding areas in the early stages of Mediterranean culture,[31] and not 'matriarchal', for which very little satisfactory evidence can be found. Reckoning of descent through the female line is common enough in peoples with a recent or incomplete grasp of the concept of paternity, and it is easy to see why among such peoples the woman remains the mysterious and dangerous center of the tribe's ritual activity: she is the sole link between the successive generations and the sole source of life to all. The sacred danger of Woman haunted Greece throughout her greatest age, a fact to which Aeschylus' play *The Eumenides* stands ready witness, and in no matter how depressed a status the Greek maintained his women, behind all his restrictions upon them, whether in the seventh century or in the fifth, lay a primitive terror of their sacred power. Every attempt to deny this power was made, including, if we may judge by *The Eumenides*, the denial to the woman of any role of consequence in the act of generation, and of any claim to represent a vital link between grandfather and father and son. Nothing, in this repressive mood, could seem more dangerous or disreputable than the reminiscences of the ritual murder of a king who was quickly replaced by another, in marriage to a queen whose permanent cultic regency would not have been questioned. That the male should enact the short life and fleeting of a changeable Dying God, that a female should remain after the dreadful murder to reign again, perhaps even participate in it, was a condition intolerable to the Greek consciousness, and the vital core of Greek literature was formed under this intolerance half-cognizant of its origins. The Homeric epics share—in so far as the materials could be purged of their ancient confusion and blood[32]—this patriarchal vehemence,[33] and the all-embracing theme (Book XIV) of the *Odyssey* is whether or not 'the race of godlike Arceisius [Odysseus' paternal grandfather] may perish nameless out of Ithaca.'[34]

Before we examine a few of the major episodes of Odysseus' travels, we should observe the framework into which they are set. First of all, the *Odyssey* is concerned not with one journey, but two: Books I-IV are largely devoted to Telemachus' increasing awareness of his inadequacy to deal with the situation in Ithaca without his father, and to his journey outward to find Odysseus or receive word of him. James Joyce seems to have been unusually sensitive to this aspect of the poem, since in *Ulysses* almost equal weight is given to each of the two principal characters, Stephen and Bloom, and the real climax of the novel occurs in their meeting, in the father-son society which they create between themselves. Secondly, Telemachus is the first member of Odysseus' family to greet Odysseus (Book XVI) upon his return to Ithaca, and plays a major role in his revenge upon the suitors. Thirdly, the last book of the poem deals with the reunion of

Odysseus and his father Laertes, who is convinced of his son's identity when Odysseus shows him the scar of the boar-wound on his leg; the book ends with the three of them, grandfather, father, and son, standing side by side to defend 'the race of god-like Arceisius' against those who have come to avenge the suitors' death.

> Then Athene, daughter of Zeus, drew near them in the likeness of Mentor both in form and in voice, and the much-enduring, goodly Odysseus was glad at sight of her, and straightway spoke to Telemachus, his dear son:
> 'Telemachus, now shalt thou learn this—having thyself come to the place of battle, where the best warriors are put to the trial—to bring no disgrace upon the house of thy fathers, for we have ever excelled in strength and in valour over all the earth.'
> And wise Telemachus answered him: 'Thou shalt see me, if thou wilt, dear father, in my present temper, bringing no disgrace upon thy house, even as thou sayest.'
> So said he, and Laertes was glad, and spoke, saying: 'What a day is this for me, kind gods! Verily right glad am I: my son and my son's son are vying with one another in valour.'[35]

And upon Athena's prompting, Laertes is first to cast his spear and kill his man. Odysseus has been the missing link in the patrilinear descent; both his son and father are helpless without him. Now, with his survival and return, the dynastic honor is joyfully restored, Telemachus comes into his manly strength, and sufficient virile power returns to old Laertes to drive a spear through a man's armor and body and out the other side. The triumph of a poem and way of life are bloodily complete.[36]

It remains for us to show how Odysseus' survival—the episodic 'fairy-tale wanderings', as Finley puts it—relates to this patriarchal triumph. In explanation, we may refer to Robert Graves's summary account: he sees in Odysseus a rebellious sacred king who refused to be murdered and replaced by another consort for the queen. 'Lotus-land, the cavern of the Cyclops, the harbour of Telepylus, Aeaea, Persephone's Grove, Siren Land, Ogygia, Scylla and Charybdis, the Depths of the Sea, even the Bay of Phorcys—all are different metaphors for the death which he evaded.'[37] With some allowance for Graves's habitual overstatement of a case, this is true, though, as in the adventure at the cavern of Polyphemus, the ritual from which any episode derives may be comparable to the others only in the more general features common to the vast majority of Mediterranean cultic practices. What will mainly concern us in each case is that it show the marks of the critical juncture of a ritual cycle, a rite of passage; that it show a possibility of death and a consequent rebirth; that Odysseus' commendable aim is to enjoy the revivifying effects of each episode without suffering the concomitant crudities; and that, in each case but one, the thematic connection of these adventures with Odysseus' final trial against the suitors for re-marriage to Penelope is strengthened by the appearance of a threatening female figure strongly associated with the more obviously ritualistic elements in the story.

The first major episode in Odysseus' wanderings,[38] his adventure in the land of the Cyclops, conforms only to the more general features of the pattern outlined above. Alone of all the principal adventures, it makes no reference to a threatening female figure, yet the cave is 'plainly a place of death,'[39] and is plainly the point from which life is renewed as well, both by reason of its symbolic appearance as the womb, the source of all life (such representations being common features of primitive ritual) and because the mariners who escape from the one-eyed monster have in the most literal sense been granted a new lease on life. There has been recent wide recognition of the probable connections of the Polyphemus legend with early ritual, but opinion has divided over the question of the particular nature of the rite involved. Two such interpretations will be particularly worth considering. In an extremely interesting section of his book *Folk Tale, Fiction and Saga in the Homeric Epics*, Rhys Carpenter has set forth, in too great detail to be summarized here, the theory that the legend is referable to a Thracian cult of immortality in which worship—and the hope of renewed life—is centered around the hibernating bear, which 'dies' every autumn and after passage to the underworld (like Odysseus himself, whose nickname used in the episode betrays ursine associations) 'returns to life' in the spring.[40] To judge from the evidence Carpenter draws upon to support his theory, the ritual included in its cruder forms the sacrifice of a bear-as-man or a man-as-bear; its basic characteristics, then, are not divergent in any important respect from those we have delineated: it would mark a critical juncture in the seasonal cycle dictated by an easily observed point in the hibernation-cycle of the bear; it would involve death, actual or symbolic, and the hope of renewed life, and in the Homeric version Odysseus manages to squirm through the lethal ritual unscathed yet in possession of its benefit of rebirth.

Gabriel Germain, on the other hand, states an excellent case for the episode as the mythical representation of a nomadic initiation-rite into a ram cult, or into adult membership in a tribe with a ram totem.[41] Thus the story itself would have been at one time a kind of 'admonition, precatechism,'[42] intended to 'strike the imagination of the women and children';[43] the cave would be the place of initiation, the awful voice of Polyphemus some kind of ritualistic noise-makers, the fire in the cave in some way connected with an ordeal by fire, and the sheep by which the men make their escape would have been the sheepskins worn by the initiated as they emerge from their trials.[44]

These two speculations do not exclude one another.[45] We may regard as a possibility that a myth reflecting the escape of a figure of the general type of sacred king, whether embodying the spirit of ram or bear, was later modified and transferred to a different purpose, that of representing to the uninitiated of the tribe the mystery and horror of the ceremony which awaited them, yet with enough of the characteristics of the original myth and practice remaining to prompt the Homeric poet to include it—however instinctively he may have done so—as a thematically relevant portion of Odysseus' adventures. In any case, as Germain himself points out, one of the important features of the initiation ceremony 'is to represent a first death of the novice, which permits him to be reborn thereafter in a transformed state of being,'[46] thus displaying the same basic pattern as that of the king-sacrifice. We may even extend this observation into a lesson of sorts: *all* primitive ritual of passage through a critical point from one stage to another of the seasons or of human life follows this pattern.[47] Realizing this will help us see that, in as much as our final concern is with the retention of cultic sequences only in so far as they affect the structures and issues of literature, and in as much as the Homeric poem's Athenian audiences were themselves in a condition of what we may call 'highly responsive ignorance', the precise identification of a ritual background as to historical origin or application is far less important than the simple fact that the underlying form of a story is indeed that of cyclical ritual. Names and places escape us after thousands of years. What remain are the habits of mind, the very design of thought, of the numberless generations whose culminative epic we survey, and those recurrent habits, primarily expressed in their ritual attempts to control the forces of life, permeate and inform every odd corner and cranny of the *Odyssey*, charging it with the issues of life and death.

The visit to Circe displays far more clearly the characteristic elements of the ritual struggle which we have claimed to be the dominant theme of the *Odyssey*. It has been convincingly argued that Circe herself is a minor solar goddess of the general type of Ishtar, the alternately cruel or beneficent courtesan-divinity of oriental origin.[48] She changes Odysseus' mariners into nine-year-old swine; we have already noted the part played by the boar in sacrificial ritual, and in addition may observe that swine played an important role in the Thesmophories, festival of the Athenian cult of Demeter, and in the Eleusian Mysteries,[49] in both places associated with the fertile Goddess. Because of the isolation of Circe's dwelling,[50] the transformed animals surrounding it, the singing, and the chalice shared by all, as well as the subsequent details of the metamorphosis and rescue, Germain argues that the cultic origin of the episode lies in a ceremony of initiation.[51] At some stage in its development this may likely have been the case, yet the narrative is internally discontinuous enough to suggest a multiple origin, and in the account of Odysseus' rescue of his men (with which neither Germain nor Carpenter deal at any length) the story shows strong liaisons with the seasonal fertility-ritual of the type we have described. Let us attend closely to the sequence of events in this rescue, the first encounter of Odysseus himself with the goddess. The hero starts out and is intercepted by Hermes, who gives him the magic herb *moly* and tells him exactly how to protect himself from Circe's enchantments. We have already noticed that Hermes, perhaps as a double of Odysseus,[52] was reputed a lover of the faithful Penelope[53] whom he visited—interestingly enough in view of the Polyphemus episode—in the form of a ram.[54] In addition, his was a very ancient divinity[55] following the general type of the Eniautos-Daimon,[56] and he was represented by a crude stone phallus guarding every doorstep in Athens, assuring fertility to those within the house.[57] In this capacity and when the phallic Herm guarded a tomb, he represented the chthonic 'power that

generates new lives, or, in the ancient conception, brings the souls
back to be born again.'[58] Yet when he appears to aid Odysseus,
it is in the far different form of the beautiful anthropomorphic
god of the Homeric pantheon, thoroughly assimilated to the
spirit of a patriarchal Olympus, and the help he gives Odysseus
is in full accord with his transformation.

Odysseus proceeds to Circe's dwelling. There she offers him
a golden cup[59] containing the charmed potion and, according to
his instructions, Odysseus drinks it without harm. When Circe
taps him with her wand, he draws his sword and rushes at her
as though he intended to kill her. She clasps his knees in suppli-
cation and, in the same breath, asks him to put his sword in its
sheath and to lie with her.[60] He agrees—and this, too, is by
Hermes' instruction—only after her solemn oath not to harm
him when he is stript, because otherwise, as Hermes has warned
him, 'she may unman you and make you a weakling.'[61]

These details show a curiously disjointed resemblance to the
fertility symbols of chalice, lance, and sword made familiar to us
by Miss Jessie L. Weston's famous study of the Holy Grail
legends, *From Ritual to Romance*.

> Lance and Cup (or Vase) were in truth connected together
> in a symbolic relation long ages before the institution of
> Christianity ... They are sex symbols of immemorial an-
> tiquity and world-wide diffusion, the Lance, or Spear, repre-
> senting the Male, the Cup, or Vase, the Female, repro-
> ductive energy.
>
> Found in juxtaposition, the Spear upright in the Vase
> ... their signification is admitted by all familiar with 'Life'
> symbolism, and they are absolutely in place as forming part
> of a ritual dealing with the processes of life and reproductive
> vitality.[62]

Miss Weston then devotes a full chapter to the sword (which
figures again in the evocation of ghosts in Persephone's Grove,
and in the encounter with Scylla), used as a similar emblem of
male virility in the fertility ritual of the sacred king or Dying
God throughout Europe, Asia Minor, and India.

Yet Homer's use of these sacred objects—if we may identify
them as such—represents a highly significant deviation from the
ritual. He has separated the cup and the sword, ordinarily found
together, and has placed them in the respective hands of the two
protagonists, one female, the other male, as potential weapons.[63]

The sword of Odysseus triumphs, and he then agrees to lie with
the goddess only if she promises not to emasculate him—for that
is the only meaning the passage and word (ἀνήνορα) can reasonably yield. The appropriate death-wound given to the god
and sacred king who embodied the principle of fertility and were
destroyed when it waned, would frequently have been that of
castration,[64] for which we find an historical counterpart in the
self-emasculation practiced by the priests of Cybele in imitation
of her divine consort Attis.[65] In later expurgated accounts of this
sacred death, the wound would of course be transferred to other
parts of the body, hence the scar on Odysseus' leg from a boar's
tusk, referred to above.

If this is not sufficient indication of a methodically distorted
basis for the Homeric story in a ritual of the general pattern with
which we are concerned, we may notice further that when the
mariners are restored from their shapes of nine-year-old swine,
they become 'men again, younger than they were before, and
far comelier and taller to look upon'.[66] Not only does Circe
return them to their original condition, but she makes them
younger as well, and this rejuvenation, we may suspect, is directly relatable both to the pattern of the original ritual whatever
it may have been, and to the Homeric rearrangement of its
details. Not only does Odysseus triumph over the tyrannical rite,
but he makes use of its restorative magic as well, on his own
terms. We need not suppose that Homer understood the meaning
of the scene, or any of the others supplied him by tradition, *as
ritual;* the chances are slim, in fact, that he could have compre-
hended directly the foundation in cultic practice of the material
which he altered. It is very difficult for us to realize the unitary
response ancient man must have made toward his experience.
Ritual supplied to him a certain very limited number of *formulations* of human or anthropomorphic divine behavior, with which
he could interpret his experience. The species of myth which we
know, from present-day savage parallels,[67] to have been recited
simultaneously with the cultic performance as corroboration and
substantiation for it, provided the first verbal reinforcements of
these formulations. Yet ancient man, unlike us, could hardly
have confined them—the image of the Dying God and his death
among them—to a 'religious' area of experience separated from
a 'secular' verbal tradition. Orally transmitted legends would
have burgeoned in secondary growth far beyond the limits of

specific ritual performance or its accompanying recitation,[68] yet
a glance at the body of Eurasian mythology is sufficient to show
that it is largely tied down to variations upon a few basic formulations with demonstrable parallels in ritual practice. This secondary growth of myth is speculative: each variation upon the
ritually-oriented original pattern is a violation and an adventure
in thinking beyond the limits of the collective tribal consciousness. The image of the Dying God is an assertion of that collective
awareness, and Homer's Odysseus is a violation of it. What
makes Homer's speculative deviation so remarkable is that it is
repeated with fair consistency within the epic, and that the issue
of *deviation itself* is integrated, as more obviously in the *Iliad*, into
the vital center of the poem's action. Odysseus insists upon living
as a man, not dying into divinity, with all that that insistence
implies of an individual consciousness emergent from the con-
fines of collective understanding.

The adventurers stay on Circe's island for a year, 'for the full
circle of a year ... and the seasons returned as the months
waned, and the long days came in their course,'[69] according to
the ritual calendar, in other words, until the season when Odysseus' ordeal should be repeated.[70] Comparisons of the *Odyssey* at
this point with Gilgamish's descent into the underworld appear
to indicate that the Shiduri-Circe figure was, from the beginning,
closely related to the hero's adventure in the land of the dead:
'the two goddesses each respectively advise the heroes at the
moment of this enterprize.'[71] Therefore it should not afford us
much surprize to find Circe prescribing a voyage to Persephone's
Grove as the occasion of his next ritual trial, particularly since
such a visit was—as instanced in those of Dionysus, Theseus, and
Heracles[72]—'an essential scene in the drama of the Eniautos-
Daimon'[73] and his counterpart, the sacred king.

Possibly because of their legendary geographical location in
the Straits of Messina, the figures of Scylla and Charybdis have
assumed a character in customary interpretation as embodi-
ments of natural phenomena, as vividly imaginative representations of the dangers of the sea. However great the Homeric
imagination, it did not function that way, though the account
in the *Odyssey* of this unpleasant pair is sufficiently abbreviated
to render interpretation in more feasible terms difficult and
tenuous. All we may be sure of is that the monsters are female,
and deadly. Nor can we conclude much from their genealogical

connections, no matter how interesting these may appear, for fear of falling into the unwarranted syncretism habitual to Greek mythographers from Herodotus onward.[74] Yet another approach yields more fruitfully to our speculative efforts. Certain motifs occur in repetition throughout the *Odyssey*, and find their counterparts in this episode as well. The first of these is the cave. Polyphemus is encountered in a cave; Scylla lives in one, Circe's description of which is significant: 'a dim cave, turned to the West, toward Erebus, even where you shall steer your hollow ship, glorious Odysseus.'[75] This chthonic orientation—for the West, the end of the sun's journey, the direction of Elysium, the abode of the primordial night-god Erebus, can mean only that[76]—seems to indicate, particularly in conjunction with the monster's murderous aspect, that her cave, like Calypso's, is the residence of the Goddess of the Underworld. Finally, Odysseus awakes from a mysteriously deep sleep on the shore of Ithaca near a strange cave with two entrances, one for mortals and one for gods, and inhabited by female spirits.

The second motif is the tree, or branch. The olive spit plays an important part in the struggle with Polyphemus (see fn. 44), Circe's dwelling is in deep forest, 'sacred glades,'[77] Odysseus is to know Persephone's Grove by its poplars and willows, he is saved by the 'fig tree with rich foliage'[78] over Charybdis; alder, poplar, and cypress grow around Calypso's cave,[79] Odysseus falls asleep under a curious double olive tree on the Phaeacian shore, covered with leaves[80] and later covers his nakedness from Nausicaa with a leafy branch;[81] finally, he awakes on the Ithacan shore under a sacred olive tree, and we are already familiar with his olive-tree bed.

The third motif is that of the entrance, the gate, the threshold.[82] Polyphemus is prominently concerned with the entrance to his cave, which he guards and controls (see fn. 44). All of the ships which passed through the mouth of the harbor at Telepylus are destroyed; Odysseus alone has moored his outside the entrance-way (characteristically) and so escapes death. Circe's island is both Gateway to the Sun and the last point of departure on the journey to the underworld. Scylla sits at the entrance to her cave, and the passage between her and Charybdis is itself a gateway. Both in Telepylus and in Phaeacia, entrance to a palace is immediately followed by an encounter with an imposing queen. The curious double entrance to the cave on the shore of

Ithaca has already been noted. And finally, Odysseus kills the suitors from the 'great threshold'[83] of his own home.

These three elements are combined in the encounter with Scylla and Charybdis, in a fashion which invites comparison with similar forms in myths and rituals recorded from areas of wide geographical separation. G. R. Levy, in *The Gate of Horn*, traces the cave-cult and its Megalithic architectural developments from northern Europe through southern Eurasia to the practices of present-day Stone Age societies in Melanesia, and it is there that the living force of this ancient species of religious belief may be most clearly understood. A terrible goddess, known as Le-hev-hev on Vao,[84] is associated with the entrance of the cave (see fn. 44) which leads to the underworld, and which is indiscriminately associated with the various rebirth-transformations which everywhere constitute the group of what we call rituals of passage.[85] Like the Scorpion Man[86] and Woman who guard the Cave of Death in the *Gilgamish Epic*,[87] and like Scylla herself, Le-hev-hev is imagined 'as a Rock ... crab, spider, or megalopod.'[88] The function as guardian of the cave's entrance, and her multibrachiate nature, receive strengthened significance from an account of ritual practice among the devotees of Le-hev-hev:

> *The Journey of the Dead*, as mimed in the ritual dances of Vao, bears the closest relation to the literary legends of our own civilisation, suggesting some common foundation in a universal ritual descended from the Stone Age of Europe and Asia. In Vao the newly-dead man is believed to arrive before the entrance to a cave on the seashore, where he encounters the dreaded Guardian Ghost. In front of the cave-mouth is a design called 'The Path', traced upon the sand by Le-hev-hev. At his approach she obliterates half the design, which the dead man must complete or be devoured ... After completing the design, he must tread its mazes to the threshold of the cave, where he may now offer the tusked boar which was sacrificed in the mortuary rites performed after his burial.[89]

The goddess is then prevailed upon to admit him to the underworld. In the Wala version the dead man carries a branch of weed on his voyage, and gnaws 'the bark of a "milk-bearing" tree' as a sign of his transformation to an infantile condition.[90] An observer of the Australian labyrinth-dances associated with this pattern and derived from the same level of culture concludes that they are, first, inevitably concerned with death and rebirth; secondly, without exception have to do with a cave or the constructed equivalent of one; thirdly, always have a maze before the entrance; and fourthly, the central figure in the rite is inevitably a woman.[91]

Let us apply the elements of this ritual pattern to Odysseus' adventure. He and his mariners approach Scylla who is sitting in the entrance to her cave, like Le-hev-hev's, facing the sea. Both possible outcomes of the confrontation of the goddess have their parallels in the *Odyssey*: six mariners, doubles of Odysseus, are snatched up and devoured, while the hero himself 'searched out the paths of the sea'[92] ($\pi\delta\varrho ov\varsigma$ $\dot{\alpha}\lambda\dot{o}\varsigma$ $\dot{\varepsilon}\xi\varepsilon\varrho\varepsilon\varepsilon\dot{\iota}v\omega v$). The phrase, which does not occur elsewhere in the *Odyssey*, appears to have transferred the maze-design found at the entrance of the cave in the Melanesian ritual, to the difficult sea-passage itself, between Scylla and Charybdis. What is important, and characteristic of Odysseus, is that the treading of the maze, however successful, does not lead to the cave—and the underworld—but away from it. Once again the basic elements of a ritual situation have been rearranged and subverted to the purposes of a hero in search of human life rather than immortality in death, a hero determined not to subordinate himself to a dominance of the female principle over that life.

In order to arrive at an intelligent hypothesis concerning Odysseus' returning encounter with Charybdis, we must add to our Melanesian parallels another, drawn out of a region almost equally remote from Greece, yet bearing traces of origins in the same cultural stratum. Beowulf, prince of the Geats, struggles and conquers a female monster in a setting remarkably similar to the Ithacan king's escape from Charybdis. Grendel's mother, in no matter how Christian a poem she appears, is unquestionably a relic of prehistoric pagan mythology. It is explicitly said of her and her son that 'they have no knowledge of a father, whether any had been begotten for them in times past, among the mysterious spirits,'[93] which is usually taken to mean simply that they were creatures without history, unable to reckon their lineage, but which may quite as easily imply an ignorance of paternity.

Their lair is described in terms reminiscent of Homer's setting for the Odyssean episode: it is found in an 'unknown land ... dangerous fen-paths, where the welling stream under the mists of headlands goes down, a flood under the earth.'[94] By comparison, Homer mentions the two high cliffs[95] in which dwell Scylla and Charybdis, and remarks that over Scylla's there is an eternal mass of clouds which never clears away.[96] Other elements present a much stronger parallel, however: the lair of Grendel's mother is reached through water, a lake 'over which hang frosted groves; the wood rooted fast overshadows the water.'[97] When Beowulf finds the lair, he recognizes it by the sight of these 'mountain trees hanging over grey stone.'[98] This latter detail, twice insisted upon in *Beowulf*, has its direct parallel in the fig tree, rooted on the cliff over Charybdis,[99] to which Odysseus clings to avoid being drawn down when Charybdis sucks in the waters of the sea.[100] Finally, Charybdis' maelstrom is itself echoed in the curious behavior of the lake in *Beowulf*: 'thence surging water rises up, darkly to the clouds, when the wind stirs evil storms, until the air turns misty, the heavens weep.'[101]

Each passage sheds light on the other. The she-monster in *Beowulf* is definitely a divinity in the *Odyssey*, whereas the localized form of Grendel's mother tells against the interpretation of Charybdis as a vague representation of a whirlpool, or general manifestation of natural powers. The crucial role of the fig tree in the *Odyssey* suggests that a greater significance than the Anglo-Saxon poet conveys, is to be attached to the grove over the lake. And whereas Charybdis' vortiginous action reveals to Odysseus only the black sand of the sea-bottom,[102] for Beowulf it is the entrance to an underworld lair, in which he will meet a more or less anthropomorphic female monster. We are again confronted with the pattern of a goddess who is associated with the opening to an underworld, with the addition of a fig tree, 'rich with foliage', or grove of trees, hanging over the watery entrance. To understand these we must refer back to the Melanesian 'milk-bearing tree,' the full significance of which we shall have occasion to discuss when we deal with the olive tree forming the foundation of Odysseus' bed. For the moment it must suffice to say that the many Mediterranean and Eurasian parallels for this peculiar tree indicate that it is a manifestation of the Goddess herself, in a beneficent, fertile aspect; in this embodiment she is the Mother and Guardian of Birth, rather than the Goddess of Death.[103] Charybdis is both of these, and her aspects are separately embodied in the two images of whirlpool (if that is what it is) and fig tree. When Odysseus approaches her, he clings to the fig tree, associated with the powers of rebirth,[104] rather than descending as Beowulf does[105] with his sword[106] into the flame-lit[107] den of the she-monster. Again it appears that Homer has altered the essential images of the original ordeal, viewing the tree as a separate means of escape rather than another form of Charybdis herself, in order to allow his hero to enjoy the beneficial effects of a passage through death to rebirth without suffering the consequences which full participation would entail.

The festivities in Phaeacia display unmistakeable parallels to the other episodes in the *Odyssey*, though because of the wealth of its detail and the deserved popularity of the tale, interpretation by classical scholars has diverged remarkably.[108] One of the most acceptable would identify Odysseus with a young olive-tree god in resurrection,[109] who is born out of the winter leaves beneath a grafted olive tree,[110] with an olive branch in his hand and surrounded by a ritual chorus of maidens who lead him in procession to the temple, where he first greets the powerful Queen-Mother (Arete) and then is wedded to her daughter the Maiden-Corê (Nausicaa), after athletic contests have determined which of the tribe is most fit to become the god in this marriage designed to promote the fertility of flocks and fields. This approach seems plausible enough, particularly when we observe that Athena, to whom the olive was sacred, [111] makes her first appearance in the chronological sequence of adventures at the side of Odysseus as his personal and immediate protector, only a few lines previous to his awakening in the leaves. From this point on she is his constant guide, meets him in disguised forms, and manipulates the actions of others to his best advantage. It is she who makes Nausicaa dream of marriage, and thereupon wash clothes on the riverbank to signify her readiness. We might also note that, after Odysseus puts in his bizarre appearance, the girls give him olive-oil with which to anoint himself, and with this cleansing 'Athene ... made him greater and more mighty to behold, and from his head caused deep curling locks to flow, like the hyacinth flower.'[112] This will recall the rejuvenation of the mariners on Circe's island, and is only the first in a rather impressive series of ablutions, usually occurring at critical and significant moments in the epic, from which Odysseus emerges younger and stronger and more beautiful than ever before; similar transformations are accorded to Laertes and Penelope, also at critical junctures.

When Nausicaa sees Odysseus come from his anointment, she

says to her maidens, 'Erewhile he seemed to me uncomely, but now he is like the gods that keep the wide heaven. Would that such an one might be called my husband, dwelling here, and that it might please him here to abide.'[113] There is more than simple admiration in this comment. In addition to the fact that she likens him to a god—comparison which Homer's Odysseus later emphatically denies, and with good reason—the form of marriage she here alludes to is decidedly matrilocal, and even without Penelope in the way, Odysseus would reject it for the same reasons that he refused to live in the house of Icarius, Penelope's Spartan father, and inherit the throne through his wife. Lively and enchanting as Nausicaa may be, Odysseus' mission is to escape the dominance of Goddess and Queen, to establish a patrilinear descent and patriarchal custom. He could not consider such a marriage.

Yet the question of marriage hangs between them. Odysseus has told Nausicaa that 'he is of heart the most blessed beyond all other who shall prevail with gifts of wooing, and lead [her] to his home,'[114] assuredly alluding to a patrilocal form of the ceremony; and Nausicaa tells him that she is afraid to let him follow her and her maidens directly home because people will gossip: 'Where found she him? Her husband he will be, her very own.'[115]

When Odysseus has been received into the house, Alcinous in his turn raises the question whether Odysseus 'is some deathless god come down from heaven.' The reply is the predictable, emphatic one: 'Alcinous, that thought be far from thee! for I bear no likeness either in form or fashion to the deathless gods, who keep wide heaven, but to men that die.'[116] For Odysseus to accept the divinity offered him, would mean his participation in the rituals of that divinity as well; he refuses immortality, just as he refused Calypso's offer in favor of mortal life.

This recurrent denial puts new meaning, also, into Odysseus' reluctance to take part in the next day's athletic contests. Such games were features of two important occasions in the ancient world which often coincided as a single event. These were: (1) the contest which selected the young man most suitable for marriage to the sacred queen; and (2) the trial which tested the old king's fitness to live and reign for another term, to make sure that his precious vital powers remained intact. The latter was, of course, a form of re-marriage, though this aspect does not appear in the epic until Odysseus reaches Ithaca. Otherwise, both applications of the athletic contest are relevant to the festivities in Phaeacia. If we assume that the competition was originally for the hand of Nausicaa (and the story gives every indication of this) we may see Odysseus' initial refusal to take part as an unwillingness to involve himself in a ritual which would both compromise his attachment to Penelope and entail, essentially, his social and religious subservience to a female principle. When Euryalus taunts him, however, he picks up a weight and casts it beyond any other mark, complaining bitterly of all he has lived through, claiming that in spite of it he is yet stronger than anyone, and throwing out an angry challenge to the crowd. Momentarily cast into the mould of the Old King who must prove himself superior to his young rivals, Odysseus triumphs over their veiled scorn; this accomplished, interestingly enough, he can afford to avoid the issue entirely by excluding Laodamas, heir-manifest to the Phaeacian throne, from his general challenge on the convenient grounds that 'he is mine host: who would strive with one that entreated him kindly?'[117] In the cultic equivalent of the story, Laodamas would stand as his chief, perhaps sole rival. King Alcinous, who plays no part in the games, is of course the actual Old King of Phaeacia, but is easily replaced here by Odysseus, who by this time has renewed his reign as archetypal Old King of several realms, and must do so again in Ithaca.

Before we proceed to a discussion of the struggle in Odysseus' homeland, another question must be satisfactorily answered. Having ignored or toyed with Odysseus for several years, why do the gods suddenly decide to hurry him to his home within a very few days? And after several drowsy years with Calypso, why is Odysseus almost impolite in his impatience with the gracious and hospitable Phaeacians, all for the sake of a few hours? Because he is homesick? Behind his yearning for Ithaca, behind Poseidon's wrath, Athena's favor, and Zeus' decrees, is a force at work more powerful than any of them: time.

The Greeks regarded time, like change, in terms of cycles, circular returns upon a former state.[118] Time was for them, as we noted in the previous chapter, not a continuous and homogenous flow but a series of personally and ritually important points[119] occurring in meaningful succession. This time is biologically determined; it is 'experienced in the periodicity and rhythm of man's own life as well as in the life of nature.'[120]

The transition from one phase to another is a crisis in which man is assisted by the community's uniting in the rituals appropriate to birth, puberty, marriage, or death ... And the manifestation of time in nature, the succession of the seasons, and the movements of the heavenly bodies were conceived quite early as the signs of a life-process similar, and related, to that of man.[121]

One may conjecture that the *Odyssey* tells the story of one of these critical junctures assisted—or rather, accompanied—by ritual, and that the sudden flurry of activity in heaven and earth owes more to the arrival of this crisis than to any need for a 'unity of time' which we may anachronistically attribute to the Homeric poet.

At the very beginning of the *Odyssey*, in addition to giving us Odysseus' stated purpose throughout the action as the 'striving to win his own life,'[122] Homer offers another interesting phrase: 'when now the year had come in the courses of the seasons, wherein the gods had ordained that he should return home to Ithaca, not even there was he quit of labours, not even among his own ...'[123] But we observe that the gods had ordained nothing of the sort, since this passage is immediately followed by their council to decide the matter, hastily summoned in the absence of Poseidon. The force at work is again time, the seasonal cycle itself. In Book V we find Odysseus sitting on the shore of Calypso's island, grieving, 'and his sweet life was ebbing away as he mourned for his return.'[124] Finally, at the beginning of Book IX, occurs the most curious phrase of all. Odysseus gives his name to the Phae-acians for the first time so that some day he will be able to return their hospitality: 'Now, first,' he says, 'will I tell my name, that ye too may know it, and that I, when I have escaped the pitiless day, may yet be your host, though my home is in a far country.'[125] Coming at this point in the epic, 'the pitiless day' ($\nu\eta\lambda\varepsilon\grave{\varepsilon}\varsigma$ $\mathring{\eta}\mu\alpha\varrho\cdot$ ix, 17) can refer to one thing only: his return to Ithaca. This is the crisis which confronts Odysseus; he must escape, not so much the plotted violence of the suitors, but the day itself.

The calendar of the ancient world was at first purely lunar, and because the cycle of the visible moon corresponded closely to the female menstrual cycle, the moon could be identified with the Goddess and worshipped as such.[126] Ritual and sacrifice were dependent upon this system.[127] With the gradual advent of the male principle into the sphere of fertility-magic, however,

the sun had to be taken into account,[128] and progressive length-
enings of the king's reigning-period would have been due to an
attempt to correlate more closely the lunar with the solar year,[129]
one such expansion occurring with an approximation at a period
of one hundred lunations,[130] or nine (the sacred number) seasons
of one year each.[131] We arrive at the third expansion of the king's
reigning-period by a doubling of the former nine-year period
according to the Greek method of inclusive reckoning,[132] i.e.,
'nine-years-and-in-the-tenth',[133] which gives us a total of twenty
years. The latter calculation seems most applicable to Odysseus;
he has been ten years at Troy[134] and nine years, finding their
completion in the tenth, has been spent on his travels. At this
point we can understand his urgency: King Agamemnon died
at the end of the first ten years, and Odysseus in his turn must
escape the 'pitiless day' and its ordeal, at the end of the second
ten. He must close with the strange forces which are robbing
him of his sweet life, and endure through the crisis into the beginning of a new cycle and a new reign.[135]

Except for Leucothea, Athena is the only woman in the epic
who grants Odysseus her undivided support in his enterprise,
and it is entirely fitting that she should do so. Odysseus shares her
characteristic qualities of cleverness and intelligence, in a relationship which appears to go back to the most ancient beginnings
of the poem.[136] More important, however, is the fact that she
was the most thoroughly assimilated of the Greek goddesses to
the father-dominated Olympian group. In one of the more
ingenious of Greek theological manoeuvers, Athena was officially
reported to be the parthenogenous daughter of Metis, whom
Zeus had swallowed to prevent her from giving birth, whereupon
the Father of Gods was plagued by a headache; he ordered
Hephaestus to crack open his skull, and Athena sprang fully-
armed from the cleft. Displaying in this way that children could
even be born without the intervention of the Goddess, Athena
was ever afterward her father's most obedient daughter.[137]
Priests were employed in her service rather than priestesses[138]
and, interesting in view of our present discussion, no male
sacrifices were offered to her.[139]

We are twice told, in Books XIV and XIX, the precise time
of Odysseus' return and vengeance; it will be in the dark of the
moon, 'as the old moon wanes and the new is born.'[140] Though
the clear ritual significance of this period may be lost to us,

neither the reversion to ancient lunar reckoning[141] nor the exactness of the image can escape our notice; and we observe that Odysseus' ordeal will occur at the completion of the moon's cycle, in the suspenseful dark between the waning and the restored, the dying and the reborn.[142]

Odysseus' central trial is that of the archery contest. His bow appears to be of very ancient and distant sources indeed; it is a double-curved type originating, not as J. A. K. Thomson supposes,[143] in the single-curved weapon of the pre-Hellenic Cretans and Myceneans,[144] but in the weapon of the Central Asian steppes.[145] The contest itself appears to be based in a widespread custom of selecting the tribal king.[146] It forms, contrary to the opinion of some scholars, one of the oldest parts of the Homeric tradition, having entered with the tribes of the migrations[147] and, as Germain points out, neither the practice of such a custom nor its appearance in legend make sense in a patrilinear society; only in a culture where the king was selected because of his vitality and prowess rather than his lineage, would such a ritual proof find an intelligible place. Instances are to be found, from the Mediterranean to China, of the drawing of a bow as an integral part of the inaugural ritual,[148] and we are told that in parts of the early Greek world the new sacred king established his reign by shooting four arrows, one in each direction, and a fifth vertically into the air.[149] This weight of ritual usage associated with the weapon may have had something to do with the disrepute into which it had generally fallen among the patriarchal Homeric Greeks as an ordinary instrument of warfare;[150] be that as it may, the bow was used in rites of marriage and inauguration.

Athena had 'disguised' Odysseus as an old man; and when the suitors are dead, the faithless servant-maids hanged, and the great hall cleaned of its blood, the expected rejuvenation occurs:

> Meanwhile ... Eurynome had bathed the great-hearted Odysseus within his house, and anointed him with olive-oil, and cast about him a goodly mantle and a doublet. Moreover, Athene shed great beauty from his head downwards, and made him greater and more mighty to behold, and from his head caused deep curling locks to flow, like the hyacinth flower. And as when some skilful man overlays gold upon silver, one that Hephaestus and Pallas Athene have taught

all manner of craft, and full of grace is his handiwork, even
so did Athene shed grace about his head and shoulders, and
forth from the bath he came, in form like to the Immortals.[151]

Then comes Penelope's test of her husband's identity: she pre-
tends that their great bridal bed has been moved, and is satisfied
by his enraged outburst:

> Who has moved my bed? That would be a difficult job for
> the best workman, unless God himself should come down
> and move it. It would be easy for God, but no man could
> easily prize it up, not the strongest man living! There is a
> great secret in that bed. I made it myself, and no one else
> touched it. There was a strong young olive tree in full leaf
> growing in an enclosure, the trunk as thick as a pillar.
> Round this I built our bridal chamber; I did the whole
> thing myself, laid the stones and built a good roof over it,
> jointed the doors and fitted them in their places. After that
> I cut off the branches and trimmed the trunk from the root
> up, smoothed it carefully with the adze and made it straight
> to the line. This tree I made the bedpost. That was the be-
> ginning of my bed; I bored holes through it, and fitted the
> other posts about it, and inlaid the framework with gold
> and silver and ivory, and I ran through it leather straps
> coloured purple. Now I have told you my secret. And I don't
> know if it is still there, wife, or if some one has cut the olive
> at the root and moved my bed![152]

Why should Odysseus react to a trivial rearrangement of his
household in so disconsolate a manner? The very force of his
speech betrays some kind of unexplained importance which he
attaches to the tree; since it is the firm foundation of Odysseus'
bed which is at stake, we may assume that such a disaster would
mean his wife's infidelity. And if our thesis is correct, it would
imply as well a disruption of the patrilineal dynasty which
Odysseus and his allies, human and divine, have struggled so
desperately to establish; worse than that, it would appear to
involve Odysseus' very life and well-being, particularly if we
regard as plausible the theory of submerged connections between
the Homeric hero and an ancient olive-tree god, and thereby
interpret the relation between hero and tree as a causal and
magical as well as symbolic one.

We have no certain knowledge of the image itself; no comparable anecdote has appeared anywhere in the ancient literature

of Asia, Africa, or Europe, which would enable us to define its place in the pattern of ritual.[153] We possess only scattered bits of evidence which seem to indicate that the image is related—and they prove nothing more—to the tangled matrix of practice and belief from which the epic emerged. We know, for example, that a branch of olive was hung before each door in Attica as a charm of harvest-fertility, and was renewed when it withered.[154] We are told that Hermes invented the cultivation of the olive tree.[155] Athena, whose sacred olive[156] originating in Lybia suggests a similar origin for the goddess,[157] was at one time engaged in a contest with Poseidon for control of Attica; with his trident Poseidon struck a spring of salt water and a horse from the rock of the Acropolis, but Athena was judged the winner by creating the olive tree with a blow of her spear,[158] a triumph which may have something to do with the rivalry of god and goddess in the *Odyssey*.[159] The identification of the milk-bearing sycamore with Egyptian Hathor and Isis, pointed out by G. R. Levy, may offer a useful analogy to the olive and Athena, who in her beginnings was as much a deity of fertility as either of her southern sisters. The goddess appears regularly, according to Miss Levy, as the sustaining, life-giving tree itself, the young god as the recipient of its sustinence.[160] A curious variation upon this relationship is recorded in the myth of Isis and Osiris: in her search for the mangled portions of her dead husband, Isis discovered the genitals of Osiris—by which she conceived Horus the Avenging Son —enclosed in a sycamore tree in Syria.[161] Let us extend our hypothetical parallel with the Homeric olive tree, by assuming that Horus stands in something of the same relation to the mythical pattern as do Orestes and Telemachus. If this is so, the olive will represent to Odysseus not only the source of his vitality, but his sexually generative ability to transmit that vitality *through the male line*. As we noted, the tree is the foundation of his bed and therefore related to his sexual powers; and we have postulated throughout this chapter a concentration of those powers toward the establishment of a patrilineage in Ithaca.

We encounter another illuminating possibility if we turn to Athens and the olive in the Pandroseion sacred to Athena.[162] A branch was cut away from this tree, and was

> called the *Moria* or Fate Tree. It was bound about with fillets and hung with fruit and nuts and, in the festival of the

Panathenaia, they carried it up to the Acropolis to give to
Athena *Polias*, 'Her-of-the-City' ...

This *Moria*, or Fate Tree, was the very life of Athens; the
life of the olive which fed her and lighted her was the very
life of the city. When the Persian host sacked the Acropolis
they burnt the holy olive, and it seemed that all was over.
But next day it put forth a new shoot and the people knew
that the city's life still lived.[163]

The situations are to a suspicious degree analogous. Neither tree
is merely symbolic, of the life of either city or hero; both are that
life incarnate, merged by the force of Greek imagination. The
rites of Athena's olive tree were celebrated at the same festival
which reverently heard the recitation of the Homeric poems for
the first time in recorded history.[164] Yet the mystery of the
Odyssean olive deepens; is, in fact, as deep as the inspiration of
the Poet himself, for as Hesiod tells us,[165] the Greek singer took
into his hand a staff made from a branch of the flowering olive
tree, without which he could not sing. Yet when all is said and
done, we still cannot explain this image at the innermost heart
of a great poem. The tree may 'stand for' the thin line of humanity Odysseus trod between god and beast. It may 'stand for'
the patriarchal triumph, or for the renewal of life in the dark of
the moon when, for the first time in the course of the epic, the
inexorable progress of Time is halted by Athena,[166] who restrains
the night and the dawn while the couple enjoy their love in the
bed with its living foundation. It has been our business to show
that Odysseus is vitally concerned with such renewal, that it is
the great object of his journey. The olive tree *is* that renewal, in
all its weird complexity, and finally we are left to confront the
concrete image itself, where more than two thousand years ago
the dimensions of spirit and matter crossed and were one. There
is indeed a secret in that bed.

*

In a Christian poem, the *Divina Commedia* of Dante, the same
motif appears in a form prescribed by orthodox Christian rituals,
though as a decidedly secondary objective. In the last canto of
the *Purgatorio* Dante is commanded to drink of the waters of

Eunoë, one of the four rivers which course down from a single spring in the Garden of Eden atop the Mount of Purgatory. The effect of this draught is remarkable:

> I came back from the most holy waves, born again, even as new trees renewed with new foliage, pure and ready to mount to the stars.[167]

The passage shows also in what sense this is for Dante a secondary objective: it is a renovation merely sufficient to prepare him for the pure vision of the *Paradiso*. In this respect it is unlike that of Statius, his momentary companion who drinks from the same stream; for Statius it is the final renewal of life before he takes up his eternal abode in Heaven. From the beginning of the *Purgatorio* onward, the reader must keep firmly in mind the fact (which the poet surely intends to be increasingly more difficult for us to retain) that Dante must repeat his journey after death. Though his levitation toward God is analogous to that of souls in the after-life, it is not of the same order. It is a journey toward understanding, not eternal life—though through his under-standing he will ultimately gain eternal life—and everything, including his renovation in the waters of Eunoë, is subordinate to that end.

Though Jessie Weston's theory concerning the medieval legends of a quest after the Holy Grail has not found favor with medievalists, alternative explanations of the legends in terms of simple knightly adventure are hardly more satisfactory. The Grail, according to Miss Weston, was originally a sacred object in ancient fertility ritual, was thence adopted in the wide-spread cult of Mithra, from which origin sprang the earliest cryptic literature of the Grail, and at a comparatively late date was Christianized. Whether or not we accept this explanation, the Grail quest represents in its Christian form the same object as in these postulated origins. Even as a symbol used by medieval Christian poets it retains its fundamental character, in that the blood of Christ which it was thought to contain granted personal grace to the beholder and assurance of his renewal out of sin.[168]

A similar motif appears in Book I of Edmund Spenser's *The Faerie Queene*, yet despite the fact that many of the features of the Red Cross Knight's quest seem directly and organically related to the Holy Grail legend of Percival,[169] it does not appear clearly that Spenser regards restoration as the principal end of Red

Cross's quest. The defeat of Duessa and Archimago, and the hero's betrothal to Una (as the religious spirit is united to Truth) seem to be the chief objects of the book, and together they constitute an end more closely approaching that of Dante: Understanding, or Truth in Action. It is true that the Red Cross Knight must be restored from his imprisonment and sickness in order to fight the dragon; it is true that in the course of this fight his strength is miraculously renewed for each day's combat; and it is true that in slaying the dragon of Sin, the hero restores the land which it has laid waste, restores Una's parents to their rightful inheritance (essentially that of innocence), and all of these facts are in the spirit of the Grail legends. It is also indicative that the Red Cross Knight's sojourn in the House of Holiness (Canto X)—the only period of intense *instruction*, as such, accorded him—is likewise conceived by Spenser as instrumental and subordinate to the knight's final triumph, a mode of preparation for his combat. Yet the best we can say is that the object and outcome of the quest after Holiness is a mixture—in about the same proportions as Christian orthodoxy demands—of both restoration and the apprehension of Truth.

In Bunyan's *Pilgrim's Progress*, however, the predominating feature of the pilgrims' arrival at their destination, is their passage through the River of Death and the attendant transformation they undergo, shedding their 'mortal garments' in preparation to receive the golden equipment of Eternal Life. Bunyan's graphic method is far better suited to depict this aspect of salvation, and, indeed, his description of the Heavenly Jerusalem itself is more naively literalistic than comprehending: golden pavements, trumpets, harps, crowns, music, and all the regular images of an evangelist's ecstasy. Knowledge is treated in *The Pilgrim's Progress* as definitely subordinate to the end of renewing the soul in salvation, not, as Bunyan's contemporary Milton would have insisted, part of salvation itself.[170]

## 2.

*Italiam non sponte sequor.*

At the outset we should observe that, by the strictest interpretation of our subject, 'the metaphor of the Journey,' the *Aeneid* does not fall within its sphere. Unlike Fulgentius, we must confess that in the main the journey of Aeneas is not a metaphor at all. Basing his story upon legend and myth which serve in lieu of historical fact, Virgil takes his hero from an actual city through an accepted geographical and mythological landscape familiar to the Mediterranean world, and sets the final action of the last six books in the backyard of Augustan Rome itself.[1] Yet his is not the familiarity which breeds contempt, nor is his subject trivial because of its literal basis. Virgil was a serious artist, and must certainly have felt that his epic attended to the ultimate concerns of men, the concerns that we in a later age would regard as the proper business of religion. The fact is that Virgil would not have felt the necessity, so compelling to many medieval poets and earlier interpreters of ancient literature, of giving his subject a metaphorical treatment.[2] In a manner closely analogous to Homer's, the realms of spirit and of the material world were for Virgil coincident.

If we wish to understand Virgil in this respect, we must momentarily resist the Christian view of Rome implicit in the Biblical concession 'Render unto Caesar that which is Caesar's.' To the great Augustan poet, Rome was not simply the vast type of purely temporal order. It was as well a city of the spirit, and the teleological resolution of all the aspirations and struggles in the ancient known world. Bailey quite rightly observes that 'to Virgil the thought of Rome was always closely bound up with his religion and especially with its deepest ideas ... [and] his highest conception of fate, in which it is at once world-wide and closely linked with the will of Iuppiter and the gods, manifests itself in the destiny of Rome.'[3]

We may observe that from the very beginning Roman religious belief and practice was always a collective affair. It was always inextricably involved with the various units of Latin social organization, and at all times owed whatever strength it possessed to the typically Roman regard for the welfare of the community as a whole. The simplest unit to find religious expression in ancient Italy, also the earliest and most enduring in Roman history, was the family.[4] Its worship was centered about the hearth and its Vesta,[5] the Janus guarding the gate of the house from spirits from without who might do evil to the family, and the *di penates*, or undifferentiated group of spirits in the household's storage-place for food. These latter were always referred to in the plural and, although this was perhaps originally due to their representing different foodstuffs in the store, we should note with Fowler that they 'form a group in a way which is characteristic of the Latins.'[6] In any event, these three centers of family worship form the very core of Rome's civilization equally with its religious experience. Throughout the greatest centuries of Roman government, the gate of Janus and the temple of Vesta stood at the spiritual and geographical heart of the city itself.[7] Not only did they symbolize the collective security and domestic order of its citizens, they were themselves that order and security. They had emerged as projections of the family's collective desire for harmonious and peaceful establishment, and throughout the long history of their worship they retained the vitality and force of these origins. To the degree that we can imaginatively reconstruct the spirit of this quiet and beautiful worship, we will be able to understand, for example, the horror the Augustan must have felt over the passage in Book II of the *Aeneid* which tells of Pyrrhus' violation of the household altars to which Hecuba and her maidens and Priam cling.[8] And our understanding will certainly reinforce the grim irony implicit in Virgil's picture of Helen as Aeneas finds her,[9] crouching under the protective shadow of Vesta's shrine. It is, of course, her adulterous violation of domestic order which has brought about the present destruction of Trojan homes, and yet in the middle of the chaos she has wrought she seeks sanctuary at the very shrine she has betrayed. The meaning of the simple image, illuminated by the flames of burning Troy, penetrates to the spiritual center of the poem.[10]

The other important unit of Roman religion, which emerged with an increasing complexity of social organization, was the city-state. Like the family cultus, this was a 'worship of civic grouping,'[11] but tended toward greater impersonality and detachment from the individual lives of the citizens as the small city-state gradually grew into the proportions of an empire. Under Augustus, however, after the turmoil and despair in which Republican Rome had met its death, the cult of the state underwent a real revival and regeneration,[12] and during the comparatively brief period of this resuscitation it seems to have been of great importance to Virgil in the creation of his great epic. Few will dispute this, and we may easily see it to be so when we reflect that the entire poem pivots about the destruction of one city-state and the creation of another, and that no other alterna-

tive, such as the Judaic or Christian imaginative construction of
an Invisible City, is considered by Virgil. Virgil makes no explicit effort whatever to transcend the material world or its
limitations in his account of a journey toward order. This tallies
with what we know of the nature of the city-state cultus, since,
as Fowler observes, 'it was ... an intensely *local* system; and the
result was, first, that the Power is localised in certain spots and
propitiated by certain forms of cult within the city wall, thus
bringing the divine into closest touch with the human population
and its interests.'[13] It is this intense spiritual localization which
produces the Virgilian emphasis, mentioned in the Preface, on
the *geography* of Aeneas' wanderings. Not only must Aeneas pass
all the familiar mythological landmarks, such as the Sirens,
Scylla and Charybdis, and Circe's island, but the moments of
greatest significance occur for him on the sites of the three
greatest cities in the ancient world. He beholds the irreparable
destruction of his home in Troy and there receives his mission.
On the site of Carthage, Rome's traditional enemy, he resists
the greatest deterrent temptation of his journey. And it is of
course necessary to Virgil that his hero should visit the future site
of Rome, which he does in Book VIII on the pretext of an appeal
for alliance with Evander. Even then the local rustics feel the
great holiness of the place: 'This wood,' Evander says, 'this hill
with its crown of leaves, though which god is uncertain, is yet
the home of a god.'[14]

One other very strong characteristic of the Roman system of
worship ought to claim our attention as well: its elaborate legal-
ism. Secular Roman law remains for any student of the ancient
world the most impressive and felicitous aspect of the City and
its Empire, and despite its occasional lapses into violence and
unpredictable despotism, it stands as a by-word in the minds of
most of us for a calm and dispassionate order in government, in
the administration of civil justice, and in a high concept of individual duty to the state, the likes of which had never been seen
before in the Mediterranean world and has not been equalled
until comparatively recent times. We have all been trained to
detect its shortcomings, its inability to cope with growing despair
and terror in the hearts of its individual citizens, its failure to
attend to their inner emotional and spiritual needs, its helplessness
before the irrational forces of the Oriental resurrection-cults. All
these shortcomings are abundantly illustrated in Virgil's *Aeneid*,

and principally in his inability to deal with figures like Dido and Turnus to our complete moral and emotional satisfaction. Yet no one may seriously claim that Roman law did not embody one of the most exalted and worthwhile ideals the world has known, nor that Aeneas' flight, on what appears to us a legalistic pretext, from the deranged love of Dido toward the order of a future Rome, is an action undertaken from inferior or selfish motives.

We find it less easy to sympathize with the fact that the Roman formulated his spiritual attitudes through the city-state cult in a fashion closely analogous to his great concept of secular law. Just as the *ius civile* ordered the relationships of one citizen to another, so there existed a highly-developed *ius divinum*, administered by a very special priesthood who were essentially 'lawyers of the spirit', which Fowler has defined as 'the law governing the relations between the divine and human inhabitants of the city.'[15] It was the function of this spiritual law, like the civil, to keep order, to maintain the *pax deorum*. The highly ritualistic form of worship which it entailed was devoted to the end of maintaining 'right relations between the citizens and their deities; as ordaining what things are to be done or avoided in order to keep a continual *pax*, or quasi-legal covenant, between these two parties.'[16] The religion of the city-state was 'a *Rechtsverkehr*, a legal process going on continually.'[17] Despite the obvious inadequacy and impersonality of such a system, however, it very probably helped 'to maintain that sense of law and order which served to keep the life of the family sound and wholesome.'[18] In fact, this impersonality is not without virtue, since it reflects the attitude that the ultimate concerns of men should be attended to in the most peaceful and orderly manner possible. If it underestimated these ultimate concerns, if it failed to appeal to the individual's emotional life, it was certainly neither a barbaric nor a violent worship, and it avoided these qualities in an age which saw plenty of both. It reflected the characteristic and, in many ways, salutory Roman feeling that 'religious law and order were indispensable parts of their whole political and social life.'[19] Though we may feel that the Roman had thus taken hold of human experience by the wrong end, this was the way Virgil viewed the cult of Rome, and it is the same impulse toward the ordering of every part of experience at work in the legalistic mode of this religion, which lends to the *Aeneid* its main outlines and the definition of Aeneas' destination.

We should briefly touch on one remaining aspect of Virgil's 'spiritual Rome'. This is the worship of the Emperor as a divinity. Concerning this fairly late development,[20] we need only point out that Augustus discouraged belief in his personal divinity to a considerably greater degree than Julius had done,[21] founding his greatest claim to Roman loyalty in his role as the ruler who had restored the *pax deorum*,[22] and the *Aeneid* seems to reflect the official position in referring to the Emperor as the 'son of Divus,' i.e., of Julius. This cautiously establishes the status of Augustus. As Bailey observes, 'he is the son of one who has attained to a special kind of godhead, Divus not *deus;* he himself is a man as yet, but with a special kind of sanctity expressed in the old ritual title.'[23] It is in the sense of this special sanctity that he embodies and helps to localize the spiritual dimension of the Rome of Virgil's *Aeneid*. He stands in the poem both as the type of Aeneas the traveller, and of Rome the destination.

In brief, then, this is Virgil's spiritual Rome, or at least the Rome he saw and portrayed. It will not surprize us to find that the ethical response to his city-religion which the good Roman found suitable is *pietas*, 'the sense of duty to family, State, and Deity.'[24] Duty is always a commitment to order; it is the adherence, often difficult and unpleasurable, to predictable patterns of behavior, patterns upon which others may rely, patterns which give to those around us the quiet assurance that the expected will occur, and which provide the basis for every human endeavor, humble or spectacular. It is the commitment of Aeneas to such patterns which makes his continual epithet *pius* meaningful; his people, past, present, and future, depend on him to bring the Trojan-Roman *gens* to its future fruition in the city of Rome, and he must not disappoint either their conscious expectations or their nescient potentialities. In his case it is very clear that the patterns to which he must adhere are dictated by the gods or by the even higher power of fate, and are only gradually revealed to the hero, yet he must follow them as they are by degrees unfolded: *sic volvere Parcas*. In his greatest moments of temptation it is the existence of a 'right relation' between himself and the absolute powers of the universe, a meaning also implicit in *pietas*, which keeps him to the predictable and the expected. He tells Dido that he does not pursue the dream of Rome of his own free will—'Italiam non sponte sequor.'[25] While he speaks in this manner, she 'sees the whole man with her silent eyes',[26] a phrase which the modern reader will be apt to understand—and probably aright—in a double sense. Yet this is only one judgment of Aeneas, and a thoroughly partial one. If we wish to see what is really the 'whole man', we need only read a very few lines further to the passage in which Aeneas is pictured as withstanding the entreaties of Anna on her sister's behalf like an oak buffeted by Alpine winds. Virgil tells us that it 'stretches its crown as far into the aetherial airs as it extends its root into hell',[27] and gains its stability from this double anchorage. The simile is, of course, very literally appropriate to Aeneas, because his father Anchises is in Hades and his mother Venus in heaven, but it is also true in the sense that Aeneas derives his stability (only gradually acquired) from the rapport granted him with the actual nature of the world's destiny, a rapport of which Dido can know or believe nothing. It is interesting that Jupiter, the constant arbiter of this destiny as it affects Aeneas, the first to reveal its great pattern,[28] and the highest representative of the all-determining Parcae to appear in the poem, was traditionally known in Rome as the 'Dius Fidius,' the god of legal obligations, contracts, and the moral bonds which these implied.[29] In a very special and factual sense, then, he was a God of Order, and in this, as in his highest rank in the Roman pantheon, it is appropriate and characteristic of the Roman sensibility that he should preside over the action of the *Aeneid*.

In view of our special interest in the poem, it hardly seems necessary or useful to trace a thematic unity through its entire action, a task successfully undertaken by a great many before us. But let us observe that if Aeneas' mission is to establish social and spiritual order, as we have maintained, then both the place from which the hero departs, and those who attempt to thwart the progress of his journey, will be characterized by disorder and violence. In this our expectations are fulfilled. Juno, for example, is consistently portrayed throughout the poem as a furious and raging harridan whose chief weapon against Aeneas is her ability to summon up wild and destructive natural or infernal forces. We first meet this 'dolens regina deum' in Book I, when she persuades Aeolus to release the winds under his custody in the hopes of overwhelming the fleet of Aeneas. Aeolus himself ordinarily has the job of taming these winds and soothing their rage: 'Aeolus sits in his high tower, holding sway, taming their spirits and tempering their rage.'[30] If he did not do so, Virgil tells us, they would confound and sweep away all land and seas and sky in their wild flight. But Jupiter, afraid of this ('hoc metuens'), piled over them great masses of mountains to hold them in check.[31] Now Juno appears and commands their release ('incute vim ventis').

We may digress briefly at this point to notice an interesting feature of Virgil's imagery, particularly in the first several books of the *Aeneid*. He presents a series of pictures to us, of which this Cave of Aeolus is only the first, which possess in common the element of some wild and violent force being constrained and contained by a controlling or merely enclosing element. Forces are being held down, held under in the poem. We may notice the same arrangement in the image of Impius Furor at the end of Jupiter's speech to Venus,[32] an image which is the last in Jupiter's introductory account of the way in which Aeneas' mission is related to the destiny of Rome. The gates of Janus' temple are closed and locked upon this violent spirit, and his arms are bound with a hundred brazen knots. Here, then, is the ultimate envisioned accomplishment of the City toward which Aeneas travels so laboriously: violence contained and controlled. Yet in Book VII Juno herself smashes open the doors, releasing Furor.[33]

In a different context, the same imagistic structure recurs in the Greek horse of Book II. It is repeatedly described with emphasis on its hollowness, its containment of weapons and armed men, and a series of adjectives (e.g., 'feta armis') are applied to it which bear the connotation of 'pregnancy'—an ironic and ghastly pregnancy, to be sure, because the horse will bring forth a child of chaos and destruction within the walls of unsuspecting Troy. In this case it is Sinon, the Greek spy, who releases these forces of disorder from their confinement, but Juno again acts in the same capacity in Book VII when she summons the dread Fury and goddess of discord, Allecto, up from the infernal regions.[34] In this instance, too, the release of violent forces is associated with an ironic image of pregnancy: first, Juno reflects[35] concerning Lavinia and her proposed marriage to Aeneas that Trojan and Rutulian blood will be her dower and Bellona will be her bridal matron, then compares her to Hecuba who, when she was carrying Paris, dreamed she bore a firebrand in her womb. Likewise, Allecto herself is commanded by Juno to arouse her fertile bosom and sow the seeds of war ('fecundum concute pectus ... sere crimina belli').

There is little need to dwell on the ways in which the Greeks of Book II are agents of disorder and chaos. Yet this characteristic is not only evident in the obvious fact that they are the destroyers of Troy; it is also apparent in the mode they employ to bring about this destruction. Everywhere Aeneas insists on their treachery and guile, their lack of faith,[36] qualities manifestly inimical to the maintenance of civil or religious order. Their pretended retreat from Troy, the astounding perjury of Sinon, the trick of the horse, all these play treacherously upon the more or less natural expectations of the Trojans, together with the fact that the Greeks attack at night when the Trojans are sunk in quiet sleep. Despite the ironically quiet moon[37]—another repressive image—under which the Greeks sail back to Troy, we may frequently equate images of night in Virgil's poem with the dark, uncontrollable, and violent forces of the nether world and of the human mind. No one can seriously doubt this who has paid close attention to the character of the frequent dreams described in the *Aeneid*, or who has observed with care the imagery in Book VI of the entrance into the infernal regions by the Sibyl and Aeneas.

It should be noticed that at one point in Book II Aeneas, whose *pietas* seems momentarily out of order, is caught up into the web of treachery and violence in which the Greeks and the whole city of Troy are involved. This is during the time when, against the explicit directions of the ghostly Hector to leave Troy with his family and household gods, he sallies forth from his house to fight the Greek invaders and dons Greek armor in order to trick his enemy. Here Aeneas characterizes himself with the words 'furor' and 'ira',[38] and when he and his warriors meet Androgeos and slay him, Aeneas likens himself in a simile[39] to a hidden and dangerous snake. One cannot help recalling the snakes of a few lines previous which have destroyed Laocoön and his sons, nor the simile a few lines after,[40] in which Pyrrhus himself, the most treacherous and brutal of the Greeks, is compared to a poisonous snake as he appears at Priam's threshold; nor should we forget, though the comparison is more remote, that Allecto is described in Book VII as having Medusan hair, and as causing Amata's fury by casting one of her serpents into the queen's bosom.[41] She arouses Turnus' fury in a similar manner, except that two snakes appear here, 'geminos. . . anguis,'[42] directly recalling the 'gemini . . . angues'[43] which destroyed Laocoön.

What Allecto actually casts into Turnus' breast, however, is a firebrand, and it is this flame which directly arouses his ire against Aeneas, and with this image we are brought back again to Book II and the fall of Troy. Throughout the story of the city's destruction, imagery of flame and fire constantly recurs: everywhere it may be said literally that Troy is falling with 'Volcano superante domus.'[44] There are two kinds of fire in the *Aeneid*: the one kind is sanctified, associated with the destiny of Rome, and is represented in the poem by the hearth-fire of Vesta[45] and by the miraculous fires which crown the head of Ascanius[46] and the tresses of Lavinia.[47] It clearly symbolizes for Virgil the spirit and order of Rome and her households. The other kind of fire, however, is that which rises over Troy. It is fire as a chaotic and destructive force, and as such it reappears, like Virgil's reptilian imagery, at intervals throughout the poem.

Our awareness of this will be of service to our interpretation of the story in Book IV of Dido's fatal love. The literal flames of burning Troy become, from the very beginning of this book onward, the metaphorical flames of the queen's insane and corrosive passion for Aeneas. The very frequent description of Dido's love in terms of such words as 'ignis', 'accensum', 'flamma', 'incensum', 'urere', 'ardere',[48] is now associated at intervals with another image, that of a wound ('volnus'), which develops in at least one place into a full-fledged simile of Dido as a deer smitten by the arrow of a 'pastor ... nescius,'[49] a shepherd unmindful of the harm he has done. The wound and fire will remind us of that which Juno ('accensa'[50]) suffers ('aeternum servans sub pectore volnus'[51]), and will be reflected again in the 'pectore flammam' and the poison of the snake which Amata harbors in her bosom, as well as in the firebrand which Turnus harbors in his own. Dido's wound and fire, in similar fashion, become literal facts at the end of Book IV when the queen kills herself with Aeneas' sword and is burned on the pyre she has ordered for herself. Had Aeneas delayed longer, however, the fire could have become literal fact in an entirely different way. Mercury appears to him in a dream and warns him that if he does not leave at once, Dido will have his ships burned;[52] and a few lines later[53] the idea suggests itself to Dido. It seems clear enough that with a little more time she might put it into practice. Such a flame, of course, would mean the thwarting of Aeneas' journey and mission; and when the Trojan women by the instigation of Iris actually set fire to the ships in Book V, the direct intervention of Jupiter is necessary to save the cause of Rome.

We have given some indication already of the fact that Amata and Turnus, too, are characterized by violence and disorder. Yet we may note other signs of this. If Virgil has not made his attitude toward Amata sufficiently clear in his continual portrayal of her uncontrolled emotionalism, it is well-defined from the first in another way. As soon as Allecto has done her work, Amata ('maius adorta nefas'[54]) gathers together the neighborhood matrons and hides her daughter Lavinia in the hills, where they all celebrate a frenzied Bacchanalia.[55] The queen is described as she 'immensam sine more furit lymphata per urbem'[56] (a phrase placing her in a parallel to Dido, who 'totaque vagatur urbe furens'[57]), and it is the phrase 'sine more' which provides the best key to her moral position in the last books of the *Aeneid*. The word survives in the cheapened and sterilized 'mores' of the modern sociological text-book, but for the Roman it possessed a rich and comprehensive sense which we can probably best translate as 'the due process and order of things'. Like Turnus, Amata is outside of this order and is without its inward counterpart, and there is no better indication of this than the reference itself to a Bacchic celebration. Livy tells us that, after the war with Hannibal (or, after the death of Dido), the Bacchanalia came secretly to Rome after being dangerously modified in Etruria and Campania. The form of the nocturnal ritual took a particularly obscene and violent turn, came to involve a good many of Rome's citizens including youngsters of noble families, was discovered, regarded as a conspiracy against both civil and religious Rome, and was quickly and effectively suppressed. It was viewed as 'externa superstitio' and therefore a violation and a contamination of the old gods of the City-state, and of the 'mos maiorum' (our word again).[58] Amata's actions are of the same kind. They are outside the whole complex of religious and civil and household law; Virgil points to the fact that the matrons 'deseruere domos'[59]—which for the Augustan meant Rome.

No such simple reference establishes Turnus' position in the epic, yet it is clearly and consistently maintained. As Allecto hurls her torch into his breast, his insane frenzy is described by the simile of a cauldron boiling over a fire.[60] This character he retains to the end, in attributive images[61] and in his violent refusal to quit what is more and more obviously a lost cause. After Amata's suicide, he stands alone, deserted even by Juno and Juturna, in his insistence on continuing the war. He is thus 'sine more' in a wider sense than Amata, because he is rebellious to the end not only against the order of things, but against the order of things to be, the unfolding destiny of Rome. It is this increasingly evident fact, that Aeneas is in harmony with the ultimate direction of events, which Turnus refuses to acknowledge or accept. Aeneas was required to face a similar situation in Book II, when Venus showed him that *all* the gods were intent upon the destruction of Troy, and it was due to his acceptance that he became a refugee and empire-founder rather than a dead hero. Now the same acquiescence is required of Turnus, and his failure means inevitable obliteration,[62] because he obstinately continues to represent 'the spirit of disunion and strife.'[63] Yet Turnus does realize his position at the end, even if it is too late to rectify it; the knowledge saps his vitality and power to act[64]:

> What paralyzes him is the discovery that the great deity of *fides, iustitia, pietas*, is his enemy. To have Jupiter as your enemy was for a Roman inconceivable: it would mean that you are an outcast from civilization, from social life and virtue. It was not for these that Turnus fought, but for individual passion, for the pride of youth and beauty, for the love of fighting. When that messenger from Jupiter has warned him that such things are of no avail, and that the course of this world is not to be ordered by them, that they have no value in the eyes of the king of gods and men—then his hand trembles as it grasps the stone ...[65]

Yet such things, caught up and treasured by reckless young men, *are* of value, and no amount of social virtue and organized civilization is capable of fully persuading us otherwise. Thus far we have dealt with the main lines of the *Aeneid*, the explicit and dominating pattern of disorder and order which determines the point of departure and the destination of Aeneas' journey. His travels begin in a center of confusion and amidst the disruption of all that makes for quiet and useful daily life,[66] and will end, as Anchises shows him in Hades,[67] in a great race of governors who shall bring again the Golden Age of peace and law ('pacique imponere morem'[68]). We have also noted briefly that Virgil's imagery when he deals with violence is often of a strangely re-

pressive kind; it contains rather than resolves the forces which
are evoked.[69] Yet containment and repression are not enough,
do not provide an adequate response to human experience, and
everywhere in the *Aeneid* we feel the strange and haunting
inadequacy of the hero who represents and seeks reason and
order and must leave so much else behind him, unforgiving, un-
resolved, and unconquered.[70] Dido, Amata, Turnus are not
unsympathetic characters. Far from it; they are splendidly conceived and portrayed so well that one may say that Virgil has
spent all the energy of his great, sad imagination upon them
which found no place in the Augustan success story of Aeneas
himself. And in doing so he has sapped the sureness of that
success and the certainty of the Roman vision of order which the
poem expounds, but it is from this weakening of the one explicit
dimension of the poem, that the *Aeneid* derives its perennial greatness. Amata in her sordid[71] suicide by hanging; Dido tempestu-
ous, majestic, and unforgiving; Creusa too late remembered;
weaponless and helpless Turnus, slain in righteous anger,[72] but
anger just the same; all these are *absunt*—in the fiercely active
sense of that verb—from the ultimate vision of the Roman
Empire. Miss Bodkin has with reason seen this, in a comparison
of Dido with the Eurydice at the end of Virgil's *Georgics*:

> Within our experience of Virgil's poetry, this ever-desired
> image presented in Eurydice has, I think, clear affinity with
> the image presented in Dido, of one wronged and for ever
> alienated amid the shades. Virgil's Orpheus, striving vainly
> to say a thousand things, seems one with that Aeneas who,
> while he faintly pleads or frames excuse, falters, knowing
> himself tongue-tied, fated to leave all unsaid. The poet who,
> like Virgil, by his poetic gift possesses those delicate intui-
> tions and sympathies with all forms of life that are commonly
> thought of as constituting feminine sensibility, and who yet
> accepts as inevitable a system of 'masculine' thought and
> morality, ignoring all such sympathies, holds a part of him-
> self unrealized. It will cry out upon him, alienated and
> suffering like Dido. It will move upward toward the light,
> like Eurydice, through the power of his song, then plunge
> back into the gloom, as he turns from poetry to actual life.[73]

Little further can be said, except that we may note how the sense
of emotional inadequacy, of leaving behind a richness and full-
ness of life, is to be found in great journey-poems other than the

*Aeneid* which take order as part of their destination. One needs only turn to Yeats's *Sailing to Byzantium* for a striking modern example of this:

> That is no country for old men. The young
> In one another's arms, birds in the trees
> —Those dying generations—at their song,
> The salmon-falls, the mackerel-crowded seas,
> Fish, flesh, or fowl, commend all summer long
> Whatever is begotten, born, and dies.
> Caught in that sensual music all neglect
> Monuments of unageing intellect.

An old man is looking back upon the country he has left behind as he speaks these lines and, knowing that the inadequacy to cope with the vibrant turmoil of life he describes lies in himself, who is 'but a paltry thing,' he must put life away for the metallic and artificial order of Byzantium. Yet the sentiments of the narrator do not lie entirely with the artifice of his destination, and the stanza we have quoted is as much a hymn to the sheer powers of biological regeneration as it is a renunciation of them. Though interpretation of the poem in a later chapter, turning upon a certain image in the last stanza, will permit a somewhat different reading,[74] the dominance of the first stanza over the others in terms of imagistic vitality and vividness cannot be denied. In this sense, though perhaps only in this sense, the poem's solution appears to come about through a process of subtraction. In this sense also, the order of art typified in the metal bird seems achieved more through the omission of concrete experience than through an attempt to order that experience itself.

A much happier resolution is attained in Dante's poem. Behind him is the ever-present image of a violent and treacherous and chaotic Florence; before him is the unfolding justice of God manifested in His otherworld kingdoms. It is true that Dante leaves Ser Brunetto and others behind with the most painful regret, and we cannot say that he is not haunted throughout the *Commedia* by a vision of the irreparable loss of his mother city. But, as Miss Bodkin points out,[75] Dante is unlike Virgil in having the figure of a woman before him in his search for order, not left behind, and Beatrice, exiled by death, stands for everything that Dante most valued in Florence. The resolution is partly achieved, also, by the fact noted above that Dante must return to the world and live out the rest of his days. He cannot return to Florence, to be sure, but he presumably comes back to a turbulent world not unlike that of his lost city. Though this becomes less and less evident in the didactic ecstasy of the *Paradiso*, the sense of Dante's fleshly nature remains with the reader who has seen the constant surprize of souls in Hell and Purgatory over the fact that Dante breathes and is yet endowed with mortal life.

In any case it seems quite clear that Dante's journey is primarily one toward order, though toward an order which already exists, as the justice of God manifesting itself in the state of souls after death. Since this justice is only gradually unfolded before Dante's eyes, the most important element in the poem is the awakening of the traveller's understanding. The journey of the *Commedia* is first and foremost a process of learning, of comprehension, and when in the last Canto of the *Paradiso* Dante's understanding has been sharpened to the furthest point of which a human being is capable, he is permitted to look upon God:

> Within its depths I saw ingathered, bound by love in one
> volume, the scattered leaves of all the universe;
> substance and accidents and their relations, as though to-
> gether fused, after such fashion that what I tell of is one
> simple flame.[76]

Here at last, in three rings of interlocked light comprising the ultimate vision of the *Commedia* and comprehending its reality, the anomalies of the universe make sense for Dante, and the traveller finds his desire and will controlled and at one, with the order of love which moves the sun and the other stars.

\*

In the last pages of this chapter we will find it useful to concentrate on a whole genre of literature which, though it can scarcely be called poetry, even by the widest definition of that flexible term, does exhibit generally the impulse toward order, and which reached its great years of artistic fruition in the second Augustan Age, only a short time before the nineteenth century itself. This is the picaresque novel, which in the eighteenth century ceased to include only those stories whose heroes are rogues (picaros), and embraced as well strong elements of the Quixotic tradition and the chivalric romance as well. In the great complex of the novelist's art which resulted from this fusion, one strong central pattern predominates. The youthful hero is ejected from the society into which he was born, whether by his own misdemeanors, the machinations of envious relatives, simple misfortune, or by a poverty which makes his continued position in the society intolerable. In any case he becomes a wanderer, and the object of his travels is to seek his 'fortune'. The word 'fortune' in its modern usage implies mainly financial security, and although this was one of its central meanings in the late seventeenth and eighteenth centuries, it included a much wider range of significance as well. We may better understand how this financial concern of the picaresque hero was merged in the greater set of values which were the object of his wanderings, if we recognize the truth of Professor Tawney's observations on society and wealth in this age:

> Society is not a community of classes with varying functions, united to each other by mutual obligations arising from their relation to a common end. It is a joint-stock company rather than an organism, and the liabilities of the shareholders are strictly limited. They enter it in order to insure the rights already vested in them by the immutable laws of nature ... The most important of such rights are property rights, and property rights attach mainly, though not, of course, exclusively, to the higher orders of men, who hold the tangible, material 'stock' of society. Those who do not subscribe to the company have no legal claim to a share in the profits, though they have a moral claim on the charity of their superiors.[77]

This means that contained within the social framework there are many who are regarded as owning no place in it, and whether we may or may not condemn this view of membership in society as ruthless and terrible in the consequences of its principle of exclusion, we should see that the picaresque hero seeking his fortune is seeking through it much more. He is seeking an order of life, a stability of position in which he may find his expectations of those around him fulfilled and the proper rewards of honest activity granted. Again and again in the novels of this period we see the hero torn loose from the society of his youth and set adrift, as an exile still floating *within* the social structure. not out of it, but without membership and without recognition.

He does not leave a Troy to found a Rome; the city which he leaves, the Carthage of his exile, and the city in which he finally finds membership are one and the same, and his behavior is always best understood in terms of his changing relation to it. During the period of his exile, his youthful trust in the strength of social obligations is shattered, and with the shedding of his first innocence comes the compensatory realization of the great powers of mobility which his classlessness—aided by an occasionally fraudulent impersonation—affords him. Since he is a member of no social class, the *picaro* can easily, albeit falsely, move through all of them, and it is due to the observations, whether satirical or not, which he makes in his multiplicity of roles, that the picaresque novel becomes a great vehicle of social experience and commentary. But although his mobility has great advantages, it has serious disadvantages too, and almost always the hero has before him a desired vision of class status, of the acquisition of 'fortune' and the social responsibilities for charity and benevolence which that acqustion entails. Before we look at a few of these novels, we may notice one curious detail of the picaresque pattern which is more evident in the later, more ethically sophisticated works. This is the way in which the hero, during the course of his exile, builds up a few solid and worthwhile friendships with people who maintain their honesty and generous good nature in a savage world where survival is all-important and a supremely individual affair. These friendships sometimes amount to the creation of a small 'true' society in contradistinction to the large 'false' one, and with the firm establishment of the hero, such friendships are usually rewarded and given some permanent form.[78]

Although it contains the basic elements of the pattern we have outlined above, Mendoza's *Lazarillo de Tormes* (1554),[79] shows almost no traces of this latter feature. Lazarillo, a servant, has no friends, only various masters, and the chapters of the book divide naturally into accounts of Lazarillo's service under each of these. The relationships are invariably those of exploitation. In Chapter I, for instance, Lazarillo is ostensibly the accomplice of a blind beggar, yet they are not shown struggling together to eke out a living from a hostile world. The really evident struggle for survival takes place between the two, and all Lazarillo's animal intelligence is employed in getting enough food from his master, not from others. When he serves a miserly priest the same situation recurs, and if he did not cheat his master he would simply starve to death. Only once does this pattern crack, when Lazarillo attaches himself to a proud though penniless hidalgo. Because this hungry nobleman is secretly in the same plight as Lazarillo, the boy displays a disinterested loyalty toward him in foraging for both, until the hidalgo shows the same irresponsibility as the other two in leaving him to face the alguazil and possible imprisonment for his master's debts.

Lazarillo's relation to society follows the general picaresque pattern in other respects, however. He is forced from home as a young boy because his mother cannot provide food for him, and in the Hobbesian state of nature which then engulfs him he quickly loses his friendly and trustful response to those around him and assumes an attitude of calculated self-interest and hostile reaction to the world. The first action of the blind beggar is to bang Lazarillo's head against a stone bull, and the boy tells us that from that moment he was 'now alone,' and had awakened from the simplicity of childhood. From that time on, he is caught in a desperate struggle against every other human being, and particularly against hunger. It is the sad moment of his disillusionment with the hidalgo, however, which represents the real turning-point in Lazarillo's wanderings, and, ironically enough, the beginning of his return to society in full knowledge of the sottish principles of 'cooperation' upon which it is based. This cooperation is exemplified in a lucrative fraud worked together by a seller of papal indulgences and the alguazil, upon the devout and unwary believers of the parish. Witnessing this unsavory performance, Lazarillo is duly appreciative and ready for his final integration into a corrupt though secure social order: he becomes the servant of a bishop who provides him with an income and marries him to his own concubine. In this way Lazarillo makes an easy exchange of his marital honor for the security of life which the bishop can offer him, and as the powerful little story draws to a close, the young man—at last—has enough to eat.

Mateo Aleman's *Guzman de Alfarache* (1599, 1604) is a very long, dull novel, thoroughly larded with unpleasant moral commentary characteristic of puritanical Spanish Catholicism of the period, yet one incident among its wealth of episodes is worthy of notice. The general pattern of the book is similar to that of *Lazarillo de Tormes* in its portrayal of a wanderer exiled and at

variance with a corrupt society, with which he ultimately comes
to questionable terms. In the course of his adventures, Guzman
uses and is used by those who hold definite positions in this
society, but it is impossible for him to establish any deep or
permanent attachments with them.[80] He gains the ability, by
acting fraudulent roles, of moving easily through the entire
hierarchical structure of society, but at the expense of his membership in it. He is irretrievably an exile. All of his liaisons of any
kind whatever are established under false pretenses and therefore
untenable for long, or contracted with the intention to defraud a
third party, and therefore necessarily opposed to and isolated
from the social structure. The episode referred to above, which is
both revealing and pathetic, is that in which Guzman, posing in
Florence as the nephew of the Spanish Ambassador, falls in love
and actually goes through the motions of contracting marriage
with a lady of quality, even though such a project is made
utterly hopeless by the imminence of his exposure. When he is
forced to leave her, she tells him, 'I loved you without knowing
you; and even if you were not what I think you are, I feel I
should not cease to love you. I should not perhaps have noticed
in a common man the qualities with which you have impressed
me; my pride of birth would not have allowed me to remark
them in an inferiour; but since they have once swayed my heart,
believe me, they can never lose their power.'[81] This is about as
close as poor Guzman comes to membership in the society which
he constantly preys upon, a society too self-involved and rigid
in its structural snobberies to regard him as himself, a society
which rejects him when he tries to play a truly honest role,[82] but
which accepts unquestioningly the least deception which he
practices. In the Florentine episode are revealed both Guzman's
wistful awareness of the terrible extent of his exile, and his
underlying concern with belonging, even though the hierarchical
order to which he would belong is corrupt and membership in
it of questionable value. Other episodes in the novel point to the
same polarity of concern: although the great majority of Guzman's frauds are perpetrated with an eye for financial gain, and
although Guzman continually reminds us that he acts in total
self-interest, yet he frequently poses at great cost as a gentleman
to satisfy his own vanity, and is thereby almost as frequently
rendered penniless. His confusion about his own motives is
apparent at every turn, and is largely due to his conflicting atti-

tudes in reacting to the strongly evident social hierarchy, the order which eventually brings his autonomous ambitions to nothing.

The position of the hero in Le Sage's great novel *The Adventures of Gil Blas* (1715) is considerably different from Guzman's. Gil Blas has far less difficulty in finding a place in society, and it is seldom a fraudulent one. Whatever his misdemeanors are, they are done within rather than against the hierarchy. The ingratitude and affectation and occasional dishonesty of which he is guilty, particularly during his first taste of precarious power at court, and which he comes to regret deeply, are of a kind all too freely sanctioned by the society in which he struggles, and much of the latter portions of the book is concerned with his creation for himself of an ethical standard independent of general morality, and with his realization of a small society of his honest friends to whom this higher standard exactly applies. He learns a great deal about the duty he owes his friends in the interval between his two careers at court. During his service with the Duke of Lerma, he quarrels with Fabricius, repays Joseph Navarro's friendship by ungratefully refusing to do him a favor because another offers money for it, and only provides his former patron Don Alphonso with a governorship out of vanity. But when he is disgraced and imprisoned, his servant Scipio displays his fidelity and devotion in keeping him company in the tower of Segovia and in eventually obtaining his release; the prison-keeper Tordesillas befriends him, and Don Gaston de Cogollos, a fellow prisoner, becomes his consolatory partner in misfortune. When he is released, Gil Blas is given an estate at Lirias by Don Alphonso. He is sincerely grateful to all of these, and is in time enabled to repay them with important services. He has learned his lesson: the folly and self-interest and affectation which had engulfed him at court make real friendship impossible. Finally Gil Blas achieves what Guzman could never win, either in fact or as a symbol of belonging: he is awarded a patent of nobility. This performs the useful function of removing the last barriers in the hero's small group of friends, between his former masters and himself, but it is totally in keeping with Le Sage's intelligent and inclusive system of values, and highly significant for the development of his hero, that Gil Blas makes no show whatever of possessing the patent. It is a sign of success in society-at-large, but in the course of Gil Blas' fight to win that kind of success, he has lost his dependence upon it.

It is when we turn to eighteenth-century English novels that our quotation above from Professor Tawney's book appears most relevant. In Daniel Defoe's *Moll Flanders* (1722), the heroine's aberrations (like Guzman's) are due largely to the frustrations of a plucky individual faced by a restrictive society: 'The heroine, it is true, is a criminal; but the high incidence of crime in our civilization is itself mainly due to the wide diffusion of an individualist ideology in a society where success is not easily or equally attainable to all its members.'[83] Unlike Guzman, however, Moll seems to Ian Watt to be fully a member of her society, operating within its structure and presumably thus indicative of a general condition:

> It is because her crimes ... are rooted in the dynamics of economic individualism that Moll Flanders is essentially different from the protagonists of the picaresque novel ... Defoe ... presents his whores, pirates, highwaymen, shoplifters and adventurers as ordinary people who are normal products of their environment, victims of circumstances which anyone might have experienced and which provoke exactly the same moral conflicts between means and ends as those faced by other members of society.[84]

To some extent this is quite true, but if Professor Tawney is correct, Moll, together with a large segment of the population, would not have been regarded in her own time as members of society at all. This is why, though Moll is in the same uncertain status as many others, she fits so well into the typical pattern of the wandering picaresque hero looking for a place in the social order. All of Moll's attempts to situate herself in a wealthy marriage occur as a most basic part of her will to respectability and membership in a society whose entrance requirements are primarily financial. She is initially removed from her position as a servant because of her sexual involvement with the sons of the house, floats from one strained and difficult relationship to another, and even in her middle age sees the American marriage she has finally won explode with her knowledge that it is incestuous. Yet no matter how crudely her endeavors are formulated, they represent a yearning toward a life without the necessity of fraud, secure and ordered.

Jonathan Swift's *Gulliver's Travels* (1726) achieves its effects often by the satirical inversion of commonly accepted literary patterns and standards of morality. Such an observation is the Swiftian critic's stock-in-trade, but we might easily overlook the fact that the movement of the entire last voyage, Gulliver's adventure in the Land of the Houyhnhnms, represents such an inversion of the usual picaresque pattern. Gulliver does not detach himself from the order of society, become an exile, and eventually find a place once more in that order. On the contrary, he gets his last glimpse of human 'society' in the form of his mutinous crew, who set him ashore in an unknown land. He discovers that he is in a community of horses possessed of the greatest wisdom and reason, who live an orderly existence entirely undisrupted by the ill effects of passion, greed, or pride. During the five years of his stay, he has always before his eyes the execrable figures of the Yahoos, evil and passionate beasts with a debased human form and a crude herd-instinct as their only form of social organization, who are happily kept under the Houyhnhnms' strict control. It is with the utmost difficulty that Gulliver succeeds in persuading his equine masters of some slight distinction between himself and the Yahoos; yet the final judgment of the Houyhnhnms in assembly is that, if there exists such a distinction, it only makes Gulliver more dangerous, not less. Therefore he is told that he must leave, and return to those of his own kind. This idea is abhorrent to him, and when he sets sail it is his intention 'to discover some small island uninhabited, yet sufficient by my labor to furnish me with the necessaries of life, which I would have thought a greater happiness, than to be first minister in the politest court of Europe; so horrible was the idea I conceived of returning to live in the society, and under the government of *Yahoos*.'[85] Found by the sailors of a Portuguese vessel and forcibly returned to Europe, Gulliver suffers a revulsion against his own kind hardly to be distinguished from insanity, and after five years has progressed in his reconciliation only to the point of being able to endure the sight of his wife in the same room, though he still cannot stand the touch of her or any other Yahoo. Having travelled, in short, through a country where society is the true product of reason and mental order, he is unfitted for membership in that which is inescapably his own.

Like *Gulliver's Travels*, the last novel we shall discuss compares favorably in stature with the greatest works in any genre of literature, and remains, or should remain, a perennial source of delight to all readers. It is Henry Fielding's comic epic *Joseph*

*Andrews* (1742). A social novel in a social age, at the same time that it follows the picaresque pattern of the hero displaced from his position in society and drifting classless within it toward a reunion, it draws to a superb height as well that other theme recurrent in the genre, the friendship between outcasts, the small society of friends.

Men in a society have two roles: on the one hand they have functions, professions, trades; on the other, they are human beings, simply, with personal particular ties to one another. This distinction is noticeably applicable to the most interesting character in Fielding's novel, Parson Adams. The ostensible hero is, of course, Joseph, a young country lad in the service of Lady Booby at her London house; she discharges him because he pristinely refuses to render other services to her beyond the terms of his contract. Throughout the remainder of the novel she serves Fielding as Nemesis, attempting at every turn to thwart Joseph's return to his parish. On his way home he meets Parson Adams, the clergyman of the parish, who is travelling to London with a vague and innocent plan of publishing his sermons. The parson soon discovers, however, that he has forgotten to take the sermons with him, and therefore decides to return with Joseph. Shortly they encounter Fanny, Joseph's sweetheart, who is worried about Joseph and so has decided to find him in London. The three of them, pitted against a hostile roadside world, join together in the return which, as we will see, is far more than a simple trip from one place to another or a collection of unrelated adventures.

The real pivotal figure of the novel is Parson Adams, not Joseph. As he becomes the center of our delighted attention because of his traits and antics, so is he the moral center of the novel, for a different reason: he is both Joseph's and Fanny's pastor, and their friend. Through most of the novel he pursues both roles rather separately from one another, and at times they seem almost at variance.

As the couple's friend, Parson Adams offers the use of all the money he has (nine shillings and three pence halfpenny), for which Joseph is understandably grateful: 'This goodness ... brought tears into Joseph's eyes; he declared, he had now a second reason to desire life, that he might show his gratitude to such a friend.'[86] It is as their friend, too, that Adams demonstrates his madcap joy at the happier events which befall them, such as their reunion after a temporary and hectic separation, when, having cast his beloved Æschylus in the fire, he is found 'dancing about the room in a rapture ...'[87] or after Squire Booby has retrieved the couple from the charge, instigated by his sister, of twig-stealing, when Adams sees Joseph in his new clothes and 'burst into tears with joy, and fell to rubbing his hands and snapping his fingers as if he had been mad.'[88] His great fists and brawny muscles, also, make him a very useful friend on several occasions, notably when he rescues Fanny from her first would-be molester by the unclerical expedient of knocking him senseless. As a friend, in short, Adams is immediately concerned with furthering the couple's most intense purpose, getting them home safe, sound, and together.

As a pastor, Adams performs a quite different and most efficacious service for the young lovers. At several points in the story, Joseph shows great impatience to marry Fanny immediately. The parson will have none of it, and insists that it can be proper only after the third publication of the banns, and in their own parish church. At one point he tells Joseph in no uncertain terms that 'he had no licence, nor indeed would he advise him to obtain one: that the church had prescribed a form—namely, the publication of banns,—with which all good Christians ought to comply, and to the omission of which he attributed the many miseries which befel great folks in marriage ...'[89] Here Adams is acting in the highest capacity of a member of the organized church in an organized society; that is, he is insisting on the due process of *ritual*, which must surround all human activity in order to give it form and meaning. The episodes concerned with the attempted rapes of Fanny appear not merely for the sake of the sensational; nor do those in which Slipslop and her mistress Lady Booby attempt Joseph's person merely for the sake of satirizing the prudery of a young man. They are instances of violence—violence done to ritual and the organization of a society headed by Deity. The only proper way the story can end is in a marriage which takes its place in the order and scheme of things. As a personal friend of Joseph and Fanny, Parson Adams wishes with all his heart that the couple be united as quickly as possible. As their pastor, he proceeds with the utmost deliberation, despite all of Lady Booby's machinations and threats, to publish the banns and perform the marriage ceremony. With this final act, he establishes the couple's legal right to settle in the

parish (i.e., an end to their peregrination, a place in society), and
finally unites in a single gesture his own two roles as friend and
churchman. No man can do more.

Every age and society must work out its attitude and relationship to the sexual act, and we may consider that Fielding's
novel performs very much the same function in this regard as
Book III of *The Faerie Queene* does for its time, or *The Waste Land*
in our own. Ironically, Fielding starts out to satirize an attitude
of sexual affectation and prudery in the works of a contemporary
novelist, Richardson, and ends with a sound and humane view
of what chastity and sexual morals really imply in the context of
a good—or bad—society, a view which develops and unfolds
with the journey of these three scatterbrained innocents, and
only appears in its full latitude and great sanity at the moment
when that journey draws to its happy close.

We have come a considerable way from the lonely ego of the
early picaresque hero. Even the later novels use friendship as a
means to give the episodes along the traveller's route a certain
coherence through the reappearance of characters, or, as the
society-in-small, friendship between the hero and others serves
to reflect the ultimate concern of the traveller with finding a
place for himself in the order of things; but yet the hero always is
seeking his own fortune, not someone else's, even though he may
defer and modify his selfish interests to an ethical dictate or
powerful custom. Even in Sarah Fielding's novel *David Simple, In
the Search of a Real Friend* (1744), which places the greatest possible strain on the altruism of the friendships it portrays, the
hero is *searching* for a friend, who will be his 'fortune' since he
already has plenty of money. But Parson Adams is simultaneously the chief character of Henry Fielding's novel, and a friend.
The fortune to be sought is not his own; through his usual forget-
fulness he has left his sermons at home, and therefore is neither
inclined nor able to pursue his own interests. But the end he
travels toward is service as a friend, in the fullest possible sense
of the word, toward a society invested in a rich and amiable
order.

\*

The reader may have noticed that the novels under discussion, unlike most of the other works with which we have had
occasion to deal, do not treat of the traveller or his destination in

a spirit we should call religious. They are to a large extent the secular products of a secular-minded age, and the destiny they postulate for men is not union with God, but social organization based upon the principles of humanity and reason. Yet perhaps they are as religious as that age would permit. If you tell a man that his world is composed of solid, unmysterious particles colliding and joining in empty space according to a universal Law, and if you allow him to set God as the Great Clockmaker so far apart from His creation that He ceases to exert any relevant or continually creative influence over it, you cannot blame such a man for regarding the order and pattern of that Law as the ultimate reality that he must consider. The step from such assumptions in the physical sciences to an analogous concern with the social order is easily made, and God becomes a slightly embarrassing and superfluous concept. Either He once upon a time created the world, and is therefore no longer necessary; or He is thought of as synonymous with the Law. Whether the subject of interest is physical particles or human beings in a society, its nature is determined not by itself but by its place in the arrangement and hierarchy of things, by its behavior according to the Law. It is little wonder, then, that the religious impulse in the eighteenth century should have been devoted to an ultimate reality in Order, nor is it surprizing that the picaresque hero should express the perennial restlessness of man as a search for a place in society, a place to give him identity and a name of his own.

But it is the conviction of the authors that a still deeper impulse unites these novels with the *Aeneid*, the *Commedia*, and the *Odyssey*. We have spoken of perennial restlessness, and that is one possible name for it. It is a fidelity to the curiosity about life and the ceaseless participation in it, a commitment to the dynamic character of the flow of experience, of space and time, which is given its literary formulation in these journeys. In part they may be journeys of fear, of looking for a hole in which to hide—but not often. For the most part the traveller, whether he be a Sun-Daimon, rotund official of London, or light-hearted rogue, is more interested in exhausting experience than in escaping from it. We recall reading long ago, at the end of a history of philosophy, an apology by the author for not having given in his book definitive and lasting answers to any of the questions which have plagued philosophers for nearly three thousand years. The excuse he gave was simple and almost commonplace: philosophy was like biological life, he said—organisms are always moving and changing, and if they cease to move, it is because they are dead. In their own way the literary journeys have attempted to imitate that motion, that flow of places and people and emotions before our focus of attention. Often, indeed, the journey in literature seems most like an exercise of what Frazer called 'sympathetic magic'; that is, in order to control a phenomenon, you imitate it and then turn the imitation in the desired direction. It seems clear enough, for example, that something like this is happening in the *Commedia* of Dante. Putting into it all his bitterness and love-hatred of Florence, his yearning after the lost Beatrice and his haunting sense that life and the cleanliness of virtue were slipping away from him, the great Catholic poet imitated his experience combined with his eschatological belief, in the form of a journey which ends in his rejuvenation, reunion with Beatrice and with the Source of Life and Order. In many works the flow of experience is imitated simply in order to bring it to an end, to a destined standstill. But perhaps we are placing ourselves too decidedly in the camp of the theologically hesitant poets of the nineteenth century, whose work we will have before us in following chapters, if we venture our opinion that, all sympathetic magic to the contrary, there is less reality in destinations than in journeys, than in the unending movement of life. Homer knew this, for as we have seen, Odysseus' journey does not end with his return to Penelope. It begins again with his travel inland to found a shrine, and we know enough of the Daimon figure behind Odysseus to conjecture that his journey is as eternal as the alternation of day and night, the succession of the seasons, the regular interchange of death and life.

# II

# THE METAPHOR

So far we have been dealing with the forms themselves of the traditional journey as it appears in poetry and prose up to the nineteenth century. We have distinguished two fundamental types of that journey controlled, respectively, by circular progression toward renewal or restoration of the traveller-hero, and by a linear progression of the hero from a state of social or intellectual disorder toward one of order. We may observe briefly that these progressions are in part dictated by a difference in the possible ways of understanding time. Odysseus' return to Ithaca is required by the completion of a nine-year cycle and the necessity of inaugurating another; for Virgil, the first great author of the Western world to philosophize upon the emotion of regret, the destruction of Troy, the unanswerable reproach of Dido to Aeneas, and the projected destiny of Rome are all products of a time which cannot return upon itself, for which the future is unique and the past irretrievable.

For the most part, the literary journeys we have discussed have strong connections with various forms of the religious impulse in Western man. In one sense or another, most of them are journeys to God, whether that God be widely or narrowly conceived, and we have tried to indicate these dimensions wherever possible, because the theological misgivings of the nineteenth century paradoxically drew its literary journeys into a relation even closer and more complex to the religious speculation of the age. The present chapter, intended as a further introduction to the study of this relation, will be concerned with the critical problems of the metaphor of the journey, presented by its intimate alliance with the exploration of religious faith.

1.

*The lovely things are god that has come to
pass, like Jesus came.
The rest, the undiscoverable, is the demiurge.*

—D. H. Lawrence

Nearing the end of his life, Peer Gynt finds an onion and begins
to peel it.

His voyages have led him into a great many trials and adventures and delinquencies; always before this moment he has
assumed that there was one 'great central contemplation,'[1] as
von Eberkopf puts it—one unifying principle to give these episodes a meaning. That principle was himself, and his insistence
on being himself. Now the onion serves as a metaphor for this
belief: Peer represents its layers both as the events of his travels
and as the various identities he has assumed during his life. If he
digs far enough in, there must be a center, a meaning.

> There's the untidy outer husk; that's the shipwrecked man
> on the wreck of the boat; next layer's the Passenger, thin
> and skinny—still smacking of Peer Gynt a little. Next we
> come to the gold-digger self; the pith of it's gone—someone's
> seen to that. This layer with a hardened edge is the fur-
> hunter of Hudson's Bay. The next one's like a crown. No,
> thank you! We'll throw it away without further question.
> Here's the Antiquarian, short and sturdy; and here is the
> Prophet, fresh and juicy; he stinks, as the saying goes, of lies
> enough to bring water to your eyes. This layer, effeminately
> curled, is the man who lived a life of pleasure. The next
> looks sickly. It's streaked with black. Black may mean mis-
> sionaries or negroes. (*Pulls off several layers together.*) There's
> a most surprising lot of layers! Are we never coming to the
> kernel? (*Pulls all that is left to pieces.*) There isn't one! To the
> innermost bit it's nothing but layers, smaller and smaller.
> Nature's a joker![2]

Peer's onion betrays him in many ways, to be sure, but only one
of these is of immediate concern to us in this essay. It is this: Peer
Gynt travels through a landscape of experiences, experiences of
things and events in a world which is *not* Peer Gynt or his ideas
of it. The onion which symbolizes this recalcitrant landscape is

of the same order; it resists being used for allegory. It is not an idea, and it is not a representation of something other than itself. It is simply an onion, and that is Nature's joke. In short, *no* onion and *no* natural landscape can 'mean' Peer Gynt or 'stand for' his search after identity. He has regarded his travels as a metaphor, and is at last forced to see that they are not; as he approaches Solveig's hut in the last scene, he says 'Backward or forward, it's just as far; out or in, the way's as narrow ... Like a wild unceasing cry I seem to hear a voice that bids me go in— go back—back to my home ... "Round about," said the Boyg! ... No; this time it's straight ahead in spite of all, however narrow be the way!'[3] Peer's awareness at this point is identical, we may observe, with that of another nineteenth-century traveller-hero, Nathaniel Hawthorne's Ethan Brand; Ethan has gone through the world looking for the Unpardonable Sin and, having found it, returns, and in response to all queries lays his finger on his own heart. Hawthorne never finished *Ethan Brand*, and we may guess that he wrote only this last chapter and scarcely a word of the journey itself, because his hero's act of reflexive awareness had at one initial stroke rendered the journey and everything connected with it irrelevant. Both Ethan Brand and Peer Gynt discard the easy geographical metaphor of the spirit's progress for a much more difficult access to salvation, an access which has nothing to do with space or time. What they discover is an existential purity of choice closely akin to a dominant and familiar impulse in the literature of our own age:

> ... we experience here—at the point of salvation—a void. It is as though the moral incommensurability of the finite and the infinite had become an article of knowledge and had been seduced into metaphysical incommensurability of absolute dualistic stringency: so that the 'journey to God' is no more a coming to oneself in the God-relationship. 'There is,' as Kafka says 'a goal, but no way; what we call the way is only wavering.'[4]

But if Peer Gynt's brusque dismissal of the journey as an acceptable allegory for the soul exhibits some of the characteristics of a modern disillusionment, it must also be seen as a common enough nineteenth-century dilemma. In Coleridge's poem *Constancy to an Ideal Object*, published twenty years after *The Rime of the Ancient Mariner*, the final and decisive image well illustrates one aspect of this distrust:

And art thou nothing? Such thou art, as when
The woodman winding westward up the glen
At wintry dawn, where o'er the sheep-track's maze
The viewless snow-mist weaves a glist'ning haze,
Sees full before him, gliding without tread,
An image with a glory round its head;
The enamoured rustic worships its fair hues,
Nor knows, he *makes* the shadow he pursues!

The landscape through which Peer Gynt passes is eventually recalcitrant; this one, however, is all too compliant. Peer finds that he cannot shape the world of his travels in his own image; Coleridge is very much afraid that he can, that no legitimate pursuit of an ideal image is possible in a world whose categories are projected by the beholder and pursuer himself. The tantalizing and valuable image which the woodman pursues is an illusory one, though behind it is not concealed another 'real' image, but the sickeningly unresistant abyss which Kant attempted to fill with a notion of the *Ding-an-sich*, Berkeley with his God. Coleridge appeals to neither.

This dilemma may be expressed in a number of different ways. We may see it as a difficulty in imposing a teleological pattern—an integral element in the fully-developed metaphor of travel—on a concretely realized and ostensibly 'natural' landscape. Though the literary and spiritual traveller must travel through such a landscape, the nineteenth-century poet was apt to feel reluctance at an arbitrary rearrangement of the sequence of objects or of the events which befall the traveller in it. Or in the terms of Ruskin's 'pathetic fallacy', we may see it as a troubled awareness that in some essential way the traveller himself and his dearest interests were not of the same order as the world of his travels, that its geography did not and could not reflect the geography and progress of his soul. Or we may simply see it as a difficulty in welding realistic narrative of episodes, on the one hand, to a pattern of inter-related 'meanings', on the other. The physical nature of things and events appeared to have very little to do with the order of mind or the nature of thought. Or, as in the case of Coleridge, it was suspected to have *everything* to do with the mind, which was hardly better.

The reasons for the severe dualism underlying the various aspects of this dilemma are not hard to find; it was the gift of eighteenth-century philosophy to its unwilling inheritors. As Coleridge observed, 'In the Hebrew poets each thing has a life of its own and yet they are all one life. In God they move and live and *have* their being; not *had*, as the cold system of Newtonian Theology represents, but *have*.'[5] Auden has summarized briefly the crucial inadequacy of this theology:

> Like the orthodox Christian God and unlike the God of Plato and Aristotle, [the Newtonian deity] is the creator of the world; but unlike the Christian God, and like that of Plato and Aristotle, God and the World have no real mutual relation. While the Greek Universe loves and tries to model itself on the unconscious self-sufficient god, the Newtonian Universe is the passive neutral stuff. God imposes rational order, which it obeys, but to which it does not respond, for the natural world is no longer thought of as an organism.[6]

William Blake appears to have recognized the doctrine at stake as that of Christ's Incarnation and to have reacted from the dualistic outlook toward a belief in the complete immanence of God, so that divine nature revealed itself only in concrete symbols, matter retrieved to the uses of spirit from the dead particles of the Newtonian Universe.[7]

> We are led to Believe a Lie
> When we see not Thro' the Eye
> Which was Born in a Night to perish in a Night
> When the Soul Slept in Beams of Light.
> God Appears & God is Light
> To those poor Souls who dwell in Night,
> But does a Human Form Display
> To those who Dwell in Realms of day.
>
> (*Auguries of Innocence*)

He also seems to have put his finger at least momentarily on the paltry and mechanical substitute which the Newtonian cosmology was able to suggest for richly 'incarnate' metaphorical structure: he called it allegory. In a scornful parody of a Newtonian's Lord's Prayer, he appears to see the device of allegory as the only remaining connection between the realms of matter and spirit: 'For thine is the kingship, (or) Allegorical Godship, & the Power, or War, & the Glory, or Law, Ages after Ages in thy descendants; for God is only an Allegory of Kings & nothing Else. Amen.'[8]

Blake, who found 'a World in a Grain of Sand,' perceived correctly that the artist and worshipper must see through the eye if he is to see truth, not through the mind. He perceived the direct connection between a sharp dualism of matter and spirit, and the prolonged mechanical identification of image and 'meaning' which we call allegory. And he knew that worshipper and poet must understand through the image, not force the image into the mould of an idea. Peer Gynt tries to force such an allegory on his onion—thereby on his travels—and fails miserably.

Yet Peer's disillusionment can be laid wholly neither at Newton's door, as Blake believed it should, nor at Descartes', as modern nostalgia for the Christian Middle Ages inclines us to do. The very character of the Western intellect, prone not only to making sharp distinctions between subject and object which are largely absent, for instance, in Indian thought,[9] but to making the concomitant distinctions between intelligible and sensible as well, has been such from its origins as practically to guarantee the useful misfortunes of nineteenth-century epistomology. Descartes and Newton's popularizers necessarily drew upon the great matrix of medieval asceticism and its notions of a God transcending phenomena and of a world irrelevant and deterrent to the progress of the soul toward Him. And it was a relatively short step from an irrelevant and despised world of phenomena to a totally separated and inanimate one, a step which, once taken, placed overwhelming strictures upon the use of the allegorical mode, which depends upon the artistic union of the sensible and intelligible realms of experience.

The reasons for Peer Gynt's troubles with an obstinate onion, then, must be traced back beyond the beginnings of modern literature, to a world in which the analytic, divisive bent of present Western culture was in a condition of emergence from the prehistoric and pre-intellectual stages of our race. Homer's *Odyssey* is illustrative of such a world, and the curious difficulty of the modern reader in accounting for this epic on his own terms merely testifies to the difference in kind. The modern reader has been trained above all to 'interpret', to react sensitively to 'meanings', to subordinate, in short, the sensible image to a unified, formal, intellectual image of the whole work which is what he carries away from his reading. Our discussion of the *Odyssey* in the last chapter was in part such an interpretation, an effort to translate the concrete presentations of poetic language into another kind of language altogether. This cannot be helped; the readers of the poem are now modern men with all the predispositions of their age. Yet a cursory examination of what we know of ancient habits of thought together with the mental characteristics of present-day primitive peoples is capable of reducing much of the misunderstanding. It is true that the Homeric Greeks were by no means savages; indeed, our reading of Homer will surely have inclined us to agree with Finley, that the central problem for the critic of Homer 'is to find the proper line between a primitive thought-world that was gone and a rationality that was yet to come.'[10] Yet these Greeks, balanced as they were between prehistoric confusion and civilization, retained both in their epic and in their devoted response to that poetry much of the immediate and unitary perception of the savage, and much of the freshness and spirituality of his contact with his simple world.

The primitive mind makes no distinction between the realms of matter and spirit,[11] and because they coincide, each physical event occurs both as something which the eye sees and as a disturbance among spiritual powers—hence the Roman *numina*[12] —which strike through and impel sensible objects on every side. The Greeks seem to have shared this attitude,[13] and Thales' statement, quoted in Aristotle's *De Anima*, that 'all things are full of gods,'[14] is simply a formulation of it. The landscape through which Odysseus passes is what we may term a 'numinal' one; to say that it is symbolic would be to draw a distinction which neither the Homeric poet nor his audience would have been likely to understand. The landscape exhibits itself as a series of concretions; it does not *mean*, it *is*. It is not illustrative of a general idea, but the idea itself in its most vital form; this is possible because the primitive mind draws little or no distinction between its own order and the order of the world which it per-ceives,[15] and when thought itself is concretely understood, there is no essential transformation required in its 'expression', its transfer to the level of communication.

It is hardly surprizing that in this state of affairs epistemo-logical questions should be inconceivable. No one in such a position asked, as Coleridge did, 'How do I know?' nor did he question the verbal and philosophical relation of subject to object. Snell has shown that the language of the Homeric epics itself will hardly allow the posing of such questions. One indication lies in the Homeric verbs meaning 'to see'. None of these —and there are several—mean only that.[16] They all include adverbial modes of seeing, like the English verb 'to gape', and none describe the simple function apart from the nature of the verb's subject reacting toward object. Only in later Greek do such verbs emerge,[17] with adverbial modifications made in separate words.[18]

The concerns of the early Ionian school of philosophy reflect this. The concern of this school was with $\Phi\acute{v}\sigma\iota\varsigma$ (nature) which in early Greek 'always means something within, or intimately belonging to, a thing, which is the source of its behaviour.'[19] As Frazer has pointed out, they were 'philosophies of Being. The end which the thinkers of these days proposed to themselves was the discovery of the ultimate reality of the physical universe; in other words, they occupied themselves with the object of Knowledge to the exclusion of the Knowing subject.'[20] We may observe that the failure of the Ionians to give an adequate account of phenomena was principally due to their failure to ask the epistemological question, to their insistence instead on forming 'a clear mental picture of the universal primitive substance.'[21] The question they wanted to ask, 'What is the one thing out of which all things are made?' led them nowhere, but the concreteness of perception which it implies indicates the experiential mode through which the great art of the Greek epics arose and by which they were judged. This art presented experience as a series of actions and images; and these images are very far indeed from allegory; they represent 'the form in which the experience has become conscious.'[22] They were derived from myth, and knit into a single form both a concretely visualized story and a formulated attitude toward spiritual forces.

2.

> The heavens declare the glory of God; and the firmament sheweth his handywork.
> Day unto day uttereth speech, and night unto night sheweth knowledge.
>
> —Psalm 19

Early in his *Allegory of Love*, C. S. Lewis provides his reader with a useful distinction between the allegorical method and what he calls the method of 'sacramentalism'.[1] Both, he observes, are based on man's perennial attempt 'to represent what is immaterial in picturable terms,'[2] yet there are two distinct approaches to the creation of 'married pairs of sensibles and insensibles.'[3] Allegory begins with an immaterial perception, pattern of thought or a mental or emotional conflict, and proceeds to *express* this perception through a series of constructed figures, a raging *Ira* contending with a meek *Patientia*, for instance. These figures remain subservient to the elements of mental reality which they represent; they are not 'true', because their only reason for coming into existence is to *illustrate* the truth:

> The allegorist leaves the given—his own passions—to talk of that which is confessedly less real, which is a fiction.[4]

The assumptions and disabilities of such a method will quickly be apparent. The image in poetry is of an order different from and lesser than the pattern of thought which arranges it. It is not used as an exploratory device but as a decoration and a necessary condescension into the material realm of explanatory communication, a descent from the 'empyrean heights' where the poetic transaction, whatever it may have been, took place. Allegory is a formal afterthought, occasionally helpful but accidental to the substance of the poem.[5]

The assumptions underlying the sacramentalist, or symbolic, method are quite different from these. The material world, the realm of sensibles, is regarded by the sacramentalist as a 'copy of an invisible world,' and by an intent examination of the former he may detect the patterns, which it imitates, of the latter, the immaterial well-spring of existence.

> The symbolist leaves the given to find that which is more real. To put the difference in another way, for the symbolist it is we who are the allegory. We are the 'frigid personifications'; the heavens above us are the 'shadowy abstractions'; the world which we mistake for reality is the flat outline of that which elsewhere veritably is in all the round of its unimaginable dimensions.[6]

Here, as for example in Plato's parable of the cave, the image is employed not as an expressive decorative fiction, but as a heuristic indicator, a signifier of the truth. Image and sensible world from which it derives are real in so far as the exploration of their terms and characteristics yield the patterns of the real-immaterial realm. In the hands of the sacramentalist, imagery is not a plaything but a sensitive, albeit limited instrument of knowledge.[7]

Though Lewis maintains that the habit of correspondence, of finding similitude between the visible and the invisible which is characteristic of both these methods of poetry, has always been in the nature of human mental activity,[8] the reader of our first chapters may feel a suitable qualification to be in order. For we have tried to show that the Homeric *Odyssey* is at least indicative of a mental habit antecedent to either approach. The olive tree is neither allegorical nor symbolic of Odysseus' life. The anxiety which Odysseus feels about its fate appears to show that the image stands in a protective, perhaps even more integral relation, to the life of the hero. At the height of his triumph, the removal of his tree would literally undercut all upon which that triumph was based. No symbol could exert itself so powerfully as this upon the action; when it ceased to be figurative of the real triumph, it would no longer be a symbol, and would cease to exert the power of truth. Both allegory and sacramentalism, as Lewis outlines them, represent a withdrawal from the divisionless immediacy with which the poet of the *Odyssey*, or at least the authors of his inherited material, confronted the sensible world. Similarity and correspondence between thought and sense-perception are by no means the same as their simple fusion; and even a principle of *similitudo* implies a distance between these two elements seldom if ever to be found in the *Odyssey*.[9] And when this principle is employed to compare a state of mind with its appropriate material symbol, a distance is created between perceiving subject and perceived object which, we may suspect, does not exist between Odysseus and the olive tree.

The tendrils of thought which would force this chasm in man's world, so fearsome to Coleridge and Ibsen, were in vigorous and expansive growth even from the centuries of the *Odyssey*'s richest and most direct acceptance. The change did not begin in Greece alone; the quotation from the Nineteenth Psalm standing at the head of this section shows that something similar was happening in Hebrew religion. The heavens are not God; they declare his glory, speak his praise and signify his existence. In their insistence on the unconditional and absolute nature of their God, which undercut the entire basis of mythopoeia and denied the validity of the 'graven image', the Jews necessarily tended toward a devaluation of sense experience and the perceptible world. God being utterly transcendent, concrete phenomena either simply suffered by comparison or found a limited value as signs of his presence.[10] In Greece itself the breakdown occurred as a concomitant feature of a gradual turn from the early philosophies of Being, such as that of Thales, to those of Epistemology; philosophers were increasingly inclined to ask, not what substance the world was made of, but how they could *know* the world. As Frazer has observed, they came to feel that 'it is impossible for man to investigate Being in itself; he can regard reality only as it is reflected in his own mind, he can reach Being only through Knowing.'[11] In the course of this discovery, the problem of knowledge was thrust like a flaming sword between man and his universe. No longer would their substances be the same; the angel of reflection stood between them.

This divisive process makes itself evident even in the early philosophy of Anaximander. Aware that the primal substance of which all things were composed could not itself be a 'thing', that is, could neither be finite nor sensorily perceptible, he introduced as the basis of all Being a concept of the 'Infinite' or the 'Boundless',[12] thereby thrusting his idea of the universe's true nature beyond the pale of concrete phenomena. Approaching the question from a slightly different angle, Heraclitus of Ephesus seems to have been the first to ask specifically whether the universe is *intelligible*, and to assume that it is: 'Wisdom is one thing. It is to know the *thought* by which all things are steered through all things.'[13] Similarly, despite the hodge-podge of traditional lore with which their doctrines were surrounded, and despite their treatment of numbers as concrete, individual entities undistinguished from the objects numbered,[14] the Pythagoreans, too, follow the trend we have spoken of. Their insistence upon regarding number and geometrical arrangements—the formal elements of experience—as the factors producing differentiation in the primal substance, was another appeal from the materiality in which mythopoeic thought had been thoroughly rooted.[15] And Parmenides in his turn follows and greatly expands the Heraclitean doctrine of the supremacy of thought over matter, showing, in his eagerness to establish that the one is dependent on the other, that they are clearly separate in his mind: 'The thing that can be thought, and that for the sake of which the thought exists, is the same; for you cannot find thought without something that is, as to which it is uttered.'[16] Yet it is with the Platonic contempt for the particulars of experience[17] that the loosening of bonds between the mental and phenomenal realms assumes its definitive and most influential form. Here, more than ever, is apparent the great change from the immediacy of the Homeric vision:

> The philosophy of Socrates, Plato, and Aristotle as distinguished from the early theories of Being was essentially a philosophy of Knowing; it turned the side of the medal which had been neglected by previous thinkers, the subject; and its theories of the object or of Being were deductions from its theories of Knowing.[18]

It can hardly be regarded as a coincidence that the history of the development of allegory corresponds closely to the period of this philosophical revolution. Even in the midst of Hesiod's genealogical syntheses of myth,[19] we may find precursive fragments of what appears to be allegorical interpretation,[20] though Hesiod, thoroughly acclimated to the personal mode of perception, always re-assimilates these fragments into the matrix of myth whenever they appear.[21] A method clearly adumbrating allegorical interpretation emerges for the first time in the sixth century with a reported effort of Theagenes of Rhegion to equate the hostilities of the gods of sun and sea with the eternal struggle of the opposites, fire and water.[22] In the fifth century, as Democritus records, Diogenes of Apollonia allegorized Zeus as the air and Metrodorus of Lampsacus is reputed to have given an allegorical interpretation of the *Iliad*.[23] From that time onward the habit of allegorizing would steadily claim greater adherence and wider application, so much so that Gilbert Murray describes allegory as the 'characteristic method' of belief practised by the later Hellenistic philosophers, who applied it to 'Homer, to the religious traditions, to the ancient rituals, to the whole world.'[24] From the work of Cornutus and the *Homeric Allegories* of Heraclitus of the first century A. D. until the death of pagan Rome in the fourth century, allegory remained the principal approach to the old poems and the old gods. By the fourth century the method had become so thoroughly ingrained that in his standard pagan catechism *On the Gods and the World*, Julian's friend Sallustius not only formulated a five-fold method of allegory for the

traditional myths (analogous to Dante's four-fold interpretation[25]), but could even claim that 'one may call the World a
Myth, in which bodies and things are visible, but souls and
minds hidden.'[26]

The reasons why the method should have attained to such
formidable employment as this are not difficult to find. From the
outset it was a mode of apologetic criticism. Neither Homer nor
the myths were moral—Plato, particularly in his dialogue
*Euthyphro*, stands witness to that—and pseudo-Heraclitus states
the case plainly enough when he tells us that 'if Homer used no
allegories he committed all impieties.'[27] The allegorists 'craved
poetry' as Murray tells us, 'and they craved philosophy; if the
two spoke like enemies, their words must needs be explained
away by one who loved both.'[28] Cosmic allegories arose in a
similar way; the strong idealism of these late pagans clashed with
the phenomena of sense experience, and only allegory could
reconcile the warring factions.[29]

To some extent the emergence of allegory as a mode of literary creativity is due to the fading of creative imagination, in
late Latin poetry, into the frozen formulae of rhetoric, with its
easy personifications and cardboard gods.[30] But, as C. S. Lewis
has amply demonstrated,[31] the character of this emergence was
only a symptom of the increasing tendency in the pagan world
to let the traditional gods harden into signs of some abstract
quality, state, or virtue; and to apotheosize certain abstract
nouns, conferring godhood on such as *Fortuna*[32] or *Fides* or *Bellum*
and *Furor*,[33] while Minerva, Janus, and Vesta, for examples,
became simple synonyms for 'wisdom', 'door', and 'hearth'. At
the same time, Lewis points out,[34] allegory was necessary to
literature in order to reconcile the pale assemblages of the old
polytheistic religion with the rising monotheism of the Mediterranean world. We have observed that natural phenomena became mere signs, for the Jews, of their God; the pantheons of
Greco-Roman civilization were similarly converted to attributes
or manifestations of a single power. When belief claimed One,
and experience protested Many, the easiest answer for the poet,
whose art depends for its life upon the diversity of experience,
was personification, allegory, and symbolism.

The method of the Christian artist, too, was strongly reinforced by this tradition. Not only did he take over the practices,
often the temperament, of pagan poets; he inherited a solid

tradition of allegorical Biblical interpretation from Judaic theology through Origen, Hilary, and Ambrose.[35] But perhaps the
most important single factor to affect his creative mode is to be
found in his models: a poet of the Middle Ages, accustomed by
writers like pseudo-Heraclitus or the Christian Fulgentius—
whose *Continentia Vergiliana* interpreted the *Aeneid* as the stages
in the life of man—to reading hidden allegorical meanings into
the great poems of antiquity upon which he based his poetic
practice, would hardly be inclined to an imitation devoid of
allegorical structure. The ancients were re-created in their late
interpretations, and imitating them came to mean imitating their
allegory.[36]

Yet for the great inheritors of the allegorical tradition, this
gift of pagan and Christian idealism posed an almost insuperable
problem, and it is the highest mark of their genius that they
triumphed over it. Great poems are not made only from the stuff
of thought or intangible spirit; they are made out of the green
of our trees, the flesh and texture of our bread, our encounters
with the neighbors we would love as ourselves and very seldom
do. They are solid with life and in the particularity of their
attention. The idealist, and his poor relative the solipsist, may
use 'the method of modeling the properties of existing beings on
the abstractions of the human intellect';[37] he may despise the
flesh, he may tell us that our bread is not bread but a symbol of
the martyred body of Christ, he may represent our societies of
love and hatred as a condescension into the material world of
seven or twelve archetypal virtues and seven archetypal vices, or
their more modern psychological equivalents. Yet the world is
not an allegory; again and again, misunderstood because its
validity is denied, it breaks in upon the visionary's edifice of
thought, haunts him as it haunted Coleridge and Ibsen with the
destructive and creative faces of its imperturbable power. Great
poetry has seldom done injustice to the imagination of man; but
it can ill afford to bleach and thin his simple, sensuous struggle
for life into the substance of such dreams.

Allegory and symbolism are bridges between two worlds,
between truth and truth. In the case of allegory, at least, we
may observe how frail and tenuous a bridge it really is, by contrast to the Homeric union of image and thought. Furthermore,
allegory generally represents a bridge from the idealist to the
sensible world, not the other way around; he creates images to

obey the laws of his mental processes, and this is exactly what they do. They are definitively finite in their implications. Unlike Homer's olive tree, Dante's Ser Brunetto, Chaucer's Wife of Bath, Keats' urn, or Peer Gynt's onion, they seldom tease us *out* of thought, because thought created (defined) them, and thought they remain. They never suggest that mental reality embodied in images is not capable of exhausting the reality of the sensible world.[38]

Three writers—Dante, Chaucer, and Bunyan—lay particular claim to our attention for having met and, with individual degrees of success solved, the problem posed by allegorical technique. Each of the three dealt with allegory's most suitable and characteristic form, the journey,[39] and each must have felt the traditional weight of allegorical interpretation which imposed itself upon that form.

### The Divine Comedy

Dante's own effort to synthesize thought and image followed, as is commonly recognized, much the same lines as that of Thomas Aquinas' life-long opposition to the method of the Platonic philosophers. This method postulated a deep split, as one Thomist has remarked, 'between intellectual knowledge and sensation.' According to these philosophers,

> Intellectual knowledge neither comes from sensible things, nor is it about them; and to say that reminiscence is a necessary moment in the origin of intellectual knowledge is to admit this precise fact, namely, that such knowledge is neither *from* nor *of* sensible things.[40]

Believing that 'since matter is a creature in a world of creatures, it has an intelligible role to play in the structure and organization of the world,'[41] Aquinas had unfolded the great course of his philosophy in defense of a view of the universe which did not achieve its unity by simply denying to the sensible, substantial world any accountable status. His essential argument was that

> the more Plato sought to discover the ultimate conditions of reality by means of a reason which had methodically cut itself off from the body and from all sensible experience, the more he was investing with the name of being the abstract essences

which were the only objects that such a methodically isolated
reason could reach; and the more abstract essences became
the center of Plato's world, the more Plato found himself
incapable of explaining those conditions of actual beings
which he could not derive from, or envisage within the eco-
nomy of, the abstract essences which were the exemplars of
his world.[42]

Standing behind the several volumes of the *Summa Theologiae* was
always the guiding shadow of the one central doctrine which
had to be defended at all costs: the Incarnation. Before Aquinas,
even St. Augustine, for all his deep affinities with the Platonic
philosophies, had observed in his reading of them, 'that the
Word was made flesh and dwelt among us I did not read there.'[43]
After him, as we noticed in Section 1, Blake would see that the
crucial issue in his own world centered around the Incarnation.
And it was similarly encumbent upon both Aquinas and Dante[44]
to preserve, in philosophy and poetry, and to amplify upon, this
mysterious coincidence of intelligible and sensible realms.

The Dante, whom C. S. Lewis confidently describes as 'the great
allegorist,'[45] seems actually to have avoided what we would
properly call the allegorical method to a progressively greater
degree as he approached the composition of his greatest poem.
The first indication of this occurs in the *Vita Nuova;* Dante
employs a figure he calls Amor who, we should observe, acts in a
highly individual way quite unbefitting an allegorical character.[46]
Even so, in Chapter XXV Dante remarks that Amor cannot after
all be regarded as a real person, a substance, since love is only an
accident occurring in a substance. And with this observation, he
puts the figure to flight; Amor does not appear again in the
*Vita Nuova.* The poet's commitment to truth, evidently, is too
great to permit even a beautiful lie, once detected, to flourish in
his work. Professor Singleton observes that in this regard Dante,
among all inheritors of the vigorous troubadour tradition, stands
alone.[47] Love can be neither god nor personification; there is
only one source of love, one source of truth.

The *Convivio* manifests a similar distrust. In it he distinguishes between the 'allegory of poets' and the 'allegory of theologians'. The poetry in the *Convivio*, he tells us, is to be interpreted
according to the former. The allegory of poets does not differ
from that of theologians in its four-fold structure; Dante enu-

merates the customary literal, allegorical, moral, and anagogical senses of interpretation[48] which are familiar to readers of the *Summa*.[49] These senses are to be found in both types. The difference is simply that the three last senses named are concealed under the literal meaning as 'una veritade ascosa sotto bella menzogna,' truth hidden under a beautiful lie. In contrast, then, to the allegorical interpretation of Scripture, the literal sense of which is to be regarded as historically true, poetic allegory deals with a literal sense which is deliberately and obviously falsified, in order that its absurdity may indicate the true philosophy beneath, as we are constantly reminded by critics from Sallustius[50] onward. Although Dante experimented with poetic allegory, of a type corresponding to the first of C. S. Lewis's two categories, it is of considerable significance that he never finished the *Convivio*; the work we possess is evidently only a fraction of that which he projected. And as Singleton points out, one of the portions never written was the 'penultimo trattato' in which Dante had planned to outline the *raison d'etre* of poetic allegory;[51] perhaps he did not regard the answer of Sallustius as sufficient. We would suggest, with Singleton, 'that Dante abandoned the *Convivio* because he came to see that in choosing to build this work according to the allegory of poets, he had ventured down a false way; that he came to realize that a poet could not be a poet of rectitude and work with an allegory whose first meaning was a disembodied fiction.'[52] In poetic allegory Lewis finds the beginnings of a brave new world of imagination, 'the marvellous-known-to-be-fiction,'[53] between 'the actual world and the world of [the poet's] own religion.' 'Go back to the beginnings of any literature,' he tells us, 'and you will not find it. At the beginning the only marvels are the marvels which are taken for fact.' Lewis may be right in his enthusiastic annunciation of this third world, yet it appears that the greatest poet of the Middle Ages would have disagreed with him. Dante's quotation of Aristotle in the letter to Can Grande, 'as a thing is in respect of being, so is it in respect of truth,'[54] pulses everywhere in the veins of the *Commedia*, less a principle of aesthetics or metaphysics than the very blood and substance of belief. Dante's entire journey through the substantiality of Hell and Purgatory is—literally—a detour to avoid the static resistance of three allegorical figures, the Leopard, the Lion, and the She-Wolf, which bar his passage up the Delectable Mountain; once he turns and leaves them, his journey is no

longer the universal, stereotyped 'cammin di nostra vita.' It
becomes his own singular experience, his own stumblings over
corporeal sinners in a tangible darkness, his own anger and pity
and dismay at the true histories of real men. Clearly we would
find great difficulty in reading his journey as a poetic allegory.

If this is so, what alternative basis may Dante have considered, upon which to build his vision? The allegory of theologians, perhaps? The idea is plausible. In his letter to Can Grande,
explaining the *Commedia* in general and the *Paradiso* in particular,
Dante tells us that his work is 'polysemos'[55]—having several
meanings—and the single example he gives of the kind of interpretation these several meanings demand is drawn, not from
mythology or any obvious allegory of poets, but from Holy
Scripture itself, the first and literal meaning of which is just as
true as the allegorical, moral, and anagogical senses which follow
from it. Whereas the parallel example Dante gives in the *Convivio* to illustrate his poetic allegory in that work, is a myth about
Orpheus drawn from Ovid, the literal sense of which is a 'bella
menzogna'. It seems highly likely, then, that Dante is fashioning[56]
his poem according to the model of Scripture. The delicate critical balance resulting from this we may best describe as an 'imitation of the Truth'.

How does this enable Dante to depict the realms of the spirit
through which he passes with unrivalled concreteness of detail,
and yet maintain, as he does, intricate doctrinal and structural
patterns throughout? First of all, God the Author of Scripture
does not signify his meaning through words alone; Aquinas tells
us that

> whereas in every other science things are signified by words,
> this science [of Scriptural interpretation] has the property
> that the things signified by the words have themselves also
> a signification.[57]

Dante echoes this when, in the letter to Can Grande, he says of
his work that 'the first meaning is that which is conveyed by the
letter, and the next is that which is conveyed by what the letter
signifies,'[58] i.e., the substance and individuality of the damned,
the hopeful, and the beatified. This looks much more, to use
Lewis's language, like sacramentalism than like allegory.[59] In
other words, Virgil and Beatrice are first *themselves*, literally and

substantially, and their signification as Natural Reason and Theology arise from these concrete centers only as accidents in substance.

It may be objected that an imitation of the truth is not the same as the Truth. Granted; but in following his model, Dante can be seen at every point to rely, not on his own inclination or fashioning-power as a poet, but upon what he would have regarded as the closest approximations of the objectively real state of souls after death that human knowledge could provide him. So, to use Professor Singleton's example, when Dante meets his old mentor and friend Ser Brunetto Latini in the Sixth Circle of the Inferno, their greeting is moving and sad beyond all human comprehension for the very reason that its truth is unavoidable:

> 'Were my desire all fulfilled,' I answered him, 'you had not yet been banished from human nature:
> for in my memory is fixed, and now goes to my heart, the dear and kind, paternal image of you, when in the world, hour by hour,
> you taught me how man makes himself eternal; and whilst I live, beseems my tongue should shew what gratitude I have for it.'[60]

But the point is that Dante's anguished wish can affect neither the banishment from human nature signified by Brunetto's death, nor the banishment Brunetto has brought upon himself by his crime of violence against nature. The poet cannot fashion and shape his characters at his own inclination, for they are the characters of God's meaning. The truth of the *Commedia* is not dependent upon Dante.

We should observe one very great advantage afforded Dante by his use of the allegory of theologians. Poets' allegory requires a constant thread of allegorical meaning running through the narrative, since the literal level, which is fictional, is justified only in terms of the truth which it conceals and conveys. Scripture, on the other hand, was recognized as conveying the three deeper senses of interpretation only intermittently, and as existing elsewhere as the uni-dimensional narrative of historical fact. By adopting such a model, Dante releases the narrative of his journey from the weight of continuous allegory without sacrificing, even in his own uncompromising judgment, its justification as an imitation of the truth.

An objection presents itself at once. If Dante has founded his poem upon the analogy of a text which is true on both literal and allegorical levels, what place in the scheme can we find for the action in Canto I of the *Inferno*, which functions in the terms of such a traditional allegorical pattern ('the journey of our life'), that it almost seems to have no literal level of meaning at all? Why does the poem begin by evoking a stock response to a figure of speech worn by constant usage and familiar to philosopher and religious enthusiast alike, from the genesis of the Orphic cults in Greece to the neo-Platonic thinkers of Africa and the pious flocks of Christendom? There are two answers to this: first, the *Commedia* is, after all, only an *imitation* of truth, not the truth itself, and by beginning his poem in what Augustine had called 'no space-occupying place,'[61] as a metaphor, Dante both warns the reader of that fact and calls his attention to a plurality of meaning in what follows when the journey becomes a singular one. Secondly, Dante here establishes the main thread of intermittent allegory in the poem; though Dante's pilgrimage through the realms of spirit can in no wise be primarily regarded as the universal Pilgrimage of Man, the poem reflects both at many points, and offers many parallels to be ferreted out by the wise and employed for the edification of the foolish.

Finally, it must be said in defense of the many readers who have tried and failed to get to Paradise through Dante, that the compelling substantiality of the poet's imagery, afforded him by the method we have outlined above, diminishes appreciably the further upward we progress. One of the first things that happens in the *Purgatorio* (Canto II) is that Dante tries to embrace his friend Casella and discovers that his hands pass through the shade without resistance. The spirits in Purgatory are in the process of being purged of their mortal dross, and with it their vivid individuality seems to lessen. In Canto V of the *Paradiso*, moreover, we see the features of a human face for the last time through Dante's eyes; before the reader lies the great sweep of twenty-eight cantos principally devoted, as many have said before, to theological teaching and light. The difficulty is simple enough: the closer Dante approaches to the immaterial God who is the end of his journey, the more impossible becomes differentiated imagery of any kind, which depends for its life upon substance, variety and mixture, the 'dappled things', as Hopkins praised them, of our earthly prison.

## The Canterbury Tales

Geoffrey Chaucer, the great master of dappled things, can not be said to differ essentially from Dante, in the full context of the *Canterbury Tales* at any rate, concerning the nature of truth and necessity of reflecting it in poetry. No one these days will agree with Matthew Arnold who, though he did not lack a sense of humor (as the pages of Trilling's study amply illustrate), did lack a sense of coordination between humor and the deepest requirements of spirit, and who therefore devaluated Chaucer's poetry because 'high seriousness' was missing from it. The *Canterbury Tales* is unquestionably a serious work, in that it exhibits profound commitments on every hand to truth and to an expansive though well-defined code of relationships between man, God, and the material universe. No matter how elusively Chaucer's point-by-point opinions on theological and social issues escape our scrutiny, we must accept the fact that the *Canterbury Tales*, like the *Commedia*, stands solitary amid a welter of Continental and English romances, secular allegories, and framed collections of racy stories, as a great imitation of the truth. Chaucer's reticence toward stringent moral condemnation is due neither to a shifting moral center in the man nor to an unwillingness to dilute pure comedy, but to an awareness that the truth is always considerably bigger, more inclusive, than we first thought it. To Chaucer the great truth is, in Dryden's words, 'God's plenty.'

Yet the same problem poses itself for Chaucer as for Dante, because 'high seriousness' in fourteenth-century England meant above all two things: belief in a transcendent God, and belief in the division and pre-eminence of thought over sensible substance. Allegories of sexual love which substituted a God of Love for the first, necessarily suffered a separation from what were regarded as the essential concerns of life, a fact which is reflected both in Dante's banishment of the figure from his *Vita Nuova*[62] and in Chaucer's unconditional disinheritance of the *Legend of Good Women* in his *Retraction* at the end of the *Tales*. And it must be agreed that almost no one in the fourteenth century, were he asked his opinion, would have questioned the second of these two assumptions, though in practice the man of the Middle Ages was no more exempt than ourselves from intellectual influences exerted by the joys of the flesh. Yet Chaucer's pilgrims, among them that most substantial lady, the Wife of Bath, are certainly no Ariels imprisoned in an earthly husk, and Chaucer is so far from holding out this view of them, that his creations are chiefly praised for their solidity, the vivid and detailed materiality of their portraits. Furthermore, we must realize that the actual fourteenth-century pilgrimages upon which Chaucer modelled his own, were by no means the efforts to transcend, the archetypes of escape to untrammelled spheres of spirit, that a later age would esteem them in its imagination. They were very earthly affairs indeed. Entirely aside from the fact that pilgrimages were made an excuse to annoy monarchs and escape their oppressive restrictions on a large transient population, or simply to see new sights and have fun, the pilgrim was a thorough-going worshipper of images. Pilgrimages, to put it somewhat extravagantly, were journeys not to God but to centers of immanent, inherent sacred power. The pilgrim travelled through what we have called a 'numinal' landscape, dominated by the forces of revered relics, miraculous images of the Virgin and the saints, and shrines which, if touched or prayed at, were known to dispense cure or indulgence or absolution almost automatically. The journeys were often undertaken, as Chaucer tells us in the general *Prologue*, in consequence of vows made in illness to some saint, which vows are, of course, a form of magic, a propitiatory pattern of action intended to control unseen and unpredictable forces. Always, though, the pilgrimages seem to have taken as their object something intermediary, something which would interpose itself between the pilgrim and the transcendent God whom he would some day have to face. As M. Jusserand points out, men in this age 'did not understand how to go straight forward; instead of opening the gates of heaven with their own hands, they imagined they could get it done by those of others.'[63] And so strong was this impulse in the pilgrim, that Lollards denounced both image-worship and pilgrimages in the same breath; therefore the recantation, on December 1, 1395, of one William Dynet of Nottingham was couched in these terms: 'Fro this day forthwarde I shall worshipe ymages, with praying and offering vnto hem, in the worschepe of the seintes that they be made after; and also I shal neuermore despyse pylgremage.'[64]

How well this state of affairs suited Chaucer's original conception of the *Canterbury Tales*, as well as the nature of his pilgrims as they are characterized by him, may be seen at a glance. Each of them[65] was to tell two tales on the way to Canterbury and, significantly, two on the way home. None of them, certainly not Chaucer himself as he began the *Tales* around 1387, in the prime of his life,[66] would have suspected that none would ever get home again. They set out in the rain and light of April, intent upon a holiday excursion set securely in the middle of their lives. They are not travelling to the City of God but to Canterbury, which is a very different and much less frightening matter, and after some pleasant exercise of religious enthusiasm they will come home again and take up the normal, impure daily life.

Throughout most of the *Canterbury Tales* this original conception and the spirit it engenders is adhered to, and in its terms alone the question of the work's 'high seriousness' is much more difficult to resolve. Yet toward the end of the *Tales* as we possess them, and toward the end of the poet's life, this conception changes rather suddenly. The difference is signalled in Furnivall's Groups H and I, which the best manuscript authority and internal evidence place consistently together.[67] These contain *The Manciple's Prologue, The Manciple's Tale, The Parson's Prologue* and *Tale*, and the *Retraction* with which the whole work ends.

The hilarious action of the *Manciple's Prologue* takes place in the morning; the scene is close to Canterbury, 'where ther stant a litel toun / Which that ycleped is Bobbe-up-and-doun, / Under the Blee, in Caunterbury Weye.'[68] This village has not been identified; perhaps it is Harbledown, one and a half miles west of Canterbury, or perhaps it is associated with 'Up-and-down Field' in the Thannington parish, but at any rate it is clear that at the end of the *Tales* the pilgrims are approaching Canterbury, not London.[69] The story told by the Manciple, which follows, is very short—only 257 lines—and yet when it is referred to in the *Parson's Prologue* immediately afterward, we are informed that it has taken all day to tell! The time is now four o'clock, the sun is setting, and Chaucer's shadow is now eleven feet long. Unlike many in the *Tales*, this discrepancy appears to be a significant one: we may suggest that while the time marked in the *Manciple's Prologue* represents simply a tentative effort of Chaucer's, like so many others, to block in the action of the pilgrimage, the time now given at great length in the *Parson's Prologue* functions without reference to previous chronology, as a metaphor for the shadows gathering in Chaucer's own life as it drew to a close. But does it not have a metaphorical function in relation to the pilgrims as well? We had best see what follows.

7

The fact that only one more tale is needed to round out the tally is plainly repeated four times in the *Prologue*, and it is clear that the Parson must tell it. The cheerful and blundering Host has collided with the Parson before, in the *Epilogue of The Man of Law's Tale*, when he swore with delight over the story just told and was reprimanded by the Parson, whom he then accused of being a Lollard. And now good Harry Bailly does it again, bumbling up to the parish priest with a bluff demand for a last fable to 'knytte up wel a greet mateere.' The Parson's reply is once again severe and dignified. He will not tell a fable because St. Paul reproved those who waive truth (Dante's problem!) and he will sow wheat, not chaff. He has no art, cannot rime or alliterate; so he will give the company a 'myrie tale in prose' if they like. Here, for the first time in the *Canterbury Tales*, allusion is made to the Eternal Pilgrimage, in the Parson's words:

> And Jhesu, for his grace, wit me sende
> To shewe yow the wey, in this viage,
> Of thilke parfit glorious pilgrymage
> That highte Jerusalem celestial.[70]

Does he mean to compare 'this viage' with the journey to God, or does he mean to *identify* them? The language is ambiguous. 'In this viage' may either mean 'in the example given by this journey of ours', or it may mean 'embodied in our journey'. Similarly 'thilke' may either mean (like Latin *ille*) 'the famous', or it can mean 'the very same'. Probably both meanings are operative here. And a similar ambivalence pervades the Host's subdued assent, as spokesman for the entire company, to the way in which the Parson proposes to 'knytte up al this feeste, and make an ende.'

> 'Telleth,' quod he, 'youre meditacioun.
> But hasteth you, the sonne wole adoun;
> Beth fructous, and that in litel space,
> And to do wel God sende yow his grace!
> Sey what yow list, and we wol gladly heere.'[71]

What follows is the longest tale in the work, a sermon on Penitence and the Seven Deadly Sins translated by Chaucer from two treatises in the Latin of thirteen-century Dominicans.[72] If suspicion of Lollardism has been cast upon the Parson for his dislike of swearing and his insistence on breaking the temporal image of the Canterbury pilgrimage as a holiday venture, it is now contradicted by the orthodoxy of his sermon,[73] and in the opening lines he uses language which is directly reflective of the merry journey behind them, and which both gently recognizes the diversity of the pilgrims themselves and their paths, and points out that a single way lies before them all; in the words of Jeremiah,

> Stondeth upon the weyes, and seeth and axeth of olde pathes (that is to seyn, of olde sentences) which is the goode wey,/ and walketh in that wey, and ye shal fynde refresshynge for youre soules, etc./ Manye been the weyes espirituels that leden folk to oure Lord Jhesu Crist, and to the regne of glorie./ Of whiche weyes, ther is a ful noble wey and a ful convenable, which may nat fayle to man ne to womman that thurgh synne hath mysgoon fro the righte wey of Jerusalem celestial;/ and this wey is cleped Penitence ...[74]

Let us remember once again that the pilgrims are approaching Canterbury, not London, and that even the image of Canterbury and its spires is quickly fading into the light of the Holy City; the travellers are actually standing upon the ways, and the Parson is seeing and asking for them which is the good way. Whether a translation or not, Chaucer's invitation, through the sermon, is very clear; it is the invitation to interpret the past events of the Canterbury pilgrimage as an allegory of what is now conceived as a far more pressing reality, the requirements of salvation. We are presented with the full panoply: the literal level being the pilgrimage to Canterbury; the allegorical level being the journey to Jerusalem Celestial; the tropological sense, the search for the 'goode wey'; the anagogical sense, the redemption of the soul by means of penitence from a motley world to eternal glory through Christ. We need not insist on this enumeration, however, because Chaucer merely signals the possibility; he has something more in store for us. This depends upon a marked change in Chaucer's conception of the governing principle of truth and its relation to the work of art. In the *General Prologue* Chaucer indicated his attitude in an apology which, however much he may have kept his tongue in his cheek, displays his early commitment to a particular relationship between the work of art and one kind of truth:

> But first I pray yow, of youre curteisye,
> That ye n'arette it nat my vileynye,
> Thogh that I pleynly speke in this mateere,
> To telle yow hir wordes and hir cheere,
> Ne thogh I speke hir wordes proprely.
> For this ye knowen al so wel as I,
> Whoso shal telle a tale after a man,
> He moot reherce as ny as evere he kan
> Everich a word, if it be in his charge,
> Al speke he never so rudeliche and large,
> Or ellis he moot telle his tale untrewe,
> Or feyne thyng, or fynde wordes newe.[75]

Here within the poem, the pilgrims, their journey, and their stories are assumed to be historically, literally true, since Chaucer is reluctant to 'falsify' even their very words. But the *Retraction* at the end of the *Canterbury Tales* represents another kind of truth by which is assumed only the reality of Chaucer himself and his redemption. The turning-point is the Parson's sermon. In so far as the Parson is himself one of the Canterbury pilgrims addressing the rest, the invitation he voices is for an interpretation of the pilgrimage based upon something like Dante's 'allegory of theologians', since the literal level is historically true, to the pilgrims themselves. But in so far as the figure of the Parson fades out in the course of the long treatise and comes to represent the voice of conscience speaking to Chaucer alone, his invitation is to view the *Canterbury Tales* as an allegory of poets, with a fictional and manipulable literal level for which Chaucer can and does hold himself morally responsible in the *Retraction*. There seems little question that the Parson does in fact speak in this dual fashion, since his advice in the sermon is this:

> Now shaltow understande what is bihovely and necessarie to verray perfit Penitence. And this stant on three thynges:/ Contricioun of herte, Confessioun of Mouth, and Satisfaccioun.[76]

This enumeration is directly reflected in the *Retraction*: Chaucer asks of Christ and Mary that

> they from hennes forth unto my lyves ende sende me grace to biwayle my giltes, and to studie to the salvacioun of my soule, and graunte me grace of verray penitence, confessioun and satisfaccioun to doon in this present lyf ... so that I may been oon of hem at the day of doom that shulle be saved.[77]

In the *Retraction* Chaucer, with a curious qualification, revokes 'the tales of Caunterbury, thilke that sownen into synne.'[78] But what about the pilgrims—Harry Bailly, the Prioress, Alisoun, the comfortable Franklin and all the rest? Did he revoke them too, with all their straggling assortment of virtues and vices, their dear and vivid lives? He had pottered among them for many years, and his change of spirit must have been heartbreaking indeed if he could deny these children of his old age. We may prefer to think that he did not; though the only evidence we can produce concerns the tone of the *Retraction*. It is not, as Professor Lawrence regards it,[79] a document of fright. Its language is too stately, it is too beautifully and—we may say it—serenely composed. It is a ritual gesture. We do not mean to imply that it was in any sense insincere; it was probably very sincere indeed. But what we do imply is that it was intended as *part* of the *Canterbury Tales*, a very important part. Had Chaucer intended to revoke his creation completely he could have burned the *Tales* and their substantial framework, at least a single symbolic copy in case other manuscripts were in circulation among his friends. But although we have stories of his death-bed repentance,[80] we have no record of his having done so, and the qualification attached to the retraction of the *Tales*, 'thilke that sownen into synne,' seems less to deny the work than to cast back over it a teleological shadow and a judgment not Chaucer's own. The pilgrims are not renounced in the negating gesture of a frightened sinner. The very fact that the Parson suggests the possibility of interpreting their journey allegorically indicates that Chaucer felt them to be sufficiently real and true, so that their reality must be related and submitted to a greater truth, the truth of God. The *Retraction* balances in Chaucer's world with the bright April morning in which the pilgrimage begins, the insouciant quest after the intermediary 'hooly blisful martir' balances against the many 'weyes espirituels that leden folk to oure Lord Jhesu Crist, and to the regne of glorie.' We may rightly feel that the *Canterbury Tales* in its present fragmentary state and with its present sudden and powerful ending is far more inclusive of truth than it would have been if Chaucer had followed the plan outlined in the *General Prologue*. Only in the sense that Dante wishes he did not have to meet his friend Ser Brunetto in the circle of the Violent Against Nature, could we wish that the *Tales* ended otherwise.

### The Pilgrim's Progress

Although several centuries, the Reformation, and correspondingly vast social and economic changes stand between Chaucer
and Dante on the one hand, and John Bunyan on the other, we
find a surprising similarity of critical concerns when we turn to
the verse *Apology* at the beginning of *The Pilgrim's Progress*. Here
Bunyan tells us that he

> writing of the way
> And race of saints, in this our gospel day,
> Fell suddenly into an allegory
> About their journey, and the way to glory ...[81]

He finds it necessary to apologize for his 'method' at considerable
length, and the term he uses in doing so will doubtless seem
familiar; he uses essentially the same argument we found in
Sallustius, that an obviously feigned first level of meaning en-
courages the reader to look beneath, combined with the notion
of the didactic sugar-coated pill familiar in Renaissance literary
criticism and refined in the pages of Sidney and Puttenham:

> If that a pearl may in a toad's head dwell,
> And may be found too in an oyster shell;
> If things that promise nothing do contain
> What better is than gold; who will disdain,
> That have an inkling of it, there to look,
> That they may find it?

Then Bunyan constructs an imaginary critic to voice approxi-
mately the same objections we have seen to be implicit in Dante's
attitude toward his art:

> Why, what's the matter? It is dark. What tho'?
> But it is feigned: What of that, I trow?
> Some men, by feigning words as dark as mine,
> Make truth to spangle, and its rays to shine.
> But they want solidness. Speak man thy mind.
> They drown'd the weak; metaphors make us blind.

With this critic Bunyan agrees, as Dante would have done, that
'solidness' is necessary to the metaphorical structure of a work
that purports to deal with the religious concerns of man; how-

ever—and here his solution comes very close to Dante's—Holy
Scripture provides the author with his precedent and pattern of
emulation:

> Solidity, indeed, becomes the pen
> Of him that writeth things divine to men;
> But must I needs want solidness, because
> By metaphors I speak? Were not God's laws,
> His gospel laws, in olden time held forth
> By types, shadows, and metaphors?

Bunyan continues further on in the *Apology* in the same vein:

> Am I afraid to say that holy writ,
> Which for its style and phrase puts down all wit,
> Is everywhere so full of all these things—
> Dark figures, allegories?

The answer is obviously no, and he draws his conclusion:

> I find that holy writ, in many places,
> Hath semblance with this method, where the cases
> Do call for one thing, to set forth another:
> Use it I may, then, and yet nothing smother
> Truth's golden beams; nay, by this method may
> Make it cast forth its rays as light as day.

It will be observed that in one important respect Bunyan is
shifting his ground, and continues to do so: it is one thing to
adopt the mode of 'poet's allegory' with its fictitious literal level,
as Bunyan seems to do here in the *Apology* and again in *The
Conclusion*, where he warns his reader to 'Take heed also, that
thou be not extreme/ In playing with the outside of my Dream.'[82]
But it is quite another matter for Bunyan to draw a direct parallel
between his work and Scripture, and to draw substantiation
from the latter for his allegorical method. The whole history of
a theological revolution stands between Dante and Bunyan in
the matter of scriptural interpretation, yet that Bunyan would
have denied the consistent historical truth of the literal level of
Scripture appears inconceivable.[83] He clearly fails to distinguish
between the allegory of theologians and that of poets, yet his
notion of 'solidness' implies more than a simple display of learn-

ing; to a certain degree it indicates a felt responsibility to the
nature of substance in God's creation. One short phrase in the
*Apology* gives away Bunyan's leanings in this direction:

> I find not that I am denied the use
> Of this my method, so I no abuse
> Put on the words, things, readers . . .

Anyone familiar with Arnold's line 'Who prop, thou ask'st, in
these bad days, my mind?' will understand what is meant by
abuse to words, and we have all been abused too often as readers
to leave any confusion on that score. But the reference to an
abuse of 'things' is of another order altogether. It may recall to
our minds St. Thomas's claim that God can 'signify His meaning,
not by words only (as man also can do), but also by things
themselves;'[84] yet it would seem unlikely in the extreme that
Bunyan is referring to so systematic an appraisal of Scriptural
allegory as this. The phrase remains a puzzling one, however,
and perhaps the best construction we can put upon it (which is
thoroughly borne out in a reading of *Pilgrim's Progress*) is that
in some sense, though intermittently, Bunyan conceives of Christian and his friends, those whom they meet, and the landscape
through which they pass as real and substantial, as 'things'. They
are not simply feigned cardboard figures, to be moved and
distorted as the exigencies of the allegorical pattern dictate. This
is further indicated in the *Apology* when Bunyan again addresses
his hypothetical critic:

> Come, let my carper to his life now look,
> And find there darker lines than in my book
> He findeth any . . .

The implications of this remark are extensive. It shows that
Bunyan thinks of his characters and their landscape, part of the
time, at least, in such a way that the meanings they conceal may
be compared with those to be found in the life and experience of
a presumably real human being. Bunyan is quick to warn us not
to go too far in playing with the outside of his dream, but he
seems to regard it at times as possessing nearly the same status
as the Dream of This Life, whose 'outside' would claim relatively
little more of his Puritan credence. As Professor Talon observes,
'. . . on sent alors avec quelle conviction Bunyan écrit son conte.

Il finit par croire à la réalité physique de ses symboles autant qu'à la doctrine dont ils sont l'expression. Et c'est par cette foi d'enfant, alliée à sa riche expérience humaine, qu'il est un grand poète.'[85]

This state of affairs is reflected often in the work itself. It appears, for example, in so simple a matter as Bunyan's choice of names for his characters. A curious fact confronts us here. Christian meets many people during his journey, often in groups or pairs, such as Simple, Sloth, and Presumption,[86] or Formalist and Hypocrisy,[87] or Timorous and Mistrust.[88] In each of these three groupings, it will be noted, adjectival names have been freely mingled with names which are abstract nouns. The confusion is significant, because when an allegorical character is called by an abstract noun it limits his sphere of activity, as Dr. Johnson pointed out, to the concerns immediately allotted to him by the quality he represents, and he can do nothing else because he *is* nothing else; he exists only for the sake of his allegorical equivalence and is unendowed with substance independent of it. If his name is adjectival, on the other hand, it is merely attributive and does not exclude the possibility of other attributions; it may imply a substance—on the literal level—capable of action independent of or only tangentially related to its principal designation. In the strictest sense, for instance, Sloth, Hypocrisy, and Mistrust might be encountered on the pilgrims' way, but they could not be conceived as themselves being pilgrims or as losing their souls on that way. Living men, not abstract nouns, have souls to lose.

Yet that is what happens to these three as to many others, and it seems very clear both that Bunyan does not make the above distinction, and that he commonly regards his allegorical characters, not as transparent and edifying fictions, but as real men. Dr. Johnson's famous criticism of allegory and personification is not applicable to *The Pilgrim's Progress*, and indeed it was one of the critic's favorite books.[89] These facts are of the utmost importance, and they can be made to account for most of the homely touches with which Bunyan brings his vast metaphorical structure to life, and which endear it to many an abysmally unpious reader even in our own age. They owe their strength to a method often verging more closely on symbolism or the allegory of theologians than on that of poets, a method Bunyan had had occasion to employ with exhausting thoroughness in an earlier

work, 'Solomon's Temple Spiritualized.'[90] It is chiefly in terms
of the critical freedom in this way accorded him that Bunyan can
have his hero meet Discretion, Prudence, Piety, and Charity in
the castle called Beautiful, who, 'after a little more discourse
with him, had him in to the family,'[91] and invited him to eat
supper with them at a 'table ... furnished with fat things, and
with wine that was well refined.'[92] It is in terms of this critical
freedom that Christian can confess to the Porter of this palace,
called Watchful, that 'My name is now Christian, but my name
at the first was Graceless.'[93] When a strictly personified figure
changes names he changes identities and characteristics as well,
but Christian can be renamed because he exists on the literal
level, in his own right. Similarly, there is a certain amount of
sense, if not truth, in Mr. By-ends' insistence that 'This is not my
name, but indeed it is a nickname that is given me by some that
cannot abide me.'[94] Though Christian decides that Mr. By-ends
is, after all, well named, that oily gentleman is sufficiently substantial so that the quarrel over his name is a meaningful one.
Likewise, as they are crossing the River of Death a despairing
Christian tells Hopeful, 'It is you, it is you they wait for; you
have been *hopeful* ever since I knew you.'[95] Hopeful's reply is
significant: 'And so have you,' he assures his companion. His
name is merely attributive, and the quality may be shared by
others. Passage over the River of Death is easier for him than for
Christian because hopefulness *predominates* in him and is his most
striking characteristic, but it is by no means his only one.

We may conclude, then, that the majority of characters encountered in *The Pilgrim's Progress* are conceived not as personifications but as types, as representatives of certain classes of
human beings. They are symbolic, in short. They possess a dual
nature: as representatives they educate Christian and his companions, as well as the devout reader, for the bewildering mazes
to be mastered or avoided in the process of saving one's soul; as
human beings beneath the symbols, they exist in their own right,
have souls to save or lose, and feed a sense of solid and homely
life into a work that might easily have been just another prescriptive desert of the Puritan mind. If it is necessary to determine a precedent for the form of Bunyan's portraits, one might
point to the Theophrastan character, a short and concise prose
delineation of a typical personality, which was a favorite exercise
among the *literati* of England in the seventeenth century and

Restoration. For his indisputable mastery of the form, and his success in welding it into the great metaphorical edifice of *The Pilgrim's Progress*, we must, however, give the laurel—or more appropriately the palm—to the sharp eye and 'excellent discerning of persons'[96] of Bunyan himself.

If the characters of the book are in the main symbolic or typical, the landscapes through which the pilgrims pass are themselves, with the prominent exceptions of Vanity Fair, the land of Beulah, and the Celestial City, also as generally allegorical in Lewis's sense of the word. They are primarily expressions of mental states experienced by the pilgrims. The Slough of Despond, the Valley of Humiliation, the Valley of the Shadow of Death (despite the authority of its Biblical prototype), the Delectable Mountains, the Enchanted Ground, and the River of Death, exist primarily as expressive equivalents for certain spiritual conditions, not as objectively realized places. Even the mouth of hell glimpsed by Christian in the middle of the Valley of the Shadow of Death is, in such a context, less the place whose existence was an article of Christian faith (as Dante's Inferno had been), than the sincere Christian's imaginative *perception* of hell's terrors, his beforehand, quaking contemplation of it as part of the process of his spiritual transformation. Vanity Fair is somewhat more difficult to fit into an exhaustive allegorical equation because not only does it represent the temptations of vanity, and provide the scene for Faithful's martyrdom, with all the equivalences which that far more severe temptation to recant implies; it seems to typify as well the world itself, since 'he that will go to the [Celestial] city, and yet not go through this town, must needs "go out of the world," '[97] and we are told that 'they that kept the fair were the men of this world.'[98] In any case, Vanity Fair is far less a construction expressive of a spiritual condition in the pilgrims themselves, than an image in which are fused symbolic overtones and a realistic picture drawn in its main elements from a trading, bustling urban England of Bunyan's time. We have listed the Land of Beulah and the Celestial City as exceptions, on the other hand, because although they are fairly easily equated with Earthly and Heavenly Beatitude, respectively, Bunyan's faith would have claimed for them both an objective reality aside from any allegorical equivalences, the Land of Beulah on the authority of Isaiah 62:4, and the Celestial City from precedents too numerous to make specific reference desirable or useful. They are the fruits of the pilgrimage, the most real of all the countries Christian has passed through, and our awareness of this fact enriches the irony of the phrase with which *The Pilgrim's Progress* in its early edition terminates: 'So I awoke, and behold, it was a dream.' We are entitled to ask, which was the dream and which the waking? The answer is not at all obvious either way.

*

We have approached the central problem of our metaphor of journey from a number of directions in the past chapters, and these have involved us at times in concerns more proper to the disciplines of anthropology, philosophy, and theology, than to literary criticism. The only excuse we may offer for our more or less superficial excursions into these fields is that our metaphor is a basic and inextricable form of the imaginative life of man. It welled up out of an ancient migratory restlessness, and will cease to exercise its primitive force only when men are satisfied, defeated, or destroyed. We might have stated the problem of the metaphor as a simple dilemma of literary criticism in a single sentence: the figure of the journey in literature tends to take the form of an extended metaphor (hence its frequent association with allegory) depending on a prolonged series of equivalences between tenor and vehicle, and the difficulty facing the author is to arrange the series, which connects image and meaning, into an intelligible whole without sacrificing the truth to experience of the component images themselves.

Yet it should be clear that we have not been confronting a simple dilemma. It is evident, indeed, that not only the solutions poets have found for themselves, but the very scruples which caused them to regard the difficulty in the first place, have been intimately associated with the deepest of theological concerns. The allegory of sexual love, and even the *psychomachia*, can be delightful and airy exercises of imagination, as Lewis has amply demonstrated; but we must ultimately agree with Dante, Chaucer, and Bunyan in their subterranean convictions when the time came to deal metaphorically with the really serious business of life. And this sense of connection between the degree of separation of God from the world, on the one hand, and the degree of separation between meaning and image in a metaphor devoted to religious application, on the other, will help us a great deal to understand why the problem and the metaphor became so difficult in the nineteenth century. The loss of faith was, of course, to mean the loss of a well-defined destination for the journey, as we have pointed out in Chapter I; but the aspect of the problem we have just been discussing emerged from the depths of Christian belief itself, and it was *because* they were Christian writers that Dante, Chaucer, and Bunyan asked and solved their great question, not in spite of it. This is the other side of the coin; for if the poets of the nineteenth century were suddenly confronted with evidences casting doubt on traditional forms of faith, they were at the same time unequipped, for the most part, to deal with such doubt. One thinks of the young poet Arnold or Tennyson in their sad alienation from the very dogmatic foundations which governed the character of their spiritual hunger. They could not have what they asked from life, because they could not ask any but the *prudens quaestio* of a faith whose answers they had rejected. Thus it was that their hesitation in poetry would be reinforced not only by the doubt from outside the faith but by that within it as well. The beginnings of a new solution would be signalled by Gertrude Stein's elvish wisdom when she asked on her death-bed, 'What is the answer?' and then, 'What is the question?'

# PART TWO

## *The Individual Quest*

by

GEORG ROPPEN

# I

# WORDSWORTH: FROM ENDLESS AGITATION

No poet in the English language has been so drawn to the journey as an imaginative structure as Wordsworth. His first poems, the thoughtful travelogues *An Evening Walk* and *Descriptive Sketches*, though marred by conventional diction, already adumbrate the way in which he later tried to exploit the possibilities of the travel metaphor. In *Descriptive Sketches* he still speaks with an eighteenth-century voice:

> Kind Nature's charities his steps attend;
> In every babbling brook he finds a friend;
> While chast'ning thoughts of sweetest use, bestow'd
> By Wisdom, moralize his pensive road.

It is in this poem also that Wordsworth first dramatises himself as a pilgrim:

> Still have my pilgrim feet unfailing found ...

In *The Borderers* we meet another type of wanderer, whose significance was later to assert itself in more ways than one: Here is Marmaduke the exile:

> a wanderer *must* I go,
> The spectre of that innocent man, my guide.
> No human ear shall ever hear me speak;
> No human dwelling ever give me food,
> Or sleep, or rest: but over waste and wild,
> In search of nothing, that this earth can give,
> But expiation, will I wander on —
> A Man by pain and thought compelled to live,
> Yet loathing life—till anger is appeased
> In Heaven, and Mercy gives me leave to die.

In a different region, as we choose at random from Wordsworth's crowd of wanderers, we find that interesting sketch of the *Old Man Travelling* (or *Animal Tranquillity and Decay*):

> The little hedgerow birds,
> That peck along the road, regard him not.
> He travels on, and in his face, his step,
> His gait, is one expression: every limb,
> His look and bending figure, all bespeak
> A man who does not move with pain, but moves
> With thought.—He is insensibly subdued
> To settled quiet: he is one by whom
> All effort seems forgotten; one to whom
> Long patience hath such mild composure given,
> That patience now doth seem a thing of which
> He hath no need. He is by nature led
> To peace so perfect that the young behold
> With envy, what the Old Man hardly feels.

And, likewise, the Old Cumberland Beggar

> travels on, a solitary Man;
> His age has no companion. On the ground
> His eyes are turned, and, as he moves along,
> *They* move along the ground; and, evermore,
> Instead of common and habitual sight
> Of fields with rural works, of hill and dale,
> And the blue sky, one little span of earth
> Is all his prospect ...

Like so many of Wordsworth's lonely wanderers, the Beggar becomes a 'silent monitor'—a moral teacher. And so does the Leech Gatherer, who is first seen by the poet in a characteristic Wordsworthian attitude—'As a huge stone', and 'Motionless as a cloud'. He is a being so bent that it seems as if his head and feet are 'Coming together in life's pilgrimage'. To the poet he is

> like a man from some far region sent,
> To give me human strength, by apt admonishment.

On the other hand, in the long ballad *Peter Bell*, Wordsworth's counterpart to Coleridge's *Ancient Mariner*, it is the wanderer whose moral being is restored through his experiences on the journey.

Wordsworth's two most ambitious works, *The Prelude* and *The Excursion*, present the poet as a traveller and a pilgrim. In *The Excursion* the hero and Teacher is a 'gray-haired Wanderer' who, like the poet-pilgrim of *The Prelude* went in quest of the good life:

> From his native hills
> He wandered far; much did he see of men,
> Their manners, their enjoyments, and pursuits,
> Their passions and their feelings; chiefly those
> Essential and eternal in the heart,
> That, 'mid the simpler forms of rural life,
> Exist more simple in their elements,
> And speak a plainer language. In the woods,
> A lone Enthusiast, and among the fields,
> Itinerant in this labour, he had passed
> The better portion of his time; and there
> Spontaneously had his affections thriven
> Amid the bounties of the year, the peace
> And liberty of nature; there he kept
> In solitude and solitary thought
> His mind in a just equipoise of love.
>                                    (lines 340-355)

This is the man who in communion with nature had corrected his own despondency and thus was able to correct that of others, just as the poet in *The Prelude* restored his imagination and moral being by returning to nature, and thus was urged to preach his gospel of the senses and of spiritual Love.

Apart from these central works, we might list the many later and lesser *Memorials* of tours in Scotland (1803, 1814), on the Continent (1820), in Italy (1837); the River Duddon sonnets, and a great many records of travels and wanderers scattered through the other sonnets and shorter poems.

We need insist no further on the frequency or importance of the theme of travel in Wordsworth's poetry, and the examples already given may suffice at this stage to indicate certain aspects of the human situation in which the poet, as a wanderer or explorer, is involved, and also certain metaphorical patterns which will be relevant to our inquiry.

This constant interest in the journey, and Wordsworth's predilection for the figure of the wanderer and the pilgrim, are features which invite closer study. In particular, we might examine the metaphor of travel in the autobiographical poem *The Prelude*, in order to determine its function and value. Throughout, the poet describes himself as a wanderer and pilgrim, and asks us to see his life as a pilgrimage. The growth of his mind—his poetic imagination as well as his moral being—is traced through a series of excursions into nature and society, and conceived of as a quest for truth and the good life. In retrospect his life is a 'course' with a distinct teleological significance: the growth of his mind was also a movement in space and time towards a definite goal. Moreover, Wordsworth uses the metaphor of the journey as a structural and unifying element in the narrative development of his poem.

Since Wordsworth invites us to see the poet-protagonist of *The Prelude* as a pilgrim, we may ask what is the relation between the descriptive and metaphorical uses of the journey, and the spiritual growth he seeks to record. In what sense and in what way does the landscape, actual or imaginary, contribute to his awareness of himself and his world? Does the landscape explored represent an effective concrete embodiment or equivalent of the spiritual process which he calls the growth of his mind? Our essay will try to answer these questions.

From the point of view of literary sources, the theme of travel in Wordsworth has drawn the attention of scholars.[1] Because of Wordsworth's enduring interest in the literature of travel, it has been natural to assume that, like Coleridge, he derived considerable imaginative material from it. After all, did he not write to his friend James Tobin that without much reading in books of travel 'my present labours cannot be brought to a conclusion.' —and that at the very moment when he planned the great work of his life, *The Recluse*?[2] Yet John Jones is undoubtedly right when he observes that 'A Wordsworthian equivalent to *The Road to Xanadu* would be dull indeed; for Wordsworth lacked the entireness of mind that makes Coleridge's borrowings relevant to his poetry ... Wordsworth scholarship remains in this respect a negative discipline: it teaches the unimportance of his sources.'[3] For reasons which will become obvious later, such borrowings will not, except in two or three cases, be important to our study.[4]

*A Pilgrim Resolute*

In terms of place and time, the introduction to *The Prelude* maintains a deliberate vagueness. We are not told whether 'that day' on which Wordsworth leaves the city—to take 'The road that pointed towards the chosen Vale'—refers to a specific day and departure.[5] It is the situation which is important. In the 1805 text, there is emphasis on the feeling that he has been 'A captive' in the 'house/Of bondage' of the City—'A prison where he hath been long immured.' In the later version this prison idea is submerged but implicit, and the controlling metaphor is that of escape, and of freedom after 'many a weary day'—freedom to go anywhere, to stay anywhere, freedom to have 'peace' and 'undisturbed delight'. And this new-won freedom has even more important meanings: A 'gift' consecrates the poet's 'joy':

> to the open fields I told
> A prophecy: poetic numbers came
> Spontaneously to clothe in priestly robe
> A renovated spirit singled out,
> Such hope was mine, for holy services.
>
> (lines 50-54)

The emotion, then, is one of overwhelming relief, mingled with an elated sense of consecration or dedication. Hence the emphasis on peaceful and pastoral elements in the landscape through which the poet paces 'With brisk and eager steps', over 'the green fields' under an 'azure sky', with 'silver clouds'. And in the 'sheltered and sheltering grove', where he rests in 'perfect stillness', he gives himself up to musings in 'gentler happiness'.

Besides this actual and objective scenery, there is another landscape vaguely emerging to the poet's inner eye: 'in what vale/Shall be my harbour?'—

> whither shall I turn,
> By road or pathway, or through trackless field,
> Up hill or down, or shall some floating thing
> Upon the river point me out my course?
>
> (lines 27-30)

And during his musings in the grove, he makes choice of a 'known Vale' and 'a cottage' as his destination, and to these he takes the road, 'as a Pilgrim resolute'. This inner landscape is a projection both of his sense of freedom and his craving for a place where he may enjoy the peace and undisturbed delight which the city has denied him.

It is only in their general Arcadian tenor that these two landscapes are inter-related. Their interest lies not so much in details of observation or reflection as in the manner in which they establish the journey as the structural metaphor both for the poet's new way of life, as a 'renovated spirit', and for his future task. The introductory lines already present the poet as a wanderer and a Pilgrim, and his life and work should be viewed, in prospect, as epic and expanding experience, discovery, quest.

The travel metaphor is sustained intermittently throughout the first Book. After a summary conclusion of the 'escape' from the city (lines 105-07: 'What need of many words?/ A pleasant loitering journey, through three days / Continued, brought me to my hermitage.'), the poet begins a wavering discussion of his 'arduous work', its possible themes, forms and images, and again the geographical teleology suggests the necessity of a plan. His imagination tentatively explores ancient groves of Chivalry and 'ever-changing scenes of votive quest', or it aspires to 'Truth that cherishes our daily life', but nowhere does it find the satisfactory theme. The poet is bewildered—his days are 'past / In contradiction', and he is tempted to shirk his great task and instead

<blockquote>
to stray about<br>
Voluptuously through fields and rural walks,<br>
And ask no record of the hours, resigned<br>
To vacant musing, unreproved neglect<br>
Of all things, and deliberate holiday.<br>
(lines 250-54)
</blockquote>

In his perplexity the poet sees himself 'Unprofitably travelling towards the grave'.[6]

It is at this point that the thought of Nature, and memories of his childhood in Cumberland, correct the despondency of the poet and bring back the false steward—or the prodigal son—to his appointed task, in his native land. This is the actual beginning of *The Prelude*, as a record of the growth of the poet's mind, and it is significant that from this point onward there is a firmer grasp of narrative and form.

In this last part of Book First the travel metaphor is not important, for the simple reason that Wordsworth is dealing with his childhood and the influence of Nature on his infant mind. It is relevant to note, however, that the idea of teleology, formerly implicit in the travel metaphor, is here explicitly transferred to Nature and her 'means' and 'aim', (lines 351, 356.) Furthermore, two important elements in the treatment of landscape begin to emerge: one the emphasis on impressions of Nature as essential events of perception, memory and consciousness, and thus of the creative imagination; and the other a situation which is characteristic and recurrent in Wordsworth's subjective landscape, where the 'tumult', 'motion' and 'agitation' of the external scene are confronted with, and yield to, a contemplative state of mind where 'all was tranquil as a dreamless sleep' (l. 463).

Book First ends on the confident metaphorical statement: 'The road lies plain before me;—'tis a theme / Single and of determined bounds.' This poetic teleology, as we shall see, corresponds to an inner teleological pattern explored and described in terms of the growth of the poet's mind under the guidance of Nature.

Book Second continues the record of childhood. For the first time the travel metaphor is used to link phases of narrative: 'The simple ways in which my childhood walked' had led the poet to love nature—'rivers, woods, and fields', and now he goes on to explore further the teleological meanings of his childhood landscape. He insists that the boyish sports which took place amid the beautiful and harmonious scenes of nature tempered his excessive pride and vain-glory, and gave him 'A quiet independence of the heart' (70). He was 'taught to feel, perhaps too much, / The self-sufficing power of Solitude.' This is an important discovery of the influence of Nature on his impressionable mind, and from now on the emphasis on Solitude recurs frequently—almost as an obsession—in his poetic landscape.

The centre of psychological interest in Book Second is the meditation around the poet's growing awareness and love of Nature. This, he claims, gradually replaces the influence of his lost parents, in particular the 'one dear Presence' of the Mother, which is shown as the force that first unifies existence for the child and connects him 'with the world'. Having lost his Mother, the child felt bewildered: 'Yet is a path / More difficult before me', a path with 'broken windings'. But Nature has already taken the

child into her care, and though the 'props of affection' are for a
time removed, his mind is 'open to more exact / And close communion.' It is now that the self-sufficing power of Solitude begins
to make itself felt through Nature, with 'sublimer joy':

> for I would walk alone,
> Under the quiet stars, and at that time
> Have felt whate'er there is of power in sound
> To breathe an elevated mood, by form
> Or image unprofaned; and I would stand,
> If the night blackened with a coming storm,
> Beneath some rock, listening to notes that are
> The ghostly language of the ancient earth,
> Or make their dim abode in distant winds.
> Thence did I drink the visionary power;
> And deem not profitless those fleeting moods
> Of shadowy exultation ...
>
> (lines 302-313)

The passage is important in that it contains the essential Wordsworthian pattern of nature worship:—on his walk, under the
quiet stars—he is gradually initiated into that 'elevated mood'
from which arises 'the visionary power'. In the lines which follow,
this experience is interpreted as part of the teleological process
of spiritual growth, in which the soul aspires to, and pursues, a
'possible sublimity'.

The landscape changes: from the 'gloom and tumult' of the
storm the poet turns to other remembered scenes, 'fair and
tranquil', which likewise awaken the mind to new energy and
awareness. He perceives 'a universal power' and 'fitness' immanent in the external objects of the landscape but corresponding
to faculties and states of the mind.[7] This, as is well known, is one
of the central ideas of *The Recluse* fragment: to show 'How exquisitely the individual Mind ... to the external World / Is
fitted', and how exquisitely, too, 'The external world is fitted to
the mind.'[8] Yet, in his treatment of landscape as a concrete equivalent of states of Mind, Wordsworth is so obsessed with the
mental event, the feeling produced by this interaction of outer
and inner 'power', that he loses his grasp of the metaphorical
process and turns his perception to the general and abstract
rather than to the particular and concrete. This weakness is
apparent in his handling of adjectives in the passage quoted

above, and also in a recurrent image like 'tranquil scene'. And it is felt again in the rest of Book Second, where his intention is obviously to demonstrate and interpret, through the objective reality of landscape, the growing awareness of his mind. A new sequence of memories is once more introduced through the travel theme:

> My morning walks
> Were early; — oft before the hours of school
> I travelled round our little lake, five miles
> Of pleasant wandering . . .

But the woods in which he sits are not a particularised individual landscape, neither is the 'jutting eminence', and neither is the Vale. The important thing is the atmosphere: Above any other moment the hour of dawn and sunrise is to Wordsworth the hour of initiation, when a 'holy calm' fills his soul and the external world seems to fade away, or become a dream landscape. This is a recurrent experience in his poetry, and its *locus classicus* is in *Tintern Abbey*.[9] In this connection the interesting feature to note is a complete subordination of the external landscape to the inner mood, in other words, a subordination of the poetic vehicle to its tenor, so that, instead of solid metaphorical form that amplifies and defines the imaginative experience, the scenery merely provides a vague setting for the poet's mood.

The same vagueness, and a correspondingly generalised phrasing also persist in the following passage, where the poet, through a rapid enumeration of the seasons and the cycles of day and night, aims at a concentration of the epic time-sequence, while the spiritual gain is emphasised: impressions from these seasonal changes 'poured forth / To feed the spirit of religious love / In which I walked with Nature.' The phrasing here deliberately stresses a cultic attitude to Nature, which implies, as usual, a marked teleological idea: it is the novice, or disciple, who walks *with* Nature.[10] Despite his ecstatic attachment to Nature, however, Wordsworth is less interested in exploring its reality than in exploring the state of his own mind, his 'creative sensibility', the 'plastic power' which sheds an 'auxiliar light' on Nature. In the projected or configurated landscape which Wordsworth unfolds as an illustration of how this power works, we again notice the lack of solid, particular detail. And when we come to the wellknown passage: 'My seventeenth year had come' the landscape vanishes or is transmuted into a simple projection of mood and feeling. The poet transfers his own 'enjoyments' to 'unorganic natures'; he communes with 'things that really are', with 'every form of creature' in the various elements, yet what is ultimately important to him is the 'bliss ineffable' and the 'sentiment of Being' which he distils from his sense experience. And thus, as in *Tintern Abbey*, the culmination of his nature worship is that passive state when the eyes cease to see, and the body sleeps undisturbed, i.e. when the sense impressions of Nature have been transcended and obviated in a mystic's trance. If this is the goal of Wordsworth's pilgrimage, it is not strange to find that the objective, solid contours of landscape fade out, and are lost in the mist of general abstractions or phrases.

Wordsworth's residence at Cambridge, recorded in Book Third, is to a large extent concerned with his response to an uncongenial place, and the distractions of social activities and convivial pleasure. His youthful instinct for companionship is felt as a temptation to lead a life not worthy of the 'holy powers and faculties' which are the essential 'native instincts' of his soul. So he often leaves his friends, the crowd and the town, to pace the level fields *alone*. Though an exile from 'the lovely sights and sounds sublime' of Cumberland, he still has moments when his mind, steeped in Nature and solitude, may return into itself and gather fresh strength. In retrospect, this was a time when the poet began to realise his own independent personality, and when he felt that he was mounting to 'community with highest truth'. It was also, apparently, a time of abstract speculation, in which he 'looked for universal things', and the world around him was more than ever a projected landscape. It is significant that his illustration of the quest for 'highest truth' again involves the travel metaphor:

> A track pursuing, not untrod before,
> From strict analogies by thought supplied
> Or consciousnesses not to be subdued.
> To every natural form, rock, fruit or flower,
> Even the loose stones that cover the high-way,
> I gave a moral life ...
>
> (lines 127-132)

And yet, though he had a world about him of his own making and which lived only to him, he also at this time 'Was searching out the lines of difference / As they lie hid in all external forms', which implies that his eyes were growing more sensitive to particular things.[11] However, all these meditations on the growing awareness of his mind are mainly a summing-up of his spiritual development up to the first months in Cambridge, providing a background and a contrast to the deterioration of life and feeling which he experienced there. His 'quiet and exalted thoughts / Of loneliness gave way to empty noise / And superficial pastimes'; and he gave himself up to 'aims / Of a low pitch—duty and zeal dismissed' (328-9). It is a betrayal of Nature, and a fall from her grace, with the result that 'the inner pulse of contemplation almost failed to beat' (334).

Though Wordsworth deplores his deviations into 'idleness and joy' at Cambridge, he justifies his preference for gay companions to those ambitious 'eager few' who sought academic rewards: 'From these I turned to travel with the shoal / Of more unthinking natures.' And he reflects that, after all, this kind of life was a useful phase in his development. So far he had been a solitary, and the image which he presents of his own youthful and undoubtedly ideal self is interesting and revealing:

> Hitherto I had stood
> ......
> Like a lone shepherd on a promontory
> Who lacking occupation looks far forth
> Into the boundless sea, and rather makes
> Than finds what he beholds ...
>                               (lines 513-519)

This is the contemplative state to which Wordsworth so often returns in his moments of high communion with Nature, and the choice of the lonely shepherd gazing into the landscape of his own making is significant. Yet Wordsworth realises that such isolation is not possible for long, nor morally desirable, and it is his duty to approach 'human business' and 'Substantial life'. It was as a 'first transit' from the isolation of early youth to the social duties of mature life that Cambridge served him so well. In these reflections the travel metaphor is again strongly in evidence: After the 'wild outlandish walks of simple youth' Cambridge was a 'midway residence' better suited to his 'visionary mind' than a sudden thrust 'into Fortune's way'. And as usual, the metaphor is accompanied by a teleological idea: this 'transit' —'by a more just gradation did lead on / To higher things' (lines 521-31).

The travel metaphor in the account of the first summer vacation in Book Fourth emerges more spontaneously from actual experience than that of the preceding Book. In the opening lines a note of gaiety is struck, and the poetic intensity and excellence of the entire book are in general better sustained. It is a story of happy reunion with his 'sweet valley' and Nature has once more supreme sway in his mind. The boy of eighteen roams the hills, 'kindled' with the 'vernal heat / Of poesy', and it is on these walks that some lovely poetic image is found—'Full-formed, like Venus rising from the sea'.[12] A mood of quiet happiness is also conveyed in the memory of how, reciting his newly composed verse, he walked with his dog:

> at evening on the public way
> I sauntered, like a river murmuring
> And talking to itself when all things else
> Are still . . .
>
> (lines 118-21).

Here Wordsworth achieves one of the rare effective combinations of general (and semi-allegorical) imagery—'public way' —and a vividly particularised image of the murmuring river—to illustrate both his sustained role of Wanderer and the individual unique moment.

The spiritual significance of these walks is emphasised in the following passage, where the teleological implications of Wordsworth's travel metaphor are again felt. Those walks, he tells us, were 'well worthy to be prized and loved—':

> Those walks in all their freshness now came back
> Like a returning Spring. When first I made
> Once more the circuit of our little lake,
> If ever happiness hath lodged with man,
> That day consummate happiness was mine,
> Wide-spreading, steady, calm, contemplative.
>
> (lines 136-41)

We should keep in mind these essential traits of Wordsworth's
experience of happiness—'steady, calm, contemplative'. Like his
statuesque solitary shepherds, he is now once more in perfect
harmony with his environment, in a state of grace, and communing with Nature and God. Hence

> Gently did my soul
> Put off her veil, and, self-transmuted, stood
> Naked, as in the presence of her God.
> While on I walked, a comfort seemed to touch
> A heart that had not been disconsolate:
> Strength came where weakness was not known to be,
> At least not felt; and restoration came . . .[13]
>
> (lines 150-56)

Once more the landscape in which the wanderer finds his restoration fades as the journey turns inward to probe the experience
of 'comfort', 'strength', and 'restoration', which, by implication,
are the equivalents of natural impressions and forms. Thus,

> —Of that external scene which round me lay,
> Little, in this abstraction, did I see;
>
> (lines 160-61)

Instead, the poet is off on one of his recurrent mystical explora-
tions, as his mind in cultic ecstasy

> had glimmering views
> How life pervades the undecaying mind;
> How the immortal soul with God-like power
> Informs, creates, and thaws the deepest sleep
> That time can lay upon her . . .[14]

From this communion the poet passes, in accordance with the
habitual direction of his search, to a blissful Garden-of-Eden
scene, with 'milder thoughts', 'love' and 'innocence' and 'repose'
in 'pastoral quiet', while the mystical introspection yields to
idyllic enjoyment in a 'sheltered coppice' where he sits musing
alone.[15] It is also interesting to notice that although the boy of
eighteen now began to find a 'freshness' in 'human life', and a
'human-heartedness', or sense of fellowship in his love of external

objects, he observes with affection 'some sheltering bower or sunny nook, / Where an old man had used to sit alone, / Now vacant'.[16]

Against this background of bliss and innocence we are invited to see what happened later during that vacation. One may suggest that something like a definite pattern of fall and redemption is beginning to assert itself in the narrative structure, ranging from the social temptations and 'aims of low pitch' at Cambridge, to the subsequent restoration in the poet's return to Nature, to be followed by a new fall. For in this vacation, too, Wordsworth —judging severely the father of the man—experienced 'an inner falling off'; and again the temptation was conviviality, 'feast and dance', and 'public revelry', luring his mind 'from firm habitual quest' and 'meditative peace'. His account of these 'vanities' culminates in a vivid picture of the kind of 'agitation' that in retrospect he so much dislikes, with 'din' and 'shuffling feet' and 'glancing forms' during a night of dancing. This memory is called up deliberately as part of the teleological pattern of fall and restoration, for after this scene follows the crucial experience on Hawkshead:

> Ere we retired,
> The cock had crowed, and now the eastern sky
> Was kindling, not unseen, from humble copse
> And open field, through which the pathway wound,
> And homeward led my steps. Magnificent
> The morning rose, in memorable pomp,
> Glorious as e'er I had beheld—in front,
> The sea lay laughing at a distance; near,
> The solid mountains shone, bright as the clouds,
> Grain-tinctured, drenched in empyrean light;
> And in the meadows and the lower grounds
> Was all the sweetness of a common dawn—
> Dews, vapours, and the melody of birds,
> And labourers going forth to till the fields.
>
> Ah! need I say, dear Friend! that to the brim
> My heart was full; I made no vows, but vows
> Were then made for me; bond unknown to me
> Was given, that I should be, else sinning greatly,
> A dedicated Spirit. On I walked
> In thankful blessedness, which yet survives.
>                         (lines 319-338)

Here, perhaps for the first time in *The Prelude*, is a successful and sustained use of landscape as an objective, concrete equivalent for the spiritual experience. The outlines and details of the scene are more sharply observed and more completely integrated than in previous episodes; the external scene corresponds to, in part engenders, the inner state of mind.

The wanderer is walking eastward into the dawn and sunrise, and light-images dominate throughout the passage. From these is derived an increasing intensity in the sense impressions, and in the feelings they call forth, from the 'kindling' of the 'eastern sky', to the shining, bright mountains, which seem, in this climactic vision, to be 'drenched in empyrean light'. To this growing intensity corresponds a rising and sinking movement in the pattern of the landscape, from 'humble copse / And open field', to the mountains, clouds and then back to 'the lower grounds' with their idyllic beauty. The landscape itself is dense —with pathways, copses, fields, sea, mountains, meadows; there are sound impressions, and human activity.

Despite the careful build-up to the grand climax of sunrise in the line: 'The cock had crowed, and now the eastern sky / Was kindling' the description of the sunrise itself has a sudden and overwhelming character: 'Magnificent the morning rose'. The verse moves now with a new and stately rhythm, underlined by sustained alliteration, and both rhythm and sound are functions of the ritual solemnity which officiates above all in the adjectival interpretation of the scene.

With all its richness and precision this Hawkshead landscape does not, in the opinion of most, express a specific mental event, in terms of either religious or poetic dedication.[17] The experience, as projected in the scenery, is religious only in the sense that most of Wordsworth's communion with Nature is religious, i.e. pantheistic (or panentheistic), and the few echoes of Biblical phrasing, 'as e'er I beheld', 'sinning greatly' and 'blessedness', do not connote any definite Christian or religious traits in the context in which they stand. Nor does 'empyrean' suggest anything more than an indirect and Miltonic link with the traditional religious idea, and its main function is to expand the cosmic impression of brightness and radiance. The culminating experience of being a dedicated spirit may, in the context of Book Fourth as a whole, simply mean that the poet's mind is restored to its sense of identity and value, to its 'firm habitual

quest' through Nature and poetry—from which there had been
'an inner falling off'. As we shall see later, Wordsworth's sense of
sin is less a Christian concept than a feeling of having betrayed
his true self and the values and truths inherent in Nature.
However, the 'pull of the context', to use a phrase from I. A.
Richards, is towards a meaning of the 'vows' which certainly
includes both religious and poetic consecration. The two are
never sharply dissociated in Wordsworth's mind in *The Prelude*,
and it is possible that the experience on Hawkshead is related
to that which he describes already in the Introduction, when
'poetic numbers came / Spontaneously to clothe in priestly
robe / A renovated spirit singled out ... for holy services.' The
core of the Hawkshead episode is a cathartic experience—a
restoration—hence the 'blessedness' in which the wanderer continues homeward.

Compared with the Hawkshead episode, the rest of Book
Fourth is an anticlimax. Surveying his memories of other important events in that summer vacation, Wordsworth is again a
'wanderer', particularly in the 1805 version, and as usual his
wanderings imply symbolic or allegorical meanings. In the 1850
text there is the praise of solitude—'When from our better selves
we have too long / Been parted ... How gracious, how benign
is solitude'. His illustration of the power of solitude seen in relation to a 'human centre', shows too much strain in the *mise en
scène*, but the passage ends with the fine lines on the feeling of
solitude on a deserted public road at night:

> Or as the soul of that great Power is met
> Sometimes embodied on a public road,
> When for the night deserted, it assumes
> A character of quiet more profound
> Than pathless wastes.
>
> (lines 366-70)

These lines belonged in the 1805 text to the following passage,
relating the incident of the lonely soldier returning home. The
travel metaphor is there used with a more personal note:

> A favourite pleasure hath it been with me,
> From time of earliest youth, to walk alone
> Along the public Way, when, for the night

> Deserted, in its silence it assumes
> A character of deeper quietness
> Than pathless solitudes.
>
> (lines 363-68)

The story of the soldier whom the poet meets at night on the lonely road is told to illustrate two main aspects of the growth of his mind; one the power of Nature and Solitude to educate the emotions of the wanderer, here the emotion of human sympathy; and the other an insight into the character and fate of the solitary wanderer, who, no matter how trivial his errand, acquires allegorical and symbolic dimensions. The figure of the soldier reminds one of Wordsworth's statuesque shepherds, and of the Leech Gatherer: there was about him a 'desolation, a simplicity', and 'his form / Kept the same awful steadiness—at his feet / His shadow lay, and moved not.' Despite his hardships and misfortunes, this man is in harmony with his world, perhaps through submission, and yet unsubdued.

Another solitary traveller who has the poet's sympathy, though in a different manner, is the Arab 'of the Bedouin tribes', in the first important episode of Book Fifth.[18] In his reflections on this strange figure who appeared to the poet in a dream, holding a stone and a shell, symbols of geometric and poetic truth, (and which were books at the same time—to be buried and preserved before an approaching catastrophe) the poet tells us that he has often remembered this 'semi-Quixote', and 'shaped him wandering upon his quest'—i.e. his effort to preserve the values which the symbols (or books) contain—and though he has felt the pathos of the figure, his feeling of reverence for a 'being thus employed' is stronger still, even to the extent that he 'could share / That maniac's fond anxiety, and go / Upon like errand.'

There can be no doubt that Wordsworth deliberately avoids a careful discussion of the 'Books' which are his chosen subject in Book Fifth. He meditates on the topic in general terms, and though his attitude to books here on the whole is different from what it is in *The Tables Turned*, it is nevertheless significant that he digresses frequently into Nature and into themes which are linked with his Nature worship, instead of showing how, and to what extent, books have contributed to the growth of his mind. True, there are books which have 'sown' pleasure and power,

and benediction, and of which the poet speaks as 'Powers'. On
the whole, however, he makes us feel that, apart from such
imaginative nurture received through books, he has not been
greatly influenced by them, and there is also the hint that books
might have been, (as they often are to him), an 'evil'—especially
such books as those used in schools. At this point we hear quite
clearly the message from *The Tables Turned:* 'This verse is dedicated to Nature's self, / And things that teach as Nature teaches.'
He deems that he and Coleridge had been fortunate:

> Where had we been, we two, beloved Friend!
> If in the season of unperilous choice,
> In lieu of wandering, as we did, through vales,
> Rich with indigenous produce, open ground
> Of Fancy, happy pastures ranged at will,
> We had been followed, hourly watched, and noosed,
> Each in his several melancholy walk
> . . .
> Led through the lanes in forlorn servitude;
> > (lines 233-241)

Here the travel metaphor illustrates both the poets' own fortunate and beneficial freedom—in reading as in actual wandering
—in their childhood, and the opposite possibility of crippling
discipline which they have escaped. With a change of meaning,
the idea of a teleology is transferred to this fatal alternative, while
free will is glorified.[19] The education of Nature, and its advantages over that of books, is in reality the main theme of Book
Fifth, and one of the illustrations used is the fine passage 'There
was a boy'.[20] Another is the memory of how the poet, then a
child, saw a drowned man by Esthwaite Lake. Here again the
theme of wandering is emphasised, along with its concomitant
idea of a moral teleology:

> When I was first intrusted to the care
> Of that sweet Valley; when its paths, its shores,
> And brooks were like a dream of novelty
> To my half-infant thoughts; that very week,
> While I was roving up and down alone,
> Seeking I knew not what . . .
> > (lines 427-32)

And the point he makes—and it is a chillingly dubious one—is that Nature, through her influence on the infant mind, had prepared it even for such sights as the drowned man and 'hallowed the sad spectacle / With decoration of ideal grace'.

After this preference for the teaching of Nature to that of books, it is not surprising to find Wordsworth claiming in the conclusion that those who have been taught by Nature have a deeper understanding of great poetry:

> that he, who in his youth
> A daily wanderer among woods and fields
> With living Nature hath been intimate,
> Not only in that raw unpractised time
> Is stirred to extasy, as others are,
> By glittering verse; but further, doth receive,
> In measure only dealt out to himself,
> Knowledge and increase of enduring joy
> From the great Nature that exists in works
> Of mighty Poets.
>
> (lines 586-595)

By implication, there is a correspondence, perhaps even an identity, between the essential objects of knowledge and joy in 'living Nature' and in the 'great Nature' of poetry, and this, as we know, is what Wordsworth argued in the Preface to *Lyrical Ballads*.

In Book Sixth Wordsworth concentrates his account of the Cambridge years, passing briefly over his reading and other interests except for 'geometric science'. Neither does he devote many lines to his second summer vacation, though it was clearly a time of varied delights to the young poet-wanderer:

> In summer, making quest for works of art,
> Or scenes renowned for beauty, I explored
> That streamlet whose blue current works its way
> Between romantic Dovedale's spiry rocks;
> Pried into Yorkshire dales, or hidden tracts
> Of my own native region, and was blest
> Between these sundry wanderings with a joy
> Above all joys ...
> ...                          blest with the presence, Friend!
> Of that sole Sister ...
> ...
> Restored to me ...          (lines 190-202)

Together they explored landscape and picturesque ruins, looking

> through some Gothic window's open space,
> And gathered with one mind a rich reward
> From the far-stretching landscape, by the light
> Of morning beautified, or purple eve;
> (lines 216-219)

From this actual landscape Wordsworth passes, in his usual manner, to more abstract meditation in which the travel metaphor is
still sustained. He now addresses himself directly to Coleridge,
who has 'wandered now in search of health' to the Mediterranean, and then makes a comparison between their lives and
backgrounds:

> I, too, have been a wanderer; but alas!
> How different the fate of different men.
> Though mutually unknown, yea nursed and reared
> As if in several elements, we were framed
> To bend at last to the same discipline,
> Predestined, if two beings ever were,
> To seek the same delights, and have one health,
> One happiness.
> (lines 252-259)

Again the teleological trend is emphatic, though still without any
clearly religious concept of predestination. The significant point
here is the linking of the metaphor of wandering with this
persistent teleological pattern and finally with the general theme
of the growth of the poet's mind. Important also is the cluster of
values which, here as elsewhere, gather the teleological perspective into focus.[21]

After the somewhat embarrassing, self-complacent compari-
son of his own character and upbringing with that of Coleridge,
Wordsworth passes to the chief event of Book Sixth—the visit
to France and the Alps—in the third summer vacation (1790).
He prepares us for 'wanderings of my own, that now embraced /
With livelier hope a region wider far.'

Wordsworth's account of the journey through France is told
with verve and fluency. The expedition begins, as so often in
*The Prelude*, with a feeling of release and escape from 'restraint',
and an anticipation of the goal is aptly placed at the outset: the
two friends 'journeyed side by side / Bound for the distant Alps.'

Meantime, before them lies the exciting prospect of travel through revolutionary France—'France standing on the top of golden hours, / And human nature seeming born again.' (lines 340-41.) The young wanderers find their tour rewarding. They land at Calais, and

> Southward thence
> We held our way, direct through hamlets, towns,
> Gaudy with reliques of that festival,
> Flowers left to wither on triumphal arcs,
> And window-garlands. On the public roads,
> And, once, three days successively, through paths
> By which our toilsome journey was abridged,
> Among sequestered villages we walked
> And found benevolence and blessedness
> Spread like a fragrance everywhere, when spring
> Hath left no corner of the land untouched:
> (lines 349-359)

Here impressions of scenery and atmosphere blend effectively with glimpses of the popular celebrations, and the swiftly developing experience of travel sustains a vivid sense of movement and exploration. In the story of their passage down the Saône the same mood prevails, and here the 'majestic ease' of the river flowing between 'lofty rocks' presents an emblematic Wordsworth landscape. On this stretch the 'lonely pair' of wanderers are caught into the 'merry crowds' celebrating the revolutionary freedom, and they obviously enjoy themselves. Yet soon there is a characteristic transition:

> Taking leave
> Of this glad throng, foot-travellers side by side,
> Measuring our steps in quiet, we pursued
> Our journey, and ere twice the sun had set
> Beheld the Convent of Chartreuse, and there
> Rested within an awful *solitude*:
> (lines 414-419)

In the 1805 version we find a brief sequel to these lines which tells us that they went 'Thence onward to the Country of the Swiss.' To the older Wordsworth who revised the poem, the word *solitude* provided a clue for dramatising the contrast between the destructive (and constructive) forces of the Revolution and the 'silence visible and perpetual calm' of the convent invaded, as we are told, by 'riotous men'. It is no lesser a power than Nature that speaks for the Chartreuse:

> 'perish what may,
> Let this one temple last, be this one spot
> Of earth devoted to eternity!'
> (lines 433-35)

The poet-wanderer, 'by conflicting passions pressed', while paying tribute to the 'patriot's zeal' and to 'new-born Liberty', joins in the plea for these 'courts of mystery', where 'life's treacherous vanities' are left far behind, and faith and 'meditative reason' achieve their 'conquest over sense'. Though the lines still echo some of Wordsworth's revolutionary ardour, (like the later passage in XI, lines 105-09), his sympathy is with the 'unworldly votaries' who pass their lives in silence and solitude; and therefore, this new geographical discovery—the most important on the journey apart from the Alps—fits well into the emotional structure of *The Prelude*.[22]

The vision which concludes this passage may have been inspired partly by the poet's memories of the 'sacred mansion', for, he now remembers, as they entered Vallombre's groves,

> we fed the soul with darkness; thence
> Issued, and with uplifted eyes beheld,
> In different quarters of the bending sky,
> The cross of Jesus stand erect, as if
> Hands of angelic powers had fixed it there ...
> (lines 481-85)

This mystical and religious experience reminds us that the wanderer was also a 'pilgrim', though more orthodox when he wrote these lines than on the actual journey. The earlier account, it is true, describes the two friends as 'brother Pilgrims' (478), but it is written more in the spirit of two 'Keen Hunters in a chase of fourteen weeks / Eager as birds of prey'. For as the story continues, we hear (in both versions) of their 'variegated journey':

> A march it was of military speed,
> And Earth did change her images and forms
> Before us, fast as clouds are changed in heaven.

Day after day, up early and down late,
From hill to vale we dropped, from vale to hill
Mounted—from province on to province swept...
                                        (lines 491-496)

Their discoveries are mainly charms of Nature—'Sweet coverts
... of pastoral life, / Enticing valleys', but also 'sanctified abodes
of peaceful man', which furnish matter for a ponderous moral
sermon on 'patriarchal dignity of mind' and 'pure simplicity of
wish and will'. In these mountain valleys Wordsworth clearly
recognises a way of life as virtuous and beautiful as that of his
Cumberland shepherds.

The Alps had been the ultimate goal of their journey, and
they had undoubtedly looked forward to Mont Blanc as a grand
climax. Yet the first sight of the peak was disappointing:

                        That very day,
From a bare ridge we also first beheld
Unveiled the summit of Mont Blanc, and grieved
To have a soulless image on the eye
That had usurped upon a living thought
That never more could be.
                                        (lines 523-528)

To make up for this, and reconcile the two dreamers to 'realities',
there was the 'wondrous Vale / Of Chamouny' far below them,
with its 'dumb cataracts and streams of ice, / A motionless array
of mighty waves', the valley which also made such a deep impression on Coleridge.[23]

Despite the power and magnificence of this landscape, it is
nevertheless, in the terms used in our introduction to this study,
compliant: a matrix into which their 'intellect and heart' could
project 'lessons of genuine brotherhood, the plain / And universal
reason of mankind, / The truths of young and old.' And, inspired
by the scenery, the two 'social pilgrims' indulge freely in 'dreams
and fictions', and a luxuriant variety of moods.

It is after this view of Chamouny that we get Wordsworth's
anticlimactic account of the crossing of the Alps. The 'sadness'
of which he speaks at the beginning is once more the disappoint-
ment of the wanderer who expects or projects too much, and who
finds a recalcitrant or real landscape, very different from his

anticipations or his dreams. They see nothing of the grandeur they had imagined, and cannot believe the peasant who gave them their bearings—'Loth to believe what we so grieved to hear, / For still we had hopes that pointed to the clouds'. Thus, without noticing it, they had *crossed the Alps!*

It is generally agreed that the following passage, dealing with 'Imagination' and a mystical experience very like that of *Tintern Abbey* intrudes on the narrative and has no connection with the actual impressions of the journey.[24] Neither does it draw on any landscape, real or imaginative, as an objective form, except for the 'vapour', the 'lonely traveller', the 'mighty flood of Nile' and the 'Egyptian plain' in the final lines. Wordsworth is here describing a purely mental event, with no reference to an outward specific scene, and it has, therefore, only indirect bearing on our study.[25]

When the poet once more returns to his narrative, he tells us that the 'melancholy slackening' was soon overcome, and now, in the rush and speed of his mind through the remembered landscape, the lines and images begin to flow with renewed energy:

> Downwards we hurried fast,
> And, with the half-shaped road which we had missed,
> Entered a narrow chasm. The brook and road
> Were fellow-travellers in this gloomy strait,
> And with them did we journey several hours
> At a slow pace. The immeasurable height
> Of woods decaying, never to be decayed,
> The stationary blasts of waterfalls,
> And in the narrow rent at every turn
> Winds thwarting winds, bewildered and forlorn,
> The torrents shooting from the clear blue sky,
> The rocks that muttered close upon our ears,
> Black drizzling crags that spake by the way-side
> As if a voice were in them, the sick sight
> And giddy prospect of the raving stream,
> The unfettered clouds and region of the Heavens,
> Tumult and peace, the darkness and the light—
> Were all like workings of one mind, the features
> Of the same face, blossoms upon one tree;
> Characters of the great Apocalypse,
> The types and symbols of Eternity,
> Of first, and last, and midst, and without end.
> (lines 619-640)

This is a scene unusually rich in concrete, sharply observed detail, in graphic outline, and movement. From the moment we enter the narrow chasm the landscape is vivid, and it is much more than a landscape, much more also than a mood and a projection. There is a subtle metaphorical transfer and interaction between the actual landscape and imaginative response. Thus once more Wordsworth has succeeded in transforming the landscape of his travel into a complex picture of his mind, without violating or discarding its sensuous reality. At the same time, to him it is a picture of cosmic range and significance, in which he recognises some of the essential aspects of the universe.

The metaphorical process is most direct and obvious in such images as that of the brook and road as 'fellow-travellers in this gloomy strait', the winds 'bewildered and forlorn', the muttering rocks, the speaking crags. This anthropomorphic transformation of the landscape (which is not animation in the eighteenth-century manner) achieves some of the usual magic of metaphor, and it is significant that here, too, the imaginative grasp weakens when metaphor is replaced by simile, and the transformation is explained: 'like workings of one mind', after which the ponderous enumeration of its meanings—as 'types' and 'symbols'—involves stock responses for everyone familiar with Wordsworth's formula of Nature. But in the landscape itself there are other imaginative processes at work, partly characteristic of Wordsworth and partly of his time. There is the Romantic grandeur of the scene—its 'immeasurable height', its 'region of the Heavens'. There are the dramatic contrasts of clear blue sky and black crags; and paradoxes—the woods decay and yet will never die, the blasts of the waterfalls are stationary (cf. lines 530-31); there are simple antitheses, like 'Tumult and peace, the darkness and the light'. In this dramatic arrangement we recognise the typical Romantic manner, one more pervasive in Coleridge's theory and practice than in Wordsworth's. It is possible that the chasm through which Wordsworth travels here owes something to *Kubla Khan* and *Hymn before Sun-rise, in the Vale of Chamouni.*

The rest of the journey did not bring any such apocalyptic glimpses of the types and symbols of Eternity. There is a fine and vivid account of the uncomfortable night they spent on Lake Como; yet, though their bewilderment and fear of the supernatural are effectively related to various aspects of the landscape, these emotions do not engender a cogent poetic discovery.

In his reflections on the spiritual and imaginative gains of that journey through the Alps, Wordsworth makes a claim that would seem rather obvious, in particular with reference to his description of the valley of Chamouny (529-540) and of the Alpine chasm (621-640.): He had not, he remembers, been overwhelmed by the natural impressions; nor had his mind been a 'mere pensioner / On outward forms'. The 'magnificent region', which he now describes as a 'Temple', had been an occasion for Nature worship, his spiritual and imaginative communion with 'the invisible world' (602), and thus, by implication, he had half received and half created, what he saw. This was possible because in Wordsworth's idea of Nature and the human mind, as we have already noted, the external world and the individual mind are exquisitely fitted to one another, so that

> whate'er
> I saw, or heard, or felt, was but a stream
> That flowed into a kindred stream; a gale,
> Confederate with the current of the soul,
> To speed my voyage . . .
>> (lines 742-746)[26]

And again, because of this correspondence and mutual fitness, and because Nature is an embodiment of the beautiful and the good, Wordsworth also insists on the moral gain:

> every sound or sight,
> In its degree of power, administered
> To grandeur or to tenderness . . .
>> (lines 746-48)

In retrospect, Wordsworth feels that this first tour on the Continent was a great and important event, which brought spiritual expansion, energy and awareness. In the exultant coda to Book Sixth he remembers that, as they were 'shortening fast / Our pilgrimage', he watched the political stir 'as a bird / Moves through the air'; moved with sympathy, but yet detached. For more important to him was the feeling that

> the ever-living universe,
> Turn where I might, was opening out its glories,
> And the independent spirit of pure youth
> Called forth, at every season, new delights
> Spread round my steps like sunshine o'er green fields.
>
> (lines 774-778)

As one may expect, the account of Wordsworth's residence in London (February to May 1791) in Book Seventh, makes less use of the travel metaphor than the Books dealing with childhood and vacations. As a boy he had journeyed to London in his daydreams:

> There was a time when whatsoe'er is feigned
> Of airy palaces, and gardens built
> By Genii of romance; or hath in grave
> Authentic history been set forth of Rome,
> Alcairo, Babylon, or Persepolis;
> Or given upon report by pilgrim friars,
> Of golden cities ten months' journey deep
> Among Tartarian wilds—fell short, far short,
> Of what my fond simplicity believed
> And thought of London . . .
>
> (lines 77-86)

But later

> Those bold imaginations in due time
> Had vanished, leaving others in their stead:
> And now I looked upon the living scene;
>
> (lines 142-144)

And though the reality he found was often disappointing, it had yet in some ways a fascination for the young explorer. What he notices, above all, is the turbulence of this 'monstrous ant-hill', its 'endless stream of men and moving things', and, a usual image of 'agitation' in Wordsworth, there is the 'quick dance / Of colours, lights, and forms; the deafening din'. So overwhelming is this hubbub that at times the wanderer can bear it no longer:

> Escaped as from an enemy, we turn
> Abruptly into some sequestered nook,
> Still as a sheltered place when winds blow loud!
>
> (lines 169-171)

A situation which reminds us both of the escape from the vast City in the Introduction, of episodes from his Cambridge time and the first summer vacation.

Despite the poet's sensitive exploration of the city and the many impressions that crowd upon him, he does not express these in terms of an extensive and coherent travel structure. Various markets and fairs are described, like the 'phantasma' of St. Bartholomew Fair, with its 'anarchy and din, / Barbarian and infernal'. One of the finest passages of the whole Book, however, is that which reveals his response to an ordinary crowd, as he moves along with it, and says to himself: 'The face of every one / That passes by me is a mystery!' And he has tried to probe that mystery,

> Until the shapes before my eyes became
> A second-sight procession, such as glides
> Over still mountains, or appears in dreams;
> And once, far-travelled in such mood, beyond
> The reach of common indication, lost
> Amid the moving pageant, I was smitten
> Abruptly, with the view (a sight not rare)
> Of a blind Beggar, who, with upright face,
> Stood, propped against a wall, upon his chest
> Wearing a written paper, to explain
> His story, whence he came, and who he was.
>                                    (lines 632-642)

Here the journey is well exploited to describe that state of reverie and subjectivism which Wordsworth knew from childhood, in which all things seemed to vanish in a gulf of nothingness. The passage in fact epitomises a characteristic pattern of experience in Wordsworth, from sense impression to a state of subjective transformation, accompanied by a feeling of unreality; from this the poet is brought back by some vivid concrete perception. Then begins—as in the lines following the passage quoted—a process of deliberate abstraction, in which the particular detail becomes a 'type' or 'symbol' of man and of the universe. Thus Book Seventh ends with a meditation on the meaning of the seemingly 'blank confusion' and the 'perpetual whirl' of the city: it is not, after all, a chaos to 'him who looks in steadiness', and with a 'feeling of the whole'; to the person who has been educated—as the poet claims he has been—by 'the works of God / Among all regions'. A mind so trained is fitted to the external world, and can 'move / With order and relation'. Therefore, somewhat para-doxically, the poet is able to claim that the 'Spirit of Nature' was upon him in London, and the 'soul of Beauty and enduring Life' —i.e. his imagination, enabled him to strike through the veil of transient things to peace and harmony. It is significant that at every stage in the growth of the poet's mind, peace and harmony recur as ultimate goals in the teleological pattern.

The theme of Book Eighth is 'Love of Nature Leading to Love of Man', and for our purpose there is no need to rehearse the poet's argument.[27] Because of the obvious *non sequitur* of Wordsworth's relationship self-Nature-man, it is the more im-portant to note the emotional and intellectual coherence with which the essential theme—the love of Nature—is sustained, and in which direction it moves. The theme expresses a nostalgic attitude, dwelling on the beauty and excellence of his native region, Cum-berland, over all other lands, and the first part of the book con-tains three contrasts which, almost in the manner of syllogisms, are intended to demonstrate this claim. In these contrasts the poet travels far in time and space, but the travel metaphor is submerged or implicit rather than functionally used. In the first, as de Selincourt has shown, Wordsworth draws on Lord Macart-ney's account of the gardens of Gehol quoted by John Barrow in his *Travels in China*:[28]

> that famed paradise of ten thousand trees,
> Or Gehol's matchless gardens, for delight
> Of the Tartarian dynasty composed
> (Beyond that mighty wall, not fabulous,
> China's stupendous mound) by patient toil
> Of myriads and boon nature's lavish help;
> There, in a clime from widest empire chosen,
> Fulfilling (could enchantment have done more?)
> A sumptuous dream of flowery lawns, with domes
> Of pleasure sprinkled over, shady dells
> For eastern monasteries, sunny mounts
> With temples crested, bridges, gondolas,
> Rocks, dens, and groves of foliage taught to melt
> Into each other their obsequious hues,
> Vanished and vanishing in subtle chase,
> Too fine to be pursued; or standing forth
> In no discordant opposition, strong

And gorgeous as the colours side by side
Bedded among rich plumes of tropic birds;
And mountains over all, embracing all;
And all the landscape, endlessly enriched
With waters running, falling, or asleep.

(lines 76-97)


Here for once Wordsworth makes good use of his reading
in travelogues, but it would appear that his painting is marred
from the beginning by his foregone conclusion, that his native
region is a 'tract more exquisitely fair / Than that famed paradise'. Thus, while Wordsworth undoubtedly delights in the imaginative scope of the scene, there is a looseness and lack of
enthusiasm about his description which reveals his underlying
prejudice. This is evident both in the two parentheses, and in
such images as 'flowery lawns, with domes / Of pleasure sprinkled
over'; further in the strange assortment of 'bridges, gondolas, /
Rocks, dens', and in the colour description with its emphasis on
the artificial and over-refined effects achieved.[29] If, as John
Jones states, this passage 'invites comparison with *Kubla Khan*'[30]
it also reveals a lack of the imaginative challenge, the firm architectonic grasp of detail that make Coleridge's Xanadu such a
remarkable achievement. To Wordsworth this landscape is seen
mainly as a foil, despite the fine concluding lines (96-7), which
are characteristic of his best imagery. Over against this landscape
Wordsworth places 'the paradise / Where I was reared'—'lovelier
far'—not as an imaginative or visual counterpoint, but as the
quintessence of virtue bestowed by Nature on man: 'simplicity, /
And beauty, and inevitable grace.' What this human ideal,
personified in the Cumberland shepherd, meant to Wordsworth
and his growing love of man we are shown in the central passage
of Book Eighth, and it is this passage which best illustrates its
subtitle:

When up the lonely brooks on rainy days
Angling I went, or trod the trackless hills
By mists bewildered, suddenly mine eyes
Have glanced upon him distant a few steps,
In size a giant, stalking through thick fog,
His sheep like Greenland bears; or, as he stepped
Beyond the boundary line of some hill-shadow,

His form hath flashed upon me, glorified
By the deep radiance of the setting sun:
Or him have I descried in distant sky,
A solitary object and sublime,
Above all height! like an aerial cross
Stationed alone upon a spiry rock
Of the Chartreuse, for worship. Thus was man
Ennobled outwardly before my sight,
And thus my heart was early introduced
To an unconscious love and reverence
Of human nature ...

(lines 262-279)

One may argue that the apocalyptic conceit of the vision is strained to breaking-point when the shepherd becomes like a cross—for worship. Yet the graphic power which controls these lines is considerable, and there is a vivid metaphorical movement in the descriptive verbs. It is obvious also that Wordsworth has carefully developed a climactic structure, for the young wanderer went 'up' the brooks, and the hills; the shepherd appears to him 'In size a giant', in 'distant sky', a 'sublime object', 'Above all height', and, finally, he seems like an 'aerial cross' on 'a spiry rock'. Impressions of aloofness and altitude, and of detachment, are emphatic, and their semi-cultic implications increase with touches of mysterious atmosphere, with the 'deep radiance of the setting sun' by which the shepherd is 'glorified'. So far Wordsworth has succeeded in giving a stately and powerful portrait of the men he liked already in his boyhood, with heroic and almost superhuman outlines. It is when he comes to his sweeping *ergo* that doubts arise as to his underlying claim—that his love of shepherds, the true sons of Nature—led to a love of man in general. On the contrary, there is ample evidence in *The Prelude* and elsewhere that love of Nature did not (necessarily) lead to a love of man, and that the shepherds, or rather his ideal image of them, thwarted rather than furthered his human sympathies. Since their 'human form' became an 'index of delight', 'Of grace and honour, power and worthiness', it was all the more difficult, as the accounts of London crowds clearly demonstrate, to accept or like those who had none of the grace and power, and above all, none of the statuesque calm, of these youthful ideals.

That Wordsworth himself is not quite at ease with his emphatic claim may be gathered from the next passage, defiantly polemic in tone. Here his moral argument is charged throughout with teleological implications and also plain assertions: 'And so we all of us in some degree / Are led to knowledge'; and: 'Starting from this point / I had my face turned toward the truth' (lines 306-7, 322-3). It may be a matter of temperamental response whether one finds Wordsworth's demonstration of his privileged access to the good life noble and legitimate, or a solipsistic complacency. As he reaches his solemn conclusion, the journey or pilgrim idea through which he so often allegorises his life, and which, as we have seen, is closely associated with his teleological concepts, is exploited once more:

> I moved about, year after year,
> Happy, and now most thankful that my walk
> Was guarded from too early intercourse
> With the deformities of crowded life ...
>
> (lines 329-332)

And thus his mind was able to rise 'to devotion'—'Into the temple and the temple's heart.' His pilgrimage, then as later, tended towards the shrine of Nature and Solitude. And it is because he unconsciously identifies himself with the lonely shepherds in their harmony and oneness with Nature that they assume such importance in his spiritual landscape.

Throughout the rest of the book Wordsworth argues his theme with similar polemic and teleological assertions, and while there is a great deal said, and convincingly said, about his love of Nature, his love of man is clearly a more ambivalent feeling exposed to contradictory impulses. His sense of duty and of ethical nobility is at odds with more deepseated attitudes. Hence the curious shift of ground, and of level, in his argument, and his claim, in one place, that man in his early youth was merely an 'Occasional, an accidental grace', subordinate to Nature, and in another, that Man stood 'In the midst'.[31] Far more interesting, and important, is his interpretation of the influence of Nature on his mind which, habitually, tended to lose its sense of identity and, when tempted into the 'magic caves' or 'far-fetched shapes' of Fancy and Imagination, felt the need of coming back to steady reality, as when the boy had clutched the tree trunk:

> I had forms distinct
> To steady me: each airy thought revolved
> Round a substantial centre, which at once
> Incited it to motion, and controlled.
>
> (lines 429-432)

And when the young man left his lonely mountains to live in the vast city of London, where every day he was surrounded by 'temporal shapes / Of vice and folly', Nature had taught him that at the heart of this endless agitation of ephemeral forms there is central peace. His exploration of London life this time leads into a Platonic cave:

> The curious traveller, who, from open day,
> Hath passed with torches into some huge cave,
> . . .
> Widening on all sides; sees, or thinks he sees,
> Erelong, the massy roof above his head,
> That instantly unsettles and recedes, —
> Substance and shadow, light and darkness, all
> Commingled, making up a canopy
> Of shapes and forms and tendencies to shape
> That shift and vanish, change and interchange
> Like spectres, — ferment silent and sublime!
> That after a short space works less and less,
> Till, every effort, every motion gone,
> The scene before him stands in perfect view
> Exposed, and lifeless as a written book! —
> But let him pause awhile, and look again,
> And a new quickening shall succeed, at first
> Beginning timidly, then creeping fast,
> Till the whole cave, so late a senseless mass,
> Busies the eye with images and forms
> Boldly assembled, . . .
>
> (lines 560-582)

If the mind, or rather here the imagination, is able boldly to assemble the fleeting, discrepant and seemingly unreal impressions, it is because it has been 'steadied' and trained by Nature. Hence Wordsworth makes the apparently paradoxical claim (as in Book Seventh, 766) that London 'Was thronged with impregnations like the Wilds / In which my early feelings had been nursed'. This time, therefore:

> The effect was, still more elevated views
> Of human nature. Neither vice nor guilt,
> Debasement undergone by body or mind,
> Nor all the misery forced upon my sight,
> Misery not lightly passed, but sometimes scanned
> Most feelingly, could overthrow my trust
> In what we *may* become ...
>
> (lines 644-650)

Wordsworth, like the Romantics in general, believes that there is a divine essence in man which accounts for his fundamental goodness and which cannot be wholly destroyed. (Cf. *Peter Bell*.) It is worth noting that the meditations which lead up to this conclusion link human nature integrally with Nature as Wordsworth sees it, with his spiritual landscape, and man therefore forms part of that subjective or compliant scenery which the cave so vividly represents. As we know, Wordsworth was not able to remain in this comfortable world of a perfect man-Nature relationship for long. Meanwhile, as the solemn conclusion to Book Eighth shows, he felt that during his first twenty-one years he had been 'drawn / To human-kind' by Nature. And once again his spiritual and moral destination is expressed in the structural metaphor. Though he often 'seemed / To travel independent of her help', Nature still retained his best love.

In the introductory passage to Book Ninth, which deals with his residence in France from 1791 to 1792, Wordsworth uses the travel metaphor to connect this book with the preceding one, and to resume the narrative left off at the end of Book Seventh:

> as a traveller, who has gained the brow
> Of some aerial Down, while there he halts
> For breathing-time, is tempted to review
> The region left behind him; and, if aught
> Deserving notice have escaped regard,
> Or been regarded with too careless eye,
> Strives, from that height, with one and yet one more
> Last look, to make the best amends he may:
> So have we lingered. Now we start afresh
> With courage, and new hope risen on our toil.
>
> (lines 9-18)

Otherwise, curiously enough, though Wordsworth is here recording a period of actual travels that marked a turning-point in

his life, he does not exploit the imaginative scope of the journey
to the same extent as before. He remembers that, having arrived
in Paris where the scars of the Revolution were still obvious,

> these various sights,
> However potent their first shock, with me
> Appeared to recompense the traveller's pains
> Less than the painted Magdalene of Le Brun ...
> (lines 74-77)

He confesses, half ashamed of his aesthetic detachment, that 'I
looked for something that I could not find'.

This 'something', which was, perhaps, the spirit and meaning
of the Revolution, he undoubtedly found at Orleans and Blois,
where he met Beaupuis. Yet despite the revolutionary ardour
fired in him by his new friend on their walks through the woods
by the Loire, he confesses again how his mind occasionally
strayed from their 'earnest dialogues'

> to other times,
> When, o'er those interwoven roots, moss-clad,
> And smooth as marble or a waveless sea,
> Some Hermit, from his cell forth-strayed, might pace
> In sylvan meditation undisturbed;
> As on the pavement of a Gothic church
> Walks a lone Monk, when service hath expired,
> In peace and silence.
> (lines 439-446)

The solitary—Hermit or Monk, the undisturbed sylvan meditation, the silence and peace, these are the recurrent traits in the
landscape of Wordsworth's pilgrimage.[32]

From the 'rich domains' of the Loire Wordsworth returned,
at the end of October 1792, to Paris. Book Tenth tells of his stay
there, but the greater part of it is devoted to the months he spent
in London after he left France, and to thoughts about the Revolution and what followed it.

Most important of these events was England's participation
in the war against France. So far in his life, Wordsworth claims,
his moral nature had suffered no shock, no setback:

All else was progress on the self-same path
On which, with a diversity of pace,
I had been travelling ...

(lines 273-75)

The English aggression was 'a stride at once / Into another region.' Grief, perplexity and rage filled the young minds who had believed and hoped in the Revolution, and Wordsworth writes two hundred lines as a lament on those woeful times. Then the mood changes, and he remembers that even that 'disastrous period' had its bright moments, like the day when the news of Robespierre's death reached him. As it happened Wordsworth was out on a holiday walk:

> Over the smooth sands
> Of Leven's ample estuary lay
> My journey, and beneath a genial sun,
> With distant prospect among gleams of sky
> And clouds, and intermingling mountain tops,
> In one inseparable glory clad,
> Creatures of one ethereal substance met
> In consistory, like a diadem
> Or crown of burning seraphs as they sit
> In the empyrean. Underneath that pomp
> Celestial, lay unseen the pastoral vales
> Among whose happy fields I had grown up
> From childhood.
>
> (lines 514-526)

This overwrought description is not among Wordsworth's best, and its strained apocalyptic effects are not redeemed by the functional purpose, which is to announce the goodness of earth and the fall of the tyrant. The goodness of earth on that day was evident everywhere: 'As I advanced, all that I saw or felt / Was gentleness and peace.' Then he meets the crowd who tell him about the fall of Robespierre, and he bursts into a 'hymn of triumph'. His mood ranges from an ecstatic hope of a new golden age to calmer thoughts of how 'The glorious renovation would proceed', and his record of the day's journey ends with the splendid lines which commemorate the times when, with his school-fellows, he travelled through the same region —

> hastening to their distant home
> Along the margin of the moonlight sea—
> We beat with thundering hoofs the level sand.

Book Eleventh, which in the 1805 version was part of the Tenth, deals with Wordsworth's attitude to the final phases of the French Revolution, the intellectual and emotional perplexity into which he was plunged and the depression he felt when he saw his high ideals debased. The story covers one year, from August 1794 to September 1795, which, as is well known, was the turning-point in his life. Perhaps it is because this was a time of crisis, when he 'Yielded up moral questions in despair' and lost 'all feeling of conviction', that the pilgrim or wanderer metaphor hardly occurs in this account.[33] It is used, however, and significantly, in connection with his effort to find a new basis for truth and action in a direction where he had not sought before, in the realm of abstract science or pure reason:

> Depressed, bewildered thus, I did not walk
> With scoffers, seeking light and gay revenge
> From indiscriminate laughter, nor sate down
> In reconcilement with an utter waste
> Of intellect; such sloth I could not brook,
> . . .
> But turned to abstract science, and there sought
> Work for the reasoning faculty enthroned
> Where the disturbances of space and time—
> . . .
> . . .            find no admission.
>
> (lines 321-333)

He became Godwin's disciple, leaving the actual world of political and moral events which had become too recalcitrant a landscape for his pilgrimage, and seeking in the uncongenial world of mathematics and pure science a scenery more compliant. The idealist cleavage is still there, and as we shall see, he is approaching the nadir of his apostasy from Nature and his true self. From the point of view of chronology, Wordsworth's account is apt to be misleading, for, as scholars have shown, his moral despair resulted from his loss of faith in Godwinism as much as from his revolutionary disillusionment. However, the main point, which he makes himself, is that his sister Dorothy at this fatal moment rescued him from despair, so that his spiritual core, his 'true self', was preserved, and so too was the Poet. Gradually Nature again comes into her own. Through the mutual assistance of Dorothy and of Nature his sense of direction and of meaning is established once more, (though not so clearly and easily as the retrospect indicates) and hence the emergence at this point of the teleological pattern underlying the history of his spiritual growth. But now the process is a more difficult one of integration and regeneration, a marriage of head and heart— 'Whence grew that genuine knowledge, fraught with peace.' (354)

The Books (twelfth and thirteenth) which tell of Words- worth's spiritual recovery—of 'Imagination and Taste—How Impaired and Restored'—are, from the point of view of argu- ment and situation, the most important parts of *The Prelude*. Having reached the crossroads of his life, Wordsworth begins with determination to correct his despondency, and it is to be expected that here as elsewhere he should impose a clearer de- sign on his past life than it actually had. A characteristic feature of these books is the way in which they identify his newly-won sense of direction with the ethical teleology always inherent, in his view, in the influence of Nature. It is fitting, therefore, that he should approach the theme of his restoration by invoking the various delights of Nature, in the sacred grove of his worship:

> And you, ye groves, whose ministry it is
> To interpose the covert of your shades,
> Even as a sleep, between the heart of man
> And outward troubles, between man himself,
> Not seldom, and his own uneasy heart:
>                                         (lines 24-28)

We are reminded of his escape from the vast city in the intro- duction to Book First, and in fact he is, in a general way, referring to the time when he left London (and Bristol) for Racedown, in 1795.[34]

As in the preceding book, there is considerable emphasis on the cleavage in Wordsworth's nature and in his world. It is the so-called dissociation of sensibility: head and heart are sundered, sense and intellect, politics and morals remain apart. During this time, the poet sees himself as a 'voyager' who is forbidden to land on a 'pleasant shore' (53-4). The gulf widened with his pursuit of abstract science, the 'new idolatry', and gradually, as he 'laboured to cut off my heart / From all the sources of her former strength', his intellect, the 'meddling intellect' of *The Tables Turned*, 'unsouled' his world and expelled those 'mysteries of being' which make it one and whole.[35] Thus, in this 'perverted' state of mind, he had murdered to dissect the 'visible Universe', with 'microscopic view', even as he had disrupted the world of man.

It is characteristic of the emotional structure of these books that ecstatic invocations of Nature alternate with confessions of error and guilt. Thus in his apostrophe to the 'Soul of Nature' Wordsworth praises the power that 'by laws divine' overflows 'With an impassioned life, what feeble ones / Walk on this earth!', which implies some agent of grace, working through Nature from a divine source. There follows a new confession: how, yielding to the 'microscopic view' of the visible Universe, Nature had become merely a pretext for aesthetic evaluation and 'comparison of scene with scene', of 'colour and proportion'. At this time he admits, the bodily eye—'The most despotic of our senses' held his mind 'In absolute dominion.' Insatiably seeking these superficial delights,

> I roamed from hill to hill, from rock to rock,
> Still craving combinations of new forms,
> New pleasure, wider empire for the sight,
> Proud of her own endowments, and rejoiced
> To lay the inner faculties asleep.
>
> (lines 143-147)

Yet from this aesthetic phase he was saved again by the grace of Nature, or rather through her early teaching, still preserved deep in his 'true self' and his imagination. Thus, once more, he experienced a renovation of spirit:

> I shook the habit off
> Entirely and for ever, and again
> In Nature's presence stood, as now I stand,
> A sensitive being, a *creative* soul.
>
> (lines 204-207)

This recalls the moment in Book First when, a 'renovated spirit', he felt dedicated to 'holy services'; and that of Book Fourth when his soul 'put off her veil' and stood 'naked' in the 'presence of her God.' (152-3.) The moment here described is one of those 'spots of time' in which the spirit is regenerated and restored. It is, of course, of little use to read a religious or Christian piety into Wordsworth's reflections here, but one may surely see in his use of certain metaphors and phrases a deliberate tendency to establish associative links between the traditional terms of fall and grace and his spiritual rebirth at this time: he appears to move his language as close to Biblical connotations as possible, as in the claim that in these 'spots of time' there is a virtue that 'lifts us up when fallen.' (218.) The two instances Wordsworth gives of such 'spots of time' are both drawn from memories of boyhood, the first a vivid description of how, while travelling over the hills to his home, he lost his way and met the girl by the pool; the other an equally vivid memory of the sense impressions he had on a day shortly before his father's death. In both incidents the travel structure is used, but in purely descriptive terms, and it is mainly in their common element of perplexity and fear, and uncertainty as to which road to choose, that the allegorical hints may be seen. The awe and mystery of the first experience leads up to reflections on the 'mystery of man', before which he feels 'lost' (273); the second provides a concrete scene —lonely sheep, the blasted hawthorn, the mist and the two roads —which form an external equivalent for his anxiety and foreboding, and which he later tended to invest with symbolic significance, like the 'types' and 'emblems' revealed to him in moments of mystical awareness.[36]

These 'types' and 'emblems' are important in Wordsworth's effort to interpret his past life and the growth of his mind. It is in Book Thirteenth that he comes to grips with the second aspect of his theme: imagination restored. Standing now at the crossroads, with Godwinism and moral despair behind him and looking at Nature with renewed sensibility, he first surveys the cognitive implications of his quest:

> Long time in search of knowledge did I range
> The field of human life, in heart and mind
> Benighted; but, the dawn beginning now
> To re-appear, 'twas proved that not in vain

I had been taught to reverence a Power
That is the visible quality and shape
And image of right reason; that matures
Her processes by steadfast laws; gives birth
To no impatient or fallacious hopes,
No heat of passion or excessive zeal,
No vain conceits; provokes to no quick turns
Of self-applauding intellect; but trains
To meekness, and exalts by humble faith;
Holds up before the mind intoxicate
With present objects, and the busy dance
Of things that pass away, a temperate show
Of objects that endure ...

                                   (lines 16-32)

The Power is Nature, and besides being, as in eighteenth-century
Platonism, the image ('type', 'emblem') of right reason, it is the
Power that upholds order, induces goodness, and above all,
points to the 'central peace' at the 'heart of endless agitation'.
Thus, in his view it satisfies both the Platonist and the realist,
and reconciles the discordant elements of existence. This reconciliation, which was a notion probably inspired by Coleridge, is
seen as a fundamental creative process in Nature in the first lines
of Book Thirteenth, and as an inestimable gift of Nature to man,
in particular to Genius—'born to thrive by interchange / Of
peace and excitation'. (5-6)

   With his recovered sense of direction, and order, Wordsworth once more recapitulates his need of leaving the City and
the world's 'tumult', where 'much was wanting':

                        therefore did I turn
To you, ye pathways, and ye lonely roads;
Sought you enriched with everything I prized,
With human kindnesses and simple joys.
                                   (lines 116-119)

It was now not so much an escape, (as in the Introduction) as a
quest for value and truth; not so much the Fugitive as the Pilgrim who set out:

Oh! next to one dear state of bliss, vouchsafed
Alas! to few in this untoward world,
The bliss of walking daily in life's prime
Through field or forest with the maid we love,
While yet our hearts are young, while yet we breathe
Nothing but happiness, in some lone nook,
Deep vale, or any where, the home of both,
From which it would be misery to stir:
Oh! next to such enjoyment of our youth,
In my esteem, next to such dear delight,
Was that of wandering on from day to day
Where I could meditate in peace, and cull
Knowledge that step by step might lead me on
To wisdom . . .

(lines 120-133)

Despite the bathetic lines in this passage, and weakening repetitions, its underlying emotional drama lends a poignancy to the fate it describes. And it suggests, moreover, one of the sources of Wordsworth's restlessness in his youth: his lack of emotional ties after the separation from Anette Vallon.

Proceeding from this teleological phase of his quest, with its deliberate advance from knowledge to wisdom, Wordsworth gains a firmer imaginative grasp of the travel metaphor in the following passage:

Who doth not love to follow with his eye
The windings of a public way? the sight,
Familiar object as it is, hath wrought
On my imagination since the morn
Of childhood, when a disappearing line,
One daily present to my eyes, that crossed
The naked summit of a far-off hill
Beyond the limits that my feet had trod,
Was like an invitation into space
Boundless, or guide into eternity.
Yes, something of the grandeur which invests
The mariner who sails the roaring sea
Through storm and darkness, early in my mind
Surrounded, too, the wanderers of the earth;
Grandeur as much, and loveliness far more.
Awed have I been by strolling Bedlamites;
From many other uncouth vagrants (passed
In fear) have walked with quicker step; but why

Take note of this? When I began to enquire,
To watch and question those I met, and speak
Without reserve to them, the lonely roads
Were open schools in which I daily read
With most delight the passions of mankind,
Whether by words, looks, sights, or tears, revealed;
There saw into the depth of human souls,
Souls that appear to have no depth at all
To careless eyes.

(lines 142-168)

The perspective is well organised and rich in suggestive detail. There is a temporal movement corresponding to the journey of life, with its characteristic Wordsworthian departure in childhood. There is also a metaphysical or mystical extension— 'beyond' the distant hill, into 'space boundless', and further still, into 'eternity'. This is both the Platonic vision of transcendental reality, and the persistent need in the poet to see things as 'types' and 'symbols', always pointing to some indestructible essence, or power. Moreover, there is the emphasis on the teleological relevance of the road to the creative and searching imagination, whose growth and progress it stimulates and visualises at the same time. Thus, in the first phase of the vision, the idea of imaginative and spiritual pilgrimage is worked out in terms of Wordsworth's favourite wayfaring symbols, the road and the hill. In the second phase he introduces the representative human figures bent on the quest—and it is interesting to note his qualifying adjectives in the description: these people are invested with 'grandeur' and 'loveliness'. In the mariner here, as in the lofty, statuesque figure of the shepherd (Book Eighth), Wordsworth visualises a human being of heroic and sublime detachment, a being who amid the agitation and tumult of the elements is nevertheless in complete harmony with the external world, and 'unsubdued'. But when he moves from the dramatic contrast of the mariner of the dark roaring sea to 'the wanderers of the earth'—a phrase which suggests allegorical and symbolic undertones—it is significant that he selects the 'strolling Bedlamites' and 'uncouth vagrants' as his most fascinating wanderers. These are the exiles from society, the solitaries, who, while they are cut off from normal human relationships, are at peace with the world through which they travel—like the soldier in Book

Fourth. In this context the crude and trivial image of 'open schools' intrudes on the poetic scenery, but it provides a useful clue for the polemic attack in the ensuing lines, where the author of *The Tables Turned* and of the Preface to *Lyrical Ballads* is strongly in evidence. On the one hand, the wanderer arrives at this negative conviction:

> —Yes, in those wanderings deeply did I feel
> How we mislead each other; above all,
> How books mislead us, seeking their reward
> From judgments of the wealthy Few, who see
> By artificial lights . . .
>
> (lines 206-210)

On the other hand, there are the truths and virtues essential to his concept of the good life:

> If virtue be indeed so hard to rear,
> And intellectual strength so rare a boon—
> I prized such walks still more, for there I found
> Hope to my hope, and to my pleasure peace
> And steadiness, and healing and repose
> To every angry passion. There I heard,
> From mouths of men obscure and lowly, truths
> Replete with honour; sounds in unison
> With loftiest promises of good and fair.
>
> (lines 177-185)

At the heart of these passages there is a tension and paradox. We hear much of human communication and companionship, yet the roads are lonely, and different from the 'talking world'. It is, at one and the same time, a world of human relationships, and also of complete freedom, a world for the outsiders, who refuse to settle down or be hedged in by society. Being a world of detachment, it also gives peace from 'angry passion'.

Thus we find in this passage that the travel metaphor expresses a sense and need of relationship, as well as a desire to escape from social bonds; hence its more inclusive range of vision, compared with such episodes as the departure of the resolute Pilgrim at the beginning of the poem.

Wordsworth insists everywhere on the journey as a mode of moral and intellectual education, and in this he was, of course, a representative of the era that produced *Wilhelm Meisters Wanderjahre* and *Wilhelm Meisters Lehrjahre*. Travelling and learning had become identical activities already to the Elizabethans and we find in Wordsworth a tendency to see youth as the proper age for the journey, though his wandering solitaries, like the Leech Gatherer, are often old. Looking back on his own experience, he feels that everything he saw and found and learnt as a 'youthful traveller' has been of enduring value (222). But apart from this function of learning and discovery, the journey is also expressive of his poetic adventure, for instance in the following passage where, as in the Preface to *Lyrical Ballads*, he proposes to 'Deal boldly with substantial things; in truth / And sanctity of passion'—to deal with 'the very heart of man, / As found among the best of those who live ... In Nature's presence'. And, gathering up the various threads of human experience, poetic dedication, the sanctity of Nature and of the human heart, his vision into the future once more links the travel metaphor with a distinct teleological perspective:

> Be mine to follow with no timid step
> Where knowledge leads me: it shall be my pride
> That I have dared to tread this holy ground,
> Speaking no dream, but things oracular;
>                                    (lines 250-253)

And he uses it again in the exalted lines which follow about 'the men for contemplation framed'—to be found 'among the walks of homely life'. Throughout this passage, and notably in the concluding lines, there is a religious pathos and intensity in the anguage rarely found elsewhere in *The Prelude*.

On his own claim, the discoveries which Wordsworth made on the 'lonely roads' as a youthful traveller helped to restore both his moral nature and his poetic sensibility and imagination. Indeed, it is more than a restoration: it is a new stage of growth in his mind from which emerges a new and higher estimate of the poet's Genius, as in the apostrophe to Coleridge:

> Dearest Friend!
> If thou partake the animating faith
> That Poets, even as Prophets, each with each
> Connected in a mighty scheme of truth,
> Have each his own peculiar faculty,

Heaven's gift, a sense that fits him to perceive
Objects unseen before, thou wilt not blame
The humblest of this band who dares to hope
That unto him hath also been vouchsafed
. . .
A privilege whereby a work of his,
Proceeding from a source of untaught things,
Creative and enduring, may become
A power like one of Nature's.

                                    (lines 299-312)

This was also Coleridge's view, as he later expounded it in *Biographia Literaria* (ch. xiii). Apart from the importance of this statement as an epitome of Wordsworth's idea of the poet (also in the Preface to *Lyrical Ballads*), it is relevant to the episode that follows, and which is introduced deliberately as an illustration of the power of the poetic imagination to transform 'life's everyday appearances' and gain 'clear sight / Of a new world'. This is the Sarum Plain episode recording the poet's walk across Salisbury Plain in the autumn of 1793.[37] His experience there, as at Hawkshead in his first summer vacation from Cambridge, was one of dedication, but this time with a more definite task in view: that of being a creative power, 'A power like one of Nature's':

                              To a hope
Not less ambitious once among the wilds
Of Sarum's Plain, my youthful spirit was raised;
There, as I ranged at will the pastoral downs
Trackless and smooth, or paced the bare white roads
Lengthening in solitude their dreary line,
Time with his retinue of ages fled
Backwards, nor checked his flight until I saw
Our dim ancestral Past in vision clear;
Saw multitudes of men, and, here and there,
A single Briton clothed in wolf-skin vest,
With shield and stone-axe, stride across the wold;
The voice of spears was heard, the rattling spear
Shaken by arms of mighty bone, in strength,
Long mouldered, of barbaric majesty.
I called on Darkness—but before the word
Was uttered, midnight darkness seemed to take
All objects from my sight; and lo! again
The Desert visible by dismal flames;

It is the sacrificial altar, fed
With living men—how deep the groans! the voice
Of those that crowd the giant wicker thrills
The monumental hillocks, and the pomp
Is for both worlds, the living and the dead.
At other moments (for through that wide waste
Three summer days I roamed) where'er the Plain
Was figured o'er with circles, lines, or mounds,
That yet survive, a work, as some divine,
Shaped by the Druids, so to represent
Their knowledge of the heavens, and image forth
The constellations; gently was I charmed
Into a waking dream, a reverie
That, with believing eyes, where'er I turned,
Beheld long-bearded teachers, with white wands
Uplifted, pointing to the starry sky,
Alternately, and plain below, while breath
Of music swayed their motions, and the waste
Rejoiced with them and me in those sweet sounds.

(lines 312-349)

This is a canvas unusually rich in suggestive detail, and one of the rare examples in Wordsworth of interaction between scenery and historical or mythical fantasy. The solemn overture, here as in the Hawkshead episode, announces an experience of mystical and far-reaching significance. There is the exultant feeling that his spirit was 'raised', and the deliberate breakdown of limits of space and time through the imaginative medium of the travel: the poet 'ranged' the 'wilds', and the 'trackless' downs, or 'paced' the roads 'Lengthening in solitude their dreary line'— all of which are recurrent features in Wordsworth's landscape. Similarly, the boundaries of time recede, and the pageant of the past begins to move before his eyes. There are three episodes or tableaux, and in the transition between the first two of these we get a clear indication that here the Poet-Prophet—in 'priestlike robes'—is officiating through the sacred medium of his imagination. Whatever the meaning of the phrase 'I called on Darkness', it functions as a magic formula through which the visionary scene changes, and the apocalyptic nature of the change is further enforced by the Biblical phrase: 'and lo!'[38] The vividness of this sacrificial tableau is heightened by a simultaneous change from past to present tense: the event happens now and the poet participates. Unfortunately, there is a bathetic break in this technique when Wordsworth comes to the third episode (336), for here his imaginative grasp is weakened by the diary parenthesis, by the comment on hypotheses concerning the Druids, and the intrusive description of his own state of mind before the third vision emerges. Yet, for all this, the passage remains one of the most interesting and satisfactory achievements in *The Prelude* of what Wordsworth calls 'Heaven's gift'—the poetic imagination, and like the Hawkshead episode and that of the Alpine chasm, it derives its structure and varied beauty from the travel metaphor.

Wordsworth reverts, in the final paragraph of Book Thirteenth, to his main theme of 'Imagination Restored', and states that it was about the time of his walk across Salisbury Plain that he gained 'clear sight / Of a new world' in 'life's every-day appearances'. This, as we know, was the poetic gift which Coleridge admired most in him, and which appointed him for the task of removing the 'film of familiarity' from the world, in *Lyrical Ballads*.[39] There is ample evidence of this regeneration of sensibility in his poetry of the subsequent years.

In the introduction to the last book of *The Prelude*, Wordsworth uses the travel structure as a means of epic connection between the present and the 'walks' and 'wanderings' in which his imagination was restored, and as a means of transition to the climactic experience on Snowdon:

> In one of those excursions (may they ne'er
> Fade from remembrance!) through the Northern tracts
> Of Cambria ranging with a youthful friend,
> I left Bethgelert's huts at couching-time,
> And westward took my way, to see the sun
> Rise, from the top of Snowdon. To the door
> Of a rude cottage at the mountain's base
> We came, and roused the shepherd who attends
> The adventurous stranger's steps, a trusty guide;
> Then, cheered by short refreshment, sallied forth.
>
> (lines 1-10)

This was still in the year 1793, and Wordsworth reached Snowdon after his walk across Salisbury Plain and the visit to Tintern Abbey. The situation of the sunrise suggests immediately a connection with the Hawkshead episode. Yet, the beginning of their quest is unpropitious:

> It was a close, warm, breezeless summer night,
> Wan, dull, and glaring, with a dripping fog
> Low-hung and thick that covered all the sky;
> But, undiscouraged, we began to climb
> The mountain-side. The mist soon girt us round,
> And, after ordinary travellers' talk
> With our conductor, pensively we sank
> Each into commerce with his private thoughts:
>                                          (lines 11-18)

Though this is realistic enough, and no doubt corresponds to the actual experience, one is struck by the elaborate and emphatic description of the fog which envelops the wanderers and which suggests a recurrent feature of both mystery and uncertainty in Wordsworth's landscape, elsewhere often more directly expressed as 'darkness', or 'trackless', or as a sense of bewilderment in the phrase 'I was lost'. There is, however, nothing sinister in the present scene, although we find the poet describing his attitude to it in a somewhat unusual manner:

>                               With forehead bent
> Earthward, as if in opposition set
> Against an enemy, I panted up
> With eager pace, and no less eager thoughts.
>                                          (lines 28-31)

The fog, with its implications of blindness and mystery, and the wanderer's complete absorption in thought, are important elements in a *mise en scène* of the dramatically unexpected moment,

> When at my feet the ground appeared to brighten,
> And with a step or two seemed brighter still;
> Nor was time given to ask or learn the cause,
> For instantly a light upon the turf
> Fell like a flash, and lo! as I looked up
> The Moon hung naked in a firmament
> Of azure without cloud, and at my feet
> Rested a silent sea of hoary mist.
> A hundred hills their dusky backs upheaved
> All over this still ocean; and beyond,
> Far, far beyond, the solid vapours stretched,
> In headlands, tongues, and promontory shapes,
> Into the main Atlantic, that appeared

To dwindle, and give up his majesty,
Usurped upon far as the sight could reach.
Not so the ethereal vault; encroachment none
Was there, nor loss; only the inferior stars
Had disappeared, or shed a fainter light
In the clear presence of the full-orbed Moon,
Who, from her sovereign elevation, gazed
Upon the billowy ocean, as it lay
All meek and silent, save that through a rift—
Not distant from the shore whereon we stood,
A fixed, abysmal, gloomy breathing-place—
Mounted the roar of waters, torrents, streams
Innumerable, roaring with one voice!
Heard over earth and sea, and, in that hour,
For so it seemed, felt by the starry heavens.
                                        (lines 35-62)

In this splendid passage we see Wordsworth once more at his best, very different from the average level of the later books of *The Prelude*. There is a firm grasp of solid visual detail, as well as of main outline, and the composition unfolds with the priestlike solemnity and assurance that Wordsworth sustains so well whenever the scene and his mood are happily interacting. The scene is characteristic of Wordsworth in its silence and breathless awe, and it blends apocalypse with discovery, although the descriptive aspect is predominant. As in the Sarum Plain episode, spatial boundaries are broken down through impressions of the 'firmament', the sea, and the vapours that 'stretched'—'beyond, / Far, far beyond'—'into the main Atlantic' which 'dwindles' and is blotted out as far as 'the sight could reach'. This lower world, half submerged in the mist, is contrasted with the 'ethereal vault' of the sky, clear and bright, with the Moon in her 'sovereign elevation'. If we attend to the phrase: 'encroachment none / Was there, nor loss', and the various adjectives through which this contrast between the upper and the lower worlds is suggested, we get a metaphor of the Platonic dualism between the ideal and the material world. The vision of the sea of mist and the unclouded sky above is one of purity and light, while below the mist things and shapes vanish and are lost, in an 'abysmal, gloomy breathing-place', perceptible through a rift. And the contrast is further sustained in the impressions of the 'roar of waters, torrents, streams' down below while the upper world, the starry sky, is so still that it seems to 'feel' the roar mounting from the abyss. Thus the scenery contains the essential dramatic opposi- tions which we found also in the Alps episode, with its 'Tumult and peace', its 'darkness and light'—which, we remember, seemed to the poet 'like workings of one mind ... the types and symbols of Eternity'. And, in fact, it is the same insight the poet gains from the present scene:

> When into air had partially dissolved
> That vision, given to spirits of the night
> And three chance human wanderers, in calm thought
> Reflected, it appeared to me the type
> Of a majestic intellect, its acts
> And its possessions ...
> ...
> There I beheld the emblem of a mind
> That feeds upon infinity, that broods
> Over the dark abyss ...
> ... a mind sustained
> By recognitions of transcendent power,
> In sense conducting to ideal form ...
> (lines 63-76)

The scene has served the poet well as an imaginative form, though his abstract speculation on it contains nothing that he has not said before. The most important and interesting point he makes is that the power which has been revealed to him in this scene, is 'the express / Resemblance of that glorious faculty / That higher minds bear with them as their own.' (88-90) It is the power of the poetic imagination, which Coleridge similarly claimed was a 'repetition in the finite mind of the eternal act of creation in the infinite I AM.'[40]

In the meditative retrospect which fills the rest of Book Fourteenth, the travel metaphor is used only once to any great extent, and the 'anticlimax' which Professor Harper has noted is here obvious:

> Oh! who is he that hath his whole life long
> Preserved, enlarged, this freedom in himself?
> For this alone is genuine liberty:
> Where is the favoured being who hath held
> That course unchecked, unerring, and untired,
> In one perpetual progress smooth and bright?—

> A humbler destiny have we retraced,
> And told of lapse and hesitating choice,
> And backward wanderings along thorny ways:
> Yet—compassed round by mountain solitudes,
> Within whose solemn temple I received
> My earliest visitations, careless then
> Of what was given me; and which now I range,
> A meditative, oft a suffering man ...
> (lines 130-143)

It would appear that for once Wordsworth's memory is flagging, for what was given him in Nature's 'solemn temple' on Hawkshead was not received carelessly. It is clear that the poet's attitude to his own past and to life in general has changed: the 'thorny ways' and the 'suffering' were not previously aspects of his 'wanderings'. There is a new note of sadness and emotional exhaustion which is due, no doubt, to the death of his brother, but also, it would seem, to an uneasiness as to the safety and 'central peace' of the goal he has reached.

Intellectually, it is true, he makes at least one more great attempt to show that he has travelled—or grown—toward spiritual Love, the power which unifies existence and makes the universe a living reality, 'Actual, divine, and true'. And, at the same time, he attempts to show that he has grown in the power of Imagination, which is an inseparable part of this Love:

> This spiritual Love acts not nor can exist
> Without Imagination, which, in truth,
> Is but another name for absolute power
> And clearest insight, amplitude of mind,
> And Reason in her most exalted mood.
> This faculty hath been the feeding source
> Of our long labour ...
> ...
> And lastly, from its progress have we drawn
> Faith in life endless, the sustaining thought
> Of human Being, Eternity, and God.
> (lines 188-205)[41]

This is a noble goal, but it is different from the one Wordsworth had hoped to find. Despite its many touches of revision, the 1850 version of *The Prelude* still retains the underlying cultic attachment to Nature of the earlier text, and points to the 'solemn temple' of Nature rather than to this more orthodox one. De Selincourt has an apt comment on these changes towards greater orthodoxy:

> By changes such as these, the last Book in particular, which is the philosophical conclusion of the whole matter, leaves a totally different impression from that created by the earlier text. The ideas he has introduced are from the brain that wrote the *Ecclesiastical Sonnets;* they were entirely alien to his thought and feeling, not only in that youth and early manhood of which *The Prelude* recounts the history, but in that maturer period when it was written; and they have no rightful place in the poem. Whether he ought to have felt them, or wished, when he was reviewing his work, that he had felt them, is another matter. The essential point for us to realize is that their intrusion has falsified our estimate of the authentic Wordsworth, the poet of the years 1798-1805.[42]

For our purpose, however, it is not strictly relevant to discover whether and how the poet went wrong, or what determined his choice of direction. We have been concerned with his use of the travel metaphor as an imaginative structure—and with the evidence now before us we might attempt some conclusions as to its general characteristics and function.

As we have seen, the extent to which the journey is used in *The Prelude*, either as descriptive account of remembered experience or as metaphor, is considerable. Wordsworth throughout the poem exploits the journey as a structure to realise moments of great spiritual significance. Of these, the Hawkshead episode, the journey through the Alps, that over Salisbury Plain and, finally, the Snowdon climb are the most important, and they carry far-reaching implications relating to the main theme, the growth of the poet's mind. In these episodes, the journey fits naturally into the narrative, since they present the wanderer actually travelling through scenery that is observed, and which at the same time lends itself well to metaphorical or symbolic extension. There are many instances, however, where Wordsworth's effort to sustain the portrait of himself as the pilgrim or *homo viator* results in statements which are not imaginatively integrated, and contribute little if anything to the metaphorical structure of the poem.[43]

As for the general characteristics of Wordsworth's travel metaphor, it charts, on the whole, a fairly varied landscape, though with emphasis on the one hand on mountain grandeur, on the other on the secluded intimacy and peacefulness of the wood or grove. The lofty vantage point is usually the place from which a sense of profound spiritual or mystical insight is achieved, so that, while groves are places of repose—of 'central peace', the mountains, like Hawkshead and Snowdon, provide scenery for ecstatic discovery of the 'types and symbols' of the Power which interfuses Nature; or of Eternity, or God.

The handling of scenery is mostly descriptive, and relies on denotation rather than connotation. But in the key passages where landscape is used definitely as a metaphor, as in the Hawkshead, Alps and Snowdon episodes, the language has a more complex quality, and the poetic process ranges over wider tracts of experience. Here the interaction between outer and inner worlds engenders splendid visions.

Apart from scenery, the road is a central and recurrent feature of the metaphor, and Wordsworth's insistence on the symbolic meaning of the road is everywhere in evidence. The road may imply either a definite geographical direction, like 'The road that pointed toward the chosen Vale', or it may be part of the teleological pattern of poetic dedication or moral growth. Or both meanings may combine. Equally, it has the opposite functions of suggesting the wanderer's bewilderment or uncertainty, or a sense of absolute freedom. In this situation however, the wanderer more often finds himself in 'trackless fields and pathless wastes', where the boundaries of time and space tend to vanish in the mystical vision.

Except for the three mountain episodes, and such incidents as the encounter with the lonely soldier in Book V, and the 'escape' from the 'vast city' in the Introduction, one is left with the impression of a somewhat stereotyped vocabulary associated with the metaphor. There is repetitive insistence on the 'quest', the 'roaming' and 'ranging' of the wanderer, with implications of a goal, or of freedom and leisure; or the teleological idea that the poet was 'led' along the way of life is stressed with a similar monotony. Though one may argue, as Louis MacNeice has done, that Wordsworth 'does not require many images because his properties [i.e. perceptions] carry their own message', it must be admitted that Wordsworth's 'properties' or perceptions are, in *The Prelude*, of a limited and uniform kind.[44] And so, one may also argue, is the 'message' they carry.

The functions of the travel metaphor in *The Prelude* are numerous and varied, and one may distinguish between its formal and structural uses, for instance as a vehicle of the time perspective, of geographical and allegorical extension, on the one hand; and, on the other, as a vehicle for the two dominant impulses in the poet's mind, that of quest and nostalgia and that of escape.

As we have seen, the poet's wanderings are used both as structural connections between past and present (in Book Thirteenth *passim*), and as a means of linking episodes and phases of narrative. They are also used to provide a natural transition in the narrative from one book to another. (I and II, III and IV, VIII and IX, XIII and XIV.) Apart from this temporal coherence and perspective, the structural uses of the travel are mainly thematic and associative, and through these a set of words and symbols are established and repeated in order to sustain the main idea of the journey of life. In this function the travel metaphor approaches an allegorical use, though only in a vague and general sense, for there is no attempt at a coherent, extended system of equation between mental and external landscape.

It is, of course, as a metaphor for the poet's dominant impulses that the journey has its most important function. Wordsworth makes the journey a symbol for his yearnings after truth, creative power, and peace, and, as we have seen, in this 'quest' we have the central imaginative vehicle for the account of his mental growth. To realise this meaning and function, Wordsworth depends to a large extent on traditional connotations of religious quest, of 'pilgrimage', and associations of exploration and discovery. This aspect of his quest is most closely related to the neo-Platonic search of the *homo viator* or *peregrinus*, travelling towards a spiritual goal, which is ultimately beyond this world. The episodes at Hawkshead, in the Alpine chasm and on Snowdon may be interpreted in terms of such spiritual insight or fulfilment, and in the meditation on the 'public way' in Book Thirteenth the transcendental perspective is obvious, for the road as seen by the poet is 'like an invitation into space / Boundless, or guide into eternity.' But since this goal in its final aspects is unknowable, it follows that the journey can function imaginatively up to a certain point only, where all becomes 'darkness', or 'radiance', or where natural forms are felt as 'types' and 'symbols' of the great cosmic Power. In this neo-Platonic perspective, Wordsworth's travel metaphor functions well through the climactic mountain episodes, but not in the diffuse meditations on his moral goal. No matter how hard he tries to demonstrate the moral growth of his mind, he seems unaware of the monotony and stock responses involved in such terms as 'led', 'guided' and 'conducted' through which his teleological idea is conveyed. The one notable exception is the passage in Book Thirteenth where the vision of the lonely road includes such human elements as 'the mariner', the 'wanderers of the earth', 'strolling Bedlamites' and 'uncouth vagrants'.

The second predominant impulse for which the journey serves as a vehicle is that of escape. Though less pervasive or explicit than the quest-impulse, it is nevertheless important. The Introduction tells us that the poet has 'escaped / From the vast city'. Later there is the memory of 'flight' into Nature in his first summer vacation from Cambridge (VI, 8), and in the third vacation the poet and his friend, 'free from restraint' set out for the Alps. Again the poet escapes when he leaves London after his second residence there. A characteristic feature of the escape is that it is a movement away from disorder, chaos, and tumult, and towards order, silence and peace. There is no need to elaborate this point, since many critics of Wordsworth have discussed its psychological import at great length. But there can be no doubt that we have here a fundamental urge in the poet's mind, and it is evidence of the force and persistence of Wordsworth's inner chaos that what he seeks throughout *The Prelude*, and other poems of that period, is 'the peace that passeth understanding'— the 'central peace' at the 'heart of endless agitation'. Hence his escape from scenes of human disorder and noise, especially in the cities. In Nature, on the other hand, the 'tumult and peace', and contrasts of sound and silence, do not similarly affect the poet, because in this nonhuman world, devoid of human misery and passion, it is possible to see the 'workings of one mind', the 'types and symbols of Eternity'. In other words, while the human crowd is recalcitrant to imaginative and emotional configuration, because it is felt to be eminently real and like himself, the natural landscape is compliant and yields more easily a symbolic and metaphorical meaning. It is true that Wordsworth does not shun or dislike elemental disorder in Nature, though storms and fogs tend to be sinister and induce fear. But what he dwells on in preference to these is the silence and calm of the 'sheltered and sheltering grove'—he is indeed like a man always seeking shelter, seeking the outward scene that may impose upon his harassed mind a pattern of order and peace. It is the yearning which we know also from the *Ode to Duty*: 'My hopes no more must change their name, / I long for a repose that ever is the same.' It is true that we do not meet in *The Prelude* such despairing desire as that which he voices in *Personal Talk*:

> Better than such discourse doth silence long,
> Long, barren silence, square with my desire;
> To sit without emotion, hope, or aim ...

Yet, though he may, in *The Prelude*, sit in a sheltering place and draw 'confidence in things to come' from his meditation, or have 'inward hopes / And swellings of the spirit', the prevalent state he enjoys is that of 'ease and undisturbed delight', or of 'holiday repose', or in any case, the absence of bustle and disorder.

It is at this point that the two main impulses in *The Prelude* meet, so that the object of his quest manifests itself at the same time as the state into which he escapes. His cognitive search, which ultimately ends in mystical experience, in 'darkness' or 'sleep', also brings him to the 'central peace' where the 'endless agitation' of the human world is no longer felt. Underlying the journey of *The Prelude*, therefore, one may see an unmistakable desire for nescience (or insentience) and even for death. (The same death-wish informs the sonnet 'Methought I saw the footsteps of a throne'.) On the discursive and meditative level of the poem, this wish is always controlled and transformed, just as the moral struggle of the poet towards a place in the general human order is controlled, here as in the *Ode to Duty*, though in different terms.

In so far as Wordsworth in *The Prelude* attempts to show how he has travelled, not only towards greater awareness as a poet, but towards greater awareness as a social and moral being, his journey corresponds to the ancient tradition of the exile who seeks a new order within a new society. It is the journey of Aeneas. Characteristic of the *homo viator* impulse in such journeys is the yearning for intellectual and social order, or a unity of knowledge, sensibility, or being which implies or imposes order.

The baffling and inconclusive impression left by Wordsworth's journey—despite his great emotional and intellectual control, and his demonstration of ethical growth—is due, to a large extent, to conflicting impulses in his relationship to society. On the surface—where will and duty hold sway—he journeys into society, into an acceptance and love of mankind. On other levels, emotional and imaginative, his journey is one of transcendence and rejection, *out* of society towards an order which implies solitude and which approaches to states of beatitude, or death. Wordsworth never managed to combine the two. This may be one of the reasons, though perhaps not the most important one, why Wordsworth does not succeed in using the travel metaphor to better and more sustained effect in his autobiographical poem.

It might be tempting here to ask why Wordsworth, who throughout his poetry is preoccupied with the journey and the wanderer, never succeeded in writing a travel poem as Coleridge did in *The Rime of the Ancient Mariner*.

Though Wordsworth, the prophet of the senses, may be generally more aware of Nature as an external reality than Coleridge, and more aware of it as a matrix for his thought and feeling, yet he is incapable of that comprehensive fusion of mental event and external relations that Coleridge achieved in such poems as *Kubla Khan* and *The Rime of the Ancient Mariner*. In the latter, the external scene explored or experienced by the traveller is completely integrated with the spiritual state, it exists not only as projection, but as something so intensely realised that it attains to objective status, as a thing of nightmare vision and yet tangibly real. It is entirely compliant scenery or sea-scape, emerging from the creative imagination with all its Coleridgian autonomy, yet its reality is vivid and actual, because it corresponds to, and figures forth, a spiritual experience of profound universal significance, and at the same time retains its sensuous concreteness. Wordsworth never quite achieves this, perhaps because he is unable to bridge, except in general and discursive terms, the inner and outer world. In *The Prelude* at least, he does not usually live or create his external landscape directly: he observes it, and then interprets it in terms of personal mood or cosmic meaning and process. Thus, thing and emotion or idea do not fuse, as they do in Coleridge's great poem; they remain in a comparative or causal juxtaposition.

This way of seeing landscape does not, of course, account for Wordsworth's failure to sustain the journey as an effective poetic structure, but it reveals a certain obsession with projective explanation that weakens his imaginative grasp of the external world. Gradually, as the poet's quest turns in upon itself and becomes a vicious circle of thesis and demonstration, the juxtapositions of mind and landscape also grow more peremptory and stereotyped. Neat similes rather than metaphors tend to occupy the boundary between outer and inner landscape, and bar the wanderer from a unified vision.

# II

# COLERIDGE AND THE MARINER'S
# SEA-CHANGE

Whether we regard it as a 'gothic' ballad story, as a personal allegory, or a poetic myth, the voyage of the *Ancient Mariner* is the most compelling expedition of its kind in English poetry. In the course of the journey, as incidents and symbols accumulate their meanings, a provocative exploration of human mind and destiny takes place, through the medium of natural and supernatural forces, sea- and cloudscape, storms and calms and elemental changes. As Livingston Lowes has observed, 'the grand structural line of the voyage is the first determining factor of the poem.'[1] To retrace this line, and examine the meanings which emerge from the interaction of outer and inner worlds, of elemental and spiritual events during the voyage, is the purpose of this chapter. Considerations of a biographical and genetic kind, of the poem's 'moral', and its possible connection with Godwin or Hartley, will not enter into our discussion. Neither will it be part of our task to determine to what extent the poem may depend on a dream experience, and thus involve patterns and processes more interesting to a psychologist than to a critic.

The structure of the journey has been charted from various angles. Livingston Lowes has shown us which sources of reading combined to make the strange seas of Coleridge's imaginative quest. To Maud Bodkin we owe a perceptive account of possible psychological processes at work—in the implicit theme of the 'night journey', or the archetypal pattern of 'rebirth.[2] Hugh I'Anson Fausset and others have argued that the experience projected into the voyage represents the poet's inner discord and the habitual rhythm of his mind, vacillating between lethargy and depression and creative outbursts.[3] More interested in the poem's background, Dr. E. M. W. Tillyard has seen the voyage as a 'spiritual adventure' stamped by the enthusiastic sense of discovery in the accounts of seventeenth-century voyages.[4] Of all the attempts made by critics to relate the complexities of the poem to one unifying scheme, the most original and ingenious is that of Robert Penn Warren, who finds two distinct themes, that of the 'One Life' or the Sacramental Vision, and that of the 'Imagination', which are developed throughout the poem and fused at important points through the 'symbolic cluster' of wind, bird, mist, moon and sun.[5] Humphry House—in what is probably the most satisfactory shorter account of *The Ancient Mariner* —agrees with Lowes that the 'chief characters' in the poem are the elements: what Coleridge called 'the great appearances of nature', and House aptly observes that

> The function of the elements and heavenly bodies is not merely to *image* the Mariner's spiritual states (though indeed they do this), but also to provide in the narrative structure of the poem the link between the Mariner as ordinary man, and the Mariner as one acquainted with the invisible world, which has its own sets of values.

And again:

> The parallels ... between the spiritual and the natural —the physical imagery not just illuminating but actually conveying the spiritual state—are what most characterise the poem.[6]

To these scholars and critics, and to others, our study of the 'grand structural line' in the poem is greatly indebted.

Lowes has plotted the voyage as an 'architectonic factor' in the poem and shown how this 'formative conception' acted as a 'magnetic field' into which were drawn the many fragments of remembered images from travelogues and books of discoveries. According to Lowes

> there were two cluster-points of the sleeping images which were stirred to peculiarly intense activity, as the plastic agency of the design exerted its attraction. For the two stretches of the actual voyage which inevitably stamped on the mind the most powerful impressions were the 'Frigida' and the 'Perusta' of the ancient maps—the tracts of calms at the Equator, and the fields of ice about the pole. And

nowhere else in the poem is there such an incredible flocking together and coalescence of scattered recollections as at these two points—when the ship is passing through the ice-packs, and when it is lying becalmed at the Line.[7]

Already at this stage—to clear the way, so to speak, for the ship's departure—we may bear in mind Dr. Tillyard's suggestion that the sea-voyage in the poem 'indicates spiritual adventure', and one may accept this notion as true and fruitful without accepting the concomitant view that the Mariner is 'an unusually inquiring spirit'.[8] In its progress, as outer and inner horizons recede, the voyage becomes both a 'great spiritual experience' and an adventure, an exploration into the realms of mind, despite the fact that the Mariner and his shipmates are mostly passive and their voyage apparently without a goal. Not only in its cumulative symbolic and visionary discovery does the journey take on this aspect of adventure; from the very outset a sense of adventure is implicit, almost paradoxically, in the mysterious vagueness of the mariners' mission and route. This vagueness has important consequences for the developing structure of the voyage as well as for the human experience, and in this connection we may observe that although Coleridge, as Lowes has shown, had quite definite historical and geographical sources for natural phenomena and imagery, there is not a single specific term in the poem, no limited topographical area involving precise ideas. Such chartings are deliberately omitted, and, as we shall see, the imagery of climate and elements is used in such a way that it brings out the general (and symbolic) course of the voyage while emphasising the mariners' ignorance of their exact position (location). This is almost too obvious to call for mention, yet it forms a salient trait of the poetic technique, and one of the chief means by which the character of the voyage as quest and adventure is revealed. The purpose it serves is not determined in any way by Coleridge's usual practice (cf. *Kubla Khan*), nor by the ballad convention within which, to a certain extent, he was writing. It inheres in the basic design of the voyage as an exploration into an unknown world, a borderland between the natural and supernatural, between waking and dream.

To begin with, we may concentrate our attention mainly on two features of the journey: the sea-scape, as a developing pattern of images, and the movement or progress, with its marked rhythm and changes. While we are not committed to a rigid symbolic scheme as a basis of interpretation, it would appear that the term symbol cannot profitably be avoided in a reading of the poem.[9] It is hardly possible to dispense with it, as a 'focus of relationships', in George Whalley's apt formulation. The evidence which Whalley produces from Coleridge's Note-Books as bearing on his preoccupation with symbolic process, is relevant to an understanding of the poetic technique in *The Ancient Mariner*:

In *The Ancient Mariner* he had fashioned a myth in narrative form, weaving it around a group of symbols, few of which — and notably the albatross — were consecrated by previous symbolic use... Coleridge's personal symbols — the moon, the blue sky, the ocean, trees, fire, the candle flame... control the power of the Moon-gloss in *The Ancient Mariner*.[10]

As the Mariner begins his tale, the first thing we notice is that the home harbour has no definite location, and the voyage no apparent or stated destination. With the ancient epic formula: 'There was a ship' we are back among the flotsam of myth and folklore—and yet the situation of the departure is vividly and concretely seen. Indeed what characterises the voyage from the outset is that while there is no forward-looking exploration, no task to be fulfilled, each moment of the passage is recorded in its immediate vivid present. As such, the voyage is related to the Romantic *voyage sans but* which, without a teleological perspective, finds its object in the experience of self-realisation and in the exciting conquest of the unknown.

The moment of departure is charged with impressions of cheerfulness and exuberant speed. It is a propitious start: 'The ship was cheered ...'—and though the implications of the human relationships in this line do not persist throughout the poem, this is nevertheless the background and the happy communal situation against which the later events of the poem may be seen.

The traditional ballad use of repetitions is exploited by Coleridge throughout, and it serves mainly two purposes: either to mark the time during speedy progress, as in the passing of the landmarks

Below the kirk, below the hill,
Below the lighthouse top.

or, later on, to sustain a sense of monotony. Another kind of steady, regular movement is felt as 'the great appearances of nature' next encompass the ship:

> The Sun came up upon the left,
> Out of the sea came he!
> And he shone bright, and on the right
> Went down into the sea.
>
> Higher and higher every day,
> Till over the mast at noon—

Intentionally naive and bare in its design, this balanced pattern has yet a peculiar fascination, and it records several things at once: the progress in time and space; the fact that the Mariner's world is emptied of solid topographical categories, so that 'left' and 'right' become the only points of orientation; finally, almost paradoxically, the monotony of the voyage and at the same time the heightened awareness in the Mariner's observations. For as regards the Mariner's record of the voyage, the thing to note is that while he has little or no understanding of what is going on, he is endowed with extraordinary senses.

It has often been remarked that the Mariner is a passive figure, and that throughout the poem events *happen* to him and to the rest of the crew, except for the central action of the Mariner's crime. This passiveness in the human participants is suggested, it seems, already from the beginning in the use of verbs, and notably in the recurrence of 'came'. Objects and sights are not discovered or arrived at on this voyage so much as they 'come' upon the ship, and this trait is brought out once more as the sea-scape changes and the 'good wind and fair weather' of the gloss turn to storm:

> And now the Storm-Blast came, and he
> Was tyrannous and strong:
> He struck with his o'ertaking wings,
> And chased us south along.

In the stanzas describing the storm, there is insistence on the movement as a flight, which helps to develop the context for the passive experience later on. Critics have attempted to discover the precise symbolic meaning of the storms and winds in the poem—as creative impulse, or outbursts of vital energy.[11] Warren, in the context of what he calls the secondary theme of the Imagination, explains the ambivalence of the storms (here and after the Mariner's redemption) in terms of the ambivalence of the creative imagination—at times pleasant and 'good', at times terrifying and hostile:

> the first storm is an 'enemy' because to the man living in the world of comfortable familiarity, complacent in himself and under the aegis of the sun, the creative urge, the great vital upheaval, is inimical.[12]

To this one may object, however, that the Mariner is no longer living in the world of comfortable familiarity. The function of this first storm, it would seem, is rather that of a configuration of the elements, as part of the general myth-making process of the poem, to bring out their personified and animated force. The noises and elemental commotion so powerfully rendered in the description of the storm might be seen, also, as a preparation— on a psychological as well as symbolic level—for the following stanzas, when the ship reaches the 'Land of ice, and of fearful sounds, where no living thing was to be seen.' The terrifying 'blow', 'yell' and roaring 'blast' of the storm appear to charge in particular one line (61) describing the icepacks, and since the attitude in both passages is wonder and fear, it is reasonable to regard the storm partly as a cause, partly as an elemental equivalent of the spiritual and moral confusion which is soon to become the centre of interest. The sense of danger and persecution provoked by the storm is still felt during the passage through the ice—until the 'pious bird of good omen' arrives.

Like the storm, this land of ice and fearful sounds *comes upon* the mariners, and the sustained function of the elements as animated forces is set against the Mariner's baffled awareness of a pervasive hostility. According to Warren, the land of ice is both beautiful and terrible, 'as is proper for the spot where the acquaintance with the imagination is to be made. Like the storm which drives the ship south, it shakes man from his routine of life.'[13] This is true if we consider the fields of ice, like the storm, as aspects mainly of what Warren calls the 'secondary theme of Imagination'. But it would appear that Coleridge is here more bent on an exploration of the land of ice as the immediate background of the Mariner's crime. It is a cold ubiquitous desert, dismal, lifeless and inhuman. There are fearful sounds which echo those from the hostile storm, and these sounds, and the endless waste, are the features most strongly emphasised. The culminating word in the description—'swound', which according to some critics is oddly or wrongly used in this connection, very aptly renders the mariner's feeling of horror, unreality and loneliness at the sight. At this point, with dramatic contrast the albatross—the harbinger of life—is introduced, and immediately there is a sense of joy and relief. Thus the 'appearances of nature' prepare us for the psychological and imaginative significance of the bird of good omen which, as the one living being in this lifeless waste, becomes a symbol or representative of the Living Order—or the 'One Life', and thus not only breaks the deathlike spell of the land of ice but also controls its forces. This function of the bird is partly brought out by its reception as 'a Christian soul' which is hailed 'in God's name', partly by the power of the bird to open a passage through the ice and guide the ship. With the bird, a principle of life, love and direction has replaced the fear and confusion of the storm and the ice. Steady sailing through peaceful, enchanting seas follows, with gaiety and good fellowship. In this context, the Mariner's act of killing the albatross is a paradox and a perversion, but a perversion which may be related to the antithetical changes in the Mariner's experience so far on the voyage, from fair winds to terrifying storms, from the Equatorial sun to the dark polar ice-fields, and thence to the white moonshine in temperate pleasant seas. It is doubtful, of course, whether Coleridge intended this violent antithetical rhythm as a direct cause or preparation for the mariner's crime, but the crime itself falls into this strongly contrasting pattern which already controls the imagery of the poem and its developing structure.

As the bird was endowed with supernatural power, and felt to be a messenger from God, so the violation of its life becomes a violation against the 'One Life' and against God. On this most critics agree, but there is less agreement on the motive. Warren and Beer tend to see the murder as a symbolic equivalent to the Fall, while to House it is a manifestation of the 'error, incomprehensibility and frustration' in which the Mariner is caught throughout the poem.[14] The latter view seems to be the one most solidly founded in the context, and in the natural background of the voyage which, as we have suggested, corresponds to the Mariner's spiritual or mental states and reflects these states. For as Coleridge later wrote in *Dejection*: 'we receive but what we give,'—the act of perception is a creative act, and through his imagination the explorer contributes to his experience. The appearances of nature as seen by the Mariner suggest that he has lost his normal sense of orientation, he is haunted by fear and wonder through the storm, and is abandoned to a state—perhaps of his own making—of desolation and horror in the lifeless waste of the polar ice. This experience persists even after the ship has gained the open seas and a steady wind once more, and ultimately it perverts the Mariner's will. To claim this is not to provide a 'naturalistic' or 'psychological' motive for his crime, but rather to indicate how the elements in their varied and changing aspects are fused—or 'intimately combined'—with the recording consciousness. Two words from E. M. Forster's *Howard's End*—'panic and emptiness'—seem most aptly to describe the Mariner's surrender to the experience of the storm and the land of ice, and it is this condition—something like the terror and indifference of Mrs. Moore in *A Passage to India*—which cuts his ties with the Living Order. Yet his killing of the albatross remains in the nature of a shocking perversion. For the murder takes place not in the desolate waste of ice, but in the beautiful moonlit waters and gay fellowship with the bird, in all of which the Mariner shares. Yet his experience of nature has suggested a bewilderment and fear which cripple his moral awareness and his sense of the Divine Living Order—the 'One Life'.

The land of ice, therefore, does not emerge clearly from the context as 'the spot where the acquaintance with the imagination is to be made', but rather as the place where the spiritual or moral conflict of the poem is first defined in physical terms, and where something like a dialectic rhythm is established. Its function, broadly speaking, is to dramatise the conflict between principles of life (the albatross) and death (the ice); between love and harmony on one side and inhuman isolation and elemental disorder on the other. If the land of ice may be related to the hostile wind through Coleridge's description of their 'fearful sounds', the conflict suggests also a fundamental dialectic of good and evil, love and hatred. Beer has noted that ice and snow 'seem to have an ambivalent position in Coleridge's symbolism'

—they may represent the 'coldness of the unawakened heart—but they are also attractive, by reason of their brightness and purity.'[15] The second aspect is not apparent or implicit here, for it is a 'dismal sheen' and nightmare noises which most characterise this desolate waste. Hence, when the albatross arrives, to deliver the crew from fear and captivity, we have a stark contrast to their experience in the land of ice. The subsequent happy sailing in more temperate seas, and the good fellowship inspired by the bird, is the background against which the Mariner's violation of life is rendered the more ghastly and perverse.

With the shock of the Mariner's crime the first part of the poem is concluded. In the dialogue between the Mariner and the Wedding-Guest the significance of this act, as a fatal peripety, is emphatically marked, and when Part II begins, we expect sinister and inevitable consequences. Such expectations are fully intended and relevant to our reading. Yet what we find is a laconic description of sun and sea-scape, which repeats the regular pattern of an earlier stanza (7), though reversed. On the naturalistic level, this reversal of the points of orientation—of sunrise and sunset—indicates that the ship is sailing north in the Pacific towards the Line. Behind this, however, we have an ironical paradox, involving a vision both of cosmic order (the cyclic diurnal movement) and of the Mariner's feeling of the destruction (or inversion) of that order through his act of killing. For the observation of sunrise and sunset functions not only as log-book information, but as part of that contrasting and antithetical pattern which underlies the developing structure of the poem, and which emerges explicitly with the moral blindness and confusion of the Mariner's shipmates, in the two following stanzas. Here, dramatised by a new antithesis—the symmetrical counterpoise of the stanzas—the crime is first condemned and then praised, and thus, as the gloss tells us, the Mariner's shipmates become 'accomplices in the crime'. In the background of this moral tension, the appearances of nature are recorded both as temporal and spatial changes, and next involve the mariners' superstition concerning the albatross and the 'good south wind'. The mist that descended on the ship in the polar regions still lingers at sunrise, but clears off as they penetrate deeper into the temperate zone. It is here that their superstition and moral blindness lead the mariners astray:

> Nor dim nor red, like God's own head,
> The glorious Sun uprist:
> Then all averred, I had killed the bird
> That brought the fog and mist.
> 'Twas right, said they, such birds to slay,
> That bring the fog and mist.

Warren, arguing the 'secondary theme of the Imagination', claims that at this point the sun becomes the symbolic cause of moral confusion in the crew, and its meaning should be defined as the light of the 'understanding', of the 'mere reflective faculty' that 'partook of Death'.[16] And thus, being the cause of the mariners' acceptance of the crime, the sun in a short while takes the mariners to the sea of death, where it appears no longer as 'glorious' and as 'God's own head', but as the 'bloody' sun of destruction.[17] There is no doubt that the sun does acquire this character and function in the tropical seas, but for the time being it is truly 'glorious', not in terms of a fatal human deception, but because it is the sun of the temperate zone and the trade winds, and welcome to the mariners after the dismal sheen and the mists of the polar ice. This sun is not yet the tropical sun, small and 'bloody', as H. House seems to assume, and the dual quality in the sun which House rightly stresses, does not, at this stage, reveal itself in the solar metamorphoses from morning to noon, but emerges at the end of the implicit passage through the temperate zone and the trade winds to the tropical calms. Unless we keep this passage in mind, and the 'natural' response to the sun as 'glorious', we cannot accommodate the exuberant stanza:

> The fair breeze blew, the white foam flew,
> The furrow followed free;
> We were the first that ever burst
> Into that silent sea.

in the development of the voyage as a structure of experience. Here, more strongly than anywhere else in the poem, the wind suggests unhampered progress, release, spontaneous joy in the sailing, and then finally wonder and excitement at the discovery of the 'silent sea'. Thus Coleridge exploits the geographical possibilities of the seas of the trade winds in a manner which is consistent with the naturalistic level on which the poem still moves, and with the moral and spiritual levels. In the naturalistic context he records the aspects of nature in order to define the meaning and function of the imagery which will be used later to explore the events in the Mariners' experience. This is not to deny, but to assert, that the sun at the same time provokes and reflects the mariners' subjective and erratic interpretation of natural phenomena. Indeed, this correspondence is brought out with the force of tragic irony as the 'glorious sun' becomes the 'bloody sun' of the tropical seas. The same antithetical change, with similar implications, occurs in the sudden transition from wind to calm:

> Down dropt the breeze, the sails dropt down,
> 'Twas sad as sad could be;
> And we did speak only to break
> The silence of the sea!

where the last line repeats and stresses the contrasting images of 'burst' and 'silent sea' in the previous stanza. Increasingly, the great appearances of nature in the poem are being shaped and controlled by stark antithetical rhythms, and forming a pattern of 'discordant opposites'. The fact that at this point in the poem we have four stanzas linked together in contrasting and antithetical pairs, which dramatise first the moral confusion of the human beings and then the elemental opposites of wind and calm, is important to our exploration of the events of the voyage on naturalistic as well as moral and symbolic levels. The stanzas prepare for, and help to define, the great and inclusive contrast between the two geographical centres of the poem—the land of ice and the tropical seas.

As we have seen, the sun in the temperate zone is 'glorious', and then in the tropical 'silent sea' turns 'bloody' and destructive. Humphry House is quite right in his insistence on the dual import of the sun, reflecting the 'moral and spiritual error' of the crew. Coleridge exploits the 'glorious' sun' and the 'fair wind' of the temperate zone to achieve a more powerful imaginative definition of the mariners' experience when they are finally becalmed. As the imagination contributes to experience, so in the guilty minds of the crew the sun—which recently was like God's own head—becomes a source of wrath and retribution, the image of the angry God, whose living Order they have violated. It is this awareness which is determined by the tropical sun and calm, and within this naturalistic and elemental framework their spiritual corruption takes place.[18] Their corrupted view of Nature is suggested both in their changing and contradictory reaction to the sun, and in their mistaken enthusiasm for their discovery of the 'silent sea'.[19]

After the storms, the roaring noises of the land of ice, and the exuberant sailing, the tropical calm is the most important natural feature in parts II, III and IV. When the sudden turn comes in the voyage:

> Down dropt the breeze, the sails dropt down,

we do not need the explicit comment:

> 'Twas sad as sad could be;

to feel that here the weather and the elements are parts of the spiritual drama of the poem. The falling movement in the repetitive verbal emphasis first marks the contrast with the rush and speed of the preceding stanzas, and next becomes gradually charged with such associations of physical and mental depression as falling hands, a sinking heart, and even more sinister suggestions of sudden death—to be more fully realised later in the poem. The obvious psychological correlatives to this naturalistic change are depression and frustration: in their superstition and moral bewilderment the crew immediately interpret the appalling calm in the light of their guilty conscience and as a direct consequence of the Mariner's crime. In another psychological context, we may, as Maud Bodkin claims, see this falling movement as the first phase of the Rebirth Archetype:

> a movement, downward or inward toward the earth's centre, or a cessation of movement—a physical change which, as we urge metaphor closer to the impalpable forces of life and soul, appears also as a transition toward severed relation with the outer world, and, it may be, toward disintegration and death.[20]

Through imagery more directly expressive of mental states, the poem now begins to explore the 'great appearances of Nature' in their fusion with spiritual events. The cloud-scape conveys sensations of pervasive, infernal heat: the 'hot and copper sky' in which the 'bloody sun' stands, metaphorically fuses, in its furnace, associations of metal and blood—'bloody' is an apt projection of the Mariner's guilty conscience. While the metaphor of the infernal furnace may not be conscious or deliberate at this point, it certainly becomes so in Part III—where the Sun 'peers'—as if through a 'dungeon grate'—'With broad and burning face.' This explicit idea of imprisonment is already implicit (Part II) in the endless monotony and fixity of the calm:

> Day after day, day after day,
> We stuck, nor breath nor motion;

It is a captivity of the mind rather than of the ship, and the Mariner renders graphically the obsessive unreality of his experience in his description of the 'painted ship / Upon a painted ocean.' In his recording consciousness, obsession corresponds to the unchanging monotony of the external scene. This sense of unreality next turns into a grim paradox:

> Water, water, every where,
> And all the boards did shrink;
> Water, water, every where,
> Nor any drop to drink.

Apart from its sustained impression of monotony, this stanza keeps the antithetical rhythms of the poem vibrating in our minds—in the contrast between the endless sweep of sea waste and the shrinking boards, and in the nightmare paradox of thirst in a world of water. Further, through its direct exploitation of the Tantalus situation the stanza develops the meaning of the experience as infernal torment.

Cut off from their natural condition, the mariners in their guilty, captive state begin to see nature as a process of corruption:

> The very deep did rot: O Christ!
> That ever this should be!
> Yea, slimy things did crawl with legs
> Upon the slimy sea.

In the following stanza, this vision is developed more explicitly in terms of elemental and spiritual chaos, of surrender to forebodings of death, while the images of 'death-fires' and burning water also sustain the sense of unreality and at the same time of infernal torment. From this nightmare vision, there is an apt transition to the explanatory stanza in which the supernatural element—the Polar Spirit—is introduced in the mariners' dream and shown to be the cause of their misery, or, in other words, the agent of retribution. The stanza also looks back to the 'land of mist and snow', and draws the two geographical centres of the poem closer together, to define more clearly the meaning of the passage from the one to the other. As a conclusion to this imaginative and symbolic course from crime to atonement, the dead Albatross is hung round the Mariner's neck—'instead of the cross'. On the part of the Mariner, this is sad self-irony, but at the same time it serves to keep the religious analogue of his experience before our eyes.

Part II, as we have seen, records a process of mental corruption, in terms of infernal torment and elemental disorder. One of the many contrasts set up in this part to dramatise the spiritual isolation of the Mariner and his fellows, is that between motion and fixity. As the mariners are imprisoned in the calm, this contrast persists in the vision of slimy things crawling about the unmoving ship, and 'death-fires dancing' in 'reel and rout' by night. This is the contrast which also controls the imaginative pattern of Part III, when the spectre bark arrives. Here again, through emphatic repetition, the captive and static monotony of the mariners' hell is conveyed, and against it is seen the swift mysterious arrival of the bark: 'It moved and moved'—'It plunged and tacked and veered'. In the verbal counterpoint of 'rested' and 'drove' in the magnificent sunset stanza the contrast is again focused:

> The western wave was all a-flame.
> The day was well nigh done!
> Almost upon the western wave
> Rested the broad bright Sun;
> When that strange shape drove suddenly
> Betwixt us and the Sun.

As the Polar spirit holds the mariners' ship captive, so this strange ship moves mysteriously without wind. We have here an important preparation for the supernatural forces and events which play such a large part later in the poem, and they are aptly

introduced in a situation of nightmare and hallucination. The
sunset stanza records an experience of beauty as well as terror,
and it points, with sinister ambivalence, to night as well as death.
While the sun is once more glorious—or at least 'broad' and
'bright'—its flames still sustain the associations of hell-fire torment from the previous part—and the water still burns. The prison metaphor which was submerged in the earlier stanzas describing the 'painted ship' which 'stuck' day after day without
motion, now emerges more explicitly, in connection with the
sun, and in the Mariner's vision the ideas of imprisonment and
infernal fire fuse through the pivotal word 'dungeon-grate' and
the image of the sun 'flecked with bars'. The outward scene
continues to reflect the inward state—the imagination contributes to the experience, and increasingly the sun is felt as a
personified force—as the power that imprisons and torments the
crew. In their diseased imagination, the sun peering through
the infernal dungeon-grate now suggests Lucifer rather than
God. Through these associations, as well as the cry: 'Heaven's
Mother send us grace!' the religious background of the poem
serves, as in the two previous parts, as a framework of reference,
and against this background the allegorical incident of Death
and Death-in-Life dicing for the Mariner and the crew takes
place. With the arrival of these allegorical figures in the spectre-
bark, the fatal moment has come, and once more the situation is
dramatised through a contrast between violent movement in the
'appearances of nature':

> The Sun's rim dips; the stars rush out:
> At one stride comes the dark;
> With far-heard whisper, o'er the sea,
> Off shot the spectre-bark.

and, on the other hand, the dumb and paralysing horror of the
mariners. There is a moment of suspense in which the strange
vision of 'The hornèd Moon, with one bright star / Within the
nether tip' appears. According to J. B. Beer, 'It is the star between its horns that represents the daemonic vengeance upon the
Mariner'—not the Moon itself.[21] At any rate, this unusual con-
stellation of moon and star, seen in the context of hallucination
and of the mariners' corrupted view of the natural order, focuses

powerfully the various impressions of human beings severed from the natural world and doomed to perish.

The antithetical contrast between motion and fixity in these two stanzas is sustained in the account of the mariners' death:

> Four times fifty living men,
> (And I heard nor sigh nor groan)
> With heavy thump, a lifeless lump,
> They dropped down one by one.

The verb 'dropped' seems to echo the verbal emphasis in the lines: 'Down dropt the breeze, the sails dropt down', and as in a musical structure it completes the theme then introduced. The first phase of retribution is concluded.

So far, we have insisted on the mariners' experience as one mainly of spiritual corruption, manifested in revulsion from living beings (the slimy things), in nightmare and superstitious visions, and brought to a climax with the arrival of the spectre-bark. This is not to ignore the physical torment which underlies the spiritual experience and partly causes it. The agony of thirst is conveyed already in Part II through imagery that suggests death: life is gradually drained from the mariners, so that their tongues are 'withered at the root'. In the opening stanzas of Part III further images graphically describe the corpse-like state of the crew—their throats are 'parched', their eyes are 'glazed', and their lips are 'black'. Through these physical symptoms the death of the mariners, although sudden and apparently caused by the sinister figures in the spectre-bark, is prepared for in the structural imagery. Apart from this imagery, there are other words drawn into the description by the powerful context of the death theme—such as the skeleton 'ribs' of the spectre-bark, and the skin of Life-in Death—'white as leprosy.'

A great deal of recent critical discussion has turned on the symbolism of the sun, as the chief natural agent, in Parts II and III. To Warren's thesis that the sun is the 'bad light' of the poem —the 'sun of death', House has rightly objected that the sun has a double character, and the error of the crew is not to perceive it.[22] Beer claims that Coleridge intended the sun to be the symbol of God, or the divine Glory, who, in the mariners' guilty conscience, turns into a destructive force.

To insist, however, as House and Beer tend to do, that the

destructive function of the sun inheres in the mariners' erratic
perception of it—that it becomes the 'angry "Typhonian" sun,
unendurable because improperly apprehended', is to stress un-
duly an aspect of the experience which is peripheral, compared
with the central design of crime and expiation. And Coleridge's
great achievement here is to derive such powerful symbolic implications from a solidly naturalistic narrative, vividly present to
the senses. Thus he steers the ship with perfect ease from the
pleasant moonlit seas where the Albatross was killed into the
tropical calm and the fire of the sun, and while the course is
plotted according to the need and logic of the spiritual experience, the 'great appearances of nature' remain all-important,
and objectively real. The sun, though changing in the mariners'
view from 'glorious' to 'bloody' and then to 'broad' and 'bright',
is the cause of their suffering, their further spiritual corruption
and, ultimately, their death. But this process is worked out with
such tightness of correspondence and interaction between outer
and inner events that the specific questions of cause and consequence have little importance. All the way on the voyage, the
imagination draws on old maps as well as on changing climates,
but it creates the reality and meaning of the outer and inner
worlds it explores. The geographical design is determined by
events in the realm of the soul, above all by the crime, corruption
and atonement, but in its turn that design, in its evolving physical
equivalents, furnishes the outer conditions through which the
spiritual experience is fully realised.

Within the 'grand structural line of the voyage' the main
points of orientation established thus far are the land of ice and
the tropical seas, and these regions emerge not only as stark
contrasts in the objective voyage, but they mark the extremes of
the inner journey from crime to expiation. We may not be entitled
to read these in the light of Coleridge's later definition of the
poetic imagination as the synthetic power that 'reveals itself in
the balance or reconcilement of opposite or discordant qualities',
but we know that already in his poetic practice Coleridge was
exploring the symbolic juxtaposition of such opposites as ice
and heat—as when in the following year he wrote *Kubla Khan*.
The fact that *Kubla Khan* was conceived in a dream shows how
spontaneously his mind was already building its imaginative
forms in dialectic structures, more explicitly formulated by him
in his favourite dictum: 'Extremes meet'.

The 'discordant opposites' of ice and heat in the main design of the voyage span the central action of the poem. In this more comprehensive antithetical pattern the significant details are worked out with a corresponding rhythm, in imagery as well as in the verbal movement, and there can be little doubt that Coleridge carefully and deliberately devised this stark rhythm, to dramatise the spiritual issues. The rhythm emerges in simple observations of the rising and setting sun, of the changes from wind to calm, of the contrast between endless water and nothing to drink; there are further the steep antitheses between fixity and motion, day and night, heat and cold, hideousness and beauty, life and death.

After the 'four times fifty living men' have dropped dead at the end of Part III, the Mariner, sole survivor of the crew, reaches his nadir of lonely agony in Part IV. As in previous stanzas (27, 28, 29) repetitions and the emphatic use of 'all' bring out the felt ubiquity of the Mariner's torment:

> Alone, alone, all, all alone,
> Alone on a wide wide sea!
> And never a saint took pity on
> My soul in agony.

The endless sea-waste mirrors his terrible mental void, and against this background is seen, in poignant ironical contrast, the dead men and the slimy things living—his only companions. The natural order seems wholly corrupted, and the Mariner views it with horror and revulsion:

> I looked upon the rotting sea,
> And drew my eyes away;
> I looked upon the rotting deck,
> And there the dead men lay.

As a felt consequence of his crime, guilt and ugliness prevail and prosper, while the beautiful and—to the Mariner—innocent men are dead. In the following stanza, describing his effort to pray, the structural imagery sustains the interaction of spiritual and physical torment: a 'wicked whisper', recalling the whisper heard from the spectre-bark, stifles the Mariner's prayer and makes his heart *as dry as dust*. These stages of revulsion and despair lead on

to an effort to retreat out of this world, yet the appearances of
nature continue to haunt the Mariner with an obsessive sense of
their connection with his crime and the innocent victims:

> I closed my lids, and kept them close,
> And the balls like pulses beat;
> For the sky and the sea, and the sea and the sky
> Lay like a load on my weary eye,
> And the dead were at my feet.

The interaction between spiritual state and natural surroundings
is rendered with powerful simplicity. In its charged imagery, the
stanza epitomises the torment inflicted by the tropical calm, and
relates it to the Mariner's burden of guilt, in the pivotal word
'load', which implies both the dead men and the albatross hung
around his neck. The 'fixedness' which the prose gloss aptly uses
to describe his experience is one of physical imprisonment, as in
the previous parts, and of incipient mental paralysis. He is now
in the throes of Life-in-Death, and longing for death to release
him. Yet despite this paralysing horror, his mind still retains an
unusual awareness of what is going on. When we insist on the
Mariner's spiritual corruption which isolates him completely
from the natural order and fills him with revulsion from the slimy
things, we tend to ignore his human attachment, his regret for
the dead men, and his effort to pray. These are redeeming
features, and so is his awareness of the ironic situation in which
he and the slimy things live on while beings innocent and beautiful have perished. Thus his isolation and despair are mainly due
to his sense of a former order that is destroyed in the world.

At the moment when the nethermost circle of hell is reached
and the Mariner's wish to die completes his descent, his peculiar
sensory awareness discovers a change in the appearance of
nature:

> The moving Moon went up the sky,
> And no where did abide:
> Softly she was going up,
> And a star or two beside—

In contrast to the burning sun and the 'load' of sea and sky which
have dragged the Mariner to his hell, there is the rising moon,
whose soft light and upward movement break the monotony of

his daylight world and fill him with wonder and delight: 'In his loneliness and fixedness he yearneth towards the journeying Moon, and the stars that still sojourn, yet still move onward'. The moon and stars, as this splendid prose-gloss suggests, reveal to the Mariner a world of beauty, and order, and peace; a world where things have their 'appointed rest', their 'native country' and their 'own natural homes', where they are received with 'silent joy'.

At this crucial point in the poem, where the verbal emphasis on movement breaks the static horror of the Mariner's hell, the elemental change hints at a restoration of balance or order in the physical as well as in the spiritual world of the poem, and this process is more fully explored in the following stanzas. The night and cool moonlight bring relief from the sun, and thus also provide the basis for a change in the Mariner's awareness. The moon is felt for the first time in the poem as a supernatural force, increasingly personified through the verbal action of the next stanza:

> Her beams bemocked the sultry main,
> Like April hoar-frost spread;
> But where the ship's huge shadow lay,
> The charmèd water burnt alway
> A still and awful red.

In the moonlight, a new vision of the natural order emerges to the Mariner's imagination, and in this and the following stanzas we observe a myth-making process transforming the outer panorama through growing spiritual and imaginative insight. The Mariner feels the change to come from without—first from the Moon and later from Mary, Queen of Heaven, but the outer world remains nevertheless a projection of his mind, or rather an interpretation.

As the Mariner sees it, the journeying moon not only breaks the spell of his mental and physical imprisonment, its cool light appears literally to temper the 'sultry main' and make of it an April field covered with hoar frost. Thus the infernal heat yields to the power and control of the moon, and a temperate balance is restored within the reach of its beams. But in the direct juxtaposition of the cool moonlit waters and the waters still burning red within the shadow of the ship, there is, perhaps, an image

of elemental contention—a struggle and conflict pointing forward to the supernatural contention and struggle in later stanzas.
Meanwhile, as the moon tempers the dark, burning sea, its
light transforms the watersnakes, or rather shows them to the
Mariner in their true, natural beauty. Since the Mariner's crime
was a violation of life and the natural order, so part of his atonement, it is now seen, has been to suffer through a corrupted view
of nature and a revulsion from living beings. The slimy things,
at first apparently bred in a process of corruption in the rotting
deep, and later despised as 'the creatures of the calm', now
appear to the Mariner as 'God's creatures of the great calm',
and significantly, their beauty is revealed to him through impressions of vivid movement and cool moonlight. In this metamorphosis of light, even fire is tempered and becomes 'golden'—
an aspect of this living, moving and beautiful sea-scape, where
the dance and splendid pageantry of the watersnakes are very
different from the Mariner's first vision of them, crawling on the
slimy sea, under the death-fires dancing by night and the water
burning—'like a witch's oils'.

When the Mariner blesses the watersnakes for their beauty
and happiness, and feels a spring of love gushing from his heart,
this spiritual change is well prepared for and defined in terms of
physical equivalents. The meaning of this act of love has been
noted by most critics: as the Mariner's crime was a murder—a
violation of a life representing the sanctity of the 'One Life' and
the natural order, so his atonement lies through suffering and
repentance and a rediscovery of the unity and beauty of all life.
When this insight is achieved, he experiences a rebirth into a
state of love and grace, and is once more admitted to the fellowship of living beings. But he himself insists on the redemption as
an act of grace, granted him by his 'kind saint', and he tells us
twice that he blessed the watersnakes 'unaware'. In this word
Coleridge focuses two important and complementary aspects of
the Mariner's experience: his lack of understanding, and his
sense of the miraculous and supernatural, both of which are
fundamental shaping factors in the poem. Indeed, part of the
unique quality of the poem depends on the subtle balance maintained in the recording consciousness between a vivid awareness
of sight and sound and of supernatural forces behind them, and at
the same time a lack of understanding of what they are or mean.
From this balance is derived that sense of wonder and fear which

controls the visionary experience in the first parts of the poem and prepares us for the direct introduction of the supernatural elements in Parts III and V. It is, moreover, in keeping with the voyage as a vividly seen but dimly realised experience that dreams at three points serve to introduce supernatural beings which either produce or explain the events.[23] Part IV ends with the external sign of redemption when the Albatross falls from the Mariner's neck and sinks like lead into the sea. The whole context is charged with religious and Christian implications: it is the kind saint who takes pity on the Mariner; he is now able to pray, and Part V opens with a praise to Mary Queen who sends the gentle sleep from Heaven. Quite aptly, the Mariner's expiation brings peace of body and soul. After his seven days and nights of lonely agonised watch, he is given the balm of sleep, and next the balm of water. The first stanzas of Part V thus record a wonderful sense of physical as well as mental relief, and the rain which finally saves him from the torment of thirst is a natural concomitant to the 'spring of love' which 'gushed' from his heart. Seen against the cumulative experience of infernal heat and drought, nothing could convey better the relief of cool moisture than these lines:

> My lips were wet, my throat was cold,
> My garments all were dank;
> Sure I had drunken in my dreams,
> And still my body drank.

And the restitution goes on: next the Mariner records with delighted wonder that he 'moved'. The same verb which introduced the moon and the watersnakes, the verb of vital action, releases the Mariner from his 'fixedness', and from now on *movement* dominates the imagery of the succeeding stanzas. Whether or not we accept Maud Bodkin's application of the rebirth pattern in its entirety, there is certainly a reinstitution of life implicit in the elemental process now unfolding:

> The upper air burst into life!
> And a hundred fire-flags sheen,
> To and fro they were hurried about!
> And to and fro, and in and out,
> The wan stars danced between.

13

As rain brought relief from thirst, so the wind—and the 'commotions in the sky and the element' bring relief from the stagnant calm. The stanza celebrates an outburst of elemental and cosmic vitality which corresponds to and expresses that of the Mariner, and now, instead of the 'death-fires' dancing at night (128), the fire-flags suggest joy, exuberance and festivity. But significantly, the element of fire persists, and like the 'golden fire' which flashed in the tracks of the watersnakes, these fire-flags are aspects of a beautiful and temperate world, and move in the cool regions of the moon and stars. The death-fires dancing in reel and rout in Part II announced cosmic disorder as seen by a corrupt imagination, but here the restoration of that order, through a rebirth of the imagination, and of love, is announced through the splendour and movement of the fire-flags.[24] In the context, these powerful stanzas describe a universal release of energy and movement, as seen by the Mariner, against the background of vast stretches of stagnant calm and 'fixedness' preceding them in the poem. In this cosmic change the moon is still felt as an active force, it is constantly kept before our eyes while the thunderstorm sweeps over the ship and in its commotion the life-giving rain and the lightning seem to fuse, once more miraculously, the elements of water and fire:

> Like waters shot from some high crag,
> The lightning fell with never a jag,
> A river steep and wide.

In the elemental and cosmic synthesis indicated here through the imagery, we may see a further development of the vision of all-embracing harmony which began with the moonlight on the sultry main and on the watersnakes—a 'reconciliation of opposite or discordant qualities'. But at the same time there is implicit in this universal commotion an aspect of tension and conflict dramatising the Mariner's precarious state of mind, his destiny of 'Life-in-Death', and preparing us for the struggle which soon begins between supernatural forces for the Mariner's soul. As the natural panorama evolves its mysterious and miraculous process, these forces are increasingly felt, and above all they are manifested in the roaring wind which never reaches the ship—as the Mariner tells us three times—and yet the ship 'moved on': it, too, is released from its fixedness. The supernatural intervention continues, and next the dead men rise and begin working the ropes. Of all the seemingly 'unmeaning marvels' of this and the following parts of the poem, this resurrection of the dead is the most enigmatic, since, as critics have pointed out, it neither serves a practical purpose, nor represents a real resurrection of the fellow mariners. House's remark that the incident 'dramatises to the Mariner's consciousness the utter ruin of the merry, unified community which had set out on the voyage' leans too heavily on one single aspect of the Mariner's experience, i.e. his incomplete atonement and his persisting sense of guilt under the curse from the dead men's eyes.[25] Clearly, this would work if one might assume that the function of the 'inspired' bodies is merely to haunt the Mariner. But the spirits who enter the dead bodies, we are told in the gloss, are a 'blessed troop of angelic spirits, sent down by the invocation of the guardian saint', and the meaning of the incident is pointed most clearly, it would appear, in the way these spirits finally relieve the ghostlike horror of the mariners' movements and silence:

> For when it dawned—they dropped their arms,
> And clustered round the mast;
> Sweet sounds rose slowly through their mouths,
> And from their bodies passed.

> Around, around, flew each sweet sound,
> Then darted to the Sun;
> Slowly the sounds came back again,
> Now mixed, now one by one.

The significance of the episode in the general movement towards redemption and reconciliation becomes more clearly defined in this development. If the crew's resurrection is only temporary, as the Mariner's redemption is only temporary, it fits the cyclic and repetitive rhythm of guilt and grace which from now on marks the Mariner's spiritual destiny. In another aspect the crew seems to represent a purgatorial trend which has been increasingly felt from Part II, and which is consistent both with the Catholic framework of the poem and with the spiritual experience of the Mariner. What Coleridge has tried to work out in the final parts of the poem by the aid of supernatural events and contending spirits, is more than anything else a vision of purgatorial struggle in which the spiritual as well as physical world is involved. As before, the physical world continues to fuse and interact with the spiritual experience, and the contention between angels and demons for the Mariner's soul (and for his shipmates) is reflected in the voyage itself and in the motion of the ship. If one objects to this view that it is too encumbered with specific dogmatic associations, there is still the supporting psychological context in which the struggle represents the effort of a mind to regain health and balance after an experience bordering on madness. This trend is implicit, but it is clearly not to Coleridge the only one, nor the most important. For the supernatural 'machinery' functions throughout towards a fusion of the outer and inner worlds, of the macrocosm and microcosm, as conceived by the Romantics in their view of the 'One Life' and the creative imagination.

We have seen, in the stanzas just quoted, how the angelic spirits through their 'sweet sounds' relieve the Mariner from the horror instilled by the dead bodies, and how in this incident a more definite vision of resurrection is achieved. J. B. Beer finds in the stanza describing the sounds darting to the Sun the very centre of the poem: the moment when the beatific or angelic vision is granted to the Mariner, when he perceives the essential harmony of the universe and is able to communicate with God.[26] According to Beer, the sun 'in the poem as a whole, is a symbol not of wrath and retribution, but of God and the image of God in human reason—as is normal in Coleridge's writings.'[27] In this common source, the aspects of light and sound are fused in a universal harmony.

The stanza referred to is important, and Beer's reading of it is consistent with the structural imagery of the poem. But Coleridge has not insisted on this vision in his usual manner of emphatic repetition, it stands rather like a passing episode, which in the context serves to introduce a much more comprehensive vision of harmony and joy. And this vision contains features which are closely bound up with, and derived from, the purgatorial experience through which the Mariner has passed, and which carry meanings more readily available both to poet and reader than a mystical conception of the sun as symbol of God. In three stanzas, Coleridge explores the cosmic harmony through impressions of sound, and the arrangement of images suggests a wedding of the One and the Many, of the supernatural and the natural. The song of the angelic spirits re-echoes from the sun and involves nature in various bird-song similes, the angel is associated with the lark, and the controlling though submerged metaphor is the music of the spheres. When the song ceases, the vision ranges to another aspect of the universal harmony, no less significant in the light of the Mariner's experience.

> It ceased; yet still the sails made on
> A pleasant noise till noon,
> A noise like of a hidden brook
> In the leafy month of June,
> That to the sleeping woods all night
> Singeth a quiet tune.

Lowes has noted the 'sylvan loveliness' of this vision, and its psychological import:

> But its beauty that falls like balm on the sailor, in moments of vision home from sea, has gained from its unwonted background a fresh poignancy; and in that heightening of beauty through the implications of a deeply human trait lies one of the most unerring imaginative perceptions of the poem.[28]

Indeed, the pastoral vision in which the Mariner's feeling of peace and harmony culminates is not only an apt psychological projection, or an apt contribution made by the creative imagination to its own experience: the vision also represents a comprehensive imaginative and symbolic synthesis of the areas traversed in the poem—from the land of ice to the courts of the sun. As a catharsis of the human experience which spans these 'discordant opposites', the pastoral vision completes the grand dialectic of the poem, which is the ancient Christian dialectic of sin, expiation and peace. Through the voyage, then, Coleridge has been exploring a possible unity or harmony within the extremes of human nature, its evil and good, indifference and charity, and the quest has taken him over untravelled seas of his imagination and reading, and yet what is discovered in the end is something very ancient and well-known: the peace in which the 'discordant opposites' of existence are resolved.

Between the land of ice (the crime) and the tropical seas (the expiation), the vision of harmony which culminates in the pastoral stanza represents what Browning calls a 'temperate and equidistant world.' Coleridge has worked out, very carefully it seems, the pastoral aspects as a direct development of the changes in the tropical climate which brought relief to the Mariner. The pleasant noise of the sails recalls a 'hidden brook', which sustains the idea of the spring of love that gushed from the Mariner's heart, as well as the lifegiving rain, and the 'sleeping woods' and 'quiet tune' link up the pastoral vision with the Mariner's 'gentle sleep' and his sense of peace after the nightmare watch. While the controlling metaphor is that of musical harmony, developed from the preceding stanzas, the visionary landscape, with its brook, leafy season, and sleeping woods, is charged above all with impressions of a balanced, temperate climate, homely and peaceful, without the cold, or the fiercely burning sun, which 'came' to the Mariner on his strange and terrifying voyage.

Meanwhile the ship moves on, though the breeze never reaches it. The dynamic verb which described the rising moon, the watersnakes, and the Mariner's release from his 'fixedness' is used also repeatedly of the miraculous progress of the ship. We are told, in the poem as well as in the gloss, that the Polar spirit 'carries on the ship as far as the Line, in obedience to the angelic troop, but still requireth vengeance' for the albatross, and thus the ship is once more becalmed. At the same time the Equatorial sun is said to have 'fixed her to the ocean'. This disruption of the newly established harmony presents one of the greatest difficulties of interpretation, mainly because it seems to be quite unrelated to the Mariner's present spiritual state. He has atoned for his violation of life and is reconciled to his fellow beings, yet it is the friend of the albatross who requires vengeance. On the other hand, as we shall hear, the Mariner is not yet freed from the spell of the dead shipmates' curse, though this fact has no bearing on the present situation. What seems to happen is that the voyage, which has already taken on a boldly supernatural and symbolic character, is used increasingly to actualise a spiritual and universal struggle, involving cycles of guilt and grace. The gloss gives us to understand that it is a conflict between the angelic troop and the demons of the South Pole, and the contention is vividly dramatised in the stanza:

> The Sun, right up above the mast,
> Had fixed her to the ocean:
> But in a minute she 'gan stir,
> With a short uneasy motion—
> Backwards and forwards half her length
> With a short uneasy motion.

It reaches a climax in the following stanza, where the ship makes a 'sudden bound'. The miraculous phase of the voyage culminates in the following stanzas, where the ship moves on so fast that the Mariner faints and while unconscious learns from the spirits that he will have to do more penance. This phase is a dream journey, and thus provides a convenient magic for speeding the ship homewards: 'The air is cut away before, / And closes from behind.' While the notion of miraculous speed is sustained in repetition and verbal emphasis, it is seen against the contrasting background of the ocean calm:

> 'Still as a slave before his lord,
> The ocean hath no blast;
> His great bright eye most silently
> Up to the Moon is cast—
>
> If he may know which way to go;
> For she guides him smooth or grim.
> See, brother, see! how graciously
> She looketh down on him.'

Thus the great appearances of nature are also kept before our eyes in the dialogue of the spirits. J. B. Beer has shown that these lines (the first stanza) derive their images from the description of the 'dance', or harmony of nature, in Davies's *Orchestra*.[29] And it would seem that the part played by these stanzas is that of retaining a vision of the enduring and essential harmony of the universe. As in the later harbour description, which develops certain traits of the imagery in these stanzas, there is insistence on calm and brightness, and on the subordination of sublunar things to celestial power. The moon, which began the redemption of the Mariner, remains the centre of order and beauty, and after its power and presence has been felt once more, the Mariner wakes to find that he is sailing in gentle weather, in calm and moonlight. Yet all is not well: the curse in the dead men's eyes is still upon him, and under the burden of guilt the Mariner again experiences a moment of despair and 'fixedness':

> I could not draw my eyes from theirs,
> Nor turn them up to pray.

Then, without any manifest act of contrition, the spell of the curse is 'snapt'—once more, one feels, through the intervention of heavenly grace. This time, however, there is no immediate sense of relief, but instead a feeling of 'fear' and 'dread'. At this point the travel metaphor is used to visualise the Mariner's guilt-haunted state and to anticipate the nature of his 'penance' in the future: He looks far forth over the ocean—turning away from the obsessive, immediate scene:

> Like one, that on a lonesome road
> Doth walk in fear and dread,
> And having once turned round walks on,
> And turns no more his head;
> Because he knows, a frightful fiend,
> Doth close behind him tread.

This pursuit echoes that in the early episode of the ship fleeing before the storm (lines 45-50) which now, in the total context of the poem, may be claimed to portend the sinister experiences of the voyage.

When relief comes to the Mariner, in this new cycle of grace, it is, significantly, again associated with refreshing wind:

> It raised my hair, it fanned my cheek
> Like a meadow-gale of spring—
> It mingled strangely with my fears,
> Yet it felt like a welcoming.

Significantly, too, there emerges once more the pastoral vision—in the 'meadow-gale of spring', with its implications of a rebirth of life in a 'temperate and equidistant world'. But this time it also serves to announce the Mariner's arrival in his own 'countree'.

The description of the harbour draws on the charged imagery of Parts IV and V, with prevailing impressions of calm and brightness, beauty and repose. It is an apt destination after the purgatorial voyage in tropical seas—a perfectly ordered world in which to the Mariner's bewildered senses, the details stand out in crystal clarity, solid and peaceful and lovely.[30] Livingston Lowes has observed that the 'impelling agency' of the poem from the shooting of the albatross to the end of Part IV is *dæmonic*, while from then on it is *angelic*. The shift 'from dæmonic to angelic,' Lowes comments, is 'an integral element in Coleridge's constructive design.'[31] It contributes, one may add, to the balanced, dialectic movement of the spiritual experience, and it is fitting, therefore, that the angelic spirits should 'leave the dead bodies, and appear in their own forms of light', as the ship arrives in the harbour. Apart from the practical and symbolic function they perform, standing 'as signals to the land' and the pilot, they represent, it would appear, a final reconciliation between the dæmonic and angelic forces—these 'discordant opposites' which play such an essential part in the Mariner's spiritual drama. The vision of this 'seraph-band' is a 'heavenly sight' to the Mariner, and sinks 'like music' on his heart. As in the first phase of redemption, impressions of light and music fuse through the structural imagery to suggest a state of harmony and reconciliation. But there appears to be another kind of fusion too. The shadows made by the seraph men on the moonlit bay are 'crimson', and this observation is emphatic. The crimson colour recalls both the 'still and awful red' burning within the shadow of the ship earlier on, and, more remotely, it harks back to the crime. In this new context, however, it also involves the sacramental symbolism of the redeeming blood of Christ. In the pervasive colour and light-symbolism of the poem, this final vision telescopes the initial crime, the purgatorial experience, and the redemption in Christ in yet another pattern of synthesis and reconciliation. At one extreme of the experience, the albatross is hung around the Mariner's neck, 'instead of the cross', at the other is the Mariner's desire to shrive his soul to the Hermit who will 'wash away / The Albatross's blood.' As another aspect of the final reconciliation suggested in the episode of the seraph-men, there is also a more definite hint that the shipmates' curse has vanished and that to them, too, peace is accorded. Through the light of the moon and the seraph-men, the charnel scene of the deck is transformed into beauty, and in the context of the vision, associating the angelic spirits with the 'lifeless and flat' bodies of the shipmates, there is also, it seems, a clearer hint at

202        STRANGERS AND PILGRIMS

spiritual resurrection.[32] To complete this comprehensive movement to harmony and order and rebirth, the ship and its victims
sink like lead—and like the albatross—into the sea. The echo
from the sinking of the albatross suggests that we have here a
further stage in the process of atonement, and yet another is
reached when the Mariner confesses to the Hermit and is,
temporarily, left 'free'. His voyage is over, yet he will always
know Death-in-Life, and from now on he is the wandering ambassador of guilt and grace:

> Since then, at an uncertain hour,
> That agony returns:
> And till my ghastly tale is told,
> This heart within me burns.
>
> I pass, like night, from land to land;
> I have strange power of speech;
> That moment that his face I see,
> I know the man that must hear me:
> To him my tale I teach.

These stanzas, and indeed the long passages showing the Mariner
obsessed by the dead men's curse, make it quite clear that he is
the guilt-haunted wanderer, related to the Cain of Coleridge's
prose fragment and to the ancient legend of the Wandering
Jew.[33] He is not, as has been suggested, a 'stranger and pilgrim
of the earth' because he has had the beatific vision, but because
the horrible consequences of his indifference to life demand remorse and penance to the end of his days.[34] It is here that the
universal significance of his experience lies: he is the prototype
of fallen man.

The trait of emotional catharsis which is so pervasive towards
the end of the poem, is expressed in the stanzas just quoted in
such a way that the Mariner's confession and relief are related to
the poet's catharsis achieved in the creative act: he 'tells' and
'teaches' his 'tale'. Hence to Warren the Mariner is the *poète
maudit*, and this may be accepted provided the curse is regarded
in terms of the human experience which the poem explores, and
not as an allegory of the poetic imagination.

Our reading of the poem has clearly not yielded any such
spectacular results in symbolic interpretation as that, for instance, of Robert Penn Warren, and neither has it been possible

to exploit his discoveries and combine them with the recent scholarship of J. B. Beer. This will be disappointing to many who might reasonably expect that any further penetration into the poem's mysteries will follow the charts of such eminent scholars and critics. What has determined our more traditional approach is a strong feeling that, despite the many valuable and illuminating observations made by these and others, like Lowes, such aspects as the 'theme of the imagination', and the sources of reading in travelogues and the mystics, are working at a much greater distance in the background of the poem than these critics would be prepared to admit. We are not made aware at any point in the poem of a crime against the creative imagination, or of an effort to construct a symbolic myth on the phases of the Isis-Osiris cult. No doubt such ancient symbols, as well as the more recent sun-symbolism of the mystics, may have gravitated to the central design of the poem, along with the myriad 'sleeping images' traced by Lowes. And it is possible that the ancient myths helped Coleridge to develop the dialectic of good and evil, guilt and charity, which forms the very nerve of the poem. But the poem as it stands does not assert these ancient Egyptian or neoplatonic myths as the main vehicle of his 'reconciliation' of the human antinomies. Instead, what we have is a Christian basis of faith, and a voyage in which seascape and the elements are emphatically active in the poetic and mythmaking process, and combined with a 'supernatural agency' which, whatever its sources, is wholly determined by the human experience and the dialectic design of the poem. We have tried, therefore, to assert that the main and essential interest in *The Ancient Mariner* remains what it always has been: its tight and palpable fabric of sensory exploration through which the spiritual meanings are coordinated and gradually revealed. The safest approach to the poem, we believe, lies on the one hand through the structural imagery, on the other through the range of human experience as reflected in the events and discoveries of the voyage. It follows that an analysis of this experience must to a large extent accept it and view it more or less as if it had been real, i.e. assume a psychological basis for it which enables us to evaluate its truth and significance in terms of a common human norm, despite the Catholic, medieval framework and the supernatural phenomena. This was precisely the goal Coleridge tried to achieve, as he tells us in *Biographia Literaria*:

my endeavours should be directed to persons and characters supernatural, or at least romantic; yet so as to transfer from our inward nature a human interest and a semblance of truth sufficient to procure for these shadows of imagination that willing suspension of disbelief for the moment, which constitutes poetic faith.

In poems like *The Ancient Mariner* the transfer 'from our inward nature' is very powerful and persuasive indeed, and as generations of readers have testified, it does lend to the situations of the poem, natural and supernatural, that 'dramatic truth' of emotion which, as Coleridge tells us on the same occasion, was part of the 'excellence aimed at' in his contributions to the *Lyrical Ballads*.

In this transfer from inner to outer nature the metaphorical medium of the voyage served Coleridge well, but the voyage involves, of course, the reverse process also, so that, in the mutual illumination and interaction of the two worlds, their boundaries vanish, and the exploration ranges far and wide over a realm of dream and fantasy and faith. Here the real action takes place, but the appearances of nature continue to lend their palpable concreteness to the scenes and situations.

We have tried to indicate that the voyage of the Ancient Mariner ranges between two opposite poles or extremes, which are defined geographically in the poetic structure, and, further, that the goal of this quest is a reconciliation between these 'discordant opposites'. We are aware of the danger of a too literal interpretation of the appearances of nature in this connection, and of the equal danger (against which House has warned) of reading into the poem an application of ideas Coleridge stated much later, in *Biographia Literaria*. Nevertheless the dialectic structure is there, in a fairly obvious and coherent form. Furthermore, it is legitimate to conclude from Coleridge's poetry and speculation about the time when he wrote *The Ancient Mariner*, that he was already greatly preoccupied with the problem of how 'extremes meet'. It is not only in *Kubla Khan* that Coleridge contemplates the 'miracle of rare device' which is the synthesis of the creative imagination. His poetic and metaphysical quest, then as later, was for order and harmonious unity in a world wrecked or threatened by disruption. Thus in *Religious Musings* and in *The Destiny of Nations* he explores through a medium of meditation the chaos unchained by evil, and searches for a harmony beyond, in a millennial future. These poems are the quarries and the preparatory essays providing some of the material for *The Ancient Mariner* and *Christabel*, and, as scholars have shown, these brought to fruition reading and speculation which Coleridge had planned to put into the much more ambitious works—the epic on the Origin of Evil, and the Hymns to Sun, Moon and Elements.

*Religious Musings* in particular dramatises the antinomies of good and evil, order and chaos, and seeks to comprehend and resolve them in a synthesis on the apologetic assumption common in the eighteenth century, that evil is the instrument of good (l. 195). The idea of anarchy resulting from the loss of God (the presence of God) is there connected with the vision of man as a lonely wanderer—a 'sordid solitary thing' (l. 149). Deformity in things is also seen as a consequence of the absence of the light of God (lines 32-33, 55, 98), and love as the power that restores all things to their true beauty and harmony. The being who feeds his soul with love transcends the curse of Cain and of earthly chaos and approaches the closest to God—source of love:

> From himself he flies,
> Stands in the sun, and with no partial gaze
> Views all creation; and he loves it all,
> And blesses it, and calls it very good!
> This is indeed to dwell with the Most High!
>
> (lines 110-114)

An oft-quoted but even more relevant passage is found in *The Destiny of Nations*:

> ... Love rose glittering, and his gorgeous wings
> Over the abyss fluttered with such glad noise,
> As what time after long and pestful calms,
> With slimy shapes and miscreated life
> Poisoning the vast Pacific, the fresh breeze
> Wakens the merchant-sail uprising.
>
> (lines 283-88)

The 'slimy shapes and miscreated life' of the 'pestful calms' of the Pacific anticipate the watersnakes as they appear to the Mariner's corrupted imagination, and the vision of redeeming Love and

the life-giving breeze also clearly point forward to the poem of
the following year.

Before we look at other relevant matter in these longer meditative poems, we may consider briefly the extracts (from *Osorio*
and *Remorse*) published as one poem under the title *The Dungeon*
in *Lyrical Ballads*. It deals with the problem of evil and human
corruption, and salvation, in terms that announce *The Ancient
Mariner*. First in the description of the prisoner's condition:

> Each pore and natural outlet shrivell'd up
> By ignorance and parching poverty,
> His energies roll back upon his heart,
> And stagnate and corrupt . . .

The imagery as well as ideas are those which Coleridge later
used to describe the Mariner's 'fixedness', and, as we read on,
we find also the process of corruption in the prisoner's (and
Mariner's) mind which alienates him from living beings—the
'slimy things' of the rotting deep:

> So he lies
> Circled with evil, till his very soul
> Unmoulds its essence, hopelessly deform'd
> By sights of ever more deformity!

This is man's cure for evil in man. Not so the cure of Nature:

> With other ministrations thou, O Nature!
> Healest thy wandering and distemper'd child:
> Thou pourest on him thy soft influences,
> Thy sunny hues, fair forms, and breathing sweets,
> Thy melodies of woods, and winds, and waters,
> Till he relent, and can no more endure
> To be a jarring and a dissonant thing,
> Amid this general dance and minstrelsy;
> But, bursting into tears, wins back his way,
> His angry spirit heal'd and harmoniz'd
> By the benignant touch of Love and Beauty.

It is significant that here too the harmony of nature and the
elements is rendered in a pastoral vision reminiscent of that in
*The Ancient Mariner*, with the same reconciliatory effects. In
*Religious Musings* the pastoral vision occurs twice: first in con-

nection with the restoration of order after the ravages of war—
order as an aim of Philosophers and Bards and all who hate
confusion. After the war-storm and 'wavy chaos' these are seen
on a summer noon, as

> Beneath some arched romantic rock reclined
> They felt the sea-breeze lift their youthful locks;
> Or in the month of blossoms, at mild eve,
> Wandering with desultory feet inhaled
> The wafted perfumes, and the flocks and woods
> And many-tinted streams and setting sun
> With all his gorgeous company of clouds
> Ecstatic gazed!
>
> (lines 250-57)

The second of these visions is more directly related to the experience of the Ancient Mariner after his first phase of redemption, and it appears in connection with the apostrophe to 'pure
Faith' to return to earth after the evil and chaos wrought by
'mitred Atheism'. With the return of Faith other blessings will
follow:

> Such delights
> As float to earth, permitted visitants!
> When in some hour of solemn jubilee
> The massy gates of Paradise are thrown
> Wide open, and forth come in fragments wild
> Sweet echoes of unearthly melodies,
> And odours snatched from beds of Amaranth,
> And they, that from the crystal river of life
> Spring up on freshened wing, ambrosial gales!
> The favoured good man in his lonely walk
> Perceives them, and his silent spirit drinks
> Strange bliss which he shall recognise in heaven.
>
> (lines 343-354)

In these visions of restored order, Coleridge dwells on refreshing
breezes, rivers and waters, woods and melodies blending in an
elemental harmony, and these aspects, as we have seen, recur
also in the cathartic experience of the Ancient Mariner. Whether
we have here the influence of Wordsworth at Alfoxden, or of the
Romantic view of prelapsarian Nature, or the remnants of the
neo-classical ideal of happy retirement, or a confluence of these

impulses, they recur with important emphasis throughout this period in Coleridge's quest for harmony and the good life.[35] Thus in the *Ode to Tranquillity* the pastoral vision also includes the 'calm' of the moon:

> But me thy gentle hand will lead
> At morning through the accustomed mead;
> And in the sultry summer's heat
> Will build me up a mossy seat;
> And when the gust of Autumn crowds,
> And breaks the busy moonlight clouds,
> Thou best the thought canst raise, the heart attune,
> Light as the busy clouds, calm as the gliding moon.

That Coleridge's 'searching soul' should find these pastoral scenes after wanderings through evil and disorder, find them so often and with such ecstatic delight, shows that they were not merely poetic clichés or conventions, and not merely ideas derived from Wordsworth. As recurrent solutions to the dialectic of human existence they point to a 'temperate and equidistant world', including and reconciling the extremes of human nature—good and evil—in the grace and *agapē* which ultimately save the Ancient Mariner.

# III

# BYRON'S PILGRIMAGE

Byron's two longest and most important works, *Childe Harold's Pilgrimage* and *Don Juan* exploit the travel structure both as an epic framework and as a means of imaginative configuration. No one would dispute the general superiority of the later poem, but nevertheless we have chosen to deal with *Childe Harold's Pilgrimage*, because here the journey as a metaphorical structure is more important than in *Don Juan;* the journey is, in fact, the poet's chief medium, while in *Don Juan* it is a fictitious scheme casually and intermittently used. There is also a fundamental difference in Byron's attitude to the journey in the two poems. In *Don Juan* the journey functions mainly in terms of picaresque adventure and satirical observation, in *Childe Harold's Pilgrimage* it represents a real exploration, inward and outward. In the first two cantos, it is true, this quest is at times a mock-serious affair, often staged to dramatise the whims and poses of the fictitious hero. In the two final cantos, however, the 'self-exiled' Byron travels for a variety of personal reasons, but most of all to escape himself and his own past and to find a novel order—be it deserts, caves or oceans—to replace the community which had cast him out. Ostensibly, Byron moves along

> as a weed
> Flung from the rock, on Ocean's foam to sail
> Where'er the surge may sweep . . .

without goal and without hope. But behind this deliberate indifference there is a desire for sheer enjoyment, and there is the paradox of his conscious and unconscious destinations; the first to 'lose my own wretched identity', the second to discover his real self at the centre of that great mystery—his implacable fate.

Furthermore, there is the instinctive search for a regeneration of his emotional and artistic vitality, and in the poem itself, in the final two cantos, we have the proof of the soundness of this instinct.

Our concern in this chapter will be mainly with the final two cantos, because it is here that the personal significance of Byron's journey is most profoundly revealed. It is here too that he achieves the finest writing in the poem. If our reading is right, it will be seen that, contrary to expectation, there is more genuine delight derived from the discoveries in the final cantos than the first ones. It will be seen also that too much has been made of the 'pageant of his bleeding heart' and that, along with much notorious egocentric misery, there is much spontaneous pleasure and restless curiosity.

There are, broadly speaking, two levels on which Byron's journey takes place. The first is the level of destructive satire, involving the long meditations on historical or national *vanitas* and the moments of personal revenge on society. On this level Byron often sees his fate reflected in history, and his own ruin manifested in the ruins along the road. One might call this the level of simple allegory, in which Byron's exilic impulses are most clearly dramatised and the escape from himself and society is enacted in objective or universal terms. On the second level the poet achieves a 'being more intense' in his sympathetic response to people and places realised in imaginative configuration, and this is where his positive discoveries of value are made. The 'pilgrim' does not find, ultimately, God or truth or peace, or—least of all—human companionship, but he does find beauty and freedom and heroic life, and the enduring splendour of art and nature. And he finds, almost to his surprise, that his heart is still capable of joy. Thus the general pattern is fairly typical of the modern restless agnostic, and though Byron could hardly be called a modern Everyman, the religious quality of his mind is revealed in a common dilemma, and his cultic substitutes are fairly common too.

The chief organising principle of the poem is Byron's un-disciplined sensibility, and unity of tone and intention is the last thing we should expect from him. At the root of most of the ambiguities in the final two cantos there is the war between self-disgust and self-rejection, and an overriding pride seeking to vindicate and even exalt the humiliated self. These impulses operate at various levels of consciousness, yet they emerge with violent energy whenever Byron rebels against the pervasive wrongness of the order of things, or when he seeks to discover the laws of Fate and accept them. He had, as du Bos aptly says, 'un besoin de la fatalité'[1]. Byron's meditation on historical vanity, on abuse of power, on ruin and degeneration draws its passionate force from the fact that most *exempla*, whether individuals, places, or nations, are various modes of dramatising his own situation. Thus he explores the working of Fate in the fallen great of history, relating their downfall more or less directly to his own, and seeking the law under which his own fate must be accepted. Not indeed as a principle for action, as the eighteenth-century sage might have sought it, but rather as an excuse and an explanation of his ungovernable character. Demon and Nemesis were the pilots with whom he travelled across Europe, and thus he invested the journey with tragic and superhuman grandeur, an epic that would dwarf and defeat those who had humiliated him.

Mario Praz has observed that the violent rhythm in Byron's temperament is due, in part, to the contradictory urges to rebel and to submit, to torture and suffer.[2] These impulses are certainly active in *Childe Harold's Pilgrimage*, and they determine much of the tone and direction of this unique travelogue. They are fatal to its unity, but in compensation they lend to it a dramatic quality which, combined with Byron's powerful grasp of the actual, are at the heart of its enduring vitality and interest.

The fictitious character of Childe Harold, as Byron himself felt almost from the beginning, was an intrusion in the poem and might have proved disastrous had Byron not so consistently, at least at the crucial moments, neglected its existence. Nevertheless, though this was an unwise point of departure, it is interesting to notice Byron's conception of his hero in the early stages of writing, and the articulate moral purpose which, apparently, fathers the Childe:

> he never was intended as an example, further than to show that early perversion of mind and morals leads to satiety of past pleasures and disappointment in new ones, and that even the beauties of nature and the stimulus of travel (except ambition, the most powerful of all excitements) are lost on a soul so constituted, or rather misdirected. Had I proceeded

with the poem, this character would have deepened as he drew to the close; for the outline which I once meant to fill up for him was, with some exceptions, the sketch of a modern Timon, perhaps a poetical Zeluco.[3]

This was written in 1813, and the character of Childe Harold, as he developed, shows a complete independence of this plan and yet in a strange way fulfils the prophecy which Byron expresses conditionally at the time—'Had I proceeded with the poem'. For the character of Childe Harold in the final two cantos, submerged and increasingly identical with himself, does *deepen*. And though the poet is anxious in the more personal discursive passages to counteract the charge of misanthropy which he usually invites, in his more unguarded meditations on man and on history he becomes indeed rather like a modern Timon, as in the celebrated stanzas on the ocean which close Canto IV. But contrary to the early conception, and with important consequences for the tone and treatment, the Childe, and the poet, do not show that 'the beauties of nature and the stimulus of travel ... are lost on a soul so constituted'. On the contrary, these become increasingly important as the human and social values are rejected or denied him in exile, and they are seized on with real delight, and not mainly as places to hide or forces to let loose in revenge on mankind.

## Grand Tour

There is scarcely any need to rehearse the negative verdicts on the first two cantos of the poem, justly denouncing the immature thought, the affectations of mood and attitude, the egocentric absurdities, the crudities of style. These are serious charges, but worse still is the discrepancy between Byron's conception of his fictitious hero and the actual experience of travel, or rather, between his poetic pose and the emotions stirred by his discoveries or by his memories of them. This dichotomy mars or falsifies the two first cantos in parts, and it makes any unity of tone impossible. And yet for all these weaknesses there are long stretches where Byron, oblivious of himself and of Harold, allows his hungry sensibility and his wonderfully agile mind free play, and here the work comes alive despite shallowness of thought and crudity of form.

Omitting the details of itinerary, we shall limit our attention to some of those aspects of the first cantos which embody valuable and enduring interest.

From the way he presents his hero and mouthpiece, Byron's intention would appear to be chiefly satirical. The character of the young Childe, 'Disporting ... like any other fly' in the sun and sin of his depraved environment, is not well conceived for serious treatment, and when we are told that

> Worse than adversity the Childe befell;
> He felt the fulness of satiety ...

and that 'With pleasure drugg'd, he almost long'd for woe', we seem to hear the unmistakable tone of the mock-epic and prepare ourselves for an ironical meaning and treatment of the 'pilgrimage'. For the Childe has no other goal for his 'weary pilgrimage' than to 'flee' his bacchanals and pleasures and 'visit scorching climes beyond the sea', deserts and caves.

However, this pose in the young hero soon dissolves as the ship approaches Portugal:

> Oh, Christ! it is a goodly sight to see
> What Heaven hath done for this delicious land ...

And, more unexpected still, the Childe contemplates the country with a vivid moral awareness:

> What fruits of fragrance blush on every tree!
> What goodly prospects o'er the hills expand!
> But man would mar them with an impious hand:
> (xv)

Yet the contrast set up is not so much that between the goodness of nature and the depravity of man, it is rather the recurrent Byronic confrontation between the natural and historical nobility of a country and its present national humiliation. If the explorer is enthusiastic about the beauties of the country and of the city of Lisbon, he is equally passionate in his scorn of the nation—'Poor, paltry slaves! yet born 'midst noblest scenes—'. (xviii)

Thus, from the beginning, the tone and manner are moralistic, even before we are told that it was the sight of Cintra and the memory of its 'martial synod' which taught the Childe to 'moralize' (xxvii). Meanwhile, before meditation fixes on him he enjoys the landscape:

> The horrid crags, by toppling convent crown'd,
> The cork-trees hoar that clothe the shaggy steep,
> The mountain-moss by scorching skies imbrown'd,
> The sunken glen, whose sunless shrubs must weep,
> The tender azure of the unruffled deep,
> The orange tints that gild the greenest bough,
> The torrents that from cliff to valley leap,
> The vine on high, the willow branch below,
> Mix'd in one mighty scene, with varied beauty glow.
>
> (xix)

Though the separate details are vividly seen and recorded, they do not quite blend into 'one mighty scene' in the stanza, for the catalogue manner is too rigid, and involves too much of the monotony of nominal enumeration. Yet for all that the description of the 'toppling convent' and the 'shaggy steep' announces Byron's characteristic verbal energy, and the stanza may serve as an example of one kind of experience that makes the Childe's pilgrimage worth while, though his feelings about it —since they are those of Byron—do not fit his character. There is no need to stress further this dichotomy between poet and protagonist, for the thing to remember is that whenever something really important happens on the journey, it is the poet in person who records it.

Some of the persistent interests and motifs which Byron sustains through the poem make their appearance in these early stanzas. Thus in his meditation on the 'Paradise' once built by Vathek, now ruined and overgrown with giant weeds, he is reminded of the vanity of human wishes:

> Vain are the plaisaunces on earth supplied;
> Swept into wrecks anon by Time's ungentle tide!
>
> (xxiii)

And the whole country—here Spain—reminds him of the vanity of the hero's fate, for how are the mighty fallen:

> See how the Mighty shrink into a song!
> Can Volume, Pillar, Pile preserve thee great?
>
> (xxxvi)

It reminds him also of past splendour and greatness, now irretrievably lost:

> Oh, lovely Spain! renown'd, romantic land!
> Where is that standard which Pelagio bore ...?
>
> (xxxv)

Cava, Talavera rise up in his memory and unfold their grand and gruesome pageant, banners flying, blood streaming, arms glittering in the air:

> By Heaven! it is a splendid sight to see
> (For one who hath no friend, no brother there)
>
> (xl)

Yet even to the traveller contemplating the battlefield with such detachment, Albuera is a 'glorious field of grief'. (xliii)[4] With the same conflicting feelings we find Byron later on the battlefield of Quatre Bras, torn between delight in the heroism and spectacular pageantry of warfare, and compassion for those who died. Albuera—as later Quatre Bras—reminds him above all of the inevitability of Fate, and of man's ignorance and helplessness in the face of doom. So too does Sevilla, which, at the time of his visit, still 'triumphs unsubdued', yet:

> Soon, soon shall Conquest's fiery foot intrude,
> Blackening her lovely domes with traces rude.
> Inevitable hour! 'Gainst fate to strive
> Where Desolation plants her famish'd brood
> Is vain, or Ilion, Tyre, might yet survive,
> And Virtue vanquish all, and murder cease to thrive.
>
> (xlv)

This is the lesson of historical *vanitas* to which Byron will return so often in his poem. As yet the treatment of it is slack and shallow, without the passionate involvement of the later cantos, when history had become a mirror of his own fate.

Though Byron, as we have seen (xxxvi), has no illusions about the enduring splendour of chivalry and fame, and no faith in historical constancy, he is ever ready to cry out his exhortations whenever liberty is at stake:

> Awake, ye sons of Spain! awake! advance!
>
> (xxxvii)

On the cause of Spanish freedom, as later on that of Greece, his attitude is unambiguous, and already his characteristic note of patriotic challenge is struck.

There is then, from the outset, ample evidence of the enthusiasm as well as the indignation of the young explorer. Byron's manner of exploration is also manifest from the beginning: the landscape may be 'delicious' or it may have picturesque magnificence, but mainly it is a two-dimensional scene—a double vision—in which the historical situation predominates. It is easy to see why this should be so, for history is a more compliant medium than landscape for the kind of discovery that Byron wants to make, about the fate of men and of nations. Though he lingers on scenes of bloodshed and violence, he reacts to his discoveries, not as a cynic reacts but as a young man with healthy instincts and a frank sense of values, of beauty, chivalry and freedom.

Byron's interests and impulses in these early stanzas are relatively simple and few, and so are the underlying attitudes. Nevertheless the experience conveyed seems rich and varied, mostly because of his keen eye and his sense of historical drama. It is also partly due to his desultory and capricious manner, and the sudden shifts of attention. But if one accepts the movements of this turbulent guide, without demanding too much unity of tone, logic or geography, then he is delightful: As when, in the middle of a passionate eulogy of the maids of Spain, so 'wildly beautiful', so beautiful that even a cynic must applaud, he breaks off to address Parnassus—'soaring snow-clad through thy native sky'—as he saw it later on his journey in Greece. Then, with a nonchalance characteristic of the whole poem, and even more so of the later *Don Juan*, Byron returns from his digression:

Of thee hereafter.—Ev'n amidst my strain
I turn'd aside to pay my homage here;
Forgot the land, the sons, the maids of Spain;
Her fate, to every freeborn bosom dear;

(lxiii)

But as he finally leaves Spain behind, he expresses his passionate concern for the freedom of this country, and for its future, where, he fears, great sacrifices will be demanded before 'Freedom's stranger-tree grow native of the soil!'

The second phase of his grand tour, Byron announces at the end of Canto I, took him through

Lands that contain the monuments of Eld,
Ere Greece and Grecian arts by barbarous hands were
quell'd.

The greater part of Canto II, however, is devoted to Albania and its people and customs, and contains some of the most vivid descriptions in the entire poem. Only the beginning and conclusion of the canto are about Greece, in the form of rambling meditations on the tragic contrast between past glory and present degradation. Byron's lament on the decline of Greece maintains some of the attitudes and ideas expressed in his meditations on Spanish history, only here, since his attachment to Greece is so much greater, his words glow with a new fervour:

Ancient of days! august Athena! where,
Where are thy men of might? thy grand in soul?
Gone—glimmering through the dream
      of things that were:
First in the race that led to Glory's goal,
They won, and pass'd away—is this the whole?

(ii)

Mouldering towers, broken pillars, a nation's sepulchre, ruined buildings, and skulls on which the poet, like Hamlet, may cogitate:

Look on this broken arch, its ruin'd wall,
Its chambers desolate, and portals foul:
Yes, this was once Ambition's airy hall,
The dome of Thought, the palace of the Soul:

> Behold through each lack-lustre, eyeless hole,
> The gay recess of Wisdom and of Wit,
> And Passion's host, that never brook'd control:
> Can all saint, sage, or sophist ever writ,
> People this lonely tower, this tenement refit?
>
> (vi)

The metaphorical transfer is not very original or subtle, but it is carefully worked out and effective, establishing a complex relationship between the builders of ancient Greece and their buildings. To this favour they must come in our world of vanity and transience. All around are the vestiges of grandeur and everywhere the ravages of Chance Time and Fate. The scene is indeed favourable to morbid meditation, as the Roman Campagna was to Chateaubriand, and Byron sits down to contemplate 'what Time hath labour'd to deface'—the Acropolis. But again his sense of the actual, and his gift of indignation, serve him well in a sudden bitter attack on Lord Elgin, 'The last, the worst, dull spoiler', who had recently removed the friezes from the temple of Pallas Athene. This episode provokes some stanzas of violent eloquence, and then there is another sudden shift of attention as Byron reverts to his fictitious hero and picks up the epic thread of the journey—at the point where Harold left Spain. There follow some exuberant stanzas recording the Mediterranean crossing in a frigate, and the explorer's fascination at the power and efficiency of the 'little warlike world within' the ship, the fun of sailing, and the magic of the 'glorious main' spreading far in the moonlight. For a brief moment 'Meditation' reminds the young man that he once loved and now is friendless, yet the sailing in moonlight offers something better than a philosophical consolation:

> Thus bending o'er the vessel's laving side,
> To gaze on Dian's wave-reflected sphere,
> The soul forgets her schemes of hope and pride,
> And flies unconscious o'er each backward year.
>
> (xxiv)

In Nature—whether on the ocean or in the 'trackless mountains' —there is companionship, and generous communication. It is the crowd that makes one lonely, Byron argues in two stanzas (xxv, xxvi) which in thought and phrasing are strongly reminis-

cent of Wordsworth in *The Prelude*. This confrontation of crowd
and solitude sends Byron on another rambling digression into
the *ennui* and world-weariness of his young hero, through a
number of slack and indifferent stanzas. The carelessness of
composition which we encountered in Canto I, notably in the
anachronistic address to Parnassus, plays havoc with the unity
of this canto too. But in one sense it allows the emergence of something like a natural rhythm in the narrative, with changes between a relaxation and tightening of interest which fit the structure of the journey. They provide, so to speak, the necessary
halts before the course may be pursued:

> Away! nor let me loiter in my song,
> For we have many a mountain-path to tread ...
>
> (xxxvi)

And the traveller is now headed for Albania. He lingers for one
moment more, however, to exalt Nature for her salubrious influence on 'that corrupted thing'—man:

> Dear Nature is the kindest mother still,
> Though always changing in her aspect mild;
> From her bare bosom let me take my fill,
> Her never-wean'd, though not her favour'd child.
> Oh! she is fairest in her features wild,
> Where nothing polish'd dares pollute her path:
> To me by day or night she ever smiled,
> Though I have mark'd her when none other hath,
> And sought her more and more, and loved her best in wrath.
>
> (xxxvii)

The stanza may seem an unfair example of Byron's attitude to
nature, yet with its undistinguished and conventional diction
and shallow feeling it tells us what is, in fact, the truth: that he
loves nature best when he hates man the most. In the two final
cantos there will be ample evidence of this emotional process,
and as a background and foil to the greater achievement in the
mature Byron the stanza quoted is not without interest.

As Byron returns to his memories of the actual travel, his
grasp on scene and situation tightens once more, and the poetic
intensity grows in his evocation of the people and places of
Albania—'rugged nurse of savage men'. Approaching the coast,

he pays due tribute to the 'barren spot, / Where sad Penelope
o'erlook'd the wave', and, on the other side of the strait, the
rock on Leucas from which Sappho leaped to death. Other great
tragic places, he tells us with convenient disingenuity, he—i.e.
Childe Harold—would 'mark unmoved'—like Actium, Le-
panto, and 'fatal Trafalgar' (and, we may add, Waterloo,
Albuera and Marathon)—'for he would not delight / In themes
of bloody fray, or gallant fight'.

> But when he saw the evening star above
> Leucadia's far-projecting rock of woe,
> And hail'd the last resort of fruitless love,
> He felt, or deem'd he felt, no common glow:
>
> (xli)

He has a glimpse of 'Dark Suli's rocks' and of Pindus, land of
convulsive storms and of the 'wilder men' whose courage he later
came to admire so highly. The pilgrim penetrates into the land
alone, and makes, in passing, comments on the vanity of religious
superstition and fanaticism, and on the fatal Actium, the place
where 'was lost, / A world for woman'. In contrast to these
human follies, the land itself is magnificent, with sublime mountains and lovely dales matching even those of Tempe and Attica.
And he who had addressed Parnassus from Spain with such cultic
veneration now boldly devaluates that 'hallow'd' mountain
under the impressions of this splendid scenery. In language not
unlike that of Wordsworth he describes the country in which is
set 'Monastic Zitza', remembering its 'rainbow tints' and 'magic
charms' and 'bluest skies that harmonise the whole'. There are
torrents and cataracts and groves and tufted hills, and fresh green
and gentle breezes beneath aged trees, and there is even the
Wordsworthian loitering indolence and rest (xlviii-l). Byron has
not quite found his own manner in these stanzas, and the pastoral
and idyllic aspects of the landscape are conveyed through awk-
ward clichés. But then suddenly the land and its ancient legendary heritage blend in a fresh and vivid perspective:

> Dusky and huge, enlarging on the sight,
> Nature's volcanic amphitheatre,
> Chimæra's alps extend from left to right:
> Beneath, a living valley seems to stir;

Flocks play, trees wave, streams flow, the mountain-fir
Nodding above; behold black Acheron!
Once consecrated to the sepulchre.
Pluto! if this be hell I look upon,
Close shamed Elysium's gates, my shade shall seek for none.

(li)

With its metaphorical double vision, its powerful concentration
of detail, and verbal drive, this stanza points forward to Byron's
technique in the later cantos. From now on the poet is immersed
in the magic of exotic names and places, which provide a splendid
and congenial challenge:

The sun had sunk behind vast Tomerit,
And Laos wide and fierce came roaring by;
The shades of wonted night were gathering yet,
When, down the steep banks winding warily,
Childe Harold saw, like meteors in the sky,
The glittering minarets of Tepalen . . .

(lv)

In fact the best stanzas in Canto II are those devoted to the
oriental quaintness and magnificence of the capital of Ali Pacha,
Albania's despotic chief.

The figure of Ali Pacha is at the same time fascinating and
repellent to Byron, for Ali, 'whose dread command / Is lawless
law' (xlvii) in this country, is a man of 'war and woes'. Yet the
oriental splendour which surrounds him compels the eye:

In marble-paved pavilion, where a spring
Of living water from the centre rose,
Whose bubbling did a genial freshness fling,
And soft voluptuous couches breathed repose,
ALI reclined . . .

(lxii)

Byron is struck by the gentle appearance of the man, seemingly
untouched by his deeds of cruelty and violence. The ironical
contrast is presented both implicitly, and directly in Byron's
puzzled reflection.

Weary with this 'Moslem luxury' and the city's commotion,
the pilgrim retreats into the country where he finds that the
people, though fierce, are not lacking in essential virtues, such

as courage and kindness. Byron remembers with tenderness and gratitude the incident when his ship was in distress off 'Suli's shaggy shore', and the Suliotes, who had a reputation as robbers, 'stretched the welcome hand', 'piled the hearth, and wrung their garments damp'. Such simple acts of kindness were apt to impress Byron who was always prepared for disillusionment, although he had not yet condemned the world as 'the same wide den—of thieves'.

Travelling south once more, with a 'trusty band' of Albanians to protect him and his company, Byron discovers new enchantment, different from the mountain grandeur he has left behind:

> Where lone Utraikey forms its circling cove,
> And weary waves retire to gleam at rest,
> How brown the foliage of the green hill's grove,
> Nodding at midnight o'er the calm bay's breast,
> As winds come lightly whispering from the west,
> Kissing, not ruffling, the blue deep's serene: —
> 
> (lxx)

It is often difficult to determine the exact tone and intention of such lush pastoral passages as this one, for they do not carry the stamp of Byron's more obvious impulses or attitudes. They seem to function, as in this case, as transitions to novel phases of experience, and their *mise en scène* tends to stress elements which in the new context will provide dramatic contrast. The scenery depicted here lends heightened effect to the episode that follows, when

> On the smooth shore the night-fires brightly blazed,
> The feast was done, the red wine circling fast: —

and suddenly, at midnight,

> The native revels of the troop began;
> Each Palikar his sabre from him cast,
> And bounding hand in hand, man link'd to man,
> Yelling their uncouth dirge, long daunced the kirtled clan.
> 
> (lxxi)

And as they dance, they half sing, half scream the warlike song to which Byron has devoted eleven rough and exuberant quatrains, ending:

Selictar! unsheathe then our chief's scimitar;
Tambourgi! thy 'larum gives promise of war.
Ye mountains, that see us descend to the shore,
Shall view us as victors, or view us no more!

Against this savage bravery, and the whole account of Albania
and its rugged people, the sudden lament on Greece is introduced
with Byron's characteristic gift of stark contrast:

Fair Greece! sad relic of departed worth!
Immortal, though no more; though fallen, great!

Byron here reverts to the theme of the opening stanzas of the
canto—Greece past and present, and his attitude and treatment
in these stanzas point all the way to 'The Isles of Greece' in
*Don Juan*. On this matter, at least, he was unambiguous and
consistent. He had scorned the 'poor, paltry slaves' of Portugal,
he had exhorted the sons of Spain to advance in the cause of
national liberty; and now, in a country he loved passionately
from the beginning, the national humiliation is much harder to
bear. Byron loved Greece probably better than any other country, and as Leslie Marchand has shown us in his great biography,
he loved the Greeks and found among them his best companions,
although they were sadly lacking in the virtues he admired so
greatly in the Albanians and the Suliotes—and even in the Turks:
courage and pride.

In his lament on fallen Greece Byron could count on the cooperation of the reader, and he finely exploits the 'stock responses', in the positive sense of Dr. Richards's phrase, inherent in the
subject. The tone is perfectly adjusted, even where the melancholy meditation gives way to preaching (lxxvi) or bitter
irony (lxxxiii). The poetic process in these stanzas depends on a
simple emotional and historical contrast: In present Greece her
'scatter'd children' live in bondage, without leaders:

Not such thy sons who whilome did await,
The hopeless warriors of a willing doom,
In bleak Thermopylæ's sepulchral strait—
Oh! who that gallant spirit shall resume,
Leap from Eurota's banks, and call thee from the tomb?
                                                (lxxiii)

Here the contrast involves also the elements of sacrifice and resurrection or rebirth, charged with mythical associations greatly extending the imaginative scope of the stanza. The hope for a rebirth of Greece, which some years later inspired Shelley's fine chorus in *Hellas*, is voiced by Byron too, but in his characteristic manner of challenge:

> When Grecian mothers shall give birth to men,
> Then may'st thou be restored; but not till then.
> A thousand years scarce serve to form a state;
> An hour may lay it in the dust: and when
> Can man its shatter'd splendour renovate,
> Recall its virtues back, and vanquish Time and Fate?
>
> (lxxxiv)

For a moment the 'Demon Thought' reminds him of the vanity of human effort, and threatens to cancel out his hopes and his exhortations; yet before him is the paradox of immortal and fallen Greece:

> And yet how lovely in thine age of woe,
> Land of lost gods and godlike men, art thou!
> Thy vales of evergreen, thy hills of snow,
> Proclaim thee Nature's varied favourite now:
> Thy fanes, thy temples to thy surface bow,
> Commingling slowly with heroic earth,
> Broke by the share of every rustic plough:
> So perish monuments of mortal birth,
> So perish all in turn, save well-recorded Worth;
>
> (lxxxv)

This appears to be a stoic's tempered outlook. But as the canto draws to a close, Byron's fervent devotion to the country tends to involve names and images with an implicit or direct cultic appeal. Despite the ravages of Time, Minerva still smiles on this country, and Apollo gilds its long summers. Its 'haunted, holy ground' still retains its mould. Greece may be a sad relic of departed worth, but a splendid relic nevertheless, a shrine worth a pilgrimage—especially for that breed of nineteenth-century pilgrims who felt no need or desire to go to Palestine. For such devoted souls Byron, no doubt, is officiating in these last stanzas of Canto II, but although it is a public performance, and to some

extent marred by the sermonising tone, this does not obscure the
fact that his act of worship is, above all, a personal act of devotion.
Whatever the meaning for Byron of the 'relics' and 'altars' in
this 'consecrated land', they were part of its unique spiritual
challenge and of that myth of beauty and heroism which for
Byron came as close as anything to the cultic substitute he needed.
Meanwhile, he also owed to Greece the happiest days he had
known so far in his life, and the feeling that this land had made
him a poet. He owed to Greece, moreover, the germinal and
conscious impulses of that defiant cosmopolitanism with which
he returned to England, and which, along with his very un-
English temperament, soon made the young traveller a real
outcast.

*Exile*

*The remedy of travel and of time*

> "Afin que cette application vous forçât de
> penser à autre chose; il n'y a en vérité de
> remède que celui-là et le temps." *Lettre du Roi
> de Prusse à D'Alembert*, Sept. 7, 1776.

The opening of Canto III presents the poet's situation
through a vivid, impressionistic shift of attention from inner to
outer scene. Standing on the deck of the ship which carries him
from England, Byron is meditating on the face of his child, whom
he was never to see again, and then:

> Awaking with a start,
> The waters heave around me; and on high
> The winds lift up their voices: I depart,
> Whither I know not; but the hour's gone by,
> When Albion's lessening shores could grieve or glad mine
> eye.

In the following stanza the ocean is turned into an apt medium
for the poet's tormented mind, notably for his exilic impulses,
and assumes a complex metaphorical function in which storm-
tossed waves (as in Canto IV, clxxxiii) are horses carrying him
to freedom. The ocean is already an ally, as it is an image of his
own turbulent fate:

15

> Still must I on; for I am as a weed,
> Flung from the rock, on Ocean's foam to sail
> Where'er the surge may sweep, the tempest's breath
>                                         prevail.

Thus, from the beginning, Byron's treatment of his second journey is more frankly personal than that of the first, and though he again seizes the theme of 'the wandering outlaw of his own dark mind'—Childe Harold—this changes the autobiographical character of the poem even less than in the first cantos. Byron's purpose in re-introducing the fictitious hero is partly the initial one of 'giving some connexion to the piece', but mainly, it appears, of providing for himself a medium of concealment and dramatisation. We have found that the part played by Childe Harold in the two first cantos was not very effective, and it might be tempting to see him as one of the 'impedimenta' which, according to Paul West, clutter up Byron's life and poetry—'the wrong woman, the wrong type of poem, the wrong reputation, the wrong stanza-form'.[5] Added to this neat list, Childe Harold would be the wrong type of hero. And in a certain sense he is. His existence can be explained, partly at least, by the impulse which West shrewdly detects behind the other Byronic impedimenta—'the insecure person's fierce need of elimination'. This, to some extent, would explain the scapegoat quality in his character, and Byron's judgement of him as repulsive and unamiable. The most conspicuous thing about him, however, is his relative lack of importance, and if Byron intended him as an alter ego, or as a persona to dramatise his own multiple personality, he soon found him useless.

However, Childe Harold reappears in the third canto to remind us that the new journey, though different from the first, is an epic sequel to it and should be seen as a developing pattern of Fate running through the poet's entire life. It is the pattern of the 'wanderers over eternity', a course plotted by demon and doom, to be discovered only *en route*, if at all. The greatest mystery in the world to Byron from now on remained himself and his fate, and for poetic purposes he believed, though perhaps unconsciously, that by exploring nature and history and the workings of fate across Europe, he would also gain insight into the workings and directions of his own fate. Objectively speaking, this method leads into a vicious circle, but it is most fruitful from the point of view of imaginative and poetic process. We should bear in mind, however, that in this imaginative exploration of Fate there is a paradoxical element involved, for while his search revolves around the poet's personal centre or penetrates far and wide only to return to his own stance, the search represents also an effort to escape from himself—'to lose my own wretched identity'. Despite his proud defiance, the scandal and humiliation in England did leave a wound not easily healed, and there is abundant evidence in Canto III and IV of a sense of guilt, a sense of failure and frustration. It is this 'blight' in his character and in his past life which Byron—though he accepts it consciously at times—is trying to escape from in the two final cantos of the poem. And his method is the fairly common one of projection and identification, of finding accomplices in the past and present, and of fitting his own person and fate into a universal pattern of tragic fall, but also of heroic struggle. This, though he may not have been aware of it, is the most important aspect of that 'application' of travel referred to in the quotation heading the canto. On the surface of things, this 'application' points to the explicitly therapeutic purpose of his journey and the poem:

> Yet, though a dreary strain, to this I cling;
> So that it wean me from the weary dream
> Of selfish grief or gladness—so it fling
> Forgetfulness around me ...
>
> (iv)

His poetic journey is a panacea deliberately used. Still, though travelling and writing undoubtedly help him to bear his recent downfall, what the poem flings around him, and around the scenes explored, are rather so many configurations of his emotional tensions and of those impulses which, in his marriage and in the English society, he was not able to control. *Plus ça change, plus c'est la même chose.*

The new journey, and the new canto, are frankly conceived as a means of flight and compensation. As the man seeks refuge from himself and from society, so the poet seeks refuge in his imagination, in 'lone caves' and the 'soul's haunted cell' where he finds the shapes and images from which he may create a new earth if not a new heaven. His refuge, then, is not a flight into passivity and peace for the weary and wicked, but, on the contrary, into fuller and more active being:

'Tis to create, and in creating live
A being more intense, that we endow
With form our fancy, gaining as we give
The life we image, even as I do now.
What am I? Nothing: but not so art thou,
Soul of my thought! with whom I traverse earth,
Invisible but gazing, as I glow
Mix'd with thy spirit, blended with thy birth,
And feeling still with thee in my crush'd feelings' dearth.

(vi)

It is interesting to note that Byron, who preferred Pope to any other poet, in this central statement on the poetic process should come so close to Coleridge's view of the creative Imagination as the faculty which gives and gains at the same time, and which may contribute something objectively real to the subjective experience. And in the idea of poetry as a life-giving activity Byron is a thorough Romantic. The statement contains, moreover, the implicit idea of sublimation and catharsis.

In the light of this poetic confession, Byron's poem of exile suggests certain emotional directions and certain artistic needs. It hints, for one thing, at his compulsion to reject his own self or character, as a personal and social identity, while vindicating the worth of what to him appears as a separable 'non-self', the 'soul' of his 'thought', which, presumably, means his intellectual and poetic gift released, in the moments of creation, from the tyranny of passions and personality. As we shall see, Byron on his poetic journey immerses himself in his experience, as in a river of oblivion, and his most ecstatic moments are those in which he is 'lost' or 'absorbed' in his contemplation of external reality. The stanza quoted suggests, moreover, a desire for mental regeneration, or rather, perhaps, a regeneration of poetic sensibility. This is one of the dimly discerned goals of his exploration, and urges him on quite as strongly as the exilic impulse. For if the refuge from 'this world of woe' on the one hand takes him to the caves of the imagination, it also takes him to fresh scenes of imaginative stimulus, and makes him a 'being more intense'.

As the poet seeks intensity of life in creation, so he seeks permanence for the forms and creations of his questing soul. Amid the turbulence of his personal life and the changing scenes of the journey, this is the only destination which appears to stand out with clarity in his mind. Obsessed by the fact of Mutability, like an Elizabethan, Byron as a poet aspires to permanence and immortality in his art:

> There is that within me which shall tire
> Torture and Time, and breathe when I expire.

If the writing of *Childe Harold's Pilgrimage* brought Byron to this goal in Canto IV, then his journey was indeed worth while.

Meantime, the setting out is fraught with bitter regret rather than anticipation. Byron's wheel of fate had come full circle, and instead of the affected misery at the beginning of Canto I there is now both mortification and cause for grief:

> And thus, untaught in youth my heart to tame,
> My springs of life were poison'd. 'Tis too late!
> Yet am I changed; though still enough the same
> In strength to bear what time cannot abate,
> And feed on bitter fruits without accusing Fate.
>
> (vii)

His wheel of fate turned out to be a vicious circle, as Peter Quennell has demonstrated in his excellent book:

> He was alone now, as he had been alone when he was obscure. How curiously fate had completed the pattern, conjuring always the inevitable out of the unexpected and circumscribing within a period of less than five years the movement from isolation to isolation that seems, in the last resort, to be the course pursued by every human life! With what patience Byron himself had aided his destiny, urging it on, and yet stepping back, horrified and distraught, when it reached the climax towards which some deep and half-hidden strain in his nature had persistently impelled him![6]

He had concluded the second canto, in a mood of despondency and grief over lost friends, with a wish to bow humbly 'before the Chastener'; and now his determination is still to accept his fate, boldly as a stoic, though he blames himself and denounces society. As the conquerors and fallen great of history met fit retributions for their passion and *hubris*, so he himself has come to grief. While this outlook provided Byron with a kind of philo-

sophical consolation and determined to a large extent the course
of his poetic journey, it is the humiliating and dreadful fact of
exile which haunts him here in the beginning. He has set up the
great tragic picture of himself as a man of untameable passion,
doomed to self-destruction. This is as far as he himself wants to
go by way of explanation or apology. As for his recent clash with
society it is too painfully close to be dealt with directly, and so
'Long absent HAROLD re-appears at last'—to perform, at a
great and almost melodramatic distance, Byron's curious version
of the conflict. It is an odd and ineffective performance, pre-
cariously balanced between concealment and revelation: Harold,
who had once more tried to mix with society 'in fancied safety'
and 'guarded coldness', protected by 'an invulnerable mind',
a mind beyond the reach of sorrow as well as joy, finds that this
safety too is an illusion (xi). Love and Fame had undone him,
and Byron confesses as much, although his manipulation of the
fictitious character tends, in this part of the poem, to confuse
the issues. It is quite true that, like the protagonist he soon
'knew himself the most unfit / Of men to herd with Man', with
whom, he adds scornfully, 'he held / Little in common'. But it
was not mainly a question of having to submit 'His thoughts to
others' or of yielding 'dominion of his mind / To spirits against
whom his own rebell'd'—(xii) although this was part of his
trouble with Annabella. He came nearer to the truth when he
saw in his untamed heart the cause of his poisoned life, the heart
which, he adds here with a wry smile, 'can never all grow old'.

The function of this interlude is to launch the exile on his
journey, to show why he must leave, and how. Yet so far there
is no actual landscape to be explored, and the metaphorical
*mise en scène*, though significant, is a somewhat stiff demonstration
of his aims and needs:

> Where rose the mountains, there to him were friends;
> Where roll'd the ocean, thereon was his home;
> Where a blue sky, and glowing clime, extends,
> He had the passion and the power to roam;
> The desert, forest, cavern, breaker's foam,
> Were unto him companionship, they spake
> A mutual language, clearer than the tome
> Of his land's tongue, which he would oft forsake
> For Nature's pages glass'd by sunbeams on the lake.
>                                                    (xiii)

Here Byron officiates in the cult of wild nature initiated by Rousseau, and his attitude, at this moment mainly determined by his exilic impulses, is simple. What he finds is splendour, magnificence, freedom, and refuge from humanity. The stanza is significant in that it foreshadows the new order with which, like a modern Aeneas, he is seeking to replace the old one. It is characteristic of Byron's sensuous and non-mystical attitude to nature that when, as in the next stanza, he shifts his attention to the stars as goals of his aspiration, the lines grow into a turgid tangle of eighteenth-century clichés of the 'immortal spark' of the soul struggling to free itself from the material Chain of Being. Very different from this is the simile used (xv) to depict the zest for freedom in the fictitious hero—'as a wild-born falcon' beating 'His breast and beak against the wiry dome' of his cage—'Till the blood tinge his plumage'. This kind of passion rarely fails Byron as a source of inspiration, and with this powerful image the actual journey to freedom begins:

> Self-exiled Harold wanders forth again,
> With nought of hope left, but with less of gloom;
>
> (xvi)

As we shall see, the defiant paradox of the final line indicates salient traits in the emotional rhythm of the two final cantos.

Nowhere in the third canto, perhaps, is the psychological process of the journey better illustrated than in the stanzas where the self-exiled poet arrives on the battlefield of Waterloo. Egocentric though he is, here Byron's smiling despair is discarded or forgotten under the powerful impact of the actual scene and its tragic memories. Less than a year ago this place had witnessed death and downfall on the largest scale, and the ground on which he stands is 'an Empire's dust'. Significantly, however, it is the sense of futility, of historical *vanitas*, which first strikes him: There is no trace now of the battle which so recently sealed the fate of Europe and plunged her greatest leader into humiliation and exile—'Ambition's life and labours all were vain'—for France and for Napoleon. Byron had been 'dazzled and overwhelmed by his character and career', yet Napoleon had met 'Fit retribution'—for the laws of fate are always just.[7]

As in his meditations on the battlefields of Spain, Byron finds in Waterloo both grandeur and pathetic tragedy, and his poetic

treatment is determined by the conflicting impulses of exhila-
ration and grief. The tension is felt not only in the heavily
moralistic stanzas which lead up to the famous description of
the eve of the battle, but above all in the dramatic changes of
mood and point of view in that splendid piece of evocation. As
usual, Byron is fascinated by the heroism and pageantry of warfare, the display of power and discipline, fascinated also by the
sense of impending doom, the swoop of fate. His sound effects
and visual organisation in these stanzas are superb, and the
situation lends itself well to his particular gift of rough verbal
drive, and above all to his sense of contrast. It is against the
background of the ball and the preparation for battle that he
works out his drama of gaiety and grief, dance and death, on
his large and crowded canvas. The conflicting impulses involved
in this antithesis are seen at work also in his description of the
departing army. He sees the pathos and misery of separation, but
for a moment it is the 'marshalling in arms' and the 'Battle's
magnificently stern array' which predominate. After the vivid
evocation of the preparations the reader's expectation is pointed
to a climactic account of the battle. Yet suddenly again Byron
shifts his attention and what he gives us is a lament for the 'unreturning brave':

> And Ardennes waves above them her green leaves
> Dewy with nature's tear-drops as they pass,
> Grieving, if aught inanimate e'er grieves,
> Over the unreturning brave,—alas!
> Ere evening to be trodden like the grass
> Which now beneath them, but above shall grow
> In its next verdure, when this fiery mass
> Of living valour, rolling on the foe
> And burning with high hope shall moulder cold and low.
>                                                   (xxvii)

In this superimposed picture, which is a fine specimen of Byron's
power of inclusive and concentrated vision, he contemplates that
aspect of existence which had become so obsessively important
to him since his own late downfall and the bereavements of
friends over the last four years. It is the fickleness of fate and the
vanity of human, even heroic, endeavour. Yet despite this implicit disillusionment, Byron's fundamental humanity is vindi-
cated in these elegiac stanzas on the unreturning brave. While

he dwells on the excitement of the scene in which the soldiers are 'forming in the ranks of war', the actual battlefield with its 'red burial' holds no interest, and instead he turns to the field as it stretches out before him on this day in June 1816, and remembers his friend Howard:

> There have been tears and breaking hearts for thee,
> And mine were nothing had I such to give;
> But when I stood beneath the fresh green tree,
> Which living waves where thou didst cease to live,
> And saw around me the wide field revive
> With fruits and fertile promise, and the Spring
> Came forth her work of gladness to contrive,
> With all her reckless birds upon the wing,
> I turn'd from all she brought to those she could not bring.
>
> (xxx)

Already, one feels, Byron's second pilgrimage is opening up emotional and poetic sources which were closed to him before. His own bleeding heart, no doubt, is his guide into these novel regions, but his usually obtrusive ego is submerged in these meditations on the 'ghastly gap' which every death has made in human relationships. And the most interesting stanza of the entire group is that in which he describes, in perfectly objective terms, the life-in-death of the desolate heart:

> Even as a broken mirror, which the glass
> In every fragment multiplies; and makes
> A thousand images of one that was,
> The same, and still the more, the more it breaks;
> And thus the heart will do which not forsakes,
> Living in shatter'd guise; and still, and cold,
> And bloodless, with its sleepless sorrow aches,
> Yet withers on till all without is cold,
> Showing no visible sign, for such things are untold.
>
> (xxxiii)

And, worse still: 'There is a very life in our despair, / Vitality of poison' (xxxiv). Byron's insight into the obsessive and self-destructive forces of the mind is deepening, and he has come a long way from the early stanzas of Canto I.

Significantly, Byron devotes a large group of stanzas to the downfall of his former hero, Napoleon, and here the contradic-

tory impulses to escape from himself—the humiliated outcast—
and his desire to come to grips with himself and his own destiny,
are at the heart of the poetic process: Napoleon's spirit was
'antithetically mixt'—'Extreme in all things!', and this made
and unmade his greatness. He was the greatest of men, and his
greatness is measured by the fact that (in Byron's apostrophe)

> thy wild name
> Was ne'er more bruited in men's minds than now
> That thou art nothing, save the jest of Fame . . .
>                                                    (xxxvii)

The emphasis in this argument clearly reveals a need of mutual
explanation, and it is relevant to our reading to be aware of this
method of self-exploration in Byron. Throughout these stanzas
there is an implicit and indirect tracing of common flaws and
failures, within the universal pattern of Fate: Napoleon's sin was
*hubris*, and fame had maddened him until he became a god unto
himself. A common and trivial observation, no doubt, and a
common flaw in human nature. And yet for all his commonplace
behaviour what a mystery is man—this turbulent microcosm
who may rule the world, but not govern his 'pettiest passion'—
'Nor learn that tempted Fate will leave the loftiest star.' (xxxviii)
Byron's fate-concept may be shallow and superstitious, but his
understanding of Napoleon's temperament and destiny is nevertheless realistic. It is a view based on ancient wisdom and
expressed with a solemnity and pathos which call up images
from tragedy and epic. As Byron probes to the core of Napoleon's
inevitable downfall, he writes one of the finest stanzas in the
canto:

> But quiet to quick bosoms is a hell,
> And *there* hath been thy bane; there is a fire
> And motion of the soul which will not dwell
> In its own narrow being, but aspire
> Beyond the fitting medium of desire;
> And, but once kindled, quenchless evermore,
> Preys upon high adventure, nor can tire
> Of aught but rest; a fever at the core,
> Fatal to him who bears, to all who ever bore.
>                                                    (xlii)

Though Byron recognises the eighteenth-century limits of man's proper station, he shows, in this *locus classicus* of the demonridden Romantic soul, how unrealistic these narrow boundaries are when applied to the great men in whom the fever of conquest and creation burns:

> This makes the madmen who have made men mad
> By their contagion; Conquerors and Kings,
> Founders of sects and systems, to whom add
> Sophists, Bards, Statesmen, all unquiet things
> Which stir too strongly the soul's secret springs,
> And are themselves the fools to those they fool;
> Envied, yet how unenviable! what stings
> Are theirs! One breast laid open were a school
> Which would unteach mankind the lust to shine or rule:
>
> (xliii)

These 'unquiet things', then, cannot help their fever and ravage. They are singled out for agony and exile, cursed by the uniqueness of their vitality and unbending zest. In the following stanza Byron reverts to the storm metaphor he used as an image of his own life at the opening of the canto:

> Their breath is agitation, and their life
> A storm whereon they ride, to sink at last,
> And yet so nursed and bigoted to strife,
> That should their days, surviving perils past,
> Melt to calm twilight, they feel overcast
> With sorrow and supineness, and so die;
> Even as a flame unfed, which runs to waste
> With its own flickering, or a sword laid by,
> Which eats into itself, and rusts ingloriously.
>
> (xliv)

In these meditations on Waterloo and Napoleon, we notice a tendency in Byron to develop his argument into something like a rhetorical structure. Thus, after the statement of theme and *exempla*—here Napoleon and his likes—follows the universal application, and ultimately the conclusion. In the final stage of this process the poetic intensity often fails him, even where he avoids perilous abstraction, and instead of a vivid and unique perception we get stiffly allegorical and moralistic scenery:

He who ascends the mountain-tops, shall find
The loftiest peaks most wrapt in clouds and snow;
He who surpasses or subdues mankind,
Must look down on the hate of those below.
Though high *above* the sun of glory glow,
And far *beneath* the earth and ocean spread,
*Round* him are icy rocks, and loudly blow
Contending tempests on his naked head,
And thus reward the toils which to those summits led.
(xlv)

Yet this trivial conclusion is not the essence of the discovery Byron has made at Waterloo. Far more important are the emotional and poetic sources which have been released through his evocation of the scene of battle, its unreturning brave and the fatal and fated Emperor. Moreover, through the scape-goat hero he has managed, while keeping himself out of the picture, to come to grips with the mystery of fate as it manifests itself in all 'unquiet things'. What he has learned above all at Waterloo is that man must accept his fate, which means accept his nature, with its passion and poison, its glory and grief. Fortitude is all, and this too he has learned from the fallen Emperor:

When the whole host of hatred stood hard by,
To watch and mock thee shrinking, thou hast smiled
With a sedate and all-enduring eye;—
When Fortune fled her spoil'd and favourite child,
He stood unbow'd beneath the ills upon him piled.
(xxxix)

When Byron dismisses these meditations, in one of his characteristically abrupt transitions, he does so in a manner which indicates both the personal significance of his argument and the habitual direction his mind will take, away from the personal obsession into the cathartic release through the journey and the landscape:

Away with these! true Wisdom's world will be
Within its own creation, or in thine,
Maternal Nature! for who teems like thee,
Thus on the banks of thy majestic Rhine?
There Harold gazes on a work divine,

A blending of all beauties; streams and dells,
Fruit, foliage, crag, wood, cornfield, mountain, vine,
And chiefless castles breathing stern farewells
From gray but leafy walls, where Ruin greenly dwells.

(xlvi)

The stanza implies the metaphor of the refuge and the sanctuary, and this in turn harks back to the two sources of life and value which were left to the exiled poet at the beginning of the canto: on the one hand the caves of the imagination in which *thought* takes refuge, in order to create and 'in creating live / A being more intense'; and on the other hand nature in her varied aspects providing both companionship and wisdom (xiii). The metaphorical transfer in the early stanzas, from the caves and lonely inaccessible places of nature to the caves of the creative mind, and equally from the poet's need of companionship and communication to the caverns and forests of nature, suggests an important correspondence between mind and nature as sources of creation, beauty and wisdom. After the unpleasant allegorical scenery drawn from the human follies at Waterloo, Byron now finds solace and delight in the scenery of the Rhine valley. Yet here too, amid the 'blending of all beauty' which he again tries to convey in a rather hasty nominal catalogue, there are emphatic touches which remind us that what he is seeing is all the time a reflection of his own mind and fate. He sees the 'chiefless castles breathing stern farewells', and the vivid paradox of Ruin dwelling 'greenly' in these desolate buildings. This metaphorical process of personification yields a more definite meaning in the further contemplation of the castles standing as 'a lofty mind / Worn, but unstooping to the baser crowd'. Yet for all these undertones of personal obsession, Byron owing to the glorious scenery is able to immerse himself in the actual and sensuously concrete, as well as in the historical dimension of the landscape. His discovery, as before, is nearly always a double vision where the vestiges of power and passion contrast with the goodness and beauty of 'maternal Nature'.

The effect of this landscape on Byron's mind may also be seen from his shy though quite deliberate method of revealing that effect on the mind of his fictitious hero. Harold feels the enchantment of the scenery 'In glens which might have made even exile dear' and his severe stoicism does not prevent him from showing that 'Joy was not always absent from his face'. Nor is even love always absent from his heart, despite his burnt-out passions. Even the most disillusioned lover, we were told in stanza xi, cannot 'view the ripen'd rose / Nor seek to wear it'; nor fail to respond to 'one fond breast' in which there is 'soft remembrance, and sweet trust'. (liii) This devotion to Augusta, which a few stanzas later he confesses more fully in the lines on 'The castled crag of Drachenfels', combines with the impressions of landscape and journey to engender in him, almost to his surprise, a tenderness for children. The mood in these stanzas is, on the whole, bright and relaxed, and Byron's enjoyment of the journey reaches a descriptive climax in the stanzas on the Drachenfels he wrote to his sister. The landscape, as usual, is packed with nominal detail, but animated by a metaphorical vividness and powerfully developed and controlled through Byron's chief poetic instrument, the verb:

> The castled crag of Drachenfels
> Frowns o'er the wide and winding Rhine,
> Whose breast of waters broadly swells
> Between the banks which bear the vine,
> And hills all rich with blossom'd trees,
> And fields which promise corn and wine,
> And scatter'd cities crowning these,
> Whose far white walls along them shine,
> Have strew'd a scene, which I should see
> With double joy wert *thou* with me.

On the whole, Byron's record of the journey up the Rhine shows that he was able to immerse himself in the enjoyment of exploration, as in a spring of ablution and rebirth. His poetic sensibility is beginning to work through a new medium and with fresh emotional energy drawn from the journey and from his poetic configuration of its varied aspects. Taking leave of the Rhine, he pays it an unusual tribute: Here if anywhere, the tormented mind of man might know peace, here

> Where Nature, nor too sombre nor too gay,
> Wild but not rude, awful yet not austere,
> Is to the mellow Earth as Autumn to the year.
>                                                                (lix)

This emblem of temperance and equipoise is delightful to the
'unquiet thing' trying to subdue his demon and his past.

Byron has now arrived on the threshold of the Alps, and he
responds to their magnificence with his grand manner:

> But these recede. Above me are the Alps,
> The palaces of Nature, whose vast walls
> Have pinnacled in clouds their snowy scalps,
> And throned Eternity in icy halls
> Of cold sublimity, where forms and falls
> The avalanche—the thunderbolt of snow!
> All that expands the spirit, yet appals,
> Gather around these summits, as to show
> How Earth may pierce to Heaven, yet leave vain man below.
>
> (lxii)

Byron does not immediately set out to explore the Alps, and
oddly enough, though they offer dramatic and congenial material, the mountains are not very important to him, save as a
spectacular background, or as a quarry for metaphor (Cf. lxvii).
Instead, he continues to pursue the historical interest of the
scenery, and its meaning for himself. First there is the battlefield
of Morat, which enables Byron to state explicitly what has been
implicit in his meditations on the battlefields of Spain and
Greece:

> While Waterloo with Cannæ's carnage vies,
> Morat and Marathon twin names shall stand;
> They were true Glory's stainless victories,
> Won by the unambitious heart and hand
> Of a proud, brotherly, and civic band,
> All unbought champions in no princely cause
> Of vice-entail'd Corruption; they no land
> Doom'd to bewail the blasphemy of laws
> Making kings' rights divine, by some Draconic clause.
>
> (lxiv)

The place reminds Byron of the shining virtues of heroism and
self-sacrifice in the dedicated patriots, and he who has recently
spoken such harsh words on the vanity of Ambition's 'labour'
(xviii) writes now this splendid stanza:

But these are deeds which should not pass away,
And names that must not wither, though the earth
Forgets her empires with a just decay,
The enslavers and the enslaved, their death and birth;
The high, the mountain-majesty of worth
Should be, and shall, survivor of its woe,
And from its immortality look forth
In the sun's face, like yonder Alpine snow,
Imperishably pure beyond all things below.

(lxvii)

Here history and scenery fuse in a powerful and unique perception gained by the poet—'a being more intense—in this exalted moment of creation.

The geographical and psychological centre of Canto III are the stanzas dealing with Byron's stay on Lake Leman. The weeks he spent here with Shelley were, probably, the happiest he had known since his first visit to Greece. Yet the beginning was not propitious, for 'There is too much of man here', and Byron, almost in the manner of Wordsworth, contrasts the magic of the still lake with the oppressive 'herd' around him. As we know, the actual situation of those first days at the Hotel D'Angleterre was justification enough, but it is interesting to note how Byron in the poem takes care to guard against the suspicion or blame of misanthropy: 'To fly from, need not be to hate, mankind', and he illustrates by a vivid metaphor the necessity of keeping one's mind 'deep in its fountain' — of Nature and solitude—'lest it overboil / In the hot throng, where we become the spoil / Of our infection'. It is again the fever working destruction in and through the 'unquiet things'—the madmen, and once more he faces the enigma of fate as it strikes, swiftly and mysteriously, in the 'contentious world':

There, in a moment we may plunge our years
In fatal penitence, and in the blight
Of our own soul turn all our blood to tears,
And colour things to come with hues of Night;
The race of life becomes a hopeless flight
To those that walk in darkness: on the sea
The boldest steer but where their ports invite;
But there are wanderers o'er Eternity
Whose bark drives on and on, and anchor'd ne'er shall be.

(lxx)

As we see from this pivotal stanza, Byron, despite his casual mode of composition, exploits certain images and metaphors of sea, storm and wandering or flight which, through their recurrence and expanding associations, acquire symbolic and structural functions. Thus the image of himself as a 'weed / Flung from the rock, on Ocean's foam to sail / Where'er the surge may sweep' here re-emerges, in conjunction with the idea of his life as a 'hopeless flight'—without a destination, and the metaphor of his life as a journey reaches its climax in the celebrated phrase— the 'wanderers o'er Eternity'—which came to stamp him as the prototype of the Romantic *poète maudit*.

Byron does not dwell on the sombre mood of this stanza, but sets about correcting his despondency in the beauty and solitude of the lake. Biographers and critics have often pointed out that Byron during those weeks opened his mind to novel influences—even to that of Wordsworth.[8] And it is true that Byron in his contemplation of the lake and mountain scenery expresses a tender and almost naive abandonment to nature which is not found in his earlier poetry. In the stimulating company of his friend Shelley, his sensibility is beginning to work through a new medium, exploring nature as a framework for personal myth, and even the regions of mystical nature worship. It is as if Byron, like Wordsworth at one time, sees his exile from society as a return of the prodigal son to nature—'maternal Nature', 'true Wisdom's world'. Although Byron does not gain any such profound insight or wisdom from nature as Words- worth does, it is obvious that he regards it as a source of wisdom (xlvi), and his immersion in nature in sts. lxxii-lxxv implies not only a mental and poetic regeneration but also profounder in- sight. It is necessary, it would appear, to make this qualification to the statement, otherwise accurate, made by Joseph Warren Beach:

> Byron speaks, like the other romantics, of the book of nature. But he does not imply, like many of them, that it is a book of wisdom, that there is actually something to be learnt from it. It is simply a 'tome' that speaks more congenially to the heart of his hero than those written in the English language, since it speaks directly to his mood and passion.[9]

The metaphor of maternity is used again as he describes the tenderness and peace he finds in the Rhone,

> Or the pure bosom of its nursing lake,
> Which feeds it as a mother who doth make
> A fair but froward infant her own care,
> Kissing its cries away as these awake; —
>
> (lxxi)

and it indicates the way in which Byron is shortly to turn the lake and Alpine scenery into a myth of human affections and relations, of emotional and natural forces. Meanwhile, he wants to state more fully his attitude to nature and what it means to him:

> I live not in myself, but I become
> Portion of that around me; and to me
> High mountains are a feeling, but the hum
> Of human cities torture: I can see
> Nothing to loathe in nature, save to be
> A link reluctant in a fleshly chain,
> Class'd among creatures, when the soul can flee,
> And with the sky, the peak, the heaving plain
> Of ocean, or the stars, mingle, and not in vain.
>
> (lxxii)

For all his professed Augustan sympathies, Byron, unlike Pope and Cowper, deplores the slavery imposed by the great Chain of Being, and like a true romantic he speaks for the unbounded freedom and aspiration of the soul, in the manner of Shelley and later Browning. It is also interesting to note how close Byron comes to Wordsworth in his confession that to him mountains are a 'feeling', delightful and wholesome, while 'the hum / Of human cities torture'. According to Beach, Byron here uses the word 'nature'

> in a comprehensive sense to include man and the external world together as a part of universal life. But the other sense [wild nature] is implicit in the sharp opposition of wild nature to the artificial world of cities and the fleshly chain.[10]

Beach is undoubtedly right in claiming that Byron is the most 'classical' of the romantic poets in his view of nature, in that he has little of 'the platonic sophistications of romantic thought, and apprehending it deeply neither on the scientific nor the religious side.'[11] Yet we can see that nature now has acquired for him a new interest and new meaning, and we found an indication of this clearly set down in st. xiii. The stark contrast between society and nature in the stanza just quoted shows that his immersion in nature is due mainly to exilic impulses, for in the freedom of wild nature there is nothing to loathe (as in mankind), and no torture as in human cities. Thus nature is both the refuge from society, and the novel order which Byron, having failed to mould mankind to his temperament, now seeks to shape in his own image. But paradoxically, he does so in these stanzas by losing himself in the ecstatic enjoyment of nature:

> And thus I am absorb'd, and this is life:
> I look upon the peopled desert past,
> As on a place of agony and strife,
> Where, for some sin, to sorrow I was cast,
> To act and suffer, but remount at last
> With a fresh pinion; which I feel to spring,
> Though young, yet waxing vigorous as the blast
> Which it would cope with, on delighted wing,
> Spurning the clay-cold bonds which round our being cling.
>
> (lxxiii)

In this stanza we may see the working of a personal myth of atonement and sacrifice, as well as of resurrection. Its central and organising metaphor is the archetypal image of rebirth, and the rebirth it describes is of something more than emotional and poetic vigour, it is a surge of spiritual energy which enables him to push his quest beyond the usual range of his mind:

> And when, at length, the mind shall be all free
> From what it hates in this degraded form,
> Reft of its carnal life, save what shall be
> Existent happier in the fly and worm,—
> When elements to elements conform,
> And dust is as it should be, shall I not
> Feel all I see, less dazzling, but more warm?
> The bodiless thought? the Spirit of each spot?
> Of which, even now, I share at times the immortal lot?
>
> (lxxiv)

Here Byron comes so close to the 'platonic sophistications of the romantic poets' that he even contemplates, if only as a possibility, the 'state of pure intellect' (Robinet's *pure intelligence*) which Coleridge tentatively anticipated as a spiritual destination for mankind. The underlying idea, in Coleridge as in Byron, is that of catharsis, purification and liberation from the flesh. Whether the stimulus comes from Coleridge or from Shelley, or from the Alpine scenery, Byron expresses here a religious and platonic fervour, and a sense of the ultimate, never voiced in his earlier poetry. So also in the following stanza:

> Are not the mountains, waves, and skies, a part
> Of me and of my soul, as I of them?
> Is not the love of these deep in my heart
> With a pure passion? should I not contemn
> All objects, if compared with these? and stem
> A tide of suffering, rather than forego
> Such feelings for the hard and worldly phlegm
> Of those whose eyes are only turn'd below,
> Gazing upon the ground, with thoughts which dare not
> glow?
> (lxxv)

A general comment by Beach may aptly be applied to this stanza:

> Byron is romantic in his exaltation of passion. He is romantic in his stress upon the wild and elemental in nature. And, most of all, he is romantic in his craving to identify himself with, to lose himself in, these wild and elemental forces.[12]

That this passion is largely 'confined to feeling, and implies in him very little of an intellectual conception of nature', as Warren Beach goes on to claim, does not in any way weaken or obscure the religious quality in Byron's response to nature, nor is it very fruitful, with reference to its poetic manifestations, to distinguish here between purely intellectual and emotional aspects.

At this point Byron, with his characteristic sense of the 'immediate' breaks off his meditation to draw a portrait of that restless ghost of these regions, Rousseau, and the portrait, like that of Napoleon, is very largely a self-projection and a study of a madman who knew 'How to make madness beautiful'. Rousseau is to Byron above all another example of that demon-ridden fated soul that creates and destroys through its ungovernable forces. And in this aspect Rousseau becomes part of that myth of emotional and natural forces for which the Alpine scenery serves as a metaphor, and we shall see what part Rousseau plays in this myth-making process in the later stanzas on Clarens (xcix-civ).

When Byron returns to the scenery, the passion and exaltation have given way to calm, and in this mood he now explores the lake:

> Clear, placid Leman! thy contrasted lake,
> With the wild world I dwelt in, is a thing
> Which warns me, with its stillness, to forsake
> Earth's troubled waters for a purer spring.
> This quiet sail is as a noiseless wing
> To waft me from distraction; once I loved
> Torn ocean's roar, but thy soft murmuring
> Sounds sweet as if a Sister's voice reproved,
> That I with stern delight should e'er have been so moved.
>
> (lxxxv)

As we have seen before, for instance in his changing appraisals of Parnassus, Byron's constancy to ideal objects is not very great. Here, for the same reasons of emphasis and superlative praise, he even betrays his old friend and ally, the ocean, for the calm idyllic lake. Byron may be a better poet of the roaring ocean than of this kind of lake stillness and breathless listening, yet the stanza, for all its deliberate, conscious tone and careful *mise en scène* is nevertheless effective. The exilic impulses are still predominant, and the stanza shows the escape, sacrifice and purification which we noted in st. lxxiii, along with the structural imagery of the 'purer spring' of emotional (and poetic) rebirth, and the wing, metaphor of freedom and renewed spiritual energy in the 'being more intense' of the poet. In the metaphor of the lake's 'soft murmuring' like a 'Sister's voice' the scenery is used once more as a myth for human affections and relations, as in st. lxxi. Within this personal myth, the Sister's voice sets the key for Byron's exploration through the next stanzas:

> It is the hush of night, and all between
> Thy margin and the mountains, dusk, yet clear,
> Mellow'd and mingling, yet distinctly seen,

> Save darken'd Jura, whose capt heights appear
> Precipitously steep; and drawing near,
> There breathes a living fragrance from the shore,
> Of flowers yet fresh with childhood; on the ear
> Drops the light drip of the suspended oar,
> Or chirps the grasshopper one good-night carol more;
>
> (lxxxvi)

There is little of the characteristic Byronic energy in this description, and yet for subtle and varied perception it matches some of the nature poetry of Wordsworth and Keats. As a new facet in Byron's poetic genius this ecstatic contemplation of a quiet, pastoral landscape is interesting. Seen in the context of the vast range of imaginative exploration of Canto III, where the 'red burial' of Waterloo marks one extreme, and this, perhaps, the other, its significance is important and obvious. Byron's sensibility is here working through the new and unaccustomed medium of Arcadian scenery, and though it does not call on his most spectacular gifts, its value to him is revealed in the more than usual care he takes in arrangement, texture and imagery, the suggestions of mood and meaning through alliteration, assonance and rhythm, and the concentration on minute, vivid sense impressions. No doubt, the critics who insist on the 'playboy' in Byron would be tempted to see this as a clever, indeed too clever performance, persuasive yet tricky. But this hardly accounts for the effectiveness of Byron's description.

The touches of Arcadian or childhood innocence which Byron introduces in these stanzas—the flowers 'yet fresh with childhood', and the grasshopper who 'makes his life an infancy' (lxxxvii) are all part of the myth-making process in which nature and its forces are felt to fuse with and illuminate those of man. It is active throughout this group of stanzas:

> All heaven and earth are still—though not in sleep,
> But breathless, as we grow when feeling most;
> And silent, as we stand in thoughts too deep:—
> All heaven and earth are still: From the high host
> Of stars, to the lull'd lake and mountain-coast
> All is concenter'd in a life intense,
> Where not a beam, nor air, nor leaf is lost,
> But hath a part of being, and a sense
> Of that which is of all Creator and defence.
>
> (lxxxix)

For once Byron has a sense of complete oneness and peace throughout the universe, and communes with that essence of being which to Coleridge and Wordsworth as well as to Shelley was life. The 'intense life' which pervades the universe in this ecstatic moment is related to the 'active, living spirit' which Shelley and the other romantics found everywhere in nature and which helped them, in an age of fading mythologies, to see natural objects as spiritual signs, and instil into these objects mysterious modes of living. Intensity of being, to live on the peaks of sensation and creation, was Byron's constant aspiration and one of the reasons why he travelled, and the life intense he discovers here in the Alpine night is one with himself as a 'being more intense' who participates in it and derives from it the power to create. So completely is his being 'absorbed' in this experience that he has even a sense of God, and nowhere in his poetry does Byron come so close to what one might legitimately call a pantheistic ecstasy. The poet of discord and tormenting conflict communes with the world of eternal harmony, and it is significant that this communion purifies from 'self', and thus emphasises the religious implications of the experience. Yet it is 'Nature's realms of worship', and not any specific religious creed which convey this 'feeling infinite':

> Not vainly did the early Persian make
> His altar the high places, and the peak
> Of earth-o'ergazing mountains, and thus take
> A fit and unwall'd temple, there to seek
> The Spirit, in whose honour shrines are weak,
> Uprear'd of human hands. Come, and compare
> Columns and idol-dwellings, Goth or Greek,
> With Nature's realms of worship, earth and air,
> Nor fix on fond abodes to circumscribe thy pray'r!
>
> (xci)

This turgid stanza turns the poet's exilic impulses against the tyranny of dogmatic religion, and consequently its main function and purpose is to glorify nature and to draw the rather unnecessary conclusion, from the mystical experience in the preceding stanzas, that nature suffices for our spiritual needs.

As the mystical and religious mood passes, the landscape changes under the impact of Byron's resourceful temperament, and now it is the spirit of freedom and rebellion which takes over the myth-making process. In these violent changes of mood and attention, and the corresponding changes in descriptive technique, the landscape becomes increasingly a picture of Byron's mind, his inner world, restless, tormented and contradictory, but above all else vital:

> The sky is changed!—and such a change! Oh night,
> And storm, and darkness, ye are wondrous strong,
> Yet lovely in your strength, as is the light
> Of a dark eye in woman! Far along,
> From peak to peak, the rattling crags among
> Leaps the live thunder! Not from one lone cloud,
> But every mountain now hath found a tongue,
> And Jura answers, through her misty shroud,
> Back to the joyous Alps, who call to her aloud!
>
> And this is in the night:—Most glorious night!
> Thou wert not sent for slumber! let me be
> A sharer in thy fierce and far delight,—
> A portion of the tempest and of thee!
> How the lit lake shines, a phosphoric sea,
> And the big rain comes dancing to the earth!
> And now again 'tis black,—and now, the glee
> Of the loud hills shakes with its mountain-mirth,
> As if they did rejoice o'er a young earthquake's birth.
>
> (xcii-xciii)

Here the 'lava of the imagination' flows copiously, and not laboriously. This cheerful and unique myth of the elements makes one reflect once more how sadly inadequate are such terms as pathetic fallacy or projection, or animation, to describe the poetic process which through vivid and original perception creates the external landscape in the image of the poet's mind.

The bitterness and despair in which Byron began his exile are now receding, and in the sheer enjoyment of nature he has experienced something like the sublimation, or the purification from self which he aspired to, and also the rebirth of emotional and imaginative vitality which was part of that aspiration from the beginning. He lives now with his favourite companions—the varied aspects of wild nature—and he lives, 'a being more intense', in his own creation. Though death and fate and a sense of futility will return and haunt him, it is this kind of being which gradually fosters in him his defiant conviction of achievement:

> There is that within me which shall tire
> Torture and Time, and breathe when I expire . . .

Where Byron abandons himself to the kind of myth-making we have seen in the 'joyous Alps', and when he deals with the immediate confrontation, whether of nature or history, he is nearly always able to turn his unique energy to good account. Where, on the other hand, he is tempted to develop his discovery into a rhetorical structure, with *exemplum* and application, he frequently loses his magic touch. That happens, for instance, when after these stanzas he meditates on the emotional equivalents and goals of tempests (xcvi), and on 'Lightning' as a word to focus his own poetic aspiration (xcvii). His wrestling with abstracts here shows that this is not his proper medium for wreaking his 'thoughts upon expression'. Yet from his experience of the Alpine thunderstorm in the night something valuable remains, something not clearly defined, but summed up in his determination to 'resume / The march of our existence'. And the passionate pilgrim who had been more disenchanted with love than with anything else moves now into Clarens, and once more the myth is active in the landscape:

> Clarens! sweet Clarens, birthplace of deep Love!
> Thine air is the young breath of passionate thought;
> Thy trees take root in Love; the snows above
> The very Glaciers have his colours caught,
> And sun-set into rose-hues sees them wrought
> By rays which sleep there lovingly: the rocks,
> The permanent crags, tell here of Love, who sought
> In them a refuge from the worldly shocks,
> Which stir and sting the soul with hope that woos, then mocks.
>
> (xcix)

Love, like himself, is an exile and has taken refuge in this region, at least so it seems to Byron with Rousseau's *Heloïse* in mind.[13] In the next stanza the mountains around Clarens provide a natural setting for a ritual act—an apotheosis of Love to regions where the god is 'a pervading life and light'. And meanwhile his myth is developed through the landscape:

> All things are here of *him*; from the black pines,
> Which are his shade on high, and the loud roar
> Of torrents, where he listeneth, to the vines
> Which slope his green path downward to the shore,
> Where the bow'd waters meet him, and adore,
> Kissing his feet with murmurs; and the wood,
> The covert of old trees, with trunks all hoar,
> But light leaves, young as joy, stands where it stood,
> Offering to him, and his, a populous solitude.
>
> A populous solitude of bees and birds,
> And fairy-form'd and many-colour'd things,
> Who worship him with notes more sweet than words,
> And innocently open their glad wings,
> Fearless and full of life: the gush of springs,
> And fall of lofty mountains, and the bend
> Of stirring branches, and the bud which brings
> The swiftest thought of beauty, here extend,
> Mingling, and made by Love, unto one mighty end.
>
> (ci-cii)

There is an almost Keatsian delight in the Arcadian beauty of the landscape, and its secret life. Like Keats, and, stranger still, like Wordsworth, Byron places the fane of love far from the 'crushing' crowd, in the prelapsarian innocence of wild nature. In his favourite recurrent paradox of 'populous solitude' (the solitude which is to him companionship) we have the formula of Byron's new order, the state of exile fashioned to his own needs. When he again resumes the myth of the god Love as an exile, he arrives at an unexpected piece of wisdom:

> He who hath loved not, here would learn that lore,
> And make his heart a spirit; he who knows
> That tender mystery, will love the more;
> For this is Love's recess, where vain men's woes,
> And the world's waste, have driven him far from those,
> For 'tis his nature to advance or die;
> He stands not still, but or decays, or grows
> Into a boundless blessing, which may vie
> With the immortal lights, in its eternity!
>
> (ciii)

Formerly, bitterness and exilic rejection followed in the wake of Byron's meditation on men's woes and the world's waste, and the destructive passion of love. Now love has become a 'tender mystery' and something capable of growing into 'a boundless blessing', with Platonic implications of transcendence or permanence.

It is the Clarens landscape which enables Byron to express this sense of the ultimate reality of love, just as the lake of Geneva initiated him into the 'life intense' permeating the universe. We see, then, that quite apart from Byron's need for change and amusement, quite apart also from his need for turning the ruins and battlefields of Europe into ciphers for the working of Fate, he gained from the journey a regeneration of emotional vitality which enabled him to rediscover, if only in glimpses, the essential values in human existence. In the bitterness of rebellion he has denied these, and will deny them again. But for the time being these values are important to him as a poet—a 'being more intense' who explores and creates and frankly records the process in all its changing and contradictory phases. As the canto draws to a close, Byron returns from his immersion in nature, to the fact of his exile, and after his passionate stanzas on the Lake Leman scenery and Clarens it is curious to find that he claims a stoical fortitude as the chief gain from his journey. It is 'a stern task of soul' to 'conceal, / With a proud caution, love or hate ... Passion or feeling, purpose, grief or zeal,—' and yet: 'it is taught.' This claim, however, is hardly borne out by the evidence. On the other hand, he has reaped from adversity and the excitement of travel a more subtle awareness of the external world, and thus been able to draw large new expanses within the range of his vision. In extending thus his poetic grasp of reality, Byron had to overcome certain prejudices, such as his dislike of the earlier romantics and their treatment of nature, and, at least for the moment, he did this. The reconciliation was well prepared for, however, in his characteristic romantic yearning to become one with nature, to be 'absorbed' into her life and share in her elemental power.

Besides this, some degree of detachment is gained, as we see from his parting shot:

> I have not loved the world, nor the world me,—
> But let us part fair foes; I do believe,

Though I have found them not, that there may be
Words which are things, hopes which will not deceive,
And virtues which are merciful, nor weave
Snares for the failing; I would also deem
O'er others' griefs that some sincerely grieve;
That two, or one, are almost what they seem,
That goodness is no name, and happiness no dream.

(cxiv)

For rhetorical purposes, or rather for the sake of argument, it is
convenient for Byron to deny here that he has indeed, throughout the canto, found evidence of solidity in and behind words,
of virtues, and even of happiness.

### The unreach'd Paradise of our Despair

> The poem ... as a mark of respect for what is
> venerable, and of feeling for what is glorious,
> ... has been to me a source of pleasure in the
> production ...
> (From dedicatory letter to John Hobhouse,
> January 2, 1818.)

The fourth and final canto of *Childe Harold's Pilgrimage* was
completed at Venice in 1817. Nearly two years had passed since
Byron wrote Canto III at Lausanne, and because of this distance
in time, and because he now pursues his exploration into Italy,
certain new metaphorical directions are to be expected. The
remedy of travel and time has not, however, furthered an emotional development along the lines suggested by the stanzas on
the Alpine scenery; there is no greater freedom from fate and
doom. On the contrary, the gloom seems to have deepened
around the poet, and his old bitterness remains. As we know, at
Venice Byron reached the nadir of his self-inflicted exile, and he
told Medwin later: 'I detest every recollection of the place, the
people, and my pursuits.'[14] Yet in the poem his attitude is not one
of detestation but of admiration and love (iii, xviii). Neither is
his fierce and dissipated life at Venice during the months of 1817
and 1818 directly reflected in the canto, though it may well
account for the sombre mood which pervades it. Moreover, his
theme is Italy past and present, and nowhere outside Greece did
he find so much lost grandeur to mourn and so much evidence

of historical futility. There is also the new congenial theme of
the exiled and persecuted poets, like Tasso and Dante, which
fires him to angry eloquence. Characteristic of the whole canto
is a density of varied detail that obliterates the sense of coherence
which, in the earlier cantos, despite pauses and deviations, the
journey to some extent imposed on the composition. Although
there is an implicit itinerary, taking the poet from Venice
through Ferrara to Florence, and thence past the lake of Thrasimene to Rome, the movement of the canto is one in time—in
history—rather than one in space. There is no forward-looking,
teleological plan, and no destination. Nevertheless, the canto
still sustains the basic idea of the journey as a quest, an exploration, and Byron intended Rome to provide a fitting climax and
conclusion.

Byron's exploration of Venice yields the usual dramatic contrast between past glory and present decay, a contrast to which
he is more than ever sensitive, and he masters this kind of
*tableau* now with ease and magnificence:

> I stood in Venice, on the Bridge of Sighs;
> A palace and a prison on each hand:
> I saw from out the wave her structures rise
> As from the stroke of an enchanter's wand:
> A thousand years their cloudy wings expand
> Around me, and a dying Glory smiles
> O'er the far times, when many a subject land
> Look'd to the winged Lion's marble piles,
> Where Venice sate in state, throned on her hundred isles!

One might have expected Byron to pronounce 'Fit retribution!'
on Venice as he has done on other tyrants of the past, for Venice
too has made slaves and been guilty of that *hubris* which Byron
detects in the fallen great. Yet the redeeming feature to him is
that this city turned her wealth into great art, she herself grew
into a work of art, and inspired artists for centuries. Hence he
mourns her present humiliation under foreign rule, but now,
instead of exhortation to fight for freedom, he invokes the libe-
rating power of art: Just as 'Redemption rose up in the Attic
Muse' after the defeat at Syracuse of the Athenian armies, so it
might be possible for Venice to regain her freedom, for her love
of Tasso if for nothing else. This idea of the bard as a national
redeemer had exercised Byron's imagination since his first visit

to Greece, and was later to be given its fullest treatment in the well-known stanzas 'The Isles of Greece' in *Don Juan*.

Amid the decaying stones of Venice live the figures with which the poetic imagination has peopled her, and these are still young and vigorous:

> The beings of the mind are not of clay;
> Essentially immortal, they create
> And multiply in us a brighter ray
> And more beloved existence: that which Fate
> Prohibits to dull life, in this our state
> Of mortal bondage, by these spirits supplied,
> First exiles, then replaces what we hate;
> Watering the heart whose early flowers have died,
> And with a fresher growth replenishing the void.
>
> (v)

The sources of emotional regeneration which he discovered in the wild nature of the Alps, he now seeks in the 'beings of the mind'—such as those of Shakespeare (iv), and again he asserts the immortality of art, and of his own art, as a goal for his journey. Here the idea of compensation and catharsis through art which he stated metaphorically in the stanza on the 'lone caves' of the imagination in Canto III is once more predominant. Yet there is also that other possibility, which, if only for the sake of defiance, the stoic faces with indomitable pride:

> If my fame should be, as my fortunes are,
> Of hasty growth and blight, and dull Oblivion bar
>
> My name from out the temple where the dead
> Are honour'd by the nations—let it be—
> And light the laurels on a loftier head!
> And be the Spartan's epitaph on me—
> 'Sparta hath many a worthier son than he.'
> Meantime I seek no sympathies, nor need;
> The thorns which I have reap'd are of the tree
> I planted: they have torn me, and I bleed:
> I should have known what fruit would spring
>     from such a seed.
>
> (ix-x)

The exilic impulse is still obvious, and so is his sense of the fit retribution he has met, a retribution which he may accept because it is part of that tragic grandeur unknown to ordinary human beings. It is this defiant pride which saves Byron's thorn metaphor from the blemish of self-pity which Shelley could not avoid. It is significant that this fatal force of self-destruction is the only trait of his character which Byron faces openly and without the usual impulse to escape or reject, for it is a flaw beyond human control and thus also beyond the censure of disgrace.

While Byron pays a splendid tribute to Venice for her beauty and great memories, and for the way in which she has stamped her image on European art, he does not record any immediate impressions of the city, and for once there is very little sense of the actual in his meditations. It is the ideal image of the city he presents, distilled or detached from the personal experiences of which he spoke to Medwin with such bitterness. And at this level of detachment he feels that, apart from the joy in seeing Art triumph over time, he owes to Venice some of the happiest moments of his life, which have also their enduring value:

> There are some feelings Time cannot benumb,
> Nor Torture shake, or mine would now be cold and dumb.
>
> (xix)

But although he owes this to Venice, it is to Alpine scenery he turns for a metaphor to body forth his stoical struggle against Time and Torture:

> But from their nature will the Tannen grow
> Loftiest on loftiest and least shelter'd rocks,
> Rooted in barrenness, where nought below
> Of soil supports them 'gainst the Alpine shocks
> Of eddying storms; yet springs the trunk, and mocks
> The howling tempest, till its height and frame
> Are worthy of the mountains from whose blocks
> Of bleak, gray granite into life it came,
> And grew a giant tree;—the mind may grow the same.
>
> (xx)

This is a more successful use of the rhetorical structure (*exemplum*) than the one we found in the more stiffly allegorical arrangement of landscape in Canto III (xlv). Yet for all the lofty

strength which the tree metaphor is meant to convey Byron
dwells in the following stanzas rather on the weakness and blight
of suffering, its obsessive quality, its latent threat—like a 'scorpion's sting'—'with fresh bitterness imbued' (xxiii). This is part
of that mystery of fate which Byron seeks to penetrate although
he knows that there is no solution to it in practical terms. And
as usual, when he has come to the dead end of his speculation,
he escapes, and finds solace, in identifying himself with a more
universal pattern of fate, whether in an historical or geographical
context:

> But my soul wanders; I demand it back
> To meditate amongst decay, and stand
> A ruin amidst ruins; there to track
> Fall'n states and buried greatness, o'er a land
> Which *was* the mightiest in its old command,
> And *is* the loveliest, and must ever be
> The master-mould of Nature's heavenly hand;
> Wherein were cast the heroic and the free,
> The beautiful, the brave, the lords of earth and sea,
>
> The commonwealth of kings, the men of Rome!
> And even since, and now, fair Italy!
> Thou art the garden of the world, the home
> Of all Art yields, and Nature can decree;
> Even in thy desert, what is like to thee?
> Thy very weeds are beautiful, thy waste
> More rich than other climes' fertility;
> Thy wreck a glory, and thy ruin graced
> With an immaculate charm which cannot be defaced.
>                                              (xxv-xxvi)

Greece alone has received similar ecstatic tributes from Byron,
with wide ranges of human value drawn into the compass. Here,
as in the final stanzas on Greece in Canto II (lxxiii, lxxxv,
lxxxviii, xciii), Byron exploits the dramatic possibilities and
tension of the oxymoron, and notably in the paradox of the final
lines he makes Italy a symbol of that Life-in-Death which, to the
tormented exile, is a form of the triumph of life. In Byron's
quest for eternity on earth, the stanzas—like those on Greece
and on the Lake Leman scenery—reveal an important discovery,
and this time not in terms of art so much as in terms of spontaneous enjoyment. It is not love, as in Shakespeare, which helps the

poet to withstand the 'rackful siege of battering days', but the loveliness of the land, transforming even ruin into glory. This is the kind of metamorphosis, otherwise possible only through art, in which Byron seeks reconciliation and catharsis. The function of landscape is still essentially cultic and ritualistic. And once more Byron immerses himself in nature, to arrest in particular one moment of splendour and loveliness:

> The moon is up, and yet it is not night;
> Sunset divides the sky with her; a sea
> Of glory streams along the Alpine height
> Of blue Friuli's mountains; Heaven is free
> From clouds, but of all colours seems to be,—
> Melted to one vast Iris of the West,—
> Where the Day joins the past Eternity,
> While, on the other hand, meek Dian's crest
> Floats through the azure air—an island of the blest!
>
> (xxvii)

As yet, the tableau is too deliberately arranged and held up for the reader to admire. In this and the following stanza Byron tries hard to express the beauty and magic of an Italian sunset, but although he writes with unusually fastidious craftsmanship the picture remains conventional, until the sight of the river, the 'deep-dyed Brenta', enables him to grasp the total experience in a single unique metaphor. The Brenta, he observes, is

> Filled with the face of Heaven, which, from afar
> Comes down upon the waters; all its hues,
> From the rich sunset to the rising star,
> Their magical variety diffuse:
> And now they change; a paler shadow strews
> Its mantle o'er the mountains; parting day
> Dies like the dolphin, whom each pang imbues
> With a new colour as it gasps away—
> The last still loveliest,—till—'tis gone— and all is gray.
>
> (xxix)

In technique as in mood, Byron is nothing if not versatile, and the dolphin metaphor reveals the poet's vivid myth-making power, which transforms a trivial experience into a memorable perception.

17

The loveliness of Italy recurs like a *leitmotif* throughout the canto, and often as in Greece this loveliness is felt to enhance the sense of loss and decay:

> Italia! oh Italia! thou who hast
> The fatal gift of beauty, which became
> A funeral dower of present woes and past,
> On thy sweet brow is sorrow plough'd by shame,
> And annals graved in characters of flame.
> Oh, God! that thou wert in thy nakedness
> Less lovely or more powerful, and couldst claim
> Thy right, and awe the robbers back, who press
> To shed thy blood, and drink the tears of thy distress;
>
> Then might'st thou more appal; or, less desired,
> Be homely and be peaceful, undeplored
> For thy destructive charms . . .
>
> (xlii-xliii)

The drama of fate and self-destructive 'gifts' continues to evolve through the medium of history and landscape. Yet again we notice the ambivalence in Byron's attitude, on the one hand accepting this national 'shame' as a consequence of the 'fatal gift of beauty', on the other hand revolting against the wrongness of things, the guilt of 'robbers', 'horde' and 'spoilers'. Italy, glorious yet disgraced, offers Byron a splendid opportunity for the ritual of revenge, but also for that of restitution:

> Yet, Italy! through every other land
> Thy wrongs should ring, and shall, from side to side;
> Mother of Arts! as once of arms; thy hand
> Was then our guardian, and is still our guide;
> Parent of our religion! whom the wide
> Nations have knelt to for the keys of heaven!
> Europe, repentant of her parricide,
> Shall yet redeem thee, and, all backward driven,
> Roll the barbarian tide, and sue to be forgiven.
>
> (xlvii)

Within this larger pattern of the national myth there emerges the theme of the wandering exiled poets, buried in foreign soil.

The tomb of Petrarch at Arqua reminds Byron that the great Renaissance poet was one of those

> who their mortality have felt,
> And sought a refuge from their hopes decay'd
> In the deep umbrage of a green hill's shade ...

The personal obsession with refuge and exile is here grafted on to the traditional idea of retirement into nature from the corrupt 'busy cities'. That Byron associates himself with the fate of Petrarch may be seen from the way in which his meditation develops:

> If from society we learn to live,
> 'Tis solitude should teach us how to die;
> It hath no flatterers; vanity can give
> No hollow aid; alone—man with his God must strive:
>
> Or, it may be, with demons, who impair
> The strength of better thoughts, and seek their prey
> In melancholy bosoms, such as were
> Of moody texture from their earliest day,
> And loved to dwell in darkness and dismay,
> Deeming themselves predestined to a doom
> Which is not of the pangs that pass away;
>
> (xxxiii-xxxiv)

Moving on to Ferrara, Byron is reminded of a different kind of poet's destiny: Tasso was there imprisoned by Alfonso, and thus became the glory and the shame of that city. Byron exploits the conflict between the two men to dramatise once more his pre-occupation with freedom and tyranny, the abuse of power and the strength of soul. Tasso was a martyr of injustice and despotism, an exile and a supreme artist, exile because of that which made him a great poet—his restless, boundless mind. Looking back on this poet's sad fate, it is a consolation to Byron to know that Tasso has been enthroned by posterity amid 'Glory without end', and consecrated with undying fame and gratitude, while Alfonso is cursed and despised. Such after all, may be the course of historical justice.

As one might expect, one of the main goals on Byron's journey south through Italy is Florence. This is how he greets it:

> But Arno wins us to the fair white walls,
> Where the Etrurian Athens claims and keeps
> A softer feeling for her fairy halls.
> Girt by her theatre of hills, she reaps
> Her corn, and wine, and oil, and Plenty leaps
> To laughing life, with her redundant horn.
> Along the banks where smiling Arno sweeps
> Was modern Luxury of Commerce born,
> And buried Learning rose, redeem'd to a new morn.
>
> (xlviii)

Here again we have a highly deliberate presentation, turgid with conventional phrasing in the opening lines, and with the usual plangency of alliteration. It is only when Byron comes to grips with the solid individual detail that his perception burns through the 'veil of familiarity' and is able to turn the Renaissance metaphor into a personal drama of life, or art, triumphant over death. This happens as he enters Santa Croce, where the sense of human greatness intensifies that of divine presence:

> In Santa Croce's holy precincts lie
> Ashes which make it holier, dust which is
> Even in itself an immortality,
> Though there were nothing save the past, and this,
> The particle of those sublimities
> Which have relapsed to chaos: here repose
> Angelo's, Alfieri's bones, and his,
> The starry Galileo, with his woes;
> Here Machiavelli's earth returned to whence it rose.
>
> These are four minds, which, like the elements,
> Might furnish forth creation: — Italy!
> Time, which hath wrong'd thee with ten thousand rents
> Of thine imperial garment, shall deny,
> And hath denied, to every other sky,
> Spirits which soar from ruin: thy decay
> Is still impregnate with divinity,
> Which gilds it with a revivifying ray;
> Such as the great of yore, Canova is to-day.
>
> (liv-lv)

To place Canova with Angelo or Galileo is a strange error of judgement, but Byron's enthusiasm is here seeking to assert a positive faith in the creative vitality of the land: The Renaissance is still going on, and it is only here, in eternal Italy, that Byron finds what he longs most of all to discover—the triumph of the human spirit over Time and circumstance, and the triumph of life and art. While Greece lives only in her great memories, Italy still lives to create. Thus, like the indomitable individual soul, Italy rises above humiliation and wrong.

Italy, then, furnishes Byron with an example of a land battered by Fate and iniquity, yet victorious, and Florence is the focal point of this glory. Yet to Byron Florence is also the town that exiled its poets, and it has, like most things in this world, its dark and vicious past:

> Ungrateful Florence! Dante sleeps afar,
> Like Scipio, buried by the upbraiding shore:
> Thy factions, in their worse than civil war,
> Proscribed the bard whose name for evermore
> Their children's children would in vain adore
> With the remorse of ages; and the crown
> Which Petrarch's laureate brow supremely wore,
> Upon a far and foreign soil had grown,
> His life, his fame, his grave, though rifled—
>      not thine own.
>
> (lvii)

Into the magnetic field of Byron's sense of exile and rejection, the great heroes and martyrs of the mind are drawn. In this brotherhood of outcasts Byron too has found a place, and hence may proudly vindicate their honour:

>                   honoured sleeps
> The immortal exile;—Arqua, too, her store
> Of tuneful relics proudly claims and keeps,
> While Florence vainly begs her banish'd dead and weeps.
>
> (lix)

At this point it is as though Byron becomes aware of the readers' expectations, naturally directed to the great art treasures of Florence and their meaning for the explorer. His nonchalant dismissal of the art galleries reminds us again that this is a private and personal performance rather than a public one: Florence may hold more marvels for the human eye, but not for his:

> For I have been accustom'd to entwine
> My thoughts with Nature rather in the fields,
> Than Art in galleries; though a work divine
> Calls for my spirit's homage . . .

and southwards he roams by the lake of Thrasimene, seeking as always his particular food for meditation. What he finds in nature is once more a battlefield, from which the vision of gore and carnage rises with bitter obsessive violence, and developing in his usual manner into a superimposed image of past and present, with nature healing the scars and the guilt of the past.

Nature's healing and regenerating power is felt everywhere in this enchanted land. Thus, passing by the river Clitymnus Byron pays tribute to its Genius:

> If on the heart the freshness of the scene
> Sprinkle its coolness, and from the dry dust
> Of weary life a moment lave it clean
> With Nature's baptism,—'tis to him ye must
> Pay orisons for this suspension of disgust.
>
>                                        (lxviii)

Here the idea of rebirth through the baptism of Nature, which has been half-consciously felt and formulated earlier in the poem, is clearly stated, and although the symbolic or ritualistic meaning of this baptism is not profound and complex as in Wordsworth, it implies nevertheless a cultic attitude. In moments like this Byron derives from nature a feeling more active than a mere 'suspension of disgust'. Nature at such times releases his mind for creative action, enables him to live a 'being more intense' in his poetic metamorphosis of elemental forces:

> The roar of waters!—from the headlong height
> Velino cleaves the wave-worn precipice;
> The fall of waters! rapid as the light
> The flashing mass foams shaking the abyss;
> The hell of waters! where they howl and hiss,
> And boil in endless torture; while the sweat
> Of their great agony, wrung out from this
> Their Phlegethon, curls round the rocks of jet
> That guard the gulf around, in pitiless horror set,

And mounts in spray the skies, and thence again
Returns in an unceasing shower, which round,
With its unemptied cloud of gentle rain,
Is an eternal April to the ground,
Making it all one emerald:—how profound
The gulf! and how the giant element
From rock to rock leaps with delirious bound,
Crushing the cliffs, which, downward worn and rent
With his fierce footsteps, yield in chasms a fearful vent!

(lxix-lxx)

Byron's myth-making power is here seen at its best, and it is
equal to the best Romantic manner. With an almost Miltonic
force Byron turns the Velino into a myth of the Fall and of Hell
torment, but also, with his characteristic sense of contrast, he
evolves a paradox of regeneration from this Hell, in the image
of the 'eternal April'. The image has an obviously personal reference, but it also contains the balancing movements of the
archetypal pattern of rebirth as defined by Maud Bodkin. In
mood and imagery, it is also related to the thunderstorm in the
Alps, and the 'fierce and far delight' of the elements in which
Byron shared with such exuberance. In both scenes the idea of
birth or regeneration is inherent in the play of the elements.
Hence the Hell-scene depicted here is not merely a place of
suffering, but rather a metaphorical attempt to connect the
destructive and creative forces in his own mind and in nature.

As Byron follows the river, the myth of rebirth develops into
a more distinct pattern:

To the broad column which rolls on, and shows
More like the fountain of an infant sea
Torn from the womb of mountains by the throes
Of a new world, than only thus to be
Parent of rivers, which flow gushingly,
With many windings, through the vale:—Look back!
Lo! where it comes like an eternity,
As if to sweep down all things in its track,
Charming the eye with dread,—a matchless cataract,

Horribly beautiful! but on the verge,
From side to side, beneath the glittering morn,
An Iris sits, amidst the infernal surge,
Like Hope upon a death-bed, and, unworn

Its steady dyes, while all around is torn
By the distracted waters, bears serene
Its brilliant hues with all their beams unshorn:
Resembling, 'mid the torture of the scene,
Love watching Madness with unalterable mien.

(lxxi-lxxii)

Thus, in something like a Coleridgian synthesis, the extremes
meet: life and death, growth and destruction, horror and loveliness, and hope on the verge of madness, concentrated in a
landscape that combines the abstract logic of allegory with the
palpable reality of symbol and myth. The scene of the Velino
waterfall has been transformed into an emblem of the poet's
inner life, and of life in general, with the redeeming core of
beauty—the still centre of Love—which survives torment and
distraction.

Byron does not announce a definite itinerary or goal for his
Italian journey, but it is inevitable that, in his pursuit of Fate
and meditation, he should end in Rome, the city which had become the symbol of the rise and fall of human glory. Gibbon had
written his great history on this theme, and among the earlier
Romantic writers Chateaubriand had struck the sombre key
which persisted *ad nauseam* throughout the nineteenth century.
Byron's attack on the great subject came relatively late, but by
then he was well prepared for it, both in life and reading, and
his whole imaginative journey through Italy leads up to this
historical and geographical climax. From the moment he surveys
Rome, he turns its destiny to personal use:

Oh Rome! my country! city of the soul!
The orphans of the heart must turn to thee,
Lone mother of dead empires! and control
In their shut breasts their petty misery.
What are our woes and sufferance? Come and see
The cypress, hear the owl, and plod your way
O'er steps of broken thrones and temples, Ye!
Whose agonies are evils of a day—
A world is at our feet as fragile as our clay.

(lxxviii)

The exile appears to seek stoical fortitude in the city whose great
and tragic destiny may help him to gain just proportions and
reconcile him to his own Fate. Yet what Byron finds in Rome is

not so much a sense of proportion with which to control his 'petty misery', as a medium through which he may experience life—and his own manifold ego—more intensely and fully. Rome, like the Alps, and the Velino, is a place for immersion and absorption into the greater life, and the 'being more intense' of creation. It is also, as Escarpit aptly puts it, a place where he may meditate in order to observe better, and in order better to observe himself meditate and observe.[15]

Byron's exploration of Rome begins with a passionate lament on her ruined greatness, and his treatment here is similar to his laments on contemporary Greece. The names of history and literature are exploited for their emotional value, and as usual, Byron makes no effort to avoid stock responses:

> Alas! the lofty city! and alas!
> The trebly hundred triumphs! and the day
> When Brutus made the dagger's edge surpass
> The conqueror's sword in bearing fame away!
> Alas, for Tully's voice, and Virgil's lay,
> And Livy's pictured page!—but these shall be
> Her resurrection; all beside—decay.
> Alas, for Earth, for never shall we see
> That brightness in her eye she bore when Rome was free!
>
> (lxxxii)

Standing now in this 'Chaos of ruins', this desert which is Rome, Byron ignores for the moment the slavery which followed in the wake of the hundred triumphs. His concern—as in fallen Greece —is with 'well-recorded worth', and its resurrection through art and through the poet-redeemer. Yet he is constantly reminded of that fatal aspect in the greatness of Rome which finally destroyed her—'the wrath of thy own wrongs', the crimes of power and ambition. Rome had its Sylla, and England its Cromwell, beneath whose fate 'the moral lurks of destiny'—:

> And show'd not Fortune thus how fame and sway,
> And all we deem delightful, and consume
> Our souls to compass through each arduous way,
> Are in her eyes less happy than the tomb?
> Were they but so in man's, how different were his doom!
>
> (lxxxvi)

Thus, sooner or later, emperors and victors came face to face with 'great Nemesis', and for all their glory they now look, to the poet, like 'puppets of a scene', such was the vanity of their struggle. Yet they were greater men than any the world has reared since, except one—and he too 'vanquish'd by himself, to his own slaves a slave'. This 'fool of false ambition', Napoleon, in his vanity had modelled himself on the real Cæsars, and now he too has met Nemesis. These vanities, ancient and modern, provoke gloomy meditations on tyrants and slavery and 'vile ambition', where the spirit of freedom, personified in Washington, is juxtaposed to the madness of France—for 'France got drunk with blood to vomit crime'. However, a triumphant positive assertion concludes this train of thought:

> Yet, Freedom, yet thy banner, torn, but flying,
> Streams like the thunder-storm *against* the wind;
> Thy trumpet voice, though broken now and dying,
> The loudest still the tempest leaves behind;
> Thy tree hath lost its blossoms, and the rind,
> Chopp'd by the axe, looks rough and little worth,
> But the sap lasts,—and still the seed we find,
> Sown deep, even in the bosom of the North;
> So shall a better spring less bitter fruit bring forth.
>
> (xcviii)

The metaphor of regeneration in nature, through which Byron has expressed his personal yearning throughout the poem, is beginning to recur with something like the frequency of a *leitmotif*—a rhythm in the poetic structure, despite its casual and incoherent character. The imagery and its implications suggest the impulses and aspirations of Shelley's *Ode to the West Wind*.

As Byron continues his exploration among the ruins and tombs, he finds the mausoleum of Metella – 'the wealthiest Roman's wife'. His paradoxical vision of Metella as one of 'Heaven's favourites' doomed to early death, seen against sunset splendour, contains features of the characteristic Byronic self-portrait, but as his contemplation of the 'ponderous tomb' expands in the following stanzas, it is the pathetic irony of the situation which fascinates him—the fact that we know nothing definite about the inmate of this sumptuous monument. The poet is reminded of the vanity of human wishes, but also of the challenge to salvage an imperishable form from these floating wrecks of the past:

> And from the planks, far shatter'd o'er the rocks,
> Built me a little bark of hope, once more
> To battle with the ocean and the shocks
> Of the loud breakers, and the ceaseless roar
> Which rushes on the solitary shore
> Where all lies founder'd that was ever dear:
> But could I gather from the wave-worn store
> Enough for my rude boat, where should I steer?
> There woos no home, nor hope, nor life, save what is here.
>
> (cv)

The *vanitas* of history intensifies his own sense of futile being, and thus the outer and inner landscapes coincide. Yet, significantly, it is not the ruined city but the ocean which, here as in the opening lines of Canto III, provides the metaphor for his own destiny. Exile and trackless ocean, and no ultimate goal for the journey of his mind! He knew well by now the misery and the splendour of his quest, and its inevitable outcome. His exile, it is increasingly evident, is not from England but from the world in general, and from his own past. There is very little nostalgia in Byron's poetry, and none at all in *Childe Harold's Pilgrimage*, though this may be partly due to his ostentatious pride. As an exile, a stranger and pilgrim, Byron is an Aeneas rather than a Ulysses, and amid the multiple splendour which he still finds in the world, he is obsessed by the lack of meaningful order: There is no goal in history, and none for the individual. In nature—in the Alps and by the Velino waterfall—Byron occasionally was able to forget this burden of *nihil*, but amid the ruins of Rome he cannot escape it. Yet in such moments of despair there still remains the panacea of sheer vitality and defiance:

> Then let the winds howl on! their harmony
> Shall henceforth be my music, and the night
> The sound shall temper with the owlets' cry . . .
>
> (cvi)

For all his disillusionment, Byron's stanzas on imperial Rome contain some of his best descriptive passages in the poem, and also some of his most typical moralistic use of scenery. Here, as a fair example, is the Mount Palatine:

Cypress and ivy, weed and wallflower grown,
Matted and mass'd together, hillocks heap'd
On what were chambers, arch crush'd, column strown
In fragments, choked up vaults, and frescos steep'd
In subterranean damps, where the owl peep'd,
Deeming it midnight:—Temples, baths, or halls?
Pronounce who can; for all that Learning reap'd
From her research hath been, that these are walls—
Behold the Imperial Mount! 'tis thus the mighty falls.

There is the moral of all human tales;
'Tis but the same rehearsal of the past,
First Freedom, and then Glory—when that fails,
Wealth, vice, corruption,—barbarism at last.
And History, with all her volumes vast,
Hath but *one* page,—'tis better written here
Where gorgeous Tyranny hath thus amass'd
All treasures, all delights, that eye or ear,
Heart, soul, could seek, tongue ask—
Away with words! draw near,

Admire, exult, despise, laugh, weep,—for here
There is such matter for all feeling:—Man!
Thou pendulum betwixt a smile and tear,
Ages and realms are crowded in this span,
This mountain, whose obliterated plan
The pyramid of empires pinnacled,
Of Glory's gewgaws shining in the van
Till the sun's rays with added flame were fill'd!
Where are its golden roofs? where those who dared to build?
(cvii-cix)

Crying in the wilderness of history, Byron has often asked this
unavailing question, and will ask it again, particularly of Greece.
However, though he knows the answer, he knows also that the
question will serve his poetic purpose.

The Palatine is indeed the best text and pretext for a sermon
on the vanity of history. Yet amid the metamorphosis of forms
and fates through which the memorials of emperors decay into
nameless fragments, there still persists the name of Trajan, who
'serenely wore / His sovereign virtue'. And down below, the
ruined Forum,

where the immortal accents glow,
And still the eloquent air breathes—burns with Cicero!
(cxii)

Here again Byron has a unique opportunity of staging a grand pageant of the past, or a drama on the theme of *hubris* and Nemesis, and once more, as when he dismissed the art galleries in Florence, he turns his back on it and leaves the fallen great buried in dust and oblivion. Instead he turns to the statue and fountain of Egeria, and his choice of enduring art for the vestiges of power leads him, away from the debris and the *memento mori* of the Palatine and the Forum, to something calm and solid and refreshing—like nature:

> The mosses of thy fountain still are sprinkled
> With thine Elysian water-drops; the face
> Of thy cave-guarded spring with years unwrinkled,
> Reflects the meek-eyed genius of the place,
> Whose green, wild margin now no more erase
> Art's works; nor must the delicate waters sleep,
> Prison'd in marble—bubbling from the base
> Of the cleft statue, with a gentle leap
> The rill runs o'er—and round—fern, flowers, and ivy
>                                       creep,
> Fantastically tangled: the green hills
> Are clothed with early blossoms, through the grass
> The quick-eyed lizard rustles, and the bills
> Of summer-birds sing welcome as ye pass;
> Flowers fresh in hue, and many in their class,
> Implore the pausing step, and with their dyes,
> Dance in the soft breeze in a fairy mass;
> The sweetness of the violet's deep blue eyes,
> Kiss'd by the breath of heaven seems colour'd by its skies.
>                                       (cxvi-cxvii)

This kind of pastoral prettiness does not show Byron at his best, but the stanzas provide something more than a quiet interlude before his emotional drama is enacted again among the ruins. The fountain group of Egeria grows into a myth of that holy and perfect love which we mortals believe to exist, while it is forever denied us. Egeria is the embodiment of our aspiration to a love which endures in its incorruptible purity, and she reminds the poet, by contrast, of that 'dull satiety which all destroys'—the 'venom' of which was known to the youthful pilgrim already in Canto I. In the meantime, his course of life had taken Byron from cynical and light-hearted anticipation of the 'dull satiety' to the actual destruction it had wrought in his mature years.

This theme of destruction, which he evolves in the following stanzas, sustains the flower imagery from the fountain group and turns it into a metaphor of emotional corruption. It is the metaphorical process of the Elizabethans, and of the cankered rose of Shakespeare's sonnets, here sprouting 'weeds of dark luxuriance ... Rank at the core'. (cxx) Interwoven with the pattern of poisoned flowers is the habitual Byronic metaphor of the waste and the desert, not, this time, as a refuge or 'dwelling place', but as a place where the 'unquench'd soul' is 'parch'd, wearied, wrung, and riven.' (cxxi) Thus Byron exploits the image of Egeria's fountain as a starting point for an unexpected twofold metaphorical development.

As usual when Byron grapples with the enigma of emotional corruption, he is brought back to the central enigma of fate. This time his discovery, which he owes to the Egeria fountain, turns out to be one of the great commonplaces of frustrated idealism. Love—perfect Love, whom he personifies into a myth and invokes so fervently in stanza cxxi, is merely a child of the mind's 'desiring phantasy', it has no objective reality. Byron draws two important and bitter conclusions from this: On the one hand: 'Of its own beauty is the mind diseased / And fevers into false creation' (cxxii). The tragedy of mind and imagination is that its very zest for beauty and ideal love leads through disillusionment to despair. And hence, also, the works of art born of this zest are—or may be—false creations, untrue and deceptive, and like Egeria's fountain they are mirages of the 'unreach'd Paradise of our despair'. In this moment of nihilistic pessimism, Byron rejects even the consolation and validity of art, which normally is his best refuge.

The other important conclusion is that Love in this aspect of 'ideal shape' is the essence of Fate, and of Nemesis:

> Who loves, raves—'tis youth's frenzy—but the cure
> Is bitterer still, as charm by charm unwinds
> Which robed our idols, and we see too sure
> Nor worth nor beauty dwells from out the mind's
> Ideal shape of such; yet still it binds
> The fatal spell, and still it draws us on,
> Reaping the whirlwind from the oft-sown winds;
> The stubborn heart, its alchemy begun,
> Seems ever near the prize—wealthiest when most undone.

We wither from our youth, we gasp away—
Sick—sick; unfound the boon, unslaked the thirst,
Though to the last, in verge of our decay,
Some phantom lures, such as we sought at first—
But all too late, — so are we doubly curst.
Love, fame, ambition, avarice — 'tis the same,
Each idle, and all ill, and none the worst—
For all are meteors with a different name,
And Death the sable smoke where vanishes the flame.

(cxxiii-cxxiv)

It is in moments like these that one feels most strongly how Byron tries to come to terms with himself by setting up a universal thesis of human life which fits the facts of his own life, or rather, some of its facts. Since we cannot know Byron's life without knowing his poetry, nor know the poetry without knowing his life, this passage reveals Byron in the paradoxical situation which we indicated at the beginning, trying at the same time to escape from himself, and to accept himself under the universal law of fate. The passage also reveals Byron in the self-conscious role of the tragic hero, and it reads like a monologue on the quandary of the great tormented souls of Shakespeare's romantic heroes.

In the following stanzas Byron anticipates something like the basic ingredients of Thomas Hardy's pessimism, particularly the idea of 'Circumstance' as a 'miscreator' which 'makes and helps along / Our coming evils'; and further, the feeling that 'Our life is a false nature: 'tis not in / The harmony of things'. To this Byron adds a touch of Calvinist predestination in the idea of the 'hard decree' of Fate as an 'uneradicable taint of sin'. And the metaphor of vegetable corruption is developed into a cosmic perspective in the image of Fate as the 'boundless upas, this all-blasting tree' (cxxvi).

It is interesting to note that Byron's sombre apocalypse of Fate, cried out in such violent language, took its rise in the calm beauty and delight he discovered in the Egeria fountain. Nothing he has seen so far in Rome—neither the Palatine nor the Forum —has led him so directly to what he conceives to be the bitter truth of his own fate. The discovery, however, has been prepared for a long time, indeed since the beginning of Canto III, and it emerges on that rhythmic wave of emotion we have noticed pre-viously, a kind of obsessive cyclic return in Byron's mind to the wounds that never heal. These moments of rage and despair achieve, however, some degree of catharsis, so that the poet is left free to shift the interest from himself to the world around him and its palpable glories. Thus the rhythm of his mind never fails to bring him back to sheer enjoyment:

> Arches on arches! as it were that Rome,
> Collecting the chief trophies of her line,
> Would build up all her triumphs in one dome,
> Her Coliseum stands; the moonbeams shine
> As 'twere its natural torches, for divine
> Should be the light which streams here to illumine
> This long-explored but still exhaustless mine
> Of contemplation; and the azure gloom
> Of an Italian night, where the deep skies assume
>
> Hues which have words, and speak to ye of heaven,
> Floats o'er this vast and wondrous monument,
> And shadows forth its glory ...
>
> (cxxviii-cxxix)

There is implicit in this vision a paradox, which Byron is shortly to give a personal application. The Coliseum is a ruin, and yet it towers like an epitome—a sum total—of all the triumphal arches of Rome. Byron's descriptive technique, deliberately or unconsciously, sustains this paradox in the peculiar (or just careless?) notion that the *glory* of the Coliseum is *shadowed* forth. The glory and the triumph do not reside in its architectural greatness alone, nor in its historical associations, but more so in the beauty and spiritual appeal which Time has lent to it. Paradoxically too, Byron shifts from his habitual idea of Time as destroyer—Shakespeare's 'devouring time'—to a vision of Time as 'beautifier of the dead / Adorner of the ruin', of Time as a 'corrector' of judgement, the 'test of truth, love—sole philosopher'. And he concludes this somewhat unusual apostrophe to Time, 'the avenger', with a prayer:

> Amidst this wreck, where thou hast made a shrine
> And temple more divinely desolate,
> Among thy mightier offerings here are mine.
> Ruins of years, though few, yet full of fate:
> If thou hast ever seen me too elate,

Hear me not; but if calmly I have borne
Good, and reserved my pride against the hate
Which shall not whelm me, let me not have worn
This iron in my soul in vain—shall *they* not mourn?

(cxxxi)

Byron through a process of metaphorical correspondence and transfer turns the Coliseum into an image of himself, and at the same time into a shrine for cultic submission to Fate. This is a simple and acceptable mode of emotional sublimation and catharsis, but it is only half the story, for as the stanza evolves the prayer implies also a compensation for courageous endurance of wrong, and it obliquely hints to those forces of hatred and fate not provoked by himself. There is a half-spoken wish that these too might come under the power of Time, the corrector and avenger. In this emotional context, and with the ancient Coliseum before him, Byron invokes the goddess of retribution, Nemesis, to rectify the wrong he has suffered, and yet, in a characteristic aside, with his usual frankness he recognises the part which he himself, with his inherited flaws of character, has played in his ruin. But for these, he feels, he shall atone; and as for the wrong inflicted by others, he demands justice of Nemesis, but a special kind of justice. Byron here (cxxxiii), in the blood-stained setting of the Coliseum, performs a ritual of sacrifice and atonement, offering his blood, his pain, up to Nemesis in order to have vengeance. There is a moment when the 'modern Timon' towers in majestic fury:

Not in the air shall these my words disperse,
Though I be ashes; a far hour shall wreak
The deep prophetic fulness of this verse,
And pile on human heads the mountain of my curse!

(cxxxiv)

Then he springs the characteristic Byronic surprise, and the paradox underlying the whole meditation on the Coliseum emerges more clearly:

That curse shall be Forgiveness ...

We are caught in one of those moments when it is hard to determine whether Byron is performing in a grand drama of emotional

concealment or whether he genuinely feels that he has much to
forgive and is capable of forgiving. He goes on insisting, in lines
that move dangerously near to self-pity, on the wrongs he has
suffered and which still sear his brain, but his splendid pride
saves him once more and carries him on a wave of rhetorical
grandeur to this conclusion:

> But I have lived, and have not lived in vain:
> My mind may lose its force, my blood its fire
> And my frame perish even in conquering pain;
> But there is that within me which shall tire
> Torture and Time, and breathe when I expire;
> Something unearthly, which they deem not of,
> Like the remember'd tone of a mute lyre,
> Shall on their soften'd spirits sink, and move
> In hearts all rocky now the late remorse of love.
>
> (cxxxvii)

This is as close as Byron ever comes to victory—over Time, Fate,
humanity and himself. Needless to say, the great stanza does not
represent more than a temporary catharsis, yet it concentrates
and releases the basic impulses of the poem, it demonstrates, in
fact, why the two final cantos were written, and what, in exile
from society and from himself, Byron tried to find and did find.
He has endeavoured to make his poetry a world of permanence
to which he belongs, and made it out of the stuff of his journeys.
In that sense the pilgrim's quest has not been altogether vain.

If one expected the poem to reach some kind of conclusion,
some goal for the pilgrim's quest, it should have ended here. Not
that the remaining stanzas could be easily spared, though there
is undoubtedly an anti-climax before the poem intones the powerful invocation to the sea. But undoubtedly also those stanzas
cancel out the magnanimous attitude to which Byron has given
voice here, and also his arrival in his realm of art. On his own
claim, the Coliseum has helped him to objectify and define the
meaning of his own fate, and now 'The seal is set'. Thus he has
come to terms with Fate and Nemesis—this 'dread power' which
dwells in the ruin. Yet what Byron discovers when he again
turns to a contemplation of the ruin is no longer its beauty
and peace, no longer the 'shrine', but the turmoil and violence
of the past, where men were slaughtered in this 'bloody Circus'
for 'imperial pleasure', or 'Butcher'd to make a Roman holiday'.

The victim, the gladiator expiring in the arena, calls up associations of exile and public cruelty, and provokes sympathetic fury, which in turn yield to the actual scene so quiet that 'My voice sounds much'—. Here, as in Byron's treatment of the Alpine scenery and the Velino waterfall, we find an unconscious and persistent desire in the poet to rule over or command, as if by magic, space and time, the process of nature as well as that of history. Byron's method is not so obviously the original or primitive one of naming things, which we find in a sophisticated modern form in James Joyce.[16] But like Joyce's poetic magic that of Byron springs from a sense of alienation and exile, and a desire for unity and permanence of being. Thus, amid the turbulence of nature and history Byron asserts the pre-eminence of his own actual being, in whose living awareness these fleeting aspects are understood, and recreated within the new order of the poet's mind. 'My voice sounds much' is also a statement of triumph: better to be alive, though battered by Fate and doomed to exile, than to share in the heroic and bloody past of this ruin.

There is in Rome another building, more perfect than the Coliseum, where the glory of enduring art is fused with other cultic meanings:

> Simple, erect, severe, austere, sublime—
> Shrine of all saints and temple of all gods,
> From Jove to Jesus—spared and blest by time;
> Looking tranquillity, while falls or nods
> Arch, empire, each thing round thee, and man plods
> His way through thorns to ashes—glorious dome!
> Shalt thou not last? Time's scythe and tyrants' rods
> Shiver upon thee—sanctuary and home
> Of art and piety—Pantheon!—Pride of Rome!
>
> Relic of nobler days, and noblest arts!
> Despoil'd yet perfect, with thy circle spreads
> A holiness appealing to all hearts—
> To art a model; and to him who treads
> Rome for the sake of ages, Glory sheds
> Her light through thy sole aperture; to those
> Who worship, here are altars for their beads;
> And they who feel for genius may repose
> Their eyes on honour'd forms, whose busts around them close.
>
> (cxlvi-cxlvii)

This is one of the rare examples in Byron of a work of art used as an effective symbol of synthesis, and the starting-point for this synthesis is the name of the building. The dome of the Pantheon in its serene permanence does not 'disdain all that man is', like the dome in Yeats's Byzantium; rather it serves man in all his various cultic needs. Again we notice in these stanzas, as in those on Greece (Canto I) the heavy emphasis on traditional terms of worship and piety, and yet the aspect of art and its permanence is sufficiently pervasive to remind us that the eternity Byron seeks, or the 'unreach'd Paradise' of his despair, is an enduring artifact—something that shall 'tire Torture and Time'.

Byron's exploration of Rome is conducted in his usual desultory fashion, and although he is naturally drawn to the great monuments, he is not subject to the hurried tourist's necessity of seeing the 'right places'. Thus, on his way from the Pantheon to the Church of Saint Peter's he pauses—too long—to touch off some indifferent stanzas on the legend of the Roman daughter who saved an old man from starvation (on the site of the St. Nicholas *in carcere*), and he devotes a mocking stanza to the 'mole which Hadrian rear'd on high'. Unintentionally, perhaps, this interlude provides welcome relaxation before the next strenuous climax:

> But lo! the dome—the vast and wondrous dome,
> To which Diana's marvel was a cell—
> Christ's mighty shrine above his martyr's tomb!
> I have beheld the Ephesian's miracle;—
> Its columns strew the wilderness, and dwell
> The hyæna and the jackal in their shade;
> I have beheld Sophia's bright roofs swell
> Their glittering mass i' the sun, and have survey'd
> Its sanctuary the while the usurping Moslem pray'd;
>
> But thou, of temples old, or altars new,
> Standest alone, with nothing like to thee—
> Worthiest of God, the holy and the true.
> Since Zion's desolation, when that He
> Forsook his former city, what could be,
> Of earthly structures, in his honour piled,
> Of a sublimer aspect? Majesty,
> Power, Glory, Strength, and Beauty all are aisled
> In this eternal ark of worship undefiled.
>
> (cliii-cliv)

It is difficult to determine the exact tone in these stanzas. There is something almost baroque in the verbal effort to achieve a magnificence adequate for the building, yet amid the towering epithets the description falls back, on the one hand, on a comparison too studded with irrelevant detail to be effective, and on the other on simple religious associations. These suggest a pious veneration not to be found elsewhere in Byron's work, and yet, though he seems genuinely moved and tries to interpret the sacred meaning of the cathedral, he fails to turn it into a great personal vision. As he enters the building, however, he achieves a clearer perception of its meaning:

> Enter: its grandeur overwhelms thee not;
> And why? It is not lessen'd; but thy mind,
> Expanded by the genius of the spot,
> Has grown colossal, and can only find
> A fit abode wherein appear enshrined
> Thy hopes of immortality; and thou
> Shalt one day, if found worthy, so defined,
> See thy God face to face, as thou dost now
> His Holy of Holies, nor be blasted by his brow.
>
> (clv)

In this incomparable cathedral Byron is moved not only to piety but to preaching, and now that we have travelled so far with this unpredictable guide, it seems futile to ask whether he really believes in his own promise of immortality and God. The only thing we may say with certainty is that in this moment Byron is more unambiguously devout than anywhere else in his work. His 'turn of mind', as he himself confesses in a letter of 1822, was so 'given to taking things in the absurd point of view', that he could not for long sustain a serious or consistent attitude to religion, any more than to morals and metaphysics, or to people. Yet, again on his own assertion, there were moments when he really believed that he was a good Christian.[17] More frequent, perhaps, were the moments when he believed in the immortality of the soul, and that the 'Mind is eternal', although life after death might not be individual existence.

From St. Peter's Byron in the usual tourist manner moves on to visit the Vatican museum, where the struggle of Laocoön is poured into a stanza of characteristic verbal intensity. There is also the Apollo Belvedere,

> With an immortal's vengeance; in his eye
> And nostrils beautiful disdain, and might
> And majesty . . .
>
> (clxi)

Clearly, the poetic zest in the exploration is abating, and we are nearing journey's end. Clearly also, the difficulties of concluding the poem are crowding in upon the poet. He dismisses finally the 'Pilgrim' of his song, who, he observes with a wry smile, 'fades away into Destruction's mass' (clxiv). Yet, he claims somewhat unexpectedly, 'My Pilgrim's shrine is won' (clxxv). Is this simply a phrase to put an epic full stop to the journey in terms of its religious metaphor, or if not, what is this shrine? Is it Rome, Italy, or the sum total of his poetic peregrination? Is it the poem itself and its concomitant sense of achievement? Or is it the temporary truce he has made with Fate—this Promethean and paradoxical submission of the incurable rebel? Or is it, finally, his feeling at this moment of having come through his turbulent life and emotional exhaustion with an indomitable zest for life, so that, for all the ruins of his past, his sufferings

> Have left us nearly where we had begun . . .

The reward, at any rate as he sees it now, looking out upon the 'blue Symplegades', is

> That we can yet feel gladden'd by the sun,
> And reap from earth, sea, joy almost as dear
> As if there were no man to trouble what is clear.
>
> (clxxvi)

Here we are moving towards the real conclusion of the pilgrimage, a complete isolation from man or mankind through nature. The poet who saw nothing to loathe in Nature and who found in the Alps and the ocean a kindred being and an ally, in fact a configuration of his own temperament, now proceeds to eliminate man even more completely than he did towards the end of Canto III. The modern Timon, unlike Shakespeare's hero, invokes the Ocean in a final ritual act of destruction and revenge.

This ritual act is introduced through solemn incantational phrasing evoking what we may now call the structural images of the poem in its exilic aspects:

There is a pleasure in the pathless woods
There is a rapture on the lonely shore,
There is society, where none intrudes,
By the deep Sea, and music in its roar:
I love not Man the less, but Nature more,
From these our interviews, in which I steal
From all I may be, or have been before,
To mingle with the Universe, and feel
What I can ne'er express, yet cannot all conceal.
(clxxviii)

In the context of the poem, there is a sardonic humour in his claim that he does not love Man less, but Nature more, through his withdrawal from mankind into Nature. His love of Man is not energetic, as the following stanzas also testify, but they reveal the other side of the picture too: Byron's need to lose his 'wretched identity' and, as a 'being more intense', to identify his mental and poetic energies with those of the cosmos, in possession of absolute freedom and power.

The ritual reunion with the Ocean implies both an act of revenge and an act of purgation, it is a sacrifice and a baptism. Usually, like Cain perhaps, the poet finds no absolute divinity for his offerings, and, worse still, no god like that of Israel to perform his revenge. But now in the image of the Ocean he evolves a cultic symbol which meets his immediate needs, and serves him well in his poetic myth. It is not a very complex apotheosis, but it concentrates the exilic impulses of Byron's proud and wounded temperament, and in its elemental power lends itself well to his violent form of worship. As a cultic symbol, the Ocean might yield to a closer analysis most of the usual divine attributes, such as omnipotence and indestructability, a force 'boundless, endless and sublime', with power to create and destroy, to inflict fit retribution, but also to liberate. True, Byron appears to temper these implicit attributes by stating that the Ocean is 'a glorious mirror' for the 'Almighty's form', and an 'image of eternity', yet the function of these phrases is not to reduce but to heighten the power and the glory of the Ocean.

In these frequently anthologised stanzas (clxxix-clxxxiii), the ritual extermination of mankind, the magic act of revenge, precedes the act of personal salvation—i.e. his reunion with the cultic symbol. This reunion is a kind of baptism—in the literal and metaphorical sense, in that the poet immerses himself in the sea. Indeed, the stanzas on the Ocean appear to work out the archetypal pattern of rebirth, and as such epitomise the fundamental impulses of the two final cantos. Thus, when we look back to the moment of departure from England, when the poet felt like a 'weed' flung on the Ocean, which was yet like a familiar 'steed' to him, carrying him to freedom, the final stanza here in its imagery and situation brings these aspects of the poem full circle:

> And I have loved thee, Ocean! and my joy
> Of youthful sports was on thy breast to be
> Borne, like thy bubbles, onward: from a boy
> I wanton'd with thy breakers—they to me
> Were a delight; and if the freshening sea
> Made them a terror—'twas a pleasing fear,
> For I was as it were a child of thee,
> And trusted to thy billows far and near,
> And laid my hand upon thy mane—as I do here.

In short, the Ocean is for Byron both means and end, the path and the goal of his pilgrimage. It is doubtful whether he ever arrived at anything more satisfactory or personally true.

### Pilgrim and Performer

With unabated zest and ingenuity, critics anatomise Byron's Promethean personality, and it would seem that the main difference between our reaction to Byron and that of his contemporary readers is that while to them he was a man of many masks, and therefore repellent and rejected, he is now gradually being accepted in all his inconsistent appearances. We understand him better, and can therefore more easily forgive. But even though his private life has ceased to shock, the many roles he plays in his poetry remain the chief obstacle whenever we try to make him 'sincere' or consistent. Mauriac, Peter Quennell and Paul West have most successfully, perhaps, explained the contradictory qualities in his personality, and the grounds on which we should try to judge his much debated sincerity. There remains a vestigial tendency to see in Byron two main *personae*— his private and his public selves. Yet it has been argued by John Wain that Byron had no identity, no real self, and his search for identity ended in failure. Hence he assumed the two different characters, the romantic and the satirical, in which he wrote his poetry.[18] Leslie Marchand makes much the same distinction between what he calls Byron's real and public selves, and finds these predominant in *Don Juan* and *Childe Harold* respectively.[19] Paul West differentiates even further and claims for Byron 'three main selves': 'First ... the exoticist of the romances; second the polemical author on literary and social themes; and third the intrusive, self-conscious creator. We have a projection, a poet in person, and a very personal impresario.'[20]

These views have their obvious bearing on *Childe Harold's Pilgrimage*, and the poem has been used as evidence for some of their main points. As the most personal record of Byron's search for identity it testifies to his failure. Indeed, the most 'personal' passages are often the ones in which the attitude, tone and intention are most difficult to determine. The degree to which concealment and his myth of the implacable fate had become second nature is perhaps the most striking symptom of Byron's exile, an exile not from England but from mankind and himself.

It is not possible, of course, to justify even on purely aesthetic grounds the all too conscious performer of *Childe Harold's Pilgrimage*. Even where he does not manipulate landscape for the sake of demonstration, and even where he does not display it grandly to our admiring eyes, Byron never for a moment allows us to forget his vociferous, unpredictable presence. He is the 'intrusive, self-conscious creator' that Paul West notes. And he is the 'fine thing' in the spectacle of 'the worldly, theatrical, and pantomimical' that already Keats knew. The wonder remains, however, that he could write the poem in this manner and yet sustain its interest over such magnificent stretches. It is this sustainment in the poem which makes it—not, needless to say, a 'rhymed Baedecker' as one critic thinks,—but an enduring artifact.

Byron's poetic journey is the record of a human isolation that in the end seems complete. Having chosen exile, he makes his poetic world a 'populous solitude', and the only person he addresses in the two final cantos is his half-sister, in the Drachenfels stanzas. The actual human element is never predominant anywhere in the poem, for the simple reason that there is no room, in the long run, for anybody but the poet himself. But still the first two cantos include situations with people, ranging from the bullfight in Spain to the court of Ali Pacha, and the homage to the Suliotes. In the final two cantos, except for a brief passing mention, there are no living people, only historical figures resurrected for special purposes. Byron is here moving in a world of much human interest, but one completely emptied of living individuals. If we judge by the many passages in which the poet hurls his hatred and scorn at mankind, and in particular if we judge by his ritual magic in the final stanzas, where he literally drowns mankind and its history in the Ocean, we might say that he was driven to this isolation mainly by his exilic impulses. But the real cause was rather the process which Paul West analyses so brilliantly in comparing Baudelaire and Byron:

> Oneself—that was a thing, like other things; and other things were mere pretexts for self-scrutiny. This possessive solitude he [Baudelaire] shares with Byron. Both found themselves rejected; both chose solitude purposely so that it should not be inflicted by others. Both felt unique. Both, though appearing to live, love and participate, refused themselves to others. Their pride fed on itself. Their sensibility rejected the natural in all its forms, eschewed immediacy. Their problem was to intensify awareness of themselves without the contrast of others.[21]

It was this problem which Byron tried to solve when he wrote *Childe Harold's Pilgrimage*, and as we have seen, Europe past and present offered him most of the compliant material he needed. The personal myth he evolves in this medium may not sound great depths of self-knowledge and neither does it cover a wide range of the common human lot. But as a poetic myth, born from an intense need of recreating the world in one's own image, it is unique. Moreover, it is a poem resourceful in its manifestation of the few obsessive themes which Byron chose, and within the compass of these he concentrates an amazing richness of detail sharply seen and transformed, in his best passages, into memorable poetry.

Though with Byron critics cannot be too cautious, it is tempting to suggest that *Childe Harold's Pilgrimage*, certainly in a sense that he did not intend, is essentially a religious poem, but a poem where the religious impulses have been perverted, despite a few references to the Chastener and the Almighty and even to God. It teems with cultic symbols and substitutes, as well as directly Christian allusions. Its shrine is the common

Romantic sanctuary of Nature, though Nature turned to a specific use, a Byronic Olympus where all the deities are so many configurations of himself and his emotional needs. If he had a wish to bow before the Chastener or the Almighty, it was not persistent nor profound, for in Byron's world there was hardly any more room for God than for man. But although this is so, and although, as Paul West observes, Byron was unable to reach the absolute, he often needed a divinity to meet his yearnings and his passionate and powerless antagonisms.

These cultic impulses in *Childe Harold's Pilgrimage* by no means exhaust the religious aspects of the poem. Equally important, though less obvious, is the impulse towards regeneration, purgation and spiritual fulfilment. And with these combined elements, the poem turned into something more like a pilgrimage than Byron ever consciously intended or wished. His Pilgrim was a mockery, at least at the outset, and yet, since he too became intolerable to the reclusive, self-sufficient poet, Byron took over his part and changed it. The adventure did not carry him very far from himself nor very near to a still centre of identity, for it was bound to end more or less where it began, with himself as a figure of myth and of public performance. Yet meanwhile through the vast spectacular eruption of the whole poem the lava of imagination flowed and brought release from madness and suffering, and even moments when the 'being more intense' in his creation felt close to the absolute.

IV

# *ULYSSES* AND TENNYSON'S
# SEA-QUEST

Probably more than any other Victorian poet, Tennyson has
been belaboured by modern critics for his simplicity, his lack of
synthetic grasp of complex impulses and attitudes. It is held that
while Tennyson was a poet of extremely varied moods and feelings, he preferred what I. A. Richards calls elimination to
synthesis in the individual poem, and thus his failure to achieve
the kind of inclusive richness which Donne and T. S. Eliot
achieve through ambiguity, paradox and irony, has made him
less attractive to critics whose criteria of greatness are mainly
based on these aspects. Yet Cleanth Brooks observed some years
ago that though Tennyson does not typically build his conflicting
impulses into the structure of his poetry as enriching ambiguities,
he is not always successful in avoiding the ambiguous and the
paradoxical, and in some of his poems this failure becomes a
saving grace.[1] As the present study will attempt to show, this is
also true of *Ulysses*, a poem in which Tennyson effects an imaginative reconciliation of the perplexities of *The Two Voices* and
*In Memoriam*.

It would appear that in much of his poetry Tennyson indeed
fails or never attempts to express these impulses in complex and
inclusive vision, and instead has recourse to a more perilous and
annoying method—that of projecting the impulses singly into
variations on the same theme, variations which tend to cancel
each other out in an endless see-saw game, like the juvenile pair
*Nothing Will Die* and *All Things Will Die*. Or, if the two voices
are allowed their say in a poem, as they often are, we get the
Tennysonian dialectic of simple discussion. The result in either
case may be loss of dramatic intensity or emotional depth.

There is one group of poems where this contradictory hand-

ling of theme is strongly in evidence, and which for convenience
we may call the poems of quest, or more generally, of the *homo
viator*. It is a fairly large and varied group, and the two voices
here claim either that the quest is good and necessary, or that
it is futile. In the first category the best known are *Ulysses*, *Sir
Galahad*, *The Sailor Boy*, *Merlin and the Gleam*, *Crossing the Bar ;* in
the second we find *The Sea-Fairies*, *The Lotos-Eaters*, *The Voyage*,
*The Voyage of Maeldune*, and *To Ulysses*.[2] The most successful of
the entire group, and the most personal, is the early *Ulysses*
(1833). In this poem Tennyson created a powerful private allegory of courage and dedication within the framework of the
Ulysses tradition, which serves as a vehicle, and whose limitations are respected, while the poet in his symbolic implications
transcends them. It is by relating the images and symbols to their
persistent meanings elsewhere in Tennyson's poetry that this
extension of the quest becomes obvious.

A different kind of complexity in the poetic process has been
noted by W. B. Stanford, in his admirable study of the Ulysses
tradition.[3] According to Stanford, no less than five distinct
voices are heard in the poem: that of Homer's Odysseus, Dante's
Ulisse, Shakespeare's Ulysses, Byron's Childe Harold, and Tennyson's own Grenville. Though the unity of the total effect is
recognised, the poem in this light—in the light mainly of various
adaptations of a traditional hero—tends to become a mosaic: a
deliberate exercise in the use of literary models or motifs, or at
least, it tends to find the generating principle in emotions and
attitudes of several odyssean heroes which are adopted and
changed or rejected in turn. To claim such a genesis for one of
Tennyson's most personal mature poems without considering
why these 'voices' were used, seems a perilous approach. Moreover, though Stanford makes out a good case for the presence of
the different voices, it is doubtful whether there is more than
one—that of Dante—which has played any important part in
the composition. Homer's voice, as Stanford points out, is the
least significant, since his hero was a nostalgic, social character,
in contrast to Tennyson's hero who scorns his people and longs
to sail away from home. This un-Homeric scorn is identified as
Byronic, yet one may ask whether Tennyson's Ulysses—this
believer in the moral value of knowledge and action—is not too
far removed from the fury and bitterness of Childe Harold to be
directly or powerfully influenced by him. What is more certain

is that Ulysses, as W. H. Auden also suggests, is a Romantic hero in the manner of Dante's tormented Evil Counsellor.[4]

As Stanford has shown, 'it was Dante who revolutionized the interpretation of Ulysses' final fate by presenting him as a man possessed by an irresistible desire for knowledge and experience of the unknown world.'[5] Tennyson may have been familiar with the *Inferno* at an early age, since Boyd's translation was in his father's library, and his interest in Dante was no doubt greatly stimulated by Arthur Hallam's enthusiasm.[6] It seems certain that by the time of *Ulysses* Tennyson knew Cary's translation of the *Inferno*, for the severe and majestic tone, as well as certain phrases and images in the account of Ulisse's last voyage (Canto 26), bear a resemblance to those in *Ulysses* which could hardly be accidental. This is what Dante's Ulisse, (in Cary's translation), tells Virgil:

> Nor fondness for my son, nor reverence
> Of my old father, nor return of love,
> That should have crown'd Penelope with joy,
> Could overcome in me the zeal I had
> To explore the world, and search the ways of life,
> Man's evil and his virtue. Forth I sail'd
> Into the deep illimitable main,
> With but one bark, and the small faithful band
> That yet cleaved to me.

At last, 'Tardy with age', they came to the 'strait pass' which Hercules had marked as 'the boundaries not to be o'erstepp'd by man', but still Ulisse urged his weary companions to persevere in the quest:

> 'O brothers!' I began, 'who to the west
> Through perils without number now have reach'd;
> To this the short remaining watch, that yet
> Our senses have to wake, refuse not proof
> Of the unpeopled world, following the track
> Of Phoebus. Call to mind from whence ye sprang:
> Ye were not form'd to live the lives of brutes,
> But virtue to pursue and knowledge high.'

Here indeed Tennyson found a zeal congenial to his own intellectual craving, but what was a sin to Dante becomes a virtue in Tennyson's hero. Between Dante and Tennyson there is the considerable distance of the medieval and modern worlds, separated by Renaissance zest for adventure and knowledge and the Romantic yearning for fresh experience and fuller life. And it would appear that the reason why Tennyson could translate Dante into such personal terms is to be sought, not so much in the literary adaptations and metamorphoses of the Ulysses myth, as in the vague Romantic idea of the value and importance of man's spiritual quest, which drew upon varied traditions, neo-Platonic and Christian, of the *homo viator*, the crusader and the pilgrim.

There are two poems by Tennyson where this conception of the search is exploited, *Sir Galahad* and *Ulysses*. In both the creative impulse is a need for dedication and fulfilment, but it is the more inclusive setting of the Ulysses theme rather than the Christian or Arthurian legend which provides the most congenial vehicle. The quest of Ulysses, as Dante told it and as the Romantics in various ways had amplified it, was one that strongly challenged Tennyson as a poet and as a man, and in the moment of crisis when *Ulysses* was written, just after the death of his friend Arthur Hallam in 1833, it appears to have provided for Tennyson something of a real catharsis:

> There is more about myself in 'Ulysses', which was written under the sense of loss and all that had gone by, but that still life must be fought out to the end. It was more written with the feeling of his loss upon me than many poems in 'In Memoriam'.[7]

While it is important to keep in mind the Ulysses tradition and its influence on the poem, particularly that of Dante, there can be no doubt that the most relevant context for an interpretation of the poem is Tennyson's personal situation in 1833, and his poetry of that and other periods which through theme or treatment or symbolism is linked with it. It will be necessary therefore to rehearse some of the biographical data.

Even before the death of Arthur Hallam, Tennyson had reached a point of crisis early in the year 1833, owing to the ruthless handling by the critics of his first collections of poetry.[8] Quite apart from his deep affection for Hallam, Tennyson needed his competent voice to assure him that the critics were wrong

and that his own poetic intuition should be obeyed.[9] Arthur
Hallam was Tennyson's 'artistic conscience' during those difficult months after the reviews by Christopher North and Croker.
By September he was dead, and there was scarcely anyone left
who believed, as Hallam believed, that Tennyson was the great
coming poet—the heir of Wordsworth and Keats.

In the following months Tennyson lived through a crisis in
which grief, perplexity and wounded pride released a chain
reaction of other emotional and intellectual disturbances, never
remote: his craving for truth and certainty concerning the fundamental questions of human existence; the conflict in his mind
between religious faith and doubt; and his ambivalent attitude
to death—partly a longing for absolute peace, for Nirvana,
partly a horror of death as the end of identity. From this painful
experience grew the direct confessions of *The Two Voices* and *In
Memoriam*, and it is significant that both these poems struggle
towards a catharsis of intellectual certainty and fulness of life.
So too, in a more indirect manner, does *Ulysses*, a poem, according to Tennyson, about 'the need of going forward and braving
the struggle for life.'[10] To appreciate the heroism of this determination one must accept the unique quality of his temperament
and bear in mind that the temptation of *The Two Voices*: 'Were
it not better not to be?' was real and persistent for a long time.
There is a dream recorded in *In Memoriam* (ciii) where Tennyson's desire to follow his friend into death is projected into a sea-
voyage over the 'tides', 'from deep to deep', in phrases that point
all the way to *Crossing the Bar*.[11]

The other impulse, the love of life and 'need of going forward', is, however, victorious in *The Two Voices* and *In Memoriam*,
and Tennyson's description of his elegy as 'The Way of the Soul',
like many passages in the poem (notably i, lxxxii, cxviii, and
conclusion) suggest that he early conceived of his adversity as a
spiritual pilgrimage through purgatorial grief and suffering towards fulfilment, truth and peace. Since the aspect of intellectual
certainty is so important in this pilgrimage, it gives new impetus
to the poet's craving for knowledge, his youthful passion

'To search through all I felt and saw,
The springs of life, the depths of awe,
And reach the law within the law.'

(*The Two Voices*)

And thus we find Tennyson planning with extraordinary determination his reading in the early months of 1834, in subjects ranging from theology to chemistry and electricity.[12] His intellectual curiosity provided in this moment of crisis a clue for the only kind of action—apart from that of writing poetry—which was still meaningful and worth while. This, then, is the situation, and the mood, from which *Ulysses* springs.

*Ulysses* is a dramatic monologue, and it has a unity of structure due partly to its compactness (70 lines), partly to the single point of view. Yet the structure is also remarkable for the varied rhythmic movement through which it develops: the perception expands and contracts, turns inward and reaches out to distant times and places; it changes from retrospect to anticipation, from the egocentric 'I' to the collective 'we'. This rhythm inheres in the temperamental dynamic of the hero, and emphasises his restlessness and discontent, his yearning for 'a newer world'. There are three main parts: the first presents the hero in situation and environment (lines 1-32); the second dramatises the hero's task through a contrast with that of his son (lines 33-43); and the third actualises his departure, and the purpose of his quest (lines 44-70).

Unlike Dante's hero, Ulysses has returned home after his long voyages, and, feeling disenchanted with his land and people, is impatient to put to sea once more. He finds himself in a paradoxical situation: he is 'an idle king', and unrecognised. Thus a conflict is set up already in the first lines between the hero and his environment, a conflict dramatised in the antithetical phrasing. Heroic travel and action is contrasted with a quiet, dull home-life, and the experienced and, by implication, cultured man with a coarse, lethargic people. The King's sense of alienation is expressed in these lines with a touch of egocentric arrogance and harshness. Yet from this sense of alienation and discontent rises the magnificent retrospect of the hero's past, and his craving for new adventure. In this situation Ulysses is seen to partake of various qualities and traditions. Dante's 'zeal . . . To explore the world . . .', and 'virtue to pursue and knowledge high' is linked with the Romantic zest for novel experience. Ulysses has lived a life between heroic extremes—'enjoy'd greatly' and 'suffer'd greatly'. Tennyson stresses his enthusiasm through a sustained use of appetitive terms: 'I will drink life to the lees'; 'always roaming with a hungry heart'; and 'drunk delight of battle'. If it is true, as W. H. Auden suggests, that the classical hero is a happy man, pleased with his past, while the Romantic hero '*ought* to be unhappy', then Ulysses in this respect stands in the classical tradition rather than the Romantic, though here too a balance is struck in the antithetical poise which characterises his speech.[13]

In the 'autobiographical' first part of the poem, Tennyson insists on the richness and fulness of the hero's past, and on the heroic measure of his experience, through the emphatic use of 'all': 'all times I have enjoy'd greatly ...'; 'but honour'd of them all'; 'I am a part of all that I have met ...'. Besides the ample use of antitheses, the stately phrasing equally sustains this effect, notably in lines like: 'when / Through scudding drifts the rainy Hyades / Vext the dim sea ...' and 'Far on the ringing plains of windy Troy.'

It would appear that Ulysses in his scorn of his people—'that hoard, and sleep, and feed'—is an arrogant Byronic alien in his own land, very different from Homer's *polytropos* hero. Yet what he seeks is not Romantic solitude, and not the favourite companionship of Childe Harold: mountains, ocean, desert, forest and cavern. His interests in the past were social and human, and far from being an outcast, he has enjoyed company and honour. The things he has seen and the values he has found are predominantly social and public values: 'cities of men / And manners ... councils, governments'; and while, like a true Romantic hero, he is proud of the legendary magnificence of his adventurous life, he equally asserts the value of his experience as knowledge and self-knowledge, and in this respect he is an Ancient Greek and a Victorian rather than a Romantic.[14] It is true that Wordsworth in *The Prelude* had recorded the growth of a poet's mind—a poet who also roamed with a hungry heart, though preferably alone. On the other hand, his hero in *The Excursion* saw much of 'men, their manners, their enjoyments and pursuits'. Yet the Romantic search often ended in emotional exhaustion (*Alastor*) or moral disillusionment (*Childe Harold's Pilgrimage*). Ulysses—and here Dante's conception of the old adventurer admirably fitted Tennyson's purpose—never tires of travel, but he has this in common with the Romantic wanderer that he dreads the boredom of the fixed abode, of the unchanging routine: 'How dull it is to pause, to make an end / To rust unburnish'd'.[15] What chiefly distinguishes Ulysses from the Roman-

tic *voyageur sans but* is the meaning of the journey itself: to him
it is not an aesthetic enjoyment, not the reckless chase after a
mirage, as in *The Voyage* (Tennyson's version of Baudelaire's *Le
voyage*):

> We know the merry world is round,
> And we may sail for evermore.

It is that in this way, and in this way only, can he 'shine in use'
—act himself out completely and to the best purpose. This usefulness, it is true, does not refer itself to a social or distinctly
ethical context (as it does in *The Sailor Boy*). But the ethical
implications are not remote, for Ulysses is throughout concerned
with the good life and with value. Hence his renewed condemnation of the sloth and inertia of those that hoard and sleep and
feed: 'As though to breathe were life.' Here again Tennyson's
hero speaks like Dante's Ulisse, but the phrase 'Life piled on
life / Were all too little' draws a more poignant meaning from
the context of such contemporary poems as *The Two Voices*,
where the voice of hope argues against the voice of despair:

> "Tis life whereof our nerves are scant,
> Oh life, not death, for which we pant;
> More life, and fuller, that I want.'

And the early passages of *In Memoriam* show a recurrence of the
same idea. Tennyson achieves a singular emotional intensity
here in contrasting the unabated life-zest of Ulysses with his
feeling of approaching death—'that eternal silence', and from
the tension thus created a new sense of urgency arises which
precipitates his determination to leave. On this impulse the
poem moves to the splendid climax which ends the first part:

> and vile it were
> For some three suns to store and hoard myself,
> And this gray spirit yearning in desire
> To follow knowledge like a sinking star,
> Beyond the utmost bound of human thought.

Here knowledge becomes identical with 'experience' (l. 19),
and in this connection it is relevant to note that while Tennyson
echoes Dante's doomed hero, even the image of the star (Phoe-

bus), the pivotal word 'knowledge', and the yearning for a larger view of the world and its meaning, are central themes in Tennyson's poetry. The idea of 'every hour' as a 'bringer of new things' links the yearning for knowledge with themes of advance and progress which also occur frequently in his early volumes, and which, for good or bad, coincided so well with the taste of his times.

In the second part of the poem, where Ulysses turns to speak of his son, we get a marked change in mood and situation. Stanford maintains that this passage is spoken in a Byronic mood, i.e. that Ulysses expresses an 'ironical contempt for the home-loving Telemachus' whom he finds 'intolerably complacent and priggish.'[16] It is difficult to accept this reading, for though it may be in character (cf. the initial words about 'an aged wife' and 'a savage race'), it would appear that the hero's attitude has changed somewhat from the scorn and rejection in which the poem begins. Now that he is taking leave, he is free to recognise the usefulness of his son's task, while he marks his own different vocation: 'He works his work, I mine.' The intention of the passage is exactly this—to dramatise Ulysses' dedication through a contrast with the 'sphere of common duties', and this contrast is fully achieved without irony. Moreover, Ulysses speaks of his son with genuine affection, as 'mine own' and 'well-loved of me'; and he no longer sees his people as 'savage', but as 'rugged' (which is a different matter), and capable of being educated and civilised. The 'labour' of Telemachus implies the rule of order and of law, and it would be strange indeed if Tennyson, whose besetting fear was of chaos and disorder, in this personal allegory should heap ridicule on 'the useful and the good.'[17] It is in this connection, however, that W. H. Auden's view of Ulysses appears to carry particular weight: 'And what is *Ulysses* but a covert—the weakness of the poem is its indirection—refusal to be a responsible and useful person, a glorification of the heroic dandy?'[18] This criticism would be even more relevant if, as the present study assumes, *Ulysses* among other things is Tennyson's poetic *Invitation au voyage*. But again the poem must be seen in the wider context of Tennyson's situation and that of his work, and when so considered, implies a wise though not consistently practised solution to the dilemma which Tennyson faced in *The Palace of Art* and *The Hesperides*.[19] Ulysses rejects the ties of society as barriers to his independent perception of value, but equally he rejects the temptation of the Hesperidian gardens, i.e. isolation, and the easy choice of the Lotos Eaters to 'live and lie reclined / On the hills like Gods together, careless of mankind.' Unlike the Lotos Eaters, Ulysses has not had enough of action and motion, he does not seek 'death, or dreamful ease', but 'some work of noble note.' It may not benefit his people or mankind directly, but it will bear witness to one essential aspect of life: 'To strive, to seek, to find, and not to yield.'

Tennyson was fully aware of the temptation to which the Lotos Eaters yielded, of the peaceful garden isle in the West, of the 'one fair vision' pursued by the mariners in *The Voyage*. But at the moment he was far more concerned with his very existence as a man and as a poet, and it is *Ulysses* which expresses his prevailing instinct. The important allegorical correlatives in the poem are such emphatic words as 'work', 'toil' and 'some work of noble note', rather than the departure from land and people. (The more traditional objection is, of course, that Tennyson did not escape fast and far enough from his people and his times, and that he tried too hard to be a useful and responsible person.) There is, needless to say, nothing more than a vague and general correspondence between the hero's determination and Tennyson's struggle to live and create during that time of distress. As Douglas Bush comments: 'Out of his grief and philosophic bewilderment the poem was born, and it expounds no ready-made moral lesson; the forces of order and courage win a hard victory over the dark mood of chaos and defeat.'[20] The lack of a definite goal—the 'indirection'—may seem a weakness, in particular if we compare *Ulysses* to Yeats' *Sailing to Byzantium*, but since this blame cuts at the poet's attitude, one may bear in mind that when Ibsen embarked for Ischia, he had no definite plan of writing *Peer Gynt*.

In the later and more directly personal allegory *Merlin and the Gleam* Tennyson insisted that he had rightly followed his 'Master's' advice:

> And so to the land's
> Last limit I came—
> And can no longer,
> But die rejoicing,
> For thro' the Magic

> Of Him the Mighty,
> Who taught me in childhood,
> There on the border
> Of boundless Ocean,
> And all but in Heaven
> Hovers The Gleam.

Hence his exhortation:

> O young Mariner,
> Down to the haven,
> Call your companions,
> Launch your vessel,
> And crowd your canvas,
> And, ere it vanishes
> Over the margin,
> After it, follow it,
> Follow The Gleam.

It would appear to be no coincidence that Tennyson in this connection reverts to the imagery and phrases which he used in *Ulysses*, as he did later in *Crossing the Bar*.

In the last part of the poem Ulysses turns to his companions of the sea, in an appeal that again recalls Dante's hero. Here too the imagery groups itself in antitheses, and the heroic measure of the future task is emphasised, as well as its paradox: 'Old age hath yet his honour and his toil.' The terms of achievement are not the classical ones of martial glory, but of work. It is indeed remarkable that Ulysses, despite his Homeric ancestry, makes only one brief reference to battle, while the bulk of the first part is concerned with experience and knowledge, and the final part with work and toil. This emphasis on endeavour and work may indicate the change in taste, and the changing conception of the hero (rather the 'great man') which announces the Victorian era, but more directly it expresses the poet's awareness of the effort and perseverance needed to gain mastery in his art, an awareness which, as we know, resulted in the 'ten years' silence'.

As the poem draws to a close, the quest-impulse reaches a new climax:

> for my purpose holds
> To sail beyond the sunset, and the baths
> Of all the western stars until I die.

The hero's stoical acceptance of the fatal possibilities of the search throws into relief his yearning as well as his courage, and here, in the dramatic contrast between the gulfs and the Happy Isles, the only reference to the poet's dead friend—'the great Achilles'—occurs. It is significant that Ulysses does not sail *in order to* reach the Happy Isles and join the great Achilles, (as the poet does in *In Memoriam* ciii). His anticipation is merely to 'touch' or visit the Isles of the Blest, and not, apparently, to enjoy for ever an elysian life. If the Happy Isles are a symbol of beatific existence, of life after death, it is clear that they do not invite him as an immediate goal. This attitude suggests that underneath the stoical control and fine imaginative handling of the quest-impulse there is Tennyson's craving, as in *The Two Voices* and *In Memoriam*, for more and fuller life rather than beatitude, the craving which justifies T. S. Eliot's remark that Tennyson's 'concern is for the loss of man rather than for the gain of God.'[21] There are some lines in *Wages* which apply to Ulysses' attitude:

> She desires no isles of the blest, no quiet seats of the just,
> To rest in a golden grove, or to bask in a summer sky:
> Give her the wages of going on, and not to die.

Whatever the private symbolic meaning of the Happy Isles, it is one of the few classical allusions in the antithetical pattern of imagery which actualises the search.

In the closing lines of the poem, the tone becomes more personal than before, and at the same time more objectively inclusive. Here the sense of loss, the weakness inflicted by time and fate, is poignantly expressed, yet it is assimilated to the mythical tradition (Dante) and expands into a universal feeling in the collective 'we'—'One equal temper of heroic hearts.' Tennyson, exploiting the medium of rhetorical exhortation, transcends the egocentric 'I' of the first part and thus achieves a more powerful cathartic effect in the conclusion. Here, more clearly than before, the painful tension which underlies the emotional structure of the poem works towards a paradoxical balance through antonyms and contrasting terms, and in this way the central experience of the poem is concentrated for the splendid release in the final line.

The heroic character which thus emerges from the poem is

remarkable both for its unity and complexity, and for the manner in which it integrates personal impulses and literary traditions. With the stoical bravery of Antiquity is linked the Romantic (and Dantesque) zeal for experience, and both are enhanced by the yearning for knowledge and self-knowledge which is both Socratic and Victorian. Arrogance and tenderness, egocentric introspection and sense of fellowship clash and mingle in the hero's pervasive sense of value and dedication. Seldom in his poetry did Tennyson achieve a similar dramatic intensity and penetration of character, or a balance of opposites more dynamic and inclusive. Ultimately, Ulysses is an embodiment of the imaginative power of the mind to create order from chaos, and unity of will from a multiplicity of impulses which threaten to shatter the sense of direction and identity in a moment of fatal choice. It is true that the search of Ulysses points to no definite goal, and thus is open to the charge of quixotic idealism, but in terms of its imaginative structure the search is justified by the desire to achieve 'some work of noble note', and the yearning to 'follow knowledge', which implies both truth and its uses. The attitude of Ulysses in this respect is determined by his conviction that though his land is barren and his people savage, and he himself idle and unrecognised, the world is a place where action is meaningful and work noble. It is, in fact, through his recognition of the essential order and beauty of the world that Ulysses acts on his impulse to follow knowledge, to strive and seek. And, as the 'hero orgulous' of the opening lines bends his will to the search, his harshness and scorn, and his egocentricity, give way to the 'magnanimous reflectiveness' which Douglas Bush notes. As for the sense of alienation which expresses itself in Ulysses' contempt of his people, it suggests the situation, and the mood, of the old poet in Yeats's *Sailing to Byzantium* rather than that of Childe Harold.[22]

The most enigmatic aspect of the poem is the hero's attitude to death. Underneath his yearning for life and knowledge there is a pervasive consciousness of death, and since this is natural in the old Ulysses, we realise once more how well Tennyson has chosen the situation of Dante's explorer to objectify his personal crisis. It would appear that the hero's acceptance of death is unequivocal: death is the 'eternal silence', 'Death closes all', and therefore, apart from the vague anticipation of the Happy

Isles, Ulysses is determined to make the most of life. The meaning of death, as the end of action and experience, is marked three times (lines 27, 51, 61), and it is integral to the emotional structure of the poem—the sense of urgency which underlies the hero's 'purpose'. Yet in this way a tension is set up between the hero's insatiable love of life and the feeling that death closes all, and in this tension we recognise the obsessive emotional conflict in *The Two Voices* and *In Memoriam*. Indeed, a unique aspect of the poem is its apparently detached attitude to the disturbing question whether man in death will be for ever 'seal'd within the iron hills?' In its own manner, however, *Ulysses* too faces this question, and the tension here too seeks release in fulfilment —in novel experience in the 'untravell'd world', in the pursuit of knowledge 'beyond the utmost bound of human thought', and the hope of finding 'a newer world', 'beyond the sunset, and the baths / Of all the western stars'. These phrases, in the context of Tennyson's poetry, carry strong connotations of spiritual quest and transcendent existence, and if we connect them with other aspects, particularly with symbolic uses of sea-scape, they form a pattern of meaning which extends the panorama in *Ulysses* considerably beyond the limits set by the explicit statement 'Death closes all'. It is true that such a reading appears to contradict the hero's view of death, but it does so only if we assume that the explicit statements and the symbols work on the same level, and are subject to the same logic. Rather it would seem that for once Tennyson has given his conflicting voices not only different keys, but different languages, and the result is a synthesis more interesting than the elimination which takes place in poems where they speak in the same discursive terms.

The symbolic pattern of the sea-scape emerges perceptibly when we relate *Ulysses* to other poems where Tennyson uses the quest-theme, thus in *Sir Galahad*, *In Memoriam* ciii, *Merlin and the Gleam*, *Crossing the Bar*, and poems which exploit the same key symbols, such as *St. Agnes' Eve*, *In Memoriam* cxxv, *De Profundis*, *Idylls of the King*, *The Ancient Sage*, and *Akbar's Dream*.[23]

The Tennysonian quest is almost always a mystical adventure and implies an exploration into the hidden meanings of existence, into the world of spiritual essence, and beyond death. The impulses active in this search are given various manifestations, but usually the Homo Viator is impelled by 'yearning' (*Ulysses*, *Tiresias*), or he is urged on by some externalised symbol of aspiration, like the 'voice' in *Youth*, the 'blessed vision' of Sir Galahad, the 'Gleam' which Merlin follows, or again it might be a 'summons' or 'call' from the sea. (*In Memoriam* ciii, *Crossing the Bar*.)

The quest, as a rule, is a voyage, and the sea thus represents the world of spiritual essence or potentiality. Even Sir Galahad leaves his charger to board a 'magic bark' on 'mountain meres', and his mystical experience, the vision of the Holy Grail, comes to him on 'dark tides'. In *The Holy Grail* (*Idylls of the King*) Galahad sails away, into death, on the 'great Sea'. In *St. Agnes' Eve* there is an anticipation of the 'sabbaths of Eternity / One sabbath deep and wide— / A light upon the shining sea—'. The dream in *In Memoriam* ciii of the poet's reunion with his dead friend records a voyage over the 'Forward-creeping tides ... From deep to deep', and after the reunion, their 'shining' ship sails towards a 'crimson cloud / That landlike slept along the deep.'[24] This dream points to the anticipation, and its conscious and definite use of 'deep' in a mystical sense, in section cxxv:

> And if the song were full of care,
>     He breathed the spirit of the song;
>     And if the words were sweet and strong
> He set his royal signet there;
>
> Abiding with me till I sail
>     To seek thee on the mystic deeps,
>     And this electric force, that keeps
> A thousand pulses dancing, fail.

Most explicit is the meaning of 'deep' in *De Profundis* (1852): 'the deep / Where all that was to be, in all that was ...'; 'that great deep, before our world begins, / Whereon the Spirit of God moves as He will—', which is the waters of Genesis, but also the Platonic world of spiritual essence: 'that true world within the world we see ...'.[25] In that sense 'deep' is used also in *Akbar's Dream*, where the 'Great Voice' (God) is synonymous with the 'true Deep'. The spiritual connotation of the word is sometimes emphasised by epithets like 'boundless'. Merlin's final vision of the Gleam is on the border of 'boundless Ocean'. In *The Ancient Sage* 'boundless deep' is again the Platonic conception, while in *Crossing the Bar* it is the world of spirit to which the soul returns. In this latter context 'deep' becomes synonymous with death, and implies this sense in both the sections quoted from *In Memoriam*, in *De Profundis* (l. 25): 'that last deep where we and thou are still', and in *The Coming of Arthur* and *The Passing of Arthur*, which are interesting for their synthesis of the symbolic meanings of 'deep' as birth and death: 'From the great deep to the great deep he goes.' The occurrence and handling of these symbols show that their meanings were realised already at the time of *St. Agnes' Eve*, *Sir Galahad* and *Ulysses*, nor indeed were they original, but they became more consciously exploited and fixed with the years.

Though Tennyson may have used these images as purely descriptive terms in *Ulysses*, or used them as symbols with a different meaning, it would appear that such phrases as 'the dark broad seas', and 'the deep / Moans round with many voices' work in their descriptive or reflective contexts towards a suggestion of a mystical, symbolic sense. This symbolic extension is felt in particular through the association of these sea-images with the idea of unending quest: 'Yet all experience is an arch wherethrough / Gleams that untravell'd world, whose margin fades / For ever and for ever when I move.' and: 'beyond the utmost bound', and again: 'beyond the sunset and the baths / Of all the western stars'.[26]

The quest-theme frequently makes use of stars, either as 'pilot stars', (*The Lotos-Eaters*, and also in *Tithonus*: 'the silver star, thy guide.') or as an image associated with the 'summons' or 'call' from the sea. *Crossing the Bar* is again a focal point for these various symbolic meanings, and here 'sunset and evening star' includes connotations of impending death and spiritual destiny which may have been realised already in the similar image in *Ulysses*. The 'sinking star' of knowledge is, however, more closely linked with the symbols of aspiration which we find in *Sir Galahad*, where the glory of the Holy Grail 'star-like mingles with the stars', and further with the 'morning star' which beckons to the Sailor Boy.[27] The passing of Sir Galahad in *The Holy Grail* describes him as a 'silver star' on the 'great Sea'. In connection with *Sir Galahad* and *Crossing the Bar* it is significant that Ulysses too sails into the night and the starlit sea.

Another recurrent aspect of this sea-scape is the fascination of the horizon—the 'margin' of the 'untravell'd world'. 'Margin' also occurs in *Merlin and the Gleam*, 'marge' in *In Memoriam* xii, while elsewhere 'brim' (*The Voyage*) and 'bourne' (*Crossing the*

*Bar*) are used. The 'untravell'd world' beckons to the explorer
in 'gleams' and 'glimpses', and these words, with connotations
of mystical insight, intuition, religious revelation, are used ex-
tensively in Tennyson's poems.[28]

In the light of this evidence, it is reasonable to suggest that
the sea-quest in *Ulysses* contains a distinct though unobtrusive
element of spiritual and transcendent meaning. It is probable,
moreover, that Tennyson in this poem (and in the contemporary
*St. Agnes' Eve*) for the first time perceived the symbolic uses to
which these sea- and quest-images might be put, at any rate his
subsequent handling of them is fairly consistent though in many
cases far more obvious.

There is further evidence which relates in particular to the
enigmatic phrase: 'the deep / Moans round with many voices'.
While this is a fine descriptive image, it also implies the projection into the sea of human utterances of grief or sadness,
possibly also of the voices of the dead. Tennyson developed this
symbolic association of sea, death, spiritual departure, and sorrow notably in the Arthurian poems, but one may conjecture
that he first became aware of it during the writing of the early
sections of *In Memoriam* (ix-xvii). In these there is a preoccupation with the voyage of the ship which carried his dead friend
to England, and they bear witness to its emotional and imaginative impact:

> For I in spirit saw thee move
>    Through circles of the bounding sky,
>    Week after week: the days go by:
> Come quick, thou bringest all I love.
>
> (xvii)

And again, as his grief-stricken mind dwells on the sea:

> Calm on the seas, and silver sleep,
>    And waves that sway themselves in rest,
>    And dead calm in that noble breast
> Which heaves but with the heaving deep.
>
> (xi)

In the following section the poet imagines himself in a trance-
like state, when 'as a dove' he leaves his body to meet the ship:

O'er ocean-mirrors rounded large,
　　And reach the glow of southern skies,
　　And see the sails at distance rise,
And linger weeping on the marge,

And saying: 'Comes he thus, my friend?
　　Is this the end of all my care?'
　　And circle moaning in the air:
'Is this the end? Is this the end?'

(xii)

In the early *Morte d'Arthur*, which was written at the time of
*Ulysses*, *Sir Galahad* and the early sections of *In Memoriam* (and
which was probably conceived as an allegory on his friend), there
are no obvious symbolic uses of sea-scape, though the dying King
Arthur is brought to a chapel that stands between the 'Ocean
and a 'great water'. When Arthur feels the end is near, he asks
Sir Bedivere to bear him to 'the margin'. On their way 'He heard
the deep behind him, and a cry / Before.' Suddenly they saw

　　　　　　　the level lake,
And the long glories of the winter moon.
　　Then saw they how there hove a dusky barge,
Dark as a funeral scarf from stem to stern,
Beneath them ...

King Arthur is received by 'stately forms' on the deck, and
among them three Queens who cry in 'an agony / Of lamen-
tation'. They sail away, and Sir Bedivere stands watching the
ship
　　　　　　　till the hull
Looked one black dot against the verge of dawn
And on the mere the wailing died away.

In 1835 Tennyson added a framework, *The Epic*, to *Morte
d'Arthur*, and in the conclusion there is an account of a dream:

　　　　　　I seem'd
To sail with Arthur under looming shores,
Point after point ...
There came a bark that, blowing forward, bore
King Arthur, like a modern gentleman
Of stateliest port; and all the people cried,
'Arthur is come again: he cannot die.'

As the poem appears in *Idylls of the King* (*The Passing of Arthur*), it is removed from the 1835 framework and fitted into the setting of the Arthurian epic through an introduction and conclusion of considerable length. Before the account of the fatal battle comes a description of Arthur's land, Lyonesse, where the mountains ended in a coast: 'and far away / The phantom circle of a moaning sea.' In the conclusion, which begins where the early *Morte d'Arthur* (without the 1835 framework) ended, Sir Bedivere is listening to the wailing from the distant ship:

> But when that moan had past for evermore,
> The stillness of the dead world's winter dawn
> Amazed him, and he groan'd, 'The King is gone.'
> And therewithal came on him the weird rhyme,
> 'From the great deep to the great deep he goes.'

This 'weird rhyme' connects *The Passing of Arthur* with *The Coming of Arthur* and the account of how Merlin and his master miraculously receive the child Arthur from the sea. Watching from the coast, they

> Beheld, so high upon the dreary deeps
> It seem'd in heaven, a ship, the shape thereof
> A dragon wing'd, and all from stem to stern
> Bright with a shining people on the decks,
> And gone as soon as seen ...

And they

>       watch'd the great sea fall,
> Wave after wave, each mightier than the last,
> Till last, a ninth one, gathering half the deep
> And full of voices, slowly rose and plunged
> Roaring, and all the wave was in a flame:
> And down the wave and in the flame was borne
> A naked babe, and rode to Merlin's feet ...

Later, when Merlin is asked whether 'these things were truth':

> The shining dragon and the naked child
> Descending in the glory of the seas—

he replies:

> 'From the great deep to the great deep he goes.'

The images and phrasing in these poems, both composed in 1870, are clearly connected with *Ulysses* as well as *In Memoriam*. The linking of sea and grief in the early sections of *In Memoriam* points forward to the more deliberate symbolic use in *The Passing of Arthur*. And the 'deep' in *The Coming of Arthur*—which is also full of voices—harks back to sections ciii and cxxv of *In Memoriam* and to *De Profundis*, as well as anticipates *Crossing the Bar*, and clinches the double meaning of 'deep' as the world of spirit from which man is born and into which he dies. This meaning connotes, of course, the unity of existence, and the immortality of the soul.

It is this same 'deep' which invites Ulysses to heroic fulfilment, and though Tennyson does not force or elaborate the symbolic implications of the image, and though, as we have seen, the 'eternal silence' and the Happy Isles are not the immediate, nor the most important goal of the hero, they together suggest a world of unlimited knowledge, experience, and noble work. Thus the quest of the old hero ultimately reaches beyond life and action into a 'newer world' of spiritual existence, an extension which includes death. In this symbolic fusion of the meanings of spiritual search and death Tennyson reconciles and masters his metaphysical perplexities, his faith and doubt, his grief and emotional exhaustion, and his conflicting feelings about death. The event which closes all that man treasures in life, which inflicts loss and grief, and yet tempts man with the relief of peace, becomes at the same time an embarkation for more and fuller life.

Thus *Ulysses* is at once a profounder imaginative vision and a finer spiritual drama than the poems where Tennyson debates the same enigmas in a discursive technique. And it is owing to this inclusive, ambidextrous handling of the quest-theme that Tennyson achieves a powerful and cathartic synthesis of the chaotic feelings of *The Two Voices*, and integrates the two worlds which Ulysses explores, that of heroic action, and that of spiritual possibility.

# V

## CHILDE ROLAND AND BROWNING'S JOURNEY TO EVIL

> Fear death? — to feel the fog in my throat,
>   The mist in my face,
> When the snows begin, and the blasts denote
>   I am nearing the place,
> The power of the night, the press of the storm,
>   The post of the foe;
> Where he stands, the Arch Fear in a visible form,
>     Yet the strong man must go:
> For the journey is done and the summit attained,
>   And the barriers fall,
> Though a battle's to fight ere the guerdon be gained,
>   The reward of it all.
> I was ever a fighter, so — one fight more,
>   The best and the last!
>
> ('Prospice')

Browning's *Childe Roland to the Dark Tower Came* like Tennyson's *Ulysses* exploits the theme of a quest that is not, strictly speaking, teleological, but an unfolding experience pointing to human fulfilment in terms of moral dedication and courage. In both poems the goal, or in the case of *Childe Roland* the meaning of the goal, lies outside the expressed awareness of the protagonists, and it is necessary to the emotional dynamic in the poems that this should be so. The experience out of which they grow is one that can be most effectively explored through symbols of landscape and discovery, but even if fully understood it could not yield an ultimate destination or arrival, because such a complete resolution of the underlying emotional conflicts and impulses would cancel out the very uncertainty on which the poems depend for their total meaning. Moreover, there are strong reasons for thinking that the experience, especially in *Childe Roland*, was not fully nor even well understood. Like *Ulysses* it is a poem of perplexity and half realised torment; its creative impulse is towards spiritual regeneration and order, and Browning like Tennyson uses the quest as a means of inward catharsis and control. Yet, as we hope to show, the means, and the entire process of organisation, is very different, for Browning is struggling to overcome and master an experience of compelling nightmare reality, the elements of which are vividly and concretely present to the senses. They are felt and expressed in a way that suggests the directness and concreteness of a myth. The medium which Browning uses to master and order this experience is the moral allegory often exploited in his poetry, indeed so often that it would have offered itself almost immediately and perhaps unconsciously to the poet's mind: it is the typical situation of impending or actual failure, fatal choice, and heroic resolution (or, in some cases, resignation). In the interaction between conscious and habitual medium—the moral allegory—and the subconscious experience—the myth element—*Childe Roland* is born. In this poetic process—one might call it a struggle between myth and allegory, one may observe an effort towards order, detachment and release, both in the articulate adjectival commentary which runs through the poem, in the hero's thinking aloud, and in the frequent Browningesque 'aside'.

*Childe Roland*, it is well known, is one of Browning's most enigmatic poems, and his personal evasiveness concerning its meaning has in itself been a challenge to scholars and critics. When asked whether he would agree to an allegorical interpretation, he replied: 'Oh no, not at all. Understand, I don't repudiate it, either ... I had no conscious intention of writing allegory ... *Childe Roland* came upon me as a kind of dream ... I had to do it.'[1] On the other hand, his statement that he had no other source for his poem than Edgar's song in *Lear* has not, of course, discouraged source hunters. A good case has been made for the influence of romance tradition on incident and landscape in the poem.[2] Browning's indebtedness to Gerard de Lairesse for horrible pictorial detail of landscape has been successfully argued.[3] That the poem arose in and from a dream, that it draws on subconscious sources is, naturally, an invitation to read its experience in terms of guilt, repression, sexual taboos, and 'displacement'. At the core of the poem a nightmare 'guilt' has been found, variously explained as 'the obverse side of the poet's humanity', or again, as a guilt arising from the poet's failure 'to deliver to mankind the full burden of the message with which he has been entrusted.'[4] More reticent critics have drawn our attention to the resemblance between the vivid pictorial detail and mysterious atmosphere in *Childe Roland* and other dream poems like Coleridge's *Kubla Khan*.[5] And there can be little doubt that the uniqueness of the poem in the Browning canon is due to the compelling force of a dream experience, or of an experience that acted upon the poet's imagination 'as a kind of dream.' The traditional and most common critical verdict is, however, that *Childe Roland* is a moral allegory, on the theme: 'He that endureth to the end shall be saved.'[6] The object of the present interpretation is to treat the poem as the outcome of a more complex imaginative process of which the allegorical medium is only one aspect, important but not more so than the nightmare substance out of which the poem is made.

The structure of the poem coheres firmly through the pervasive single point of view. It is a dramatic monologue, recording a personal experience in the past, but actually taking place in the present of vivid memory. While impersonal observation of landscape seems to prevail throughout the poem, the personal 'I' is asserted in the greater number of the stanzas. The epic theme: a knight riding in quest of the Dark Tower is only superficially linked with romance tradition, and significantly, the story told is one of passive experience and not one of action.

The story begins casually, as so often in Browning, and draws the reader immediately into the world of the poem. We are not asked to suspend our disbelief so much as to become involved, from the very outset, in an act of identification with the recording consciousness, and the reality of the actual situation emerges through the powerful emotional response of the 'I' to a repellent human figure, the hoary cripple. He is such a creature as suddenly occurs in dreams, as an embodiment of fear and anxiety, and his malicious 'pleasure' at having trapped one more 'victim' sets the tenor of the poem and its quest into an evil, hostile and diseased world. At the same time, while his presence is vividly and tangibly felt, and his ugliness dwelt on with something like the compulsive fascination of a nightmare, the 'victim' masters the encounter simply by understanding what is going on:

> My first thought was, he lied in every word,
>     That hoary cripple, with malicious eye
>     Askance to watch the working of his lie
> On mine, and mouth scarce able to afford
> Suppression of the glee, that pursed and scored
>     Its edge, at one more victim gained thereby.

He follows the evil advice, but not because he is the dupe of the ogre. In the highly conscious reflection of the first line: 'My first thought was' a process of control and detachment begins working upon the sinister experience. This reflective process continues in the first line of st. ii, where the discursive questions as to the part played by the cripple, posted at the crossroads, serve both as a means of creating distance, and of presenting further aspects of the situation. We are here in a 'dusty thoroughfare' where travellers are waylaid and lost. Again, in the comment: 'I guessed what skull-like laugh / Would break' we see the victim's mind both at grips with its object of revulsion, and in an attempt of grim awareness to master and overcome it—if only in an act of resignation. There is a significant shift in the imagery here from deformity to death, and the 'skull-like laugh' in the dusty road suggests the end to which travellers through this desert may come.

In st. iii the exposition continues in the same indirect and subtly casual manner, and we hear that to follow the cripple's advice means to enter the *ominous* tract in which the Dark Tower stands. Now the teleology of the story begins to emerge more clearly: the Dark Tower is the 'end' of the traveller's journey, and it is anticipated with an ironical and ambiguous play on two basic meanings of the word 'end', as death rather than arrival:

> If at his counsel I should turn aside
>     Into that ominous tract which, all agree,
>     Hides the Dark Tower. Yet acquiescingly
> I did turn as he pointed; neither pride
> Nor hope rekindling at the end descried,
>     So much as gladness that some end should be.

Thus, before we know who the protagonist is and why he allows himself to fall a victim to the evil guide, his prevailing mood of weary resignation and fatalism is associated with his approach to the Dark Tower, the goal of his journey. This reticence as to the protagonist's identity, as well as to the ultimate meaning of the Dark Tower, is part of a suspense technique which is effectively used in the poem to intensify its implications of mystery and horror, and the effectiveness of this manner in the first three stanzas becomes obvious when the autobiographical retrospect is unfolded in stanzas iv and vii, for by then the reality of the quest is established through our direct participation in it. Here, suddenly, the spatial and temporal dimensions of the poem open up in emphatic phrasing: 'my whole world-wide wandering'—'search drawn out thro' years'. This expansion contrasts dramatically with the confession that even the hope which had stimulated the traveller's search had 'dwindled into a ghost', which carries on the mood of resignation from the previous stanza, and indeed enforces it into something curiously vivid and active, in the image of his heart 'leaping' (an unusually strong word in this context) at the probability of failure.

The morbid suggestions—'skull-like', 'epitaph', 'end'—of the first four stanzas are epitomized in the 'aside' of v and vi, which functions both as an illustration of the wanderer's despairing mood, and as a means of creating distance between him and his anticipated doom. This aside is interesting in the way it shows the process of control at work: the conscious mind imposes a fictitious pattern—an analogue of 'as if'—on the subconscious, nightmare experience.

The direct personal retrospect continues in stanza vii, and here a justification is given for the wanderer's resignation to failure: he belongs to a dedicated brotherhood of knights, a 'Band', who all, except him, have failed in their quest for the Dark Tower. With this stanza the epic and teleological perspective is finally developed, and the proper expectations are set up for the story to move on.

A salient feature of these introductory stanzas is the way in which they combine subtle, oblique exposition of situation with introspective analysis. From the beginning we are caught up into the obsessive awareness of a mind at the cross-roads, literally, between life and death. So far, the poetic process seems a highly deliberate and intellectual treatment, and its language, apart from the description of the cripple, is laboriously abstract. Yet the result is effective for two reasons: it asserts the quality of the mind through which we are going to experience the world of the poem, and it provides a medium through which the poet may work his metaphorical transfer, both in the general sense of an 'objective correlative' of emotional states, and also of the interaction between the two aspects which we have called allegory and myth. Finally, of course, in these introductory meditations the moral issue of the poem is stated: it is Browning's arduous exploration into the meaning of success and failure.

The journey of the poem, as a sustained imaginative structure, begins in stanza viii, and at once the landscape emerges in its metaphorical function, as an objective equivalent of a nightmare experience. Significantly, here and throughout, nature tends to embody vivid anthropomorphic qualities, as in the image of the day shooting 'one grim / Red leer to see the plain catch its estray', which carries a complex sense of pervasive hostility and evil, of constrictive struggle, and lost direction. In stanza ii the lies of the malicious cripple were felt to 'ensnare / All travellers', and now the landscape begins to work through the metaphors as a trap, and this meaning, as we shall see, is sustained as an important element of the nightmare experience, or 'myth'.

Despite the strained emphasis on irrevocable choice, stanza ix is interesting for its sudden dream-like transition and for the concomitant impressions of unreality which the shifting movement throws on the landscape. The stanza also enforces the feeling of being trapped, and inevitably urged on towards doom, and at the same time, paradoxically, of deliberate choice of such a course.

As the landscape, the objective equivalent, unfolds in the next stanzas (x-xiii), we are made aware of its compelling hideousness and of the way in which the traveller's mind tries to keep it, as it were, at a distance, in cogitation and soliloquy. The reflective cast of phrases like: 'I think I never saw / such starved ignoble nature', and 'You'd think', shows the medium of control which we noted already in the first line of stanza i. Through the emphatic adjectival commentary here very much in evidence Browning achieves a double effect—a dwelling on the hideousness of the 'starved ignoble nature' and at the same time a reaction against it. The things seen are oppressively ugly and mean:

So, on I went. I think I never saw
    Such starved ignoble nature; nothing throve:
    For flowers—as well expect a cedar grove!
But cockle, spurge, according to their law
Might propagate their kind, with none to awe,
    You'd think: a burr had been a treasure-trove.

No! penury, inertness, and grimace,
    In some strange sort, were the land's portion. 'See
    Or shut your eyes,' said Nature peevishly,
'It nothing skills: I cannot help my case:
'Tis the Last Judgment's fire must cure this place,
    Calcine its clods and set my prisoners free.'

Stanza xi sustains the anthropomorphic idea, and also that of imprisonment, in the cynical words of Nature. That the 'Last Judgment's fire' must purge the place implies that it is blighted by evil. One sees in this strangely tense stanza once more the interaction of the myth—the tangible presence of horror and evil—and the moral, in the idea of purgation and release.

The blight in the landscape is, on the one hand, partly suggested or explained in terms of the biological struggle for survival. This, it would appear, is the 'law' referred to in x and further visualised in xii, where the 'bents' are 'jealous', and a 'brute' has been ravaging, 'pushing their life out'. This vision of struggle or fight, as an aspect of the evil in this waste world, is pervasive in the poem, and emerges next in the powerful image of the mud 'kneaded up with blood' (xiii). On the other hand, the evil of the landscape is expressed in terms of disease and deformity. Thus the 'stiff horse ... thrust out past service from the devil's stud' calls up the figure of the malicious cripple in the first stanzas, and again Childe Roland's revulsion is violent: the cripple was 'hateful' (viii) and as for the horse: 'I never saw a brute I hated so—'. In such instances of explicit revulsion, as well as in the continuous adjectival commentary, we sense a sustained effort to master an overwhelming experience of horror. Or, perhaps, the paralysing effect of neurotic fixation.

An apt psychological peripety takes place in stanza xv, where Childe Roland, unable to bear the sight of the landscape, shuts his eyes and seeks relief in memories of a happy past, that he may be better prepared for the impending contest. Yet even this source of vitality is denied him, for what he remembers is the corruption and failure of his once honourable friends. In these retrospective glimpses, too, the same vivid, palpable presence of dream objects is felt, and also their sudden shifts and transitions.

Another such transition occurs when the knight again faces the landscape: 'A sudden little river crossed my path / As unexpected as a serpent comes.' Even these ancient symbols of life and fertility are here expressive of evil and destructive forces. Browning achieves an unusually powerful image in seeing the river as 'a bath / For the fiend's glowing hoof', as when a red-hot iron is thrust into the bath of a forge. The 'mediaeval' associations are proper in the ballad context; and the river, as a vehicle for evil, develops the general pattern of the landscape, in its vivid, anthropomorphic quality: 'So petty yet so spiteful'. Bushes are seen kneeling down over it, as in a prayer for mercy; others are torn loose and swept away —a 'suicidal throng' —and their 'mute despair' echoes Roland's own state of mind, when 'quiet as despair' he turned into this blighted land. The river, we are told, is the source of 'all the wrong' which the surrounding vegetation suffers, and once more we recognise the pervasive idea of corruption: there is a cumulative sense of horror and revulsion in the next stanza, where even human beings, as Roland fears, may have fallen victims to the river, or to his own sounding spear:

> So petty yet so spiteful! All along,
>     Low scrubby alders kneeled down over it;
>     Drenched willows flung them headlong in a fit
> Of mute despair, a suicidal throng:
>     The river which had done them all the wrong,
>     Whate'er that was, rolled by, deterred no whit.
>
> Which, while I forded,—good saints, how I feared
>     To set my foot upon a dead man's cheek,
>     Each step, or feel the spear I thrust to seek
> For hollows, tangled in his hair or beard!
>     — It may have been a water-rat I speared,
>     But, ugh! it sounded like a baby's shriek.

The stanzas present an unusually dense and inclusive cluster of sense impressions, action and emotion, and the pivotal word, 'tangled', relates the episode to the recurrent pattern of trap or prison.

Another sudden change in mood and situation introduces stanza xxii: 'Glad was I when I reached the other bank. / Now for a better country.', which provides dramatic relief after the episode of the river, but at the same time contrasts ironically with the ensuing vision of the 'toads in a poisoned tank, / Or wild cats in a red-hot iron cage.' The idea of hostility and fight, as a manifestation of evil, is carried over from the landscape stanzas x-xiii, but here the strife is no longer explained as a struggle for survival, or jealousy. It is a mystery: 'What kept them there, with all the plain to choose?' No footprints lead to the scene of battle, none out of it. And with this feeling of an unfathomable, aggressive evil is linked again the sense of constriction: the 'poisoned tank' and 'red-hot iron cage' represent a climax in the structural imagery of the nightmare prison, and nowhere in the poem is the revulsion against it more evident, in the frenzy suggested by the staccato rhythms as well as in the violent images.

The vision of evil and constriction in stanzas xxii-xxiii develops with associations of human evil in the images of 'galley-slaves' and the engine of torment—'Tophet's tool'. Then, with another sudden change of attention, the sterile, ugly landscape once more predominates, revealing its corrupt and ruined life:

> Now blotches rankling, coloured gay and grim
>> Now patches where some leanness of the soil's
>> Broke into moss or substances like boils;
> Then came some palsied oak, a cleft in him
> Like a distorted mouth that splits its rim
>> Gaping at death, and dies while it recoils.

Disease, deformity and death are here insisted on in the images of 'boils', and the 'palsied oak' with a 'distorted mouth ... gaping at death.'

Through seventeen stanzas the poem has been immersed in exploration of landscape, or episodes apparently unconnected with the main epic structure of the quest, and representing Childe Roland's aimless journey in a maze of horror. In stanza xxvii, however, the epic teleology of the poem is once more stated, and we are reminded that it is still evening (as in dreams the sense of time has been lost) and that Childe Roland is hoping for an 'end' to his journey. Paradoxically, the idea of a goal involves a sense of lost direction (as in st. ix). But in the seemingly in-consequent idea that the black bird —'Apollyon's bosom friend' —may be the guide he seeks to the Dark Tower, there is the most definite hint so far that the Tower hides something evil —perhaps the evil power that blights the landscape.

Again, in stanza xxviii, there is a sudden transition, as the landscape changes and Roland to his surprise finds himself among mountains. Two features of this experience are empha-sised: that the hills are ugly, and that they are somehow active in a plot against him. Then, as he reflects upon the situation, he recognises in it a 'trick of mischief' of the kind, significantly, which occurs in a 'bad dream'. With this awareness of mischief and remembered nightmare emerges once more the feeling of being trapped, of being 'inside the den'.

Each of the following stanzas presents sudden, unpredictable changes of focus and attention, and yet on closer inspection there is a careful development of the teleological pattern —each new phase of vision brings Childe Roland nearer to the goal: 'Burn-ingly it came on me all at once, / This was the place'. At the same time, the various motifs and aspects of the nightmare myth are sustained in the further exploration of landscape, thus in the animation of the mountains seen as 'two bulls locked horn in horn in fight', where the evil aggression noted in stanzas x, xii, xxii, xxiii, is associated with the sense of being entangled and trapped.

The Tower itself receives scant description, and there is only one suggestion of what it really *is*: 'Blind as the fool's heart' (xxxi) which seems to imply unthinking cruelty, and there is a further hint in stanza xxxi (lines 4-6), of its destructive force. On the other hand, the Tower stands as an epitome of all the evil and corruption of the surrounding landscape, and Childe Roland's exploration of this landscape is at the same time a discovery of the agency symbolised by the Tower.

In the final stanzas of the poem, the landscape is again charged with anthropomorphic analogues: the hills are like giants at a hunting; the game is at bay, and the whole scene is set for a contest with insuperable odds. (The sinister desert stillness which has brooded over the landscape now yields to the tolling of bells.) And now that the goal is reached, the fatal issue of the contest emerges in Childe Roland's memory of his lost friends, who failed, not because they were weak or wicked, but despite their virtue and courage.

In the final development of the anthropomorphic landscape, as the poem rises to its visionary climax in the last stanza, there is a veritable resurrection of the dead: 'There they stood, ranged along the hill-sides'. Surrounded by these witnesses of failure, trapped in a final confrontation with evil, Childe Roland in his weariness and despair is called upon to accomplish a seemingly hopeless task. Thus, his act of defiance, the slug horn blast, takes on the added force of the unexpected and the impossible.

We may ignore for the time being the possible meanings of Roland's achievement, and consider how the triumphant *finale* of the poem contrasts with its psychological structure as a whole. From the beginning, Browning dwells on the weariness and fatalistic quiescence of the protagonist, and we are shown (iii-vi) how his life-long wandering has drained him of vitality and hope. When he finally turns into the tract which hides the Dark Tower, he is 'quiet as despair'. Through the following stanzas his journey is one of passive observation and bewildered reflection, and though his emotional responses are alert and vivid, their general tenor is revulsion at an experience in which the mind is held captive. There are, as we have suggested, various means by which control and release are achieved, partly at least, but in this connection it is more relevant to notice that in the one instance where Roland deliberately recoils from the horrible scenery in introspective memory (xv-xvii), he is brought back to the sinister vision of the present only because the past is worse. Twice in the poem the traveller expresses gladness (iii, xxii), but it is relief and not joy. For the rest his prevailing mood, when not revulsion, is resignation and fatigue, or fear (xxi). In this emotional structure, the word 'dauntless' really does sound a new note of courage and zest. And it is only in the passing mention of a life spent 'training for the sight', and in Roland's consistently vigilant reaction against the evil and horror of the landscape, that we find the motivation for his final defiance.

We have suggested that *Childe Roland* is the outcome of a tension and interaction between two processes of mind, one related to the emergence of myth, the other to an allegorical interpretation and ordering of existence; one a vivid, obsessive dream experience crowding the field of vision with horrible detail, in a shifting and apparently disconnected stream; and the other a conscious and habitual moral attitude that works to shape this experience into a definite epic time-structure—the journey—and simultaneously into a symbolic structure of the issue of failure or triumph in a struggle with evil.

As our analysis may have indicated, this process results, not in the reduction of myth to the status of simple allegory, nor in the shapeless predominance of visionary, shifting detail, but in a balance that retains the vigour, immediacy and inclusive suggestiveness of myth, while it establishes and maintains the ordered relations of allegory. In this fusion and reconciliation, operating through a twofold poetic perception that grasps and rejects, suffers and judges at the same time, lies the finest achievement of the poem and the secret of its unusual power.

It has been customary to interpret *Childe Roland* above all in the light of its obvious moral issue, as stated in stanzas iv, vii, xxxiii and xxxiv, and to trace this issue to Browning's public failure as a poet over many years. But this issue is pervasive in Browning from the time of *Paracelsus* on, and it is bound up with his total response to existence. As for the immediate, personal experience out of which the poem arose, it would seem futile to speculate on its causes. All we can say is that an obsessive experience has been drawn up from its inarticulate, subconscious depths to a level where the poet may control it by making it part of a poetic structure he often used. Yet the main substance of the experience persists in the sense of evil and horror, and its concomitant fear. Throughout the poem Browning insists on nothing so much as on the reality of evil, and it would seem reasonable to claim that *Childe Roland* is Browning's most personal and embittered grappling with evil—evil not only as an historical event or as an abstract moral problem, but as something overwhelmingly potent and actual. And it is because of this profound sense of the fact of evil that the issue of failure or success in *Childe Roland* is presented with so much force and conviction.

It has been maintained that the most remarkable characteristic of the poem is its 'macabre and brutal imagery', which is seen as a manifestation of 'the obverse side of Browning's buoyant optimism, his humanity'.[7] But surely the most important thing to note is the way in which Browning controls his obsessive experience of hideousness, evil and death through such formal means as reflective 'asides', analogies, and above all through the running adjectival commentary. This may not seem a subtle method, but it achieves a twofold result: to establish the objective reality of the world of the poem and at the same time the traveller's subjective reaction to it. Nowhere, unless one mistakes the tone of the poem, is there a perverse enjoyment of the horror thus externalised in landscape, and nowhere in the poem does the contemplation of it imply acceptance of the evil it represents, despite the fatalism and resignation of the questing knight. On the contrary, he is constantly passing moral judgement on his discoveries, and it is in this way that the epic structure of the journey and the moral issue of Childe Roland's quest become integrated with the powerful metaphorical vehicle to make of the poem a complex and splendid symbol of human destiny.

In this context, the ending is not as enigmatic as some would think, for whatever the outcome of Childe Roland's confrontation with the Dark Tower, his spiritual and moral triumph in that final act of courage, seen in relation to the total experience of the journey, achieves an adequate catharsis and fulfilment of the emotional impulses from which the poem springs. After his discoveries in a world where everything seems blighted by evil, Childe Roland completes his journey in an heroic effort that takes him to the very borderline of action in life, as well as of knowledge. The tone on which the poem ends is not one of despair, but of promise and exultation.

The more difficult trend to unravel in this ending is not whether Roland fails or succeeds, but the meaning of his triumph (if this be assumed) for those who failed before him. The knights of the 'Band' emerge, in the final scene, not only as vivid symbolic witnesses of Childe Roland's fatal moment, but—in the context of the poem—as an objective fact and a condition, paradoxically though it may seem, of his indomitable will. For Roland the issue of the quest is bound up, from the beginning, with the fate of his lost brotherhood, and his dedication, one feels, is to redeem them through a fulfilment of their common task. Therefore, although it may be argued that, in the final stanzas, even his resurrected friends have become part of the hostile landscape, with the giants watching the hunt and waiting for Roland's inevitable defeat, the implication of his quest is that if he succeeds, his friends will be restored to their former honour and even, within the symbolical and supranatural scope of the poem, to new life. The ancient myths and folklore stories of the one act of virtue and courage which removes the blight of evil from the whole land, and brings the victims of the ogre back to life, liberty, or to human shape, is not without foundation in reality. In *Childe Roland* there is, admittedly, scant evidence to substantiate such a reading, yet one may venture to trace in it the vestiges of the saviour archetype, of the redemption and regeneration of the many by the one. On this thesis, we may see ritual implications in the light- and fire-imagery towards the end: 'Burningly it came on me all at once', and 'in a sheet of flame / I saw them and I knew them all', which suggests ancient symbols of purgation and sacrifice.[8]

The structure of the journey is used in this poem with remarkable success. It provides, on one level, a convenient romance quest fraught with danger and moral challenge, with things mysterious and supranatural, discovered in a borderland between waking and dream. Browning does not, however, exploit the conventional elaborate machinery of romance and ballad, and the anonymity and vagueness of Roland's quest has an important effect on the treatment. It leaves the poet free to pursue his exploration into a highly personal and individualised landscape, so that he may develop his various symbolical motifs, such as the cripple, the trap, and the struggle, with cumulative force, and unhampered by trivial stock responses.

The journey is, above all, an effective vehicle for the visionary experience of the poem, with its densely crowded detail, its vivid and restless perception. Only within the teleological structure and movement of a journey could such rich and varied imagistic material be used, and such powerful effects of complex unfolding symbolism be achieved.

# VI

## MATTHEW ARNOLD'S
## SCHOLAR GIPSY

And there are some, whom a thirst
Ardent, unquenchable, fires,
Not with the crowd to be spent,
Not without aim to go round
In an eddy of purposeless dust,
Effort unmeaning and vain.

*Rugby Chapel*

There is a touch of irony in the fact that Matthew Arnold wrote one of his best poems about a 'truant boy' who shirked his social and academic duties and gave himself to wanderings which, at a first glance, look more like a Romantic *voyage sans but* than a serious Victorian quest. The Scholar Gipsy comes into Arnold's poem and moves out of it without, apparently, having received the spark from Heaven, and he is destined, therefore, in his particular kind of immortality to continue his search. Thus, of the poetic journeys of the nineteenth century, this is one of the most inconclusive, though Tennyson's *Ulysses* and *Merlin and the Gleam* offer parallel cases.

Better than any other poem of that baffled Victorian age, Arnold's elegy states its spiritual and poetic *impasse*, and the absence of teleology in the Scholar's wandering reflects a general loss of direction and ultimate goals. The journey here is not strictly speaking a journey at all, but a roaming and straying, and a flight. Nevertheless it implies a goal, and it has a metaphorical function in that the landscape explored illumines a spiritual situation. The structure of the journey is determined by Arnold's complex emotional and intellectual attitudes, and by his divided loyalties.

This complexity has led to a wide range of critical opinion.

For a long time there was agreement on the main theme of the poem, expressed with clarity by Lionel Trilling: '"The Scholar Gipsy" is a passionate indictment of the new dictatorship of the never-resting intellect over the soul of modern man.'[1] Then followed indecision, best exemplified by F. R. Leavis who fluctuates between his early opinion of the poem as one of Arnold's best and most characteristic, the Scholar Gipsy being 'Arnold's most successful symbol for his soul', and his later verdict of the poem as showing 'weak confusion' and 'intellectual debility'.[2] More recently, two such eminent critics as Wilson Knight and A. E. Dyson have arrived at very different results concerning the Scholar and his quest. Wilson Knight in a subtle analysis claims that the Scholar embodies oriental wisdom, as contrasted with Western rationalism; he represents Arnold's ideal of the fresh questing mind moving through 'fields unexplored'. To A. E. Dyson he is, on the contrary, the 'embodiment of an illusion', a symbol of an earlier age with its 'optimistic and chimerical hopes', which serves mainly as a foil to Arnold's practical liberalism and his 'stoical acceptance of unpalatable realities'.[3]

Wilson Knight finds a clue to the poem in the Tyrian trader: *The Scholar-Gipsy* aspires to and predicts a synthesis of Oriental and Western cultures. But although his reading helps to integrate the heterogeneous final tableau, it would appear that this kind of message or allegory is not sufficiently developed in the main body of the poem. On the other hand, to see the Scholar Gipsy as the 'embodiment of an illusion', or of life in an earlier happy age to which it is impossible to return, would certainly conform with Arnold's outlook as a critic of life and of culture. Yet Arnold the poet is usually something very different from the essayist, and if one stresses the implications of the 'illusion' and lack of reality in the protagonist, as something childish which must be put by, then the main human sympathy in *The Scholar-Gipsy* is in danger of being ignored, and an intolerable burden is placed on the liberalism and faith in progress which we find almost exclusively in Arnold's prose works.[4] If anything is emphatic and explicit here, as in so many of Arnold's best poems of that period, it is the gathering force of his criticism of the age, with its 'sick fatigue', its 'infection of our mental strife'; in fact the life of 'doubts, disputes, distractions, fears' of *Memorial Verses*, and the life 'Hideous, and arid, and vile' denounced in *Rugby Chapel*.

*The Scholar-Gipsy* is a complex poem, but like *Thyrsis* and like most of the other *Elegiac Poems* its emotional and poetic energy derives from a simple contrast between life as it ought to be, or might be, and as it actually is, and in this contrast Arnold habitually makes use of a pastoral setting on the one hand for the good life and, on the other hand, of the city for modern life. (Cf. also *The Future*). It is, to a large extent, the contrast between 'agitation' and 'peace' in Wordsworth, with much the same moral and artistic implications, and of course, it has roots much more ancient—in the *beatus vir* tradition of Antiquity. Strange though it may seem, Arnold the urbane prophet of culture sought 'retired ground', whether in the Cumner country or in Kensington Gardens, to confess himself fully in poetry. It is remarkable that two of Arnold's best poems are pastoral elegies, and it is remarkable also that both of them use the idyllic Oxford countryside as a setting for two complementary myths of the scholar and poet: the Scholar Gipsy preserves his youthful zest because he remains in this 'haunt beloved', while Thyrsis lost his 'happy, country tone' when he left it and was caught by the 'storms that rage outside our happy ground'. Both these poems are nostalgic and retrospective, and it is no mere coincidence that the legendary Scholar Gipsy emerges again in the elegy on Arnold's friend Clough, as a symbol of their common 'quest' through the Cumner country. In both poems the Scholar Gipsy stands for something personal and very important; he is Arnold's *alter ego* and he is an embodiment of the ideal condition of the creative mind. At the same time he is used as a definite foil in Arnold's criticism of his age.

To state all this within the framework of the Glanvil legend was no easy task, and there can be no doubt that Glanvil's story in some ways was an impediment rather than a help for the multiple meanings which Arnold wanted to express.[5] According to the story the Scholar, in Dyson's words, is 'committed to a discredited art'. But in the poem this commitment is made deliberately vague so that the context may define its meaning, and what emerges ultimately is a figure much more like a Scholar-poet or artist than a frustrated scholar who leaves Oxford in order to learn hypnotism. If the 'art' or 'skill' which the Scholar pursues is literally mesmerism, then that art would be a crude irrelevance in the context of the poem, and in the context of Arnold's praise of his splendid *one aim*. On the other hand, poetry to the Romantics as well as to the Victorians was an art to 'rule' the 'workings of men's brains' and to 'bind them to what thoughts they will', and only in this sense does the Scholar's quest present a worthy objective, although it has in addition religious and metaphysical implications. Arnold's description of the behaviour of the reclusive Scholar, and his insistence on the aspect of inspiration—that it needs 'heaven-sent moments for this skill', and that it will fall like a 'spark' from heaven, suggest very strongly the creative pursuit of the artist. In this sense the Scholar stands for something to which Arnold was very strongly attached indeed.

And yet the poem as a whole failed, according to Arnold, to perform the highest task. He wrote to Clough:

> I am glad you like the Gipsy Scholar—but what does he *do* for you? Homer *animates*—Shakespeare *animates*—in its poor way I think Sohrab and Rustum *animates*—the Gipsy Scholar at best awakens a pleasing melancholy. But this is not what we want.
>
>> The complaining millions of men
>> Darken in labour and pain—
>
> what they want is something to *animate* and *ennoble* them—not merely to add zest to their melancholy or grace to their dreams.[6]

Here speaks the critic of culture and poetry. But if the writer of *The Scholar-Gipsy* had betrayed his high practical ideal, it was not the first time, nor was it the only time in poetry when he chose the 'impossible loyalties' rather than the platform of duty. It would appear that in a real sense *The Scholar-Gipsy* is Arnold's equivalent to Tennyson's *Ulysses*—not an illusion or chimera, but an embodiment of his profoundest instinct—that what the poet needs more than anything is freedom and dedication. The unique thing about the poem, however, is that it manages to express this instinct, through the interaction between Scholar and landscape, while it also offers a great deal of direct criticism of contemporary attitudes. Thus, even while presenting a picture of the good life and of the ideal condition for the creative mind, Arnold at the same time demonstrates that function of poetry which to him was so important: a criticism of life.

Arnold's love of 'retired ground' and his choice of the pastoral setting as a contrast to the 'sick hurry' of city life do not mean, of course, that he preaches a return to Nature in the manner of Wordsworth. It is true that the Scholar's retirement is like the flight of Wordsworth to the central peace of Nature, but Arnold never for a moment suggests that the 'retired ground' which the Scholar seeks holds spiritual meanings like the 'types' and 'symbols' in Wordsworth's landscape. The impulses from the vernal woods of the Cumner country are not like the workings of the 'one Mind' in the universe, and they do not teach the Scholar much about man. But on the other hand they fill him with hope and rapture, and it is probably this influence from the landscape which Arnold has in mind when he claims in *Thyrsis:* 'And still the haunt beloved a virtue yields.'

It is not necessary in this connection to discuss in detail Arnold's attitude to Nature, for the function of nature in this poem is a simple one—to provide the beauty and freedom and peace which are essential to the main theme. That Arnold in other poems expresses an ambiguous and confusing attitude to Nature is not relevant to this reading, for he is not here dealing with metaphysical aspects of nature nor with the problem of good or evil or indifference.[7]

On the other hand, it may be relevant to an understanding of the poem to turn to those hints in Arnold's earlier work which point forward to the function of Nature in *The Scholar-Gipsy.* And here it seems that *Quiet Work* is significant, and contains an embryo of the paradox later more fully developed—this is the lesson of 'two duties kept at one ... Of toil unsever'd from tranquillity!' —

> Yes, while on earth a thousand discords ring,
> Man's fitful uproar mingling with his toil,
> Still do thy sleepless ministers move on,
> Their glorious tasks in silence perfecting;
> Still working, blaming still our vain turmoil,
> Labourers that shall not fail, when man is gone.

This is the ideal which underlies Arnold's longing in *The Scholar-Gipsy* too; this, and not what Mr. Leavis calls an 'eternal weekend'.

The poem which most directly points forward to *The Scholar-Gipsy* is *Resignation.* Here, as Tinker and Lowry rightly note in their commentary, we have some of the main elements of the later poem. Thus in the picture of the poet contemplating the calm and beauty of Nature:

> He leans upon a gate and sees
> The pastures, and the quiet trees.
> Low, woody hill, with gracious bound,
> Folds the still valley almost round;
> . . .
> Before him he sees life unroll,
> A placid and continuous whole—
> That general life, which does not cease,
> Whose secret is not joy, but peace;
> . . .
> The life of plants, and stones, and rain,
> The life he craves—if not in vain
> Fate gave, what chance shall not control,
> His sad lucidity of soul.

While this sad lucidity does not fit the character of the Scholar Gipsy, there are other feelings which do, such as the 'Rapt security' of the poets who keep aloof:

> They, winning room to see and hear,
> And to men's business not too near,
> Through clouds of individual strife
> Draw homeward to the general life.

There is also a significant association, though in contrast, of gipsies and the poet, in the words Arnold attributes to Fausta:

> *Those gipsies,* so your thoughts I scan,
> *Are less, the poet more, than man.*
> *They feel not, though they move and see;*
> *Deeper the poet feels; but he*
> *Breathes, when he will, immortal air,*
> *Where Orpheus and where Homer are.*
> *In the day's life, whose iron round*
> *Hems us all in, he is not bound;*
> *He leaves his kind, o'erleaps their pen,*
> *And flees the common life of men.*
> *He escapes thence, but we abide—*
> *Not deep the poet sees, but wide.*

Here, it would appear, we have both the theme of the later poem, and some of its language and structural images. The connection between the two poems is further evidence that Arnold had the poet rather than the philosopher or scholar in mind when he started the academic exile on his wanderings. It is probable also that certain words in Glanvil's tale suggested to him the possibility of making the Scholar Gipsy a symbol of the poet withdrawing from the world of men to a life of contemplation or imagination. Glanvil's story, in the extract which Arnold quotes as a note to the poem, tells us that the gipsies 'could do wonders by the power of imagination, their fancy binding that of others'. The emphasis on inspiration is also relevant in this context, and it is possible that the recurrent image of the 'spark' of inspiration is derived directly from Goethe's celebrated 'Göttliche Funke'.

Arnold's treatment of the figure of the Scholar Gipsy makes it necessary to see him as a symbol. Arnold resurrects him from Glanvil's page, launches him on his quest through the Cumner country where, through generations, he has been a living legend, and claims for him the immortality of the fictitious and legendary character. This is the kind of myth on which poet and reader must agree. But within the myth the Scholar Gipsy functions above all as medium of a special kind of awareness, and this is our main concern.

The first three stanzas of the poem provide the natural and imaginative setting for the Scholar's quest. Arnold freely exploits the pastoral convention with its associations of virtue and happiness and peace, but in a realistic and actual scene where the shepherds are real shepherds and not symbols or allegorical figures. They, like the reapers, help to get the scenery into focus, as something solid and close. The 'quest' of the shepherd appears also to focus, by way of prolepsis, the main action of the poem.

The early stanzas also serve an organic function as a *mise en scène* for the story-teller—they place the poet in the landscape in such a manner that he is invited, by the scenery and the occasion, to tell the tale of the Scholar Gipsy and at the same time to participate in it, through a common withdrawal from the world. As the Scholar moves through this landscape before the poet's eyes, he changes from a figure of legend into an actual human being and at the same time an undying archetype, a symbol. His presence is so vividly recorded that gradually we cease to regard him as an imaginary figure, and he takes over, as it were, the poet's awareness of the landscape. This is how Arnold visualises his own pastoral retirement, which is soon to be that of the Scholar:

> Screen'd is this nook o'er the high, half-reap'd field,
>    And here till sun-down, shepherd! will I be.
>       Through the thick corn the scarlet poppies peep,
>    And round green roots and yellowing stalks I see
>       Pale pink convolvolus in tendrils creep;
>          And air-swept lindens yield
>    Their scent, and rustle down their perfumed showers
>       Of bloom on the bent grass where I am laid,
>       And bower me from the August sun with shade;
>    And the eye travels down to Oxford's towers.

With this solid abundance Arnold creates the world of the poem, and it is solid indeed. Critics have rightly noted that these early stanzas owe a great deal to Keats's odes in mood and in the density of their sensuous images, and it is a measure of Arnold's poetic freedom that here he abandons himself to this characteristic Keatsian delight, for as a critic Arnold was still a long way off from his maturer judgement of Keats as ranking with Shakespeare in 'the faculty of naturalistic interpretation'.[8] The landscape described in *The Scholar-Gipsy* is not meant to be part of an illusion, any more than the woods in the Nightingale ode or the fruits in 'Autumn' are illusory. But these poetic sceneries are different and distant from the world where 'youth grow pale, and spectre-thin, and dies'; distant from the life of mortal men with its change and shocks, and Arnold marks that distance through his emphatic use of words suggesting seclusion, shelter and peace —words which gradually acquire a structural weight, as in Wordsworth's *Prelude*. The poet is 'screen'd' in a 'nook', and the grass 'bowers' him with shade, so that, while he is hidden from the world, he may yet observe it from this high vantage point. Though more lush and elaborate than the pastoral retreat of the Ancients, this is the kind of place to which poets and sages have withdrawn since Antiquity to enjoy contemplation and the life of the mind.

As the scenery unfolds through the poem two marked features stand out: there are the wide expanses of fields which, more than any other feature, reflect a great variety of mood and impression —like *high, still, wide, lone, shy*. They reflect also the unbounded freedom of the landscape and its dwellers. On the other hand there is the shelter of the narrow, secluded place, the 'shy retreats' of the Cumner country. Both these elements are developed in close connection with the myth of the Scholar seeking freedom and seclusion, and again we are reminded of the poet of *The Prelude*. Otherwise there is nothing in this landscape which suggests allegorical or abstract moralistic meanings. On the contrary, with its profuse sensuous detail and ecstatic contemplation of natural beauty it is a landscape one should enjoy for its own sake, like that of Keats. In these early stanzas, Arnold has carefully noted impressions of space and light and their changes through the hours of the day, from noon-time sun on the high cornfields to the 'moon-blanch'd green'.

On such a 'summer-morn' Glanvil's Gipsy Scholar 'forsook' Oxford and began roaming the countryside. Arnold devotes only two stanzas to the story and then goes on to trace the Scholar on his quest through the landscape. He depends on two complementary elements in working out the myth—one the precise geographical location and the concreteness of scenery, and the other a sustained use of hearsay and vague reporting. Much of the effectiveness and charm of Arnold's story inheres in this subtle blend of fact and mystery:

> But rumours hung about the country-side
>    That the lost Scholar long was seen to stray,
> Seen by rare glimpses, pensive and tongue-tied,
>    In hat of antique shape, and cloak of grey,
>       The same the gipsies wore.
> Shepherds had met him on the Hurst in spring;
>    At some lone alehouse in the Berkshire moors,
>    On the warm ingle-bench, the smock-frock'd boors
> Had found him seated at their entering,

> But, 'mid their drink and clatter, he would fly.
>    And I myself seem half to know thy looks,
>       And put the shepherds, wanderer! on thy trace;
>    And boys who in lone wheatfields scare the rooks
>       I ask if thou hast pass'd their quiet place;
>          Or in my boat I lie
>    Moor'd to the cool bank in the summer-heats,
>       'Mid wide grass meadows which the sunshine fills,
>       And watch the warm, green-muffled Cumner hills,
>    And wonder if thou haunt'st their shy retreats.

In this manner Arnold brings the Scholar out of the legend and
the past into the actual present, where the scenery and those who
see him lend reality to his elusive figure. While Arnold transfers
his own experience of the landscape to the Scholar, as something
shared, he defines the mood and purpose of the Scholar's wanderings through words like 'haunt' and 'shy'. What fascinates
him above all in the Scholar is that he is 'lost' to society, even
to the gipsies. His wanderings appear to be just as much a flight
as a quest, and Arnold has elaborated this trend with such care
that critics have found a moral significance in the kind of people
who are able to see the Scholar at all: they are mainly young
and innocent people, while the Oxford view of the Scholar, we
are told, is the wintry one when he is bound for Hinksey. But
surely the thing to note in all these reported glimpses is that the
people who see the roaming Scholar are there not for their
own sake or for the sake of any allegorical meaning, but merely
to observe and thus lend credibility to the legend. It is through
these glimpses that the mystery as well as fact of the Scholar's
'quest' are unfolded, and throughout Arnold uses the landscape
to bring out certain moods and states of mind, such as joy, peace,
and delight in natural beauty. He also uses geographical locali-
sation to suspend our disbelief, and make us share in the exploration. Hurst and Wychwood, the Fyfield elm and the bridge
at Godstow, Bagley Wood and Hinksey's wintry ridge, these
and other precise chartings are made against the ever-present
background of the Cumner hills. The function of these names is
important and extensive, for they provide the actual and vivid
scene within which the legendary figure grows increasingly
real.

Here, more than in any other poem we have examined, the
meaning of the journey is defined by the landscape rather than
by the stated or implicit purpose, at least this is true up to the
point (st. 14) where Arnold begins his explicit 'criticism of life'.
And thus it is to the interaction of landscape and protagonist
that we should pay the closest attention.

The landscape is, in fact, often a direct translation or metaphor of the Scholar's mind. This 'pensive' solitary may be seen
at lone alehouses or in a quiet place in the pastoral landscape,
where the river banks are refreshingly cool in the summer heat,
and wide meadows open up their free and sunlit spaces. There
are, too, the bowers and 'shy retreats':

For most, I know, thou lov'st retired ground!
Thee at the ferry Oxford riders blithe,
    Returning home on summer-nights, have met
Crossing the stripling Thames at Bab-lock-hithe,
    Trailing in the cool stream thy fingers wet,
        As the punt's rope chops round;
And leaning backward in a pensive dream,
    And fostering in thy lap a heap of flowers
    Pluck'd in shy fields and distant Wychwood bowers,
And thine eyes resting on the moonlit stream.

Throughout, the landscape is used as a medium through which the poet identifies his own awareness of beauty and peace with that of the wandering hero.

While there is much emphasis on the Scholar's shyness, we find two episodes which reveal his human sympathy and a kind of detached interest. The first is where he gives 'stores' of flowers to the girls going to dance around the Fyfield elm, but without speaking to them. The other is at the lone homestead where, like the poet in *Resignation*, he leans on a gate watching 'the general life'—here the threshers in the barn. But otherwise, what emerges from these stanzas is the figure of a man who avoids people to be alone with his own mind, in a landscape that favours his 'pensive dream'. He is either seen in meditative repose, with 'vague eyes, and soft abstracted air' sitting on the river bank, or passing slowly through the woods

Rapt, twirling in thy hand a wither'd spray,
And waiting for the spark from heaven to fall.

Though the Scholar appears to indulge in idle and purposeless wandering, Arnold reminds us in the lines just quoted of his 'aim', and the constant emphasis on pensiveness also suggests mental activity. It indicates, moreover, the recipient calm of the artist's mind. And through the metaphorical interaction of hero and landscape we are reminded also of nature's slow and silent growth—as presumably in the Scholar's mind—reminded in fact of the *Quiet Work* of Arnold's favourite sonnet.

The spring and summer landscapes which predominate tend to imply that the Scholar's life is an easy holiday existence, but the one winter episode (st. 13) shows us both the hardships of the exile he has chosen, and the irrevocable nature of that choice, as the Scholar turns his back on the lights in Christ Church to sleep in 'some sequester'd grange'. This is not the life of a weak man, but of a dedicated man, who abides by his choice.

When Arnold from stanza 14 onwards returns from his poetic dream, it is in order to denounce the life of his times through a contrast with that of the Scholar Gipsy. Into this criticism Arnold carries our awareness of the freedom, peace and beauty explored in the earlier stanzas. And now, since the Scholar Gipsy remained from the beginning a poetic fiction resurrected through the magic of the landscape, Arnold may turn him into a symbol, an ideal, immune to the 'lapse of hours' and the 'repeated shocks' which 'Exhaust the energy of strongest souls'. But Arnold's quarrel is not with Mutability, it is with modern dissipation:

> Thou hast not lived, why should'st thou perish, so?
> Thou hadst *one* aim, *one* business, *one* desire;
>     Else wert thou long since number'd with the dead!
> Else hadst thou spent, like other men, thy fire!
>     The generations of thy peers are fled,
>         And we ourselves shall go;
> But thou possessest an immortal lot,
>     And we imagine thee exempt from age
>     And living as thou liv'st on Glanvil's page,
> Because thou hadst—what we, alas! have not.

It is at this point that the second main impulse of the poem is released with full force. For if the first part explores the beauty and freedom of the dedicated life, the second completes this central vision through an attack on its opposite—the life splintered through lack of purpose and passion, the modern life with its 'dissociation of sensibility' and divided or impossible loyalties. Arnold's method is that of dramatic antithesis, through which the two impulses continue to interact and mutually illumine each other. In the following stanza his hero looms, with 'powers / Fresh ... Firm ... Free', above the idle, purposeless drift of modern men. And we notice that the Scholar Gipsy attains to this superhuman and immortal status because the fire of dedication unifies his whole being, and because he keeps his freedom and aloofness, instead of immersing himself in the destructive element, the ordinary life. The three emphatic words—Fresh, Firm, Free carry with them emotional and metaphorical energy from the earlier pastoral stanzas, and in turn help to define the Scholar's quest. The Scholar's 'immortal lot' in this context implies more definitely the particular immortality of the poet or artist to whom, Arnold tells us in *Resignation*, dedication and detachment are alike essential.

At this point, however, Arnold's criticism of his times involves a religious element which for a moment blurs the central idea:

> Thou waitest for the spark from heaven! and we,
>   Light half-believers of our casual creeds,
>     Who never deeply felt, nor clearly will'd
>     . . .
> Ah! do not we, wanderer! await it too?

But the new emphasis is a consequence of Arnold's diagnosis; he surveys the many symptoms of this 'strange disease of modern life' — religious, moral, and artistic. And it is significant that the person whom he places opposite the Scholar-Gipsy on the 'intellectual throne' is not a religious teacher but one whose function is rather more like that of the author, recording his 'sad experience' and all the various phases of mental and emotional conflict.[9]

Having exposed the 'sick fatigue' of modern life, Arnold launches the Scholar Gipsy once more on his quest, which, in the new context, takes on a greater urgency. Yet first the myth of the early pastoral stanzas must be revived, and their mood:

> But none has hope like thine!
> Thou through the fields and through the woods dost stray,
>   Roaming the country-side, a truant boy,
>   Nursing thy project in unclouded joy,
> And every doubt long blown by time away.

Within the 'sad lucidity' of Arnold's poetic soul, struggling with his sense of duty and the force of public opinion, the impulse towards freedom must have been very strong indeed. In the next stanzas what we have called the two main impulses of the poem are seen in a process of closer interaction. First with emphasis on the critical attack and the necessity of exile:

O born in days when wits were fresh and clear,
  And life ran gaily as the sparkling Thames;
    Before this strange disease of modern life,
  With its sick hurry, its divided aims,
    Its heads o'ertax'd, its palsied hearts, was rife—
      Fly hence, our contact fear!
Still fly, plunge deeper in the bowering wood!
  Averse, as Dido did with gesture stern
  From her false friend's approach in Hades turn,
Wave us away, and keep thy solitude!

The legendary figure has become an effective foil within the terms of his life in the early stanzas, and we realise now to what extent his appeal depends on the beauty of his rural retirement. It is to this beauty that Arnold next turns to focus the central vision, in a continued apostrophe to his hero:

Still nursing the unconquerable hope,
  Still clutching the inviolable shade,
    With a free, onward impulse brushing through,
  By night, the silver'd branches of the glade—
    Far on the forest-skirts, where none pursue.
      On some mild pastoral slope
  Emerge, and resting on the moonlit pales
  Freshen thy flowers as in former years
    With dew, or listen with enchanted ears,
From the dark dingles, to the nightingales!

This is the world of Keats, and indeed the Scholar Gipsy at this ecstatic climax is rather like Keats in his own poems. For all the limitations which he found in Keats, and even in Wordsworth, Arnold the poet sides with them here. This does not mean that he himself is able to follow the Scholar Gipsy: With his 'sad lucidity of soul' he remains behind in the sick world, incapable of anything but a longing for the values symbolised by the Scholar and his world. It is not a question here of warning against an illusion, but of lamenting with genuine grief a life no longer possible—at least not to a man who chooses to stay in the busy Victorian world. As the final parable of the Tyrian trader shows, there is no hope of a reconciliation between the two worlds of the poem, but if any definite meaning may be said to emerge from this episode, it is a celebration of freedom above all other things. If we bear in mind the emphasis on freedom through the poem, this grand conclusion is justified, although it does, admittedly, abandon the geographical context of the poem and also its structural images.

Of the finer poetic journeys in the nineteenth century, the wanderings of Arnold's Scholar Gipsy remain probably the most inconclusive. This, as we said in the introduction, is an inevitable aspect of the spiritual dilemma which the poem describes. And yet we may justly claim that for the strength of his argument, and his myth, Arnold has not told us quite enough about the hero's aim and desire, except in negative terms. As initially stated, the Scholar's aim is not worthy of the poem as a whole with its expanding religious, moral and artistic implications. Even if we insist, as we must, on the broader meaning of the 'art' the Scholar wants to learn, it remains a thin concept and not forceful enough for the later confrontation. But in the meantime Arnold has overcome this weakness through the emergence of two supreme values — beauty and freedom — born of the Scholar's imaginary exploration.

There is, perhaps, another reason for Arnold's reticence, for at this time he was far more concerned with his public duties as a poet than at the time when he chose — against several arguments — to deal with the 'idyllic side' of Clough in a Thyrsis myth of the same Oxford landscape. Yet although *The Scholar-Gipsy* only in a rather vague way is a poet's myth about an important personal yearning, like Tennyson's *Ulysses*, its theme and treatment are closely linked with Arnold's personal meditations on the poet's life and dedication, which recur frequently in some of his best poems from *Resignation* (1849) to *Thyrsis* (1866). The problem of poetic dedication is often bound up with an impulse to leave the world, the public platform with its strife and commotion, and withdraw into pastoral quiet. It is a withdrawal of the self in order to have freedom; as in *Resignation:*

> Blame thou not, therefore, him who dares
> Judge vain beforehand human cares;
> Whose natural insight can discern
> What through experience others learn;
> Who needs not love and power, to know
> Love transient, power an unreal show;
> Who treads at ease life's uncheer'd ways—
> Him blame not, Fausta, rather praise!

Rather thyself for some aim pray
Nobler than this, to fill the day;
Rather that heart, which burns in thee,
Ask, not to amuse, but to set free;
Be passionate hopes not ill resign'd
For quiet, and a fearless mind.
And though fate grudge to thee and me
The poet's rapt security,
Yet they, believe me, who await
No gifts from chance, have conquer'd fate.
They, winning room to see and hear,
And to men's business not too near,
Through clouds of individual strife
Draw homeward to the general life.

The attitude and choice in this poem are not quite the same as in *The Scholar-Gipsy*, yet the ideas of freedom, detachment, and dedication to a task, emerge with great emphasis. And the 'poet's rapt security' is very like that of the Scholar Gipsy, very different from Arnold's resignation to the 'sad lucidity of soul' and to the sick world. In most of Arnold's poems of these years, freedom and dedication are inseparably bound up with the problem of identity, as in *Mycerinus*, another myth of pastoral retirement:

It may be on that joyless feast his eye
Dwelt with mere outward seeming; he, within,
Took measure of his soul, and knew his strength,
And by that silent knowledge, day by day
Was calm'd, ennobled, comforted, sustain'd.

Again, in *The Buried Life*, it is a withdrawal of the self in order to discover one's identity:

But often, in the din of strife,
There rises an unspeakable desire
After the knowledge of our buried life;
A thirst to spend our fire and restless force
In tracking out our true, original course;

It is this fire which makes the Scholar Gipsy eternally young while other men spend it and decay. He, true to himself and his dedication, preserves his identity — 'undiverted to the world without'. There is in *The Scholar-Gipsy*, as in Arnold's best poems of that period, a deep sense of the beauty of the undivided personality, rooted in a central source of energy and firmly directed towards a goal. Thus in *Rugby Chapel*:

> And there are some, whom a thirst
> Ardent, unquenchable, fires,
> Not with the crowd to be spent,
> Not without aim to go round
> In an eddy of purposeless dust,
> Effort unmeaning and vain.

But still, these are the great men, like Thomas Arnold, the 'helpers and friends of mankind', and Arnold does not claim for himself a similar fire, nor would he claim it for the Scholar Gipsy. These great leaders were also to Arnold the greatest poets, because they animated men through their imitation of action. Through their great poetic action Homer and Shakespeare animate, while *The Scholar-Gipsy* 'at best awakens a pleasing melancholy'. By this standard the poem belongs to the 'minor current' in English literature; it belongs, for more than one reason, with Wordsworth and Keats.

While there is no action in the poem directed outwards across the insuperable gulf of Arnold's 'iron time', there is, nevertheless, the central idea of the quest, and of imaginative activity, and this idea, too, links up with Arnold's frequent meditations on the poet's task. With his yearning for dedication there went a desire to combine activity and peace, as in the metaphor of the 'quiet work' of Nature — 'toil unsever'd from tranquillity'. In *Lines Written in Kensington Gardens* (1852) Arnold, like the Scholar Gipsy attracted to retired ground, indulges in a Keatsian delight in the life of Nature:

> Here at my feet what wonders pass
> What endless, active life is here!
> What blowing daisies, fragrant grass!
> An air-stirr'd forest, fresh and clear.

It is again the ideal condition of imaginative creation, and Arnold prays:

Calm soul of all things! make it mine
To feel, amid the city's jar,
That there abides a peace of thine,
Men did not make, and cannot mar.

Arnold, like Wordsworth, yearns to combine this peace with duty to others, with a 'useful' task, and with the 'power to feel with others', yet he, like his predecessor, was more strongly attached to the beauty of individual freedom than to the world of action. And it is an interesting reflection on their poetry that whenever they left their 'bowers' they performed their public duty at the expense of great poetry.

Though Arnold placed Wordsworth in the 'minor current' of English literature, he paid him a significant tribute:

He too upon a wintry clime
Had fallen—on this iron time
Of doubts, disputes, distractions, fears.
He found us when the age had bound
Our souls in its benumbing round;
He spoke, and loosed our heart in tears.
He laid us as we lay at birth
On the cool flowery lap of earth,
Smiles broke from us and we had ease;
The hills were round us, and the breeze
Went o'er the sun-lit fields again;
Our foreheads felt the wind and rain.
Our youth return'd . . .

Perhaps Arnold would have liked to do the same; perhaps he too would have preferred to restore in his poetry 'The freshness of the early world' rather than diagnose over and over again the strange disease of modern life. *The Scholar-Gipsy* and other poems certainly point in that direction. Though *The Scholar-Gipsy* is the elegy of a paradise lost, it seeks to re-enact something of the freshness of that early world. Yet the chief impulse in the poem remains Arnold's needs as a poet—his yearning for artistic integrity, for freedom. Since these remain impossible ideals in a world of unpalatable duties, his poetic journey becomes an exile, wistful and interminable, steeped in a sense of *Et in Arcadia Ego*. At the same time, however, Arnold pursues the exploration through a landscape he loved, and he is able, therefore, in terms

of that landscape, to evoke a vision of perennial delight, relevant
to life as well as to art. The landscape of Arnold's wanderings is
effective in two ways; it is palpably real with its rich descriptive
splendour, and it suggests values essential to the good life and
to the creative imagination. Though we do not see the landscape
directly from the Scholar Gipsy's point of view, we are made to
share his experience through the poet's participation in his quest,
and gradually what we discover is what the scholar, too, finds.
Thus the geographical determinant is strong in this journey too,
despite its vague, rambling character and lack of teleology. Like
Wordsworth's *Prelude* and Tennyson's *Ulysses*, Arnold's poem
points to a goal which is not conclusive or final, but rather a
continuous process, like that of Nature.

# VII

# YEATS: TO BYZANTIUM

For various reasons, the Romantics and Victorians could best express their spiritual conditions, private and public, through the structure of the journey as an unending quest; or if a goal was hinted, it was left vague enough to accommodate a wide range of symbolic meaning. As faith and myth receded and the traditional patterns of Christian teleology lost their hold on the poetic imagination, the value of the image of life as a journey was sought in the actual process of discovery of the self, or the splendour of action, or the greatness of the past. Combined with the idea of a voluntary exile from a barren present the journey might lead, if not to religious certainty, then at least to freedom and self-realisation, 'beyond the utmost bound of human thought', or in the retired ground of the Oxford countryside.

The poets of the twentieth century have achieved an intellectual toughness unknown or rare in their immediate forbears, and with their greater sense of paradoxical action, they have emerged from the perplexities and darkling plains of the Victorians to strike out boldly towards goals of religion and myth which science and doubt seemed to have closed for ever. If we were to single out modern poems which in kind and quality succeed worthily to the ones we have chosen from the nineteenth century, it would have to be Eliot's *Journey of the Magi* and Yeats's two Byzantium poems. Eliot's treatment of the journey, however, is modern only from the point of view of technique, and it does not include the complex impulses of spiritual and aesthetic search which we found in Wordsworth, Byron, Tennyson and Arnold. Yeats's Byzantium poems gather these impulses into a great vision of the destiny of the creative soul.

Taken together, *Sailing to Byzantium* and *Byzantium* work out a myth of spiritual and artistic rebirth. This view is not new nor very different from that argued, in one form or another, by most critics. It implies an acceptance of Yeats's mythical system in *A Vision* and 'Anima Mundi' as important to their poetic process and their value. For Yeats's myth, fantastic though it appears, is a product of his poetic imagination and as such helps him, as he shows in poem after poem, to unify his sensibility and integrate his poetic structures, and notably those concerned with transcendence, immortality and rebirth.

In *A Vision* Yeats has explained his choice of Byzantium as a spiritual goal, and though often quoted, the passage must be recorded here:

> I think if I could be given a month of Antiquity and leave to spend it where I chose, I would spend it in Byzantium a little before Justinian opened St. Sophia and closed the Academy of Plato. I think I could find in some little wineshop some philosophical worker in mosaic who could answer all my questions, the supernatural descending nearer to him than to Plotinus even, for the pride of his delicate skill would make what was an instrument of power to Princes and Clerics and a murderous madness in the mob, show as a lovely flexible presence like that of a perfect human body.
> I think that in early Byzantium, maybe never before or since in recorded history, religious, aesthetic and practical life were one, that architect and artificers—though not, it may be, poets, for language had been the instrument of controversy and must have grown abstract—spoke to the multitude and the few alike. The painter, the mosaic worker, the worker in gold and silver, the illuminator of sacred books, were almost impersonal, almost perhaps without the consciousness of individual design, absorbed in their subject-matter and that the vision of a whole people.[1]

To Yeats, who hated the disruption of modern life as strongly as Matthew Arnold and T. S. Eliot, Byzantium stood for unity of being, splendour and creative force. In the first poem, *Sailing to Byzantium*, Yeats's nostalgia for these things feeds on yet another impulse—a need to leave the paradise of the senses, the Ireland of the young:

That is no country for old men. The young
In one another's arms, birds in the trees
—Those dying generations—at their song,
The salmon-falls, the mackerel-crowded seas,
Fish, flesh or fowl, commend all summer long
Whatever is begotten, born, and dies.
Caught in that sensual music all neglect
Monuments of unageing intellect.

It has been noted that there is a paradoxical tension in this
stanza due to the magnificence which Yeats lavishes on the land
he rejects: wistful attachment and regret contend with scorn and
keep the stanza subtly balanced for the play of its other intricate
relations. The country of the young, as N. Jeffares has shown, is
Ireland.[2] We find the ageing poet in a human situation closely
resembling that of the old Ulysses in Tennyson's poem. Yeats
marks his sense of alienation in the emphatic syntax: 'That'
country and 'Those dying generations' are already distant in his
mind. The initial antithesis of old and young turns into a paradox
in the claim that the dying generations are the young not the
old men. Its main effect is to shift the emphasis from the physical
—that which is transient—to the spiritual, the unageing intellect. And yet it is physical splendour which predominates in the
first stanza, and for all his personal scorn Yeats gives the country
of the young a grand valediction. Around the centre of human
love-making the panorama extends in a careful organisation of
detail, each adding to the impression of beauty, strength and
abundance. Yeats achieves his finest images here in combinations
of nouns and verbs or verbal nouns, suggesting form and action
simultaneously, as in 'salmon-falls' and 'mackerel-crowded
seas', where precise denotation enforces the impression of natural
energy and proliferation. Further abundance is added in the
incantatory 'Fish, flesh, or fowl', which, though spoken in contempt, sustains the solemn alliterative music of the stanza. Apart
from alliteration there is a strong element of ritual formalism
in the groups of triple enumeration (again in 'Whatever is begotten, born, and dies').
Another contradictory relation in this stanza inheres in the
vast extent and vitality of the natural world set off against the
brevity of life. '*All* summer long' underlines the same paradox
through the ironical use of 'all' to describe the brief season of

summer. The old man's disdain for the natural world and the young is finally focused in the verb *caught*, suggesting not only nets and snares but also the neo-Platonic captivity of the soul by matter, and the verb completes one metaphorical pattern hinted already in the embrace of the young. The final line further dramatises the antithesis between old and young and defines the old poet's sense of alienation. Cleanth Brooks has noted the self-irony of the image—'monuments of unageing intellect', and this irony is part of the paradox of feeling, tone and intention which underlies the whole stanza.

The most important metaphor set up in the first stanza is that of the song—the sensual music. It is linked most closely with the image of the birds, the natural birds in the trees, and we should remember these when we come to the artificial birds singing in the final stanza.[3]

The second stanza begins with a masterly and unexpected development of the image of old men as monuments:

> An aged man is but a paltry thing,
> A tattered coat upon a stick, unless
> Soul clap its hands and sing, and louder sing
> For every tatter in its mortal dress,
> Nor is there singing school but studying
> Monuments of its own magnificence:
> And therefore I have sailed the seas and come
> To the holy city of Byzantium.

The transition heightens the irony of the monument-image and at the same time states in a more implacable form the antithesis between the sensual music and that of the soul or intellect, i.e. between body and soul, nature and art. In the context of birds and song the scarecrow image is apt and vivid, and suggests that here already there is a process of metamorphosis at work, part inevitable physical decay, part spiritual and artistic regeneration, with the underlying idea of the latter born of the former through struggle and suffering. The song of soul now counterpoints the sensual music of the first stanza, and the process of learning and of regeneration implies two time-honoured aesthetic principles, i.e. that art is sublimation, and is furthered, like the marksman-ship of Philoctetes, by wounds that never heal. Yet in the world of art as in life individual skill must grow by tradition, by the 'monuments of its own magnificence', and it is this tradition — in a sense wider than that of song or poetry — which beckons the old poet to Byzantium. Thus, by redefining 'monuments' in this new context the ironical yet proudly defiant phrase of the first stanza finds justification and new force. Monuments is an image sufficiently spacious to accommodate the meanings of all the arts.[4] The emphasis is on the enduring quality of the world of soul and art, and its unity through 'singing school' or tradition, in contrast to the transience of the world of nature. The fact that it is the old man not the young who seeks the singing school sustains the paradox of sensual music and the song of the soul. The stanza is wholly concerned with art as a means of spiritual regeneration, and though the situation is painful, it is viewed from great height and with the kind of acceptance which makes even the tragic a source of joy. For the singing of the soul in pain is joyful, because the process of mortal decay is felt as necessary to the new existence it is about to enter.

The actual journey of the poem is limited to the swift yet stately movement of the last lines, but the spiritual quest which is the main theme spans with its rich metaphorical implications the distance between Ireland and Byzantium. To appreciate what this quest means to Yeats, one must bear in mind his idea of that city in *A Vision*, as a place of 'incredible splendour' and unity of existence. In this first poem, however, the quest is defined in terms of rejection and aspiration rather than in the scenery explored, although, once in Byzantium, there are remarkable discoveries indeed:

> O sages standing in God's holy fire
> As in the gold mosaic of a wall,
> Come from the holy fire, perne in a gyre,
> And be the singing-masters of my soul.
> Consume my heart away; sick with desire
> And fastened to a dying animal
> It knows not what it is; and gather me
> Into the artifice of eternity.

A new phase begins in the poetic metamorphosis. Through the image of soul in the preceding stanza, we are prepared for the religious function of song in this process, and for the solemn ritual invocation with its repetitive stresses on *holy* fire. It is significant that Yeats invokes 'sages' to be his singing-masters — men who have gone through all the phases of experience and reached what Yeats in his 'system' called the 'condition of fire'. From this high position they are called upon to 'perne in a gyre' or redescend through the cycles of experience (like a spindle winding thread) to perform the ritual of purgation.[5] The strange image is effective here more because of its ring of magic and incantation than because of its relation to Yeats's system of the gyres or cycles of history which man, the microcosm, shares with the macrocosm.

As invocation turns to prayer, the religious fervour reaches a climax in the phrase 'Consume my heart away'. The metamorphosis from scarecrow to a soul singing triumphantly from the deep source of its pain is here all but completed in a sacrificial act, in which the religious and poetic forces coincide or become identical. In this ritual of purgation, the dualistic awareness of the first and second stanzas is gathered to new intensity in the image of the dying animal from which the poet desires his soul to be freed.

The 'artifice of eternity' to which the old poet aspired must be reached through purgatorial fire. Apart from the traditional cultic significance of the fire symbol, Yeats intended it, as Cleanth Brooks has shown, to draw meaning from his metaphysics in 'Anima Mundi':

> There are two realities, the terrestrial and the condition of fire. All power is from the terrestrial condition, for there all opposites meet and there only is the extreme of choice possible, full freedom. And there the heterogeneous is, and evil, for evil is the strain one upon another of opposites; but in the condition of fire is all music and all rest.[6]

In this condition the soul 'puts on the rhythmic or spiritual body or luminous body and contemplates all the events of its memory and every possible impulse in an eternal possession of itself in one single moment.' This idea of metamorphosis (or metempsychosis) as a kind of rebirth into a new existence is central to Yeats's system. 'Human life', he states in the 'fifth proposition' in *A Vision*, 'is either the struggle of a destiny against all other destinies, or a transformation of the character defined in the horoscope into timeless and spaceless existence.'

Cleanth Brooks has indicated the relevance of the fire symbol to another passage in 'Anima Mundi'. From the Great Memory,

the Anima Mundi, Yeats believed, two kinds of influences or in-
flowings came to man; first the natural inflowing, shared by
man and animal alike, and then the second, 'which is not
natural but intellectual ... is from the fire.'

It is a 'luminous body', born from the fire, which Yeats's
soul seeks in Byzantium, as his 'artifice of eternity', an eternity
which is 'all music and all rest':

> Once out of nature I shall never take
> My bodily form from any natural thing,
> But such a form as Grecian goldsmiths make
> Of hammered gold and gold enamelling
> To keep a drowsy Emperor awake;
> Or set upon a golden bough to sing
> To lords and ladies of Byzantium
> Of what is past, or passing, or to come.

The consummation through fire is both a liberation and a creative act, like that of the artist. Thus the dualism sustained from
the first stanza is here finally resolved in the triumph of the
spirit and of art over nature, the sensual music, as the poet
achieves his 'Mask' or artifice in the golden bird. Of course,
pedantically speaking, the bodily form of the bird is taken from
nature, yet Sturge Moore's criticism of this point cannot be
seriously considered, and Yeats would hardly have written the
second Byzantium poem mainly to mend the flaw.[7] 'Bodily
form' means *kind* rather than *shape*, and the golden bird of the
final stanza is certainly as far removed from 'those dying generations' of the first stanza as Yeats could wish. The important
thing for Yeats was to find a symbol which would contrast with
the natural birds—the sensual music—and yet sustain the structure of song and effect its transformation from nature into art,
from body into spirit. Though the emphasis appears to be on
art in this process, both the process and its outcome, the artifact,
would be meaningless except as a myth hinting through symbols
and images the destiny of the poet's soul. That the creative
forces of art should be active and predominant in this destiny is
what we might expect, since the poet's soul is here exploring,
and sharing in, a world where all life is one, and where the soul
manifests itself completely through works of art, in this 'holy
city'.

As Jeffares has shown, there were legends of artificial birds and trees which helped Yeats to choose the form of his 'artifice'.[8] Yeats himself has a vague reference to such legends. But apart from these sources, there is surely something like a Phoenix myth embedded in the whole symbolic structure. More important, however, than the individual symbols is the total symbolic context as it emerges through the linking and interaction of the images of the bird and the golden bough. While the individual images tend to stress the element of art in this metamorphosis, they together bring into focus the basic idea, that of spiritual rebirth.

It would appear that the idea of eternity which is conveyed in the bird-symbol gains depth and precision if we recognise the 'golden bough' in both Byzantium poems as the mythical Golden Bough which Frazer explored in his famous 'Study in Magic and Religion.' Yeats was, of course, familiar with this work, and in 1926, when he wrote *Sailing to Byzantium*, he also found in Frazer's study the idea for the first stanza of *Two Songs from a Play*.[9]

The myth of the Golden Bough is best known from Virgil's *Aeneid*, Book VI, where Aeneas is able to descend into Hades and return to earth, having planted the bough on the 'threshold' of the entrance to Hades, as a gift to Proserpine. In myth and ritual, according to Maud Bodkin, the bough has represented the 'power of renewal in vegetation and in other forms of life', and in *The Aeneid* it functions as a 'symbol of the transition from death to life.'[10] It is this meaning which Yeats has exploited so directly and yet unobtrusively in both the Byzantium poems. Drawing on the wealth of mythical and ritual association which the bough provides, Yeats was able to link his image of the golden bird, the perfect and enduring artifact, with the ancient symbol of rebirth into a new mode of existence. The component parts of the bird-bough image thus interact to lend a richer and more definite meaning to the process of regeneration, as an act of spiritual rebirth.

That Yeats had this complex significance in mind when he came to write the second *Byzantium* may be seen from his use of the bird symbol in the third stanza, where the bird — 'Planted on the star-lit golden bough, / Can like the cocks of Hades crow.' According to Richard Ellmann, 'Yeats had learned from Eugenie Strong's *Apotheosis and After Life* that the cock, as herald of the sun, became 'by an easy transition the herald of rebirth' on Roman tombstones.'[11]

The golden bough thus stands as a threshold symbol—a passport to that purer and more perfect state of being into which the poet's soul will be born, and it enforces the rebirth idea which Yeats focused in the bird itself. He chose this form not as an eccentricity, but for this traditional symbolic meaning, and because he needed an image to complete the main antithesis of the poem and one which at the same time would sustain the structural metaphor of song, or poetry. It is the ritual of a poet's death and rebirth we are attending, and we might expect that in the intricacies of Yeats's symbolism the ways of his art and his soul would coincide, so that what is in reality and above all an immortality myth appears to be rather a dream of the artist to survive through his artifact. But this superficial and facile kind of immortality was not Yeats's concern in these poems.

It has been suggested that the poem ends where it began, for 'what is past, or passing, or to come' is really the same thing as 'those dying generations'.[12] Yet the range of time and experience suggested as topic for the song concerns something more universal and less sensual than the world of the young and their brief summer. Rather it means that the poet, having assumed the 'luminous body' of the bird, will contemplate 'all the events of its memory and every possible impulse in an eternal possession of itself in one single moment.' In these words, as in the poem itself, it is the artist's yearning to conquer time and space which speaks.

Yeats's exile from the world of nature is prompted, in part at least, by his urgent desire for impersonal modes of being and creating, for transcending his human personality.[13] Thus, though finally he appears to return to the world of sensual music and of change, he is in fact performing a ritual in which he divests himself of his personal limitations—the dying animal—in order to become that 'monument of unageing intellect' which can be only imperfectly realised in his mortal state. The main development in the symbolic structure concerns the transformation of the old poet from neglected mortal scarecrow into the glorious imperishable bird, eloquent of wisdom and triumphant over time and mutability.

Needless to say, Yeats intended his esoteric symbols of bird and bough merely to indicate the nature of the spiritual rebirth to which he aspired. On a literal level the images make no sense, not even if we interpret the total symbolic structure as representing simply the poetry which the poet leaves as immortal works of art to posterity. Yet though art and its processes are most important in the rebirth which the poem celebrates, it is only a means pointing to that ultimate condition of the soul, where all is 'music and all rest'.

Despite their graphic precision, then, the images in *Sailing to Byzantium* suggest a wide field of undefined symbolic meaning, and Yeats must have felt on concluding the poem that there was still a great deal of gold which had not been hammered out. This undeveloped richness in theme and imagery, rather than the pedantic criticism of Sturge Moore must have been the source that engendered the second *Byzantium*, which is an elaboration of the first, more than a sequel.

From the point of view of the journey, *Sailing to Byzantium* is remarkable for the steep antithesis between its two geographical centres, and for the richness of metaphorical meaning which the voyage between them conveys, as death and rebirth on the one hand, and as conquest of the realms of art on the other. The two final stanzas involve things seen or explored, but apart from the mosaic there is little which represents a discovery with metaphorical implications. In *Byzantium*, on the other hand, the oriental city which Yeats chose as his spiritual destination lends more concrete detail to his rebirth myth:

> The unpurged images of day recede;
> The Emperor's drunken soldiery are abed;
> Night resonance recedes, night-walkers' song
> After great cathedral gong;
> A starlit or a moonlit dome disdains
> All that man is,
> All mere complexities,
> The fury and the mire of human veins.

The antithesis between nature and art in *Sailing to Byzantium* remains, and, as we shall see, there is a parallel development in the symbolic structure. Yet here instead of a rich naturalistic scenery we have, from the beginning, *images :* the city is explored with the artist's awareness, and hence the ground is prepared for a more subtle and intricate symbolism. The direction and movement of the poem corresponds to that in the first one, for the 'unpurged images' here are like the 'dying generations' of Ireland. And there is also 'sensual music', of a crude kind, with soldiery and revellers singing in the darkened streets. These belong, however, to the day-time world, the world of nature, which is represented as more coarse and less bitterly regretted than the land of the young in the former poem. In the middle of the stanza, amid the noises of soldiery and night-walkers, falls the heavy sound of the cathedral gong, and with this turn the world of art and religion begins to gain ascendancy over the world of nature. The antithesis between these worlds is drama-tised in the following lines through the image of the dome, towering over 'the fury and the mire of human veins.'

As Cleanth Brooks has shown with reference to Yeats's system, a starlit dome belongs to phase one, the dark of the moon, and a moonlit dome to phase fifteen, or the full moon. These phases represent complete objectivity and subjectivity, and in these phases man cannot exist, since human nature is a mixture of both. Hence the starlit or moonlit dome, existing in a state of purity and perfection, disdains man, the creature of 'mere com-plexities'. Again, in the images of 'fury and mire' Yeats gives us a picture of the sensuality and paltriness of the human animal more scornful than in the first poem. In contrast to it, the dome, though built by human hands, has gone through a process of purification and reached the state of the superhuman. For the sake of poetic logic, one must assume that now in the starlit or moonlit night, at the historical moment which Yeats has chosen according to his system, the purity of phases one and fifteen reigns over the city, and the moment would seem to correspond to the discovery of the sages in 'God's holy fire'. Since the human beings and their sensual music now recede (and there is ritual emphasis on the verb), this change means death to the human animal, the body, and the world of nature. In the next stanza we are in a dim borderland between the two worlds, and the old poet, dying, pursues his quest amid images now of a different kind:

> Before me floats an image, man or shade,
> Shade more than man, more image than a shade;
> For Hades' bobbin bound in mummy-cloth
> May unwind the winding path;
> A mouth that has no moisture and no breath
> Breathless mouths may summon;
> I hail the superhuman;
> I call it death-in-life and life-in-death.

The tentative shifts of the syntax hint at the dissolution of the day-time world, and the mystery and uncertainty of the world into which the poet is being led by his *images*. The fleeting nature of these images also suggests the state of artistic creation or composition, so that all the time the processes of spiritual metamorphosis and those of creative art are related, as in *Sailing to Byzantium*, but now with more detailed points of reference. As for the mystery of 'man or shade', Cleanth Brooks has discovered a passage in 'Hodos Camelionis' which throws light on it. Yeats is here meditating on the Great Memory:

> Is there nation-wide multiform reverie, every mind passing through a stream of suggestion, and all streams acting and reacting upon one another no matter how distant the minds, how dumb the lips? A man walked, as it were, casting a shadow, and yet one could never say which was man and which was shadow, or how many the shadows that he cast.'[14]

The shades or images, then, are both spiritual manifestations, and here they seem to emerge as they emerge in dreams or in artistic perceptions. As for the manner in which Yeats thought of the soul as being able to manifest itself, T. R. Henn quotes an interesting passage from Yeats's essay on Swedenborg:[15]

> It may be that More but copies Philoponus who thought the shade's habitual form, the image that it was as it were frozen in for a time, could be again 'coloured and shaped by fantasy', and that 'it is probable that when the soul desires to manifest it shapes itself, setting its own imagination in movement, or even that it is probable with the help of daemonic co-operation that it appears and again becomes visible, becoming condensed and rarefied.

The relation here between spiritual manifestation and the working of the imagination seems to be the idea which Yeats has exploited in this obscure second stanza.

'Hades' bobbin', as commentators have noted, is an image, drawn from Yeats's system, of the soul unwinding after death the experience it has wound up during life. The image, which is deliberately non-sentimental and crude, alludes to Yeats's idea that all existence is a series of cycles or gyres winding and unwinding experience (as on a spindle or perne).[16] The symbolic situation corresponds to that of the prayer to the sages in *Sailing to Byzantium*, to 'perne in a gyre' to the poet and gather him into eternity. Here a soul manifesting itself as shade or rather as image, having 'no moisture and no breath', is returning along the 'winding path' of experience to summon the dying or dead poet, and to guide him. And being thus initiated into the other world, the poet hails this image as part of the true reality, the superhuman, and his invocation—'I call it death-in-life and life-in-death', like his prayer to the sages in 'God's holy fire' aims at transcending his human and earthly limitations, in order to reach the 'artifice of eternity'. The spiritual or superhuman is the power which bridges the two worlds, and through this power the old explorer passes on to contemplate the eternal form, the Mask, which he aspires to in the world of the superhuman:

> Miracle, bird or golden handiwork,
> More miracle than bird or handiwork,
> Planted on the star-lit golden bough,
> Can like the cocks of Hades crow,
> Or, by the moon embittered, scorn aloud
> In glory of changeless metal
> Common bird or petal
> And all complexities of mire and blood.

The device of syntactical indecision is repeated, again to stress the mystery of this vision, for which no earthly or natural categories can serve. At the same time, the repetition of the words miracle, bird, golden handiwork lends ritual and incantational magic to the lines. Unlike the 'thing' made by Grecian goldsmiths, this bird defies definition in words, and the emphasis on its miraculous nature reminds us that it is the product of the inscrutable processes of art as well as of the supernatural.

With the image of the bird the other symbol of rebirth from *Sailing to Byzantium*, the golden bough, appears, and through the interaction of these the symbolic structure of rebirth in the former poem emerges once more. Amid the star-lit splendour and purity of this world of spirit and art, the golden bough which supports the bird stands on the threshold to admit the poet into eternity. To emphasise this transition as a rebirth Yeats relates the golden bird to the cocks of Hades, the traditional symbol of rebirth on Roman tombstones. We should also bear in mind that Yeats in

his system used the phrase 'bird born out of the fire' to describe
the supernatural, and the word 'born' indicates that the symbol
of the bird was consciously associated with the idea of rebirth
and hence came to predominate in his pilgrimage to Byzantium.

The difficulties of this stanza are partly due to the syntactical
turn in 'Or, by the moon embittered', and partly to the obscurity
of this image itself. The bird may either sing of a new existence
beyond nature and death, or it may scorn the world of nature,
like that other work of art, the dome. In the latter case, the
antithesis, and even antagonism, between these worlds is made
more fierce than in *Sailing to Byzantium*. Hence we may accept
T. R. Henn's suggestion that the bird is embittered by the moon
because the moon is the principle of change in nature, the femi-
nine principle.[17] By linking the bird and the dome in a common
scorn of 'the fury and mire of human veins', Yeats insists on his
idea of Byzantium as a place where purity and permanence are
achieved.

The rest of the poem performs a ritual of purgation corresponding to that in the third stanza of *Sailing to Byzantium*,
though here as elsewhere in the poem the symbolic texture is
more intricate. The holy fire burns again in the mosaic:

> At midnight on the Emperor's pavement flit
> Flames that no faggot feeds, nor steel has lit,
> Nor storm disturbs, flames begotten of flame,
> Where blood-begotten spirits come
> And all complexities of fury leave,
> Dying into a dance,
> An agony of trance,
> An agony of flame that cannot singe a sleeve.

The flames are once more the 'holy fire', begotten of flames in
the workshops and, as works of art, remain beyond the powers
of nature. Though these flames in their turn have no power over
physical nature, they have the power to purify the spirit, from
its 'dying animal', the body, and its fury and mire. In this
borderland between nature and art, life and eternity, these
mosaic flames represent the 'condition of fire' for which they
purge the soul. In their ritual dance of death the spirits partake
of the movement of these flames, and the 'agony of trance' which
they experience suggests both sacrificial fervour and the artist's
creative intensity.[18] Thus the aspects of spiritual rebirth and

artistic creation continue to interact in this metamorphosis, and one might say that in this stanza they are fused in a 'mutual flame'.

The fifth stanza completes the journey from nature to art, life to eternity, and here the legend of Arion and the dolphin is exploited to sustain the symbolic structure of the song:

> Astraddle on the dolphin's mire and blood,
> Spirit after spirit! The smithies break the flood,
> The golden smithies of the Emperor!
> Marbles of the dancing floor
> Break bitter furies of complexity,
> Those images that yet
> Fresh images beget,
> That dolphin-torn, that gong-tormented sea.

There is a frantic tension between opposites in this stanza, which may be viewed as the final agonising struggle between nature and art, body and soul, which began in the first stanza of *Sailing to Byzantium*. While the world of art and its forces prevail, it is still superimposed upon the images of the world of nature, from which its own images are made and hammered into perfection. There is a kind of double vision in which we observe not only the flames and dolphins in the Emperor's pavement, but at the same time the sea of sensual music—'that dolphin-torn, that gong-tormented sea' of nature. Thus, in one intense focus, Yeats holds together the two extremes of his spiritual journey, and he achieves a singular concentration in this stanza by crowding together the central images and ideas of the two poems. Paradoxically, though *Byzantium* explores the mystery of spiritual rebirth and artistic creation which *Sailing to Byzantium* only hinted at, the conclusion here is less serene, and though here too we have an ultimate triumph of art and a celebration of the metamorphosis from creature to artifact, body to soul, it is the vision of nature, particularly in the first and final lines, which is most powerfully rendered. In the sombre grandeur of the final line, Yeats focuses once more the antithesis between nature and art (dolphin, gong) and the painful struggle from which the new spiritual being, as well as the work of art, are born. Those images', it would appear, refer to the 'bitter furies of complexity' (and the 'unpurged images of day') which give birth to, or are transformed into, the image of art.

The second *Byzantium*, then, is more concerned with the mystery of the two-fold metamorphosis than with the ultimate goal, the 'artifice of eternity'. While the poem therefore throws fascinating light on this process, as Yeats sees it, it does not clarify the symbol of the artifice itself, except for the greater elaboration of the underlying idea of rebirth. As his contemporary and later poems show, Yeats was too deeply immersed in the dolphin-torn' and 'gong-tormented sea' of life to pursue further his quest for the ultimate, the 'artifice of eternity'. Yet in the city of Byzantium as he imagined it he found an amazing richness of symbols and images through which he was able to unify, above the central antithesis, the worlds of nature and art, in the idea of a creative process in which the spirit is reborn through the operation of forces which also engender the enduring work of art. A unified vision of existence, and life abundant through the metamorphoses of art and spirit, was the goal which Yeats reached in his pilgrimage to Byzantium. Rarely has a symbol enabled a poet so to integrate his sensibility and fuse the energies of religious, intellectual and artistic aspiration.

# NOTES

PARTS ONE AND TWO

355

NOTES – PART I

CHAPTER I

¹ We should notice that the restoration-motive in a highly modified form plays an important part also in the journey of Aeneas. Not only does Aeneas undergo a restorative initiation, involving traces of a purificatory process and rebirth (cf. W. Warde Fowler, *The Religious Experience of the Roman People* (London, 1911), pp. 419-422; also the very interesting thesis of W. F. Jackson Knight, *Cumaean Gates* (Oxford, 1936), esp. Chapt. IX.), but one of the stated purposes of the journey from Troy to Rome is to restore the *collective* life of the Trojan *gens*, its gods and its city (cf. Fowler, pp. 69-70). As Aeneas says, 'illic fas regna resurgere Troiae,' (I. 206) and the word 'resurgere' should be read in its widest literal and figurative sense, though, true to Roman preoccupations, the renewal is social, collective, oriented to community rather than individual concerns. Rome, then, is a 'rebirth of social and religious order'.

² W. F. Jackson Knight, *Vergil's Troy* (Oxford, 1932), p. 7.

³ Lucien Lévy-Bruhl, *La Mentalité Primitive* (Paris, 1922), p. 93; for further discussion see also Martin P. Nilsson, *Primitive Time-Reckoning* (Lund, 1920), pp. 9-10.

⁴ H. and H. A. Frankfort, *et al.*, *Before Philosophy* (Penguin, 1949), p. 30.

⁵ See Gabriel Germain, *Essay sur les Origines de Certains Thèmes Odysséens et sur la Genèse de l'Odyssée* (Paris, 1954), p. 536.

⁶ Gabriel Germain, *La Mystique des Nombres dans l'Epopée Homérique et sa Préhistoire* (Paris, 1954), p. 97 and *passim*.

1

[This interpretation of the *Odyssey* is revised and considerably abridged from the following: Richard J. Sommer, 'The *Odyssey* and Primitive Religion,' *Acta Universitatis Bergensis: Series Humaniorum Litterarum* (1962), No. 2.]

¹ Gabriel Germain, *Essai sur les Origines de Certains Thèmes Odysséens et sur la Genèse de l'Odyssee* (Paris, 1954), p. 333.

² Rhys Carpenter, *Folk Tale, Fiction and Saga in the Homeric Epics* (Berkeley, 1958), p. 146; First pub. vol. XX of Sather Classical Lectures, 1946. New light has been shed, however, upon the necromantic rites which Odysseus performs in the underworld. On April 12, 1960, *The New York Times* carried a special from Athens announcing the discovery by Greek archaeologists of a large Necromanteion (Oracle of the Dead) at the confluence of the Kokytus and Acheron rivers in Epirus, in the northwest region of Greece. In this massive structure were found evidences of libations of honey and white barley, together with burnt sacrifices of sheep and bulls. Among the artifacts uncovered were a small clay statue of Persephone and one of Cerberus. The inner temple room, used for oracular consultation with the dead, is reached by a complicated and dark labyrinth with three arched gates. These details will have important bearing on later discussion in this chapter. The Necromanteion itself dates from the third Century B. C., but was reared on the site of another much earlier building used probably for similar purposes. The use of honey and mention of it in the Homeric account may have some relation to the episode of the Sirens, and hints of labyrinthine structures appear in several

of the others, including the story of Charybdis. Honey appears also in the sacred cave in the Bay of Phorcys, the place where Odysseus is finally deposited at his return to Ithaca.

3 All whom, incidentally, appear to be pre-Hellenic, testifying to the antiquity of their place in the *Nekyia*. See Germain, p. 332; Denys Page, *The Homeric Odyssey* (Oxford, 1955), p. 39., finds the meeting with Agamemnon one of the original episodes of a visit to the underworld.

4 See the legend of the feud between the houses of Atreus and Thyestes. This relation by blood (in a double sense) between Aegisthous and Agamemnon establishes their point of strong resemblance to the Celtic king-and-tanist, to Cain and Abel, Gilgamesh and Enkidu, Castor and Polydeuces, and the hundreds of other stories of fratricide or severe twin-rivalry associated with ritual and royal succession, which together with stories of patricide and succession to the father's throne, fill the world's mythologies. See Lord Raglan, *The Hero* (New York, 1956), p. 194. First pub. 1936.

5 Since Ikarios and Tyndareos were brothers, Penelope daughter to the former, Clytemnestra to the latter.

6 *Odyssey*, xi. 442 ff., trans. W. H. D. Rouse (Mentor Book, 1951), p. 124. First pub. 1937.

7 *Odyssey*, xi. 454-456. These lines are missing in many of the ancient editions of the epic. The possibility that they are late, perhaps Athenian interpolations, offers no great hindrance to our hypothesis to be suggested in this chapter. Recent criticism, especially that of Professor Cedric Whitman, tends to indicate a greater degree of Athenian modification of the epic than hitherto supposed. This Athenian attitude seems completely in accord with the Homeric transformation of the original ritual elements of the poem, and it is true, also, that even if the *Nekyia* as a whole is a late addition to the poem, the *catabasis* which it relates is one of the oldest elements to be found in the traditional literature and legendary annals of Eurasia and Africa. In short, we can hardly accept the view of the *Odyssey* (presented by D. Page and others) as a poem ready to fly apart and disappear into patches and pieces at the least examination of linguistic and vocabulary characteristics. The paradoxical youth-and-age of the *Nekyia* is a case in point, showing up the futility of this kind of disintegrative criticism.

8 *Agamemnon*, 915 ff.

9 There can be little question that this is their underlying motive in besieging Penelope. For the argument and evidence, see George Derwent Thomson, *Studies in Ancient Greek Society*, Vol. I, *The Prehistoric Ægean* (New York, 1949), p. 424.

10 E. O. James, *The Cult of the Mother-Goddess* (London, 1959), passim.

11 Also see G. R. Levy, *The Gate of Horn* (London, 1948), p. 86 ff.

12 J. G. Frazer, *Lectures on the Early History of the Kingship* (London, 1905), p. 161.

13 J. A. K. Thomson, *Studies in the Odyssey* (Oxford, 1914), p. 58.

14 Ibid., p. vii.

15 Loc. cit.; see also Martin P. Nilsson, *Primitive Time-Reckoning* (Lund, 1920), p. 97.

16 For instance, xvi. 172 ff. It is interesting, however, that Homer seems al-

most to protest too much, and the fact that Odysseus is taken for a god on these occasions may be indicative of an aura of divinity which the poet uneasily felt must be rendered innocuous. See Gilbert Murray, *The Rise of the Greek Epic* (Oxford, 1911), pp. 158-159, and *Five Stages of Greek Religion* (London, 1935), p. 62.

17 Leonard Cottrell, *The Anvil of Civilization* (New York, 1957), p. 23; G. D. Thomson, p. 158.

18 Frazer, pp. 291-292.

19 Germain, p. 137.

20 Cf. Lord Raglan, pp. 187-188.

21 Quoted in J. A. K. Thomson, pp. 104-105.

22 *Odyssey*, xi. 134-137. Classicists sometimes find it convenient to dismiss the Telegoneia as an imitative post-Homeric fancy, but the extract given seems to indicate very ancient sources indeed, and we would do well to follow the hint thrown out long ago by Andrew Lang, that the cruder, more incomprehensible forms of a story are far oftener the more primitive forms, rather than degenerations of a highly developed version. (See Andrew Lang, *Custom and Myth* (London, 1898), pp. 178-179.) It seems unlikely that Eugammon would have been ignorant of the Homeric story or would have disregarded it if he wrote after Homer, though the discrepancies between the two accounts are obvious (J. A. K. Thomson, p. 106), unless Eugammon, whether writing before or after Homer, were in contact with a genuine alternative tradition.

23 Eugammon's poem itself, one is inclined to suspect, shows evidence of superficial expurgation or a misunderstanding of traditional materials; we may even wonder (with J. A. K. Thomson, p. 59) whether originally Telemachus, as another consort-lover-son-god, married Penelope, and Telegonus Circe; other lands, other customs.

24 W. B. Stanford, *The Ulysses Theme* (Oxford, 1954), p. 88.

25 Pindar and Herodotus. See J. A. K. Thomson, pp. 46-47, who accepts the tradition as ancient and authentic; also Pausanias, viii. 12. 5-6.

26 *Odyssey*, xviii. 158-162; S. H. Butcher and Andrew Lang, trans. *The Odyssey*, in *The Complete Works of Homer* (New York: Modern Library, n.d.), p. 283.

27 See, however, G. D. Thomson, pp. 71-72.

28 Twelve is a number applied most frequently to sacrificed animals or slaughtered human beings, in the *Iliad*; here it may thus indicate a ritual origin for the hangings. In a similiar fashion, Scylla has 12 tentacles, and Odysseus tells us in Bk. ix that his ill-fated ships originally numbered twelve, as did the men who followed him into the cave of Polyphemus. Gabriel Germain, *La Mystique des Nombres dans l'Epopée Homérique et sa Préhistoire* (Paris, 1954), pp. 17-18; for a parallel hanging of twelve maidens, with strong indications of its possessing the character of sacrifice, see Aeschylus, *Suppliants*, 465; also Elizabeth Hazelton Haight, *The Symbolism of the House Door in Classical Poetry* (New York, 1950), p. 21.

29 *Odyssey*, xxii. 424; Butcher and Lang, trans., p. 351.

30 J. A. K. Thomson, p. 169.

31 Cf. Pausanias, i. 2. 6; and G. D. Thomson, pp. 98-99, 113, 140-143, 146, 149-150, 154 and *passim*; who regularly confuses the two, despite protestations to the contrary.

32 Ibid., p. 61.

33 Ibid., p. 58.

34 *Odyssey*, xiv. 180-182; trans. Butcher and Lang, p. 214. Lines 174-184 were apparently suspect to Aristarchus, since Eumaeus would have been ignorant of the ambush. These seem like tenuous grounds for rejection, but if they are interpolations, we are entitled to employ the same argument used in fn. 7, to deal with another set of lines similar in their almost programmatic intent. (See A. T. Murray, trans. *The Odyssey* (Cambridge, Mass., 1953), vol. II, p. 46, fns. 1, 2.)

35 *Odyssey*, xxiv. 502 ff.; trans. A. T. Murray, vol. II, pp. 438-441.

36 Although see D. Page, pp. 101-102, 114.

37 Graves, 170. 1; for a similar view of the episodes as repetitions of a single basic ritual pattern, see Levy, fn. 2, p. 268.

38 His sojourn in the land of the Lotus-eaters is first, but since debate over the nature of this cryptically described anecdote is among the most violent and purely conjectural in classical criticism, we decline to comment on it. Graves's view (*The Greek Myths* (Penguin, 1955), 170. 2) is interesting but hardly more than a possibility with the vigorous stamp of Graves's imagination upon it: he thinks that the Lotus is *cordia myxa* confused with the apple-like *rhamnus zizyphus*, and signified the sacred apple which the goddess gives to the hero to insure his passage after the ritual death to the Elysian Fields (just as Eve gives the apple to Adam, and as, Graves thinks, Aphrodite in the nubile aspect of the three-phased Goddess gave the apple to Paris, not, as in the later 'garbled' version of the myth, the other way around.) We need not question that the apple meant a death which Odysseus declines to accept, but the sparse details of Homer's story give us no indication that the Lotus is an apple at all, except that it can be eaten and makes the eater lose interest in going home. For our purpose it is enough to notice that at the outset of this arduous journey the mariners are tempted not to undertake it at all.

39 Graves, 170. 3; the absence of a female figure may possibly find its explanation by analogy with a Melanesian Stone-Age culture in which, as in the Mediterranean area, a patrilinear organization is superimposed on a matrilineally-based system of fertility magic. The men of Papuan Kiwai hold a cave-type ceremony similar in several respects to the incidents in the cave of Polyphemus, at which the bull-roarer is called the Yam-Mother, a carved statuette of a female figure is displayed, and yet women are excluded. Exclusion of and central concern with the female principle may be as meaningful a polarity to the savage as the virginity-fertility association, echoed in cultic practices the world over; or the double meaning of 'sacred' as 'holy' and 'condemned', and for much the same reasons. See Levy, pp. 152-153.

40 Carpenter, Chapts. VI, VII.

41 Germain, *Genèse*, pp. 78-86.

42 Ibid., p. 127.

43 Ibid., p. 126.

44 See D. Page, p. 13; though as usual in the Homeric stories the specific identity of Polyphemus remains obscure, his general type is well represented by close parallels both in ancient times and in present-day Stone Age cultures. No one appears to have noticed his obvious associations

with the *entrance* to the cave; these may, however, be compared to the attributes of other entrance-deities. A Melanesian parallel is the Guardian-Ghost Le-hev-hev, admittedly regarded by the natives as sexless or female, but given power of admission through the cave-entrance to the other world, like Cerberus and possibly Polyphemus conceived as the Devourer of the Uninitiated Dead, and is identified in the New Hebrides with the tusked boar. Polyphemus's single eye is probably, as A. B. Cook has contended, representative of the solar disk; and this is further confirmed by his association with the ram. The Golden Fleece story seems to corroborate this relation, and the authors of the present book have in their possession several Egyptian amulets, one at least identifiable with Ammon-Ra, showing a ram's head with a rayed solar disk between the horns, in a position easy to conceive of as a 'single eye'. Polyphemus is then of the Solar-Earth Spirit type, Guardian of the Entrance, and associated with the chthonic Goddess. Besides its resonant association with the olive of Athena, Odysseus' olive-stake appears to play a role in this episodic distortion of ritual similar to the golden bough of Aeneas, the branch covered with previous stones in the story of Gilgamish's descent, the 'branch of weed' in the Wala Melanesian voyage of the dead man, the branch of the Egyptian and Mesopotamian milk-yielding sycamore or other species, and countless others with which any reader of Frazer will be familiar. The difference in the *Odyssey* is that while Odysseus uses the olive-stake for protection in the time-honored way, he does *not* use it for entrance to the other-world, but for the disruption of the ceremony and re-escape to the living world by the same entrance through which he entered. (For references to Melanesia, see Levy, pp. 154-157.)

[45] For evidence of human sacrifice at bear-cult initiations of Brauron, see G. D. Thomson, p. 278; for evidence by Melanesian parallel that the earliest rites of a type markedly similar to the occurrences in Polyphemus' cave were undifferentiated, the practices for birth, marriage, tribal initiation, and the journey of the dead overlapping 'even in its later developments', see Levy, p. 160.

[46] Germain, *Genèse*, p. 79; see also Levy, pp. 52-53, 154-157, 160.

[47] G. D. Thomson, pp. 45-46.

[48] Germain, *Genèse*, pp. 272-273.

[49] Ibid., pp. 139-140.

[50] See, however, Levy, pp. 102-106.

[51] Germain, *Genèse*, pp. 131-132.

[52] J. A. K. Thomson, pp. 28-29; see also Pausanias, viii, 4. 6.

[53] See further, Charles Seltman, *The Twelve Olympians* (London, 1952), p. 75.

[54] Graves, 26. b; see Pausanias, ii. 3. 4; Herodotus, ii. 145; for the variety of attributions of the paternity of Pan, see Scholion to Theocritus I. 3. With the supplementary material collected by C. Wendel, *Scholia in Theocritum Vetera* (Leipzig: Teubner, 1914), pp. 27-32; for the version that Hermes in the form of a ram begot Pan on Penelope, see Philarg. Verg. *Buc.* II. 32 (Wendel, p. 30); Servius Danielis on Verg. *Aen.* II. 44 (Wendel, p. 32), however, makes the transformation not to a ram, but a goat (*in hircum*).

[55] G. D. Thomson, pp. 172-173.

[56] J. A. K. Thomson, p. 29.

⁵⁷ Charles Seltman, *Women in Antiquity* (London, 1956), p. 99.

⁵⁸ Murray, *Five Stages*, p. 55; see also D. Page, p. 117., for Hermes as Psychopompos.

⁵⁹ Shidura—or Sabitum—in the *Gilgamesh Epic* is repeatedly referred to as 'cup-bearer', though the meaning of the epithet is even more obscure than here. See William Ellery Leonard, *Gilgamesh, Epic of Old Babylonia* (New York, 1934), pp. 46-50., Tablet X.

⁶⁰ *Odyssey*, x. 333-335; the juxtaposition is obviously meaningful.

⁶¹ *Odyssey*, x. 299-300; trans. Rouse, p. 111.

⁶² Jessie L. Weston, *From Ritual to Romance* (Garden City, 1957), p. 75. First pub. 1920.

⁶³ If we assume that Circe's wand represents the lance, then she would be in possession of the two symbols ordinarily juxtaposed; Odysseus' sword would make a hostile third. For evidence that in the Grail legends the sacred objects were sometimes separated, though not in this unfriendly fashion, and borne in procession each by a youngster of the sex they represented, see Weston, p. 76. Not only in Gottfried's redaction of the story of Tristan and Isolt, but as well in a portion of the far earlier Sigurd story in the Poetic Edda (from the *Sigrdrífumál* through the *Brot af Sigurðarkviðu*, pieced out with the equivalent passages in the *Volsunga Saga*), we see the sword used in the same ambiguous representation found in the *Odyssey*: Sigurd takes the shape of his foster-brother Gunnar in order to ride through a circle of magic fire and claim Brynhild as his (Gunnar's) bride; once within the circle, the Sigurd-Gunnar sleeps three nights with Brynhild, but places the naked sword—ambiguously representative of Sigurd's sexual and other powers, as well as of his hostile renunciation of the sexual act—*between* their bodies. They then return to the outside world, Sigurd changes shapes with the real Gunnar, and the latter weds Brynhild. Sigurd does not fare as luckily as Odysseus, however. Brynhild eggs Gunnar on to kill Sigurd, and only afterward tells her husband of the sword between them. She is the humanized Deadly Female here, to be sure; and it is worthy of note that in her former aspect as the valkyrie Sigrdrifa (in the *Sigrdrífumál*) she shares the pedagogic character of Circe and the Sirens, in teaching Sigurd runic wisdom.

⁶⁴ Weston, pp. 22-23, 44-45; for possible Gilgamesh parallel, see Haupt's theory, summarized in Morris Jastrow and Albert T. Clay, *An Old Babylonian Version of the Gilgamesh Epic* (New Haven, 1920), p. 49.

⁶⁵ E. g., see Pausanias, vii. 17. 10-12.

⁶⁶ *Odyssey*, x. 394-395. (trans. Loeb, A. T. Murray).

⁶⁷ See Bronislaw Malinowski, *Magic, Science and Religion* (New York, 1948), p. 107 ff.

⁶⁸ Malinowski's category of *Kukwanebu* seems to show this type in transition from ritual utility; pp. 102-104.

⁶⁹ *Odyssey*, x. 469-470; trans. Butcher and Lang, p. 158.

⁷⁰ Cf. Gilgamesh's repudiation of Ishtar in Tablet VI, Jastrow and Clay, p. 50.

⁷¹ Germain, *Genèse*, p. 357.

⁷² Graves, 27. k; 103. 5-6; 134. 1.

⁷³ J. A. K. Thomson, p. 30.

[74] A habit the beginnings of which appear in Hesiod's syntheses of external resemblances between deities in terms of divine genealogies. One such chain involves Scylla: she was the daughter of Phorcys and Hecate, transformed to the monster seen in Homer by Amphitrite for having an affair with the latter's spouse Poseidon. The attendant beasts of Circe and Hecate's hell-hounds, a common panoply of Eurasian fertility goddesses, are faintly suggested in Scylla's voice, that of a puppy. The relation between these three is otherwise strengthened through Medea: she is spoken of as calling upon Hecate and as being a witch in her own right, and is of course the niece of Circe through her father Aeëtes. The only conclusion from this is pallid enough, and will be readily granted: that these ladies share the chthonic and sexual aspects of the ubiquitous Goddess. (H. J. Rose, *A Handbook of Greek Mythology* (London, 1938), pp. 64, 121-122, 202, also 235-236. First pub. 1928; rev. 1933, 1945, 1953.) Polyphemus is also of the family, being grandson of Phorcys (*Odyssey*, i. 71-73.)

[75] *Odyssey*, xiii. 80-83; trans. A. T. Murray.

[76] See *Odyssey*, x. 526-530; Odysseus is instructed to turn the heads of his sacrificial victims 'toward Erebus,' i.e., toward Persephone's Grove, the Land of the Dead; while he is to turn himself backward, setting his face 'towards the streams of the river,' i.e., toward the Land of the Living, to which he is determined to return. The action is of course highly appropriate and characteristic of him, if our theory is correct. (See fn. 2, above.) Notice too, that Odysseus and his sacrificed sheep are in parallel circumstances: presumably the direction of their heads guarantees the passage of their vital powers to the underworld; the position of Odysseus' ensures that his will not do likewise. The danger to his life is implicit in the nature of the instructions. The legend of Orpheus leading Eurydice up from the underworld has, it will be observed, an element analogous to this.

[77] *Odyssey*, x. 275.

[78] *Odyssey*, xii. 103.

[79] *Odyssey*, v. 63-64.

[80] *Odyssey*, v. 474 ff.

[81] *Odyssey*, vi. 127 ff.

[82] See Elizabeth Hazelton Haight, *The Symbolism of the House Door in Classical Poetry* (New York, 1950), Chaps. I-III, IV and passim.

[83] *Odyssey*, xxii. 2; for another association of threshold and bow, see Haight, p. 24.

[84] Levy, p. 154.

[85] Ibid., p. 160; for parallel Greek associations of the woman with entrances, see Haight, pp. 43 and 54 ff. The sexual symbolism of the gate as receptive female organ, the act of passing through the entrance as both birth and generative impregnation, is too universal and obvious to require explanation; the necessity of a guard at the gates will be likewise clear.

[86] Corresponding to Taghar, Le-hev-hev's daimon-consort; Levy, p. 155.

[87] Levy, fn. 2, p. 155.

[88] Loc. cit.

[89] Ibid., p. 156.

[90] Ibid., pp. 156, 161.

[91] Ibid., p. 157.

[92] *Odyssey*, xii. 259.

[93] C. L. Wrenn, ed. *Beowulf, with the Finnesburg Fragment* (Boston, 1953), vv. 1355-1357.

[94] Ibid., vv. 1357-1361.

[95] Comparable in their juxtaposition with the Goddess' cave to Mt. Mashu, 'the lost ancestral mountain' of the Sumerians, from which the ziggurat-architecture is supposed to have emerged; see Levy, p. 168 ff.

[96] *Odyssey*, xii. 73-76.

[97] *Beowulf*, vv. 1363-1364.

[98] Ibid., vv. 1414-1415.

[99] *Odyssey*, xii. 103. For a similar Greek juxtaposition of sacred grove and underworld entrance, see Haight, pp. 34-35. The association is common in classical literature. The authors remember having seen several others (one in Apuleius) though unable to relocate them. They appear to indicate regularly the sacred precincts of a goddess. For those of Athena, see *Odyssey*, vi. 291 ff.

[100] *Odyssey*, xii. 431.

[101] *Beowulf*, vv. 1373-1376.

[102] *Odyssey*, xii. 242-243.

[103] See p. 66 ff.

[104] As indicated by the Melanesian parallel (see Levy, pp. 120 ff. and passim.), and also represented with admirable clarity in the burial chamber of Tuthmosis III, Thebes, where a sycamore tree is depicted offering the breast to the king; see the Skira edition, Arpag Mekhitarian, *Egyptian Painting* (New York, no date), Eg. 18, p. 38. A honey-dripping tree appears in an ancient Buddhist parable, transmitted through Persian, Arabic, Georgian, and Greek into Latin, as part of the legend of Barlaam and Josaphat. Cf. J. Jacobs, *Barlaam and Josaphat* (London, 1896), pp. lxx-lxxii; *Harvard Theological Review*, XXXII (1939), 131-9. Also Loomis and Willard, *Medieval English Verse and Prose*, p. 379.

[105] Carpenter, p. 137.

[106] *Beowulf*, vv. 1441 ff. and 1557 ff.

[107] See Levy, p. 161; and cf. *Beowulf*, vv. 1570-1572. For the theory that *Beowulf* was directly influenced by the *Aeneid* in these passages, see Charles W. Kennedy, *The Earliest English Poetry* (New York, 1943), pp. 92-97. It is the opinion of the authors that this theory is at the very least tenuous, and at least as doubtful as the alternative notion that what few literary parallels of this kind are demonstrable, are the product of parallel culture and parallel mythic representations.

[108] Cf. Germain, *Genèse*, p. 306 ff., for summaries of the more interesting.

[109] It has been claimed that one such has been made out on the larnax of the Haghia Triada; J. Sundwall, *Acta Acad. Aboensis*, 14, 10, 1943.

[110] Pausanias, viii. 37., mentions a tree answering this description in the sanctuary of the Mistress in Arcadia, the reputed cultic origin of Odysseus and Penelope. The sanctuary contained an altar of Poseidon Hippios, associated with Odysseus also (viii. 14. 4-6.) as well as the altars of other gods.

[111] Pierre-Maxime Schuhl, *Essai sur la formation de la Pensée Grecque* (Paris, 1934), p. 133.

[112] *Odyssey*, vi. 229-231; trans. Butcher and Lang, p. 93.

[113] *Odyssey*, vi. 242-245; trans. loc. cit.

[114] *Odyssey*, vi. 158-159; trans. Butcher and Lang, p. 91.

[115] *Odyssey*, vi. 276 ff.; trans. Butcher and Lang, p. 94.

[116] *Odyssey*, vii. 207 ff.; trans. Butcher and Lang, p. 103.

[117] *Odyssey*, viii. 208; trans. Butcher and Lang.

[118] R. G. Collingwood, *The Idea of Nature* (Oxford, 1945), pp. 13-14.

[119] See also W. Warde Fowler, *The Religious Experience of the Roman People* (London, 1911), pp. 440-441.

[120] H. and H. A. Frankfort, *Before Philosophy* (Penguin, 1949), p. 32.

[121] Loc. cit.

[122] *Odyssey*, i. 5; trans. Butcher and Lang, p. 1.

[123] *Odyssey*, i. 16-19; trans. loc. cit.

[124] *Odyssey*, v. 151-153; trans. Butcher and Lang, p. 75.

[125] *Odyssey*, ix. 16-18; trans. Butcher and Lang, p. 126.

[126] Graves, p. 13; 'mensis' from μην see Nilsson, *Primitive Time-Reckoning*, p. 168.

[127] Or, at least in Greece, the other way around; see Nilsson, pp. 345-6, 353, 366.

[128] Murray, *Five Stages*, p. 30.

[129] See Gabriel Germain, *La Mystique des Nombres dans l'Epopée Homerique et sa Préhistoire* (Paris, 1954), p. 68.

[130] Graves, p. 18.

[131] Gilbert Murray, *The Rise of the Greek Epic*, (Oxford, 1911), fn., p. 156; for the puzzling relation of this period to the *Oktaeteris*, see Nilsson, p. 364; and Raglan, pp. 161-162. This peculiar discrepancy seems to be synthesized in the concrete terms of myth by the Iliadic Homer. See *Iliad*, II. 303 ff., where a portent of eight nestlings and a mother-bird devoured by a serpent, which Zeus turns to stone, is interpreted as the nine years of war and the fall of Troy in the tenth. The separate character of *both* ninth and tenth years, as mother-bird and serpent, are thus imagistically accounted for.

[132] Nilsson, pp. 326, 329.

[133] See Murray, *Rise of the Greek Epic*, fn., p. 156; or Germain, *Nombres*, pp. 27, 69.

[134] *Odyssey*, v. 105-108.

[135] We may term this critical completion of the sacrificial cycle very exactly 'Fate'. The Greek Fates, the Moerae, like the Latin Parcae and the Norse Norns, were female and three in number—that is, the Triple Goddess, corresponding to the three phases of the moon—and were simultaneously regarded as deities of both Time and Fate. In all three cases, too, they were weavers or spinners. Although it is perhaps just coincidence due to Homer's observation of Greek housewives, Circe, Calypso, and Penelope are all found at the loom. What Calypso is weaving is not specified; Circe is weaving 'a great imperishable web, such as is the handiwork of goddesses,' (*Odyssey*, x. 221 ff.) and Penelope weaves a shroud for Laertes which she unravels by night—a suitable Homeric understanding, if it is so, of ancient materials.

[136] J. A. K. Thomson, p. 165.

[137] She also engaged in a contest with Poseidon for control of Attica, which may be an indication of the god's hostility toward her protégé in the epic; for an interesting interpretation of that contest, see G. Thomson, pp. 266-267, and Varr. *ap*. Aug. CD. 18. 9.

[138] Graves, 9. 1; G. Thomson, p. 417.

[139] Germain, *Nombres*, p. 40.

[140] *Odyssey*, xiv. 161-164; trans. Butcher and Lang, p. 214.

[141] See Nilsson, p. 86 and *passim*.

[142] Germain calls attention to an interesting Chinese parallel; when an eclipse had occurred — similarly a Dark of the Moon — a bow was drawn in order to 'reconstituer l'espace ritual et à rétablir l'ordre du monde.' *Genèse*, p. 45; see also our reference above to the festival of Apollo Neomenios, and Gjerstad, p. 191. For the association of the moon with fertility, renewal of life, resurrection, see G. D. Thomson, p. 213.

[143] J. A. K. Thomson, p. 170.

[144] Germain, *Genèse*, p. 39.

[145] Ibid., p. 40.

[146] Ibid., p. 31.

[147] Ibid., p. 52.

[148] Ibid., pp. 40-48.

[149] Graves, 126. 2.

[150] Germain, op. cit., pp. 37-8, 40.

[151] *Odyssey*, xxiii. 152 ff.; trans. Butcher and Lang, p. 359.

[152] *Odyssey*, xxiii. 181 ff.; trans. W. H. D. Rouse, p. 242.

[153] Germain, *Genèse*, p. 215.

[154] Andrew Lang, *Myth, Ritual and Religion* (London, 1906), vol. II, p. 102.

[155] Graves, 17. h.

[156] See Herodotus, VIII. 55.

[157] Graves, 16. 4; Levy, p. 252.

[158] Seltman, *The Twelve Olympians*, p. 59.

[159] Germain, *Genèse*, p. 309.

[160] Levy, p. 120 ff.

[161] A. Moret, *The Nile*, p. 89, fn. 2 (Pyr. texts, para. 1485); quoted in Levy, p. 121.

[162] G. D. Thomson, p. 261.

[163] Jane Ellen Harrison, *Ancient Art and Ritual* (London, 1951), p. 180. First pub. 1913; rev. 1918.

[164] The analogy between the two trees might be regarded, together with the prominence of Athena in the epic and several other details, as substantiation of Cedric Whitman's theory that the *Odyssey* passed the most important period of its development in Athens; see Cedric H. Whitman, *Homer and the Heroic Tradition* (Cambridge, Mass., 1958), Chapts. III-IV.

[165] Hesiod, *Theogony*, vv. 30-31.

[166] *Odyssey*, xxiii. 241-246.

[167] *Purgatorio*, XXXIII. 142-5; trans. Thomas Okey. London, 1952. First pub. 1901.

[168] We might call attention to the possibility that the journey toward an evil object, such as Melville's *Moby Dick* or Browning's 'Childe Roland to the Dark Tower Came,' is at least a thematic descendant of a part of the Grail legends, the story of the Perilous Chapel, (cf. Jessie L. Weston, *From Ritual to Romance*, Chapt. XIII.) or of other literature dealing with a pagan ritual quest which has been Christianized and misunderstood (Miss Weston's thesis has, of course, met with the massive disapproval of most medievalists). Certainly in both of these nineteenth-century works, the

object has damaged and maimed, defeated and imprisoned, and there seems to be an assumption in each that if the evil object can be found and destroyed, the former state of its victims will be restored. In this sense these are works of the first type we have enumerated.

[169] Edmund Spenser, *The Works*, ed. Edwin Greenlaw, *et al.* (Baltimore, 1932), vol. I, 399.

[170] This form of destination in the metaphor of journey is by no means limited to the traditional modes we have outlined; it persists into our own age with undiminished strength. A good example is the excellent French poem *Anabase*, by St.-John Perse. Here we are confronted by the journey of repeated military conquest and nomadic migration or, as T. S. Eliot has put it, 'a series of images ... of destruction and foundation of cities and civilizations of any races or epochs of the ancient East.' (T. S. Eliot, trans. *Anabasis* (New York, 1949), p. 10. No one can fail to be impressed by the vitality of Perse's literary conception, nor to notice that the precise point of the poem is the renewal of spirit implicit in the eternal cycle of destruction and creation and restless moving-on. There is no fixed destination in *Anabase* and this fact points once again to the primitive foundations of the metaphor.

2

[1] For the possibility that Virgil was following legendary traces of actual historical migrations in his geographical arrangement of Aeneas' journey, see Knight, *Cumaean Gates*, pp. 149-159.

[2] Though in its main outlines this is true of the *Aeneid*, we should note that Virgil seems to have intended certain identifications at various points in the poem, e.g., Aeneas-Augustus, Dido-Cleopatra. Yet these identifications are not pressed far, and are usually more in the nature of simple implied comparisons between personages steadily regarded as historical. Dido is not Cleopatra; she is like Cleopatra (or vice versa).

[3] Cyril Bailey, *Religion in Virgil* (Oxford, 1935), p. 275.

[4] Fowler, pp. 68-69.

[5] Ibid., p. 73.

[6] Ibid., p. 74.

[7] Ibid., p. 126.

[8] vv. 512-559.

[9] vv. 567-570.

[10] An interesting parallel to Aeneas' vision of Troy's destruction and his subsequent exile is the great lament of the Anglo-Saxon *Wanderer* in the Exeter MS. This poem, like the *Aeneid*, is polarized to the concern with order and disorder; it depicts the destruction of the former warm and personal organization of an Anglian comitatus, and the painful and defenseless position of the thane who has survived his lord's death. In a cold, empty world of sea-birds and snow, the exile dreams of his lord's hall (vv. 39-48) and his own former place in a tightly-knit society of warriors. With his ejection from this society or its presumed dissolution, his lament naturally turns to the grandly medieval themes of *ubi sunt* and *sic transit*, using as imagery in one passage (vv. 97-98) what is likely to have been the mysterious and misunderstood Roman arches in Britain. The Wanderer's vision is one of chaos, of a world ruined by time and the natural elements, without ties of affection or law; he is an exile without a Rome.

[11] Fowler, p. 266.
[12] Ibid., p. 429.
[13] Ibid., p. 11.
[14] VIII. 349-352.
[15] Fowler, p. 169.
[16] Loc. cit.
[17] Ibid., p. 170.
[18] Ibid., p. 228.
[19] Ibid., p. 225.
[20] Ibid., p. 12.
[21] Bailey, p. 191.
[22] Fowler, p. 438.
[23] Bailey, p. 194.
[24] Fowler, p. 409.
[25] *Aeneid*, IV. 361.
[26] *Aeneid*, IV. 362-364.
[27] *Aeneid*, IV. 445-446.
[28] *Aeneid*, I. 257-296.
[29] Fowler, p. 130.
[30] *Aeneid*, I. 56-57.
[31] *Aeneid*, I. 58-62.
[32] *Aeneid*, I. 293-296.
[33] *Aeneid*, VII. 620-622.
[34] *Aeneid*, VII. 323-340.
[35] *Aeneid*, VII. 317-322.
[36] E. g., *Aeneid*, II. 65-66.
[37] *Aeneid*, II. 255.
[38] *Aeneid*, II. 316.
[39] *Aeneid*, II. 378-382.
[40] *Aeneid*, II. 469-475.
[41] *Aeneid*, VII. 341-355.
[42] *Aeneid*, VII. 450.
[43] *Aeneid*, II. 203-204.
[44] *Aeneid*, II. 311.
[45] *Aeneid*, II. 293-297.
[46] *Aeneid*, II. 681-686.
[47] *Aeneid*, VII. 71-80; for an account of this fire, see J. G. Frazer, *Lectures on the Early History of the Kingship* (London, 1905), Lecture VII, p. 221 and *passim*.
[48] Some of the references occur in the following lines: 2, 23, 54, 66, 68, 101, 300, 364, 384, 472.
[49] *Aeneid*, IV. 70-73.
[50] *Aeneid*, I. 29.
[51] *Aeneid*, I. 36.
[52] *Aeneid*, IV. 566-568.
[53] *Aeneid*, IV. 594-629.
[54] *Aeneid*, VII. 386.
[55] *Aeneid*, VII. 373-405.
[56] *Aeneid*, VII. 377.
[57] *Aeneid*, IV. 68-69.

[58] Fowler, pp. 346-349.

[59] *Aeneid*, VII. 394.

[60] *Aeneid*, VII. 456-466.

[61] See *Aeneid*, XII. 101-102.

[62] See W. Warde Fowler, *The Death of Turnus* (Oxford, 1919), pp. 154-156.

[63] Ibid., p. 3.

[64] *Aeneid*, XII. 895.

[65] Fowler, *Turnus*, p. 153.

[66] This is well embodied in the cheerful and dignified Parentalia of Book V.

[67] *Aeneid*, VI. 756 ff.

[68] *Aeneid*, VI. 847-853.

[69] One of the most interesting of these, also the last in the *Aeneid*, is the scepter of Turnus (XII. 206-211), by which he swears to the treaty which is shortly broken by the Latins. Recalling the semi-living golden bough which Aeneas carried into Hades (VI. 201-211; 635-636), it is a living branch which will never bear leaves because it has been cased ('inclusit') in bronze. Turnus swears that, just as the scepter will never burst into life, the treaty will never be broken. A few lines later, of course, it *is* broken, and the interesting thing is that, as the not wholly sympathetic reader of the *Aeneid* will have suspected all along, the life and vitality contained by the bronze is equated with the violence of war and personal passion tenuously controlled by the treaty. Life is violence, then; the suppression of the one means the suppression of the other. This one aspect—for it is only that—of the *Aeneid*, is adequately resolved just once in the poem, in the image of the golden bough with its dual nature.

[70] Knight, *Cumaean Gates*, pp. 169-170.

[71] Fowler, *Turnus*, pp. 112-114.

[72] Ibid., pp. 154-156.

[73] Maud Bodkin, *Archetypal Patterns in Poetry* (London, 1934), pp. 202-203.

[74] See Part II, Chapter 7, below, on W. B. Yeats.

[75] Bodkin, p. 200.

[76] *Paradiso*, XXXIII. 85-90; trans. P. H. Wicksteed, London, 1958. First pub. 1899.

[77] R. H. Tawney, *Religion and the Rise of Capitalism* (New York, 1958), p. 160. First pub. 1926; Holland Memorial Lectures, 1922.

[78] We may notice how Le Sage's Gil Blas learns to resist the deceitful and affected and selfish society of the court for that of his true friends, and we leave him at the end of the novel in a small society partly of his own making, based upon reciprocal gratitude and generosity. In a book with the interesting title *The Life and Adventures of Bamfylde-Moore-Carew, the Noted Devonshire Stroller and Dog-Stealer. As related by himself* ... (1745), we are treated to the story of a young man who, though of good family, becomes a *pícaro* voluntarily and joins the society of the gypsies, whom he considers his closest friends, and who are outside the pale of society in general: 'We shall therefore ... choose to account for some of the actions of our hero, by desiring the reader to keep in mind the principles of the government of the mendicants, who are, like the Algerines and other states of Barbary, in a perpetual state of hostility with most other people; so that whatsoever strategems or deceits they can over-reach them by, are not only allowed by their laws, but considered as commendable and

praiseworthy ...' (*The Adventures of Bamfylde-Moore-Carew, King of the Mendicants.* London: William Tegg, no date.) There is a continual preoccupation in the novels of this period with the small society-within-society, either as what sociologists used to call the 'sociopathic group' (e.g., the society of rogues, whose interests and collective aspirations run counter to those of society in general), whose ethical code is evident in Defoe's Moll and her comrades in thievery, and satirized by Fielding in the treachery of Jonathan Wild toward his accomplices; or as the small, virtuous group of friends—as in *Gil Blas*—who create their own society because the greater social organization is not ethically adequate, a situation reflected again in Sarah Fielding's *Adventures of David Simple*, the tearful hero of which requires 'so perfect a Union of Minds, that each should consider himself but as a Part of one entire Being; a little Community, as it were of two, to the Happiness of which all the Actions of both should tend with an absolute disregard of any selfish or separate Interest.' (*The Adventures of David Simple* (London: A. Millar, 1744), I, pp. 35-6.) Miss Fielding later tells us that '. . . it is impossible for the most lively Imagination to form an Idea more pleasing than what this little Society enjoyed, in the true Proofs of each other's Love: And, as strong a Picture as this is of real Happiness, it is in the power of every Community to attain it, if every Member of it would perform the Part allotted him by *Nature*, or his *Station in Life*, with a sincere Regard to the Interest and Pleasure of the whole.' (II, p. 319.) From this and other evidences we may conclude that in novels of the kind we are discussing, the preoccupation of the hero with integration into a social order is repeated and reflected in his attitude toward his friends during the course of his wanderings, as well as in his final acquisition of 'fortune' at their conclusion.

79 One of the earliest and best of the genre. Authorship is uncertain, and a fourteenth-century manuscript (Brit. Mus. MS. 10E. IV.) has come to light which illustrates some of the episodes of the later novel in a series of drawings; cf. J. J. Jusserand, *English Wayfaring Life in the Middle Ages*, trans. Lucy Toulmin Smith (London, 1905), Illust. 61. First pub. of trans. 1889; see edition of 1920. Illust. no. 68, and p. 21.

80 For example, in the service of a captain at Barcelona, Guzman works a series of frauds which culminate in the daring plunder of an aged jeweler for one hundred and twenty crowns. The captain is pleased by this neat bit and certainly profits by the proceeds, but is nevertheless capable of cutting off the liason when it might endanger his own interests: 'Although he alone profited by the roguery, he determined to get rid of the rogue. He was afraid that in the end I might implicate him in some of my tricks ...' (Edward Lowdell, trans. *The Amusing Adventures of Guzman of Alfaraque* by Mateo Aleman (London, 1883), p. 196.) Guzman himself is aware of his disinterested loyalty, but understands his dismissal in this way: 'I ought not to have been so very surprized at his procedure. I received the usual reward of the wicked. So long as they are useful, their services are accepted; like as the medicinal qualities of vipers and scorpions are extracted ere the refuse carcasses are thrown away.' (Ibid.) Likewise, the Spanish Ambassador resolves to get rid of Guzman when the story of his ride on the pig becomes well-known, because of the shadow which it rightly casts on his own reputation.

[81] Mateo Aleman, *The Amusing Adventures of Guzman of Alfaraque*, trans. Edward Lowdell (London, 1883), p. 321.
[82] As in the struggle against Alessandro's influence in Bologna.
[83] Ian Watt, *The Rise of the Novel* (London, 1957), p. 185.
[84] Ibid., p. 94.
[85] Jonathan Swift, *Gulliver's Travels into Several Remote Nations of the World; also The Battle of the Books and The Tale of a Tub* (New York, 1937), p. 207.
[86] Henry Fielding, *The History of the Adventures of Joseph Andrews and his friend Mr. Abraham Adams* (New York, 1904), p. 51.
[87] Ibid., p. 134.
[88] Ibid., p. 266.
[89] Ibid., p. 140.

CHAPTER II

1

[1] Henrik Ibsen, *Eleven Plays* (New York, 194*), p. 1104.
[2] Ibid., p. 1161-2.
[3] Ibid., p. 1183.
[4] Stanley Romaine Hopper, *Spiritual Problems in Contemporary Literature* (New York, 1957), p. 159.
[5] Quoted in Auden, p. 54.
[6] Ibid., p. 49.
[7] Ibid., p. 53.
[8] Quoted in ibid., p. 48.
[9] For a different placement of the Scholastic philosophers, a view nonetheless consonant with our treatment of Aquinas in Chapter III, see Ananda K. Coomaraswamy, *The Transformation of Nature in Art* (New York, 1956), p. 11; but for a more complex view of the Indian subject-object reciprocation, see Ernst Cassirer, *Language and Myth*, trans. Susanne K. Langer (New York, 1946), pp. 73-79.
[10] M. I. Finley, *The World of Odysseus* (New York, 1954), p. 143.
[11] Andrew Lang, *Custom and Myth* (London, 1898), p. 136.
[12] Lévy-Bruhl, p. 511; for the earlier meanings of *numen*, see W. Warde Fowler, *The Religious Experience of the Roman People* (London, 1911), pp. 117-119.
[13] Gilbert Murray, *Five Stages of Greek Religion* (London, 1935), pp. 12-13.
[14] R. G. Collingwood, *The Idea of Nature* (Oxford, 1945), p. 34.
[15] Andrew Lang, *Myth, Ritual and Religion* (London, 1906), I, p. 49.
[16] Bruno Snell, *Die Entdeckung des Geistes* (Hamburg, 1948), pp. 18-19.
[17] Ibid., p. 21.
[18] Ibid., p. 18.
[19] Collingwood, p. 44.
[20] James G. Frazer, *The Growth of Plato's Ideal Theory* (London, 1930), p. 1.
[21] Collingwood, p. 43.
[22] H. and H. A. Frankfort, *et al.*, *Before Philosophy* (Penguin, 1949), p. 15.

2

[1] C. S. Lewis, *The Allegory of Love* (Oxford, 1946), pp. 44-48.
[2] Ibid., p. 44.
[3] Loc. cit.
[4] Ibid., p. 45.

⁵ Dante uses these terms in speaking of the figure of Amor in his *Vita Nuova*: 'Amore non è per sè si come sustanzia, ma è uno accidente in sustanzia.' (XXV.)

⁶ Lewis, p. 45.

⁷ It was because the symbolic theophanies of Johannes Scotus Erigena were not sufficiently *limited* as instruments, that his pantheistically-inclined works fell into disrepute and were officially condemned in 1225. For a discussion see Edgar de Bruyne, *Études d'Esthétique Médiévale* (Brugge, 1946), vol. I, 339 ff.

⁸ Lewis, p. 44.

⁹ Consider, for example, our treatment of the episode of Circe; Odysseus triumphs because of a simple rearrangement, nothing more, of ritual actions and objects — Cup, Sword, and Lance.

¹⁰ H. and H. A. Frankfort, *et al.*, *Before Philosophy* (Penguin, 1949), pp. 237-242.

¹¹ James G. Frazer, *The Growth of Plato's Ideal Theory* (London, 1930), p. 1.

¹² Frankfort, p. 254.

¹³ See Frankfort, p. 255.

¹⁴ Pierre-Maxime Schuhl, *Essai sur la Formation de la Pensée Grecque* (Paris, 1934), p. 259.

¹⁵ R. G. Collingwood, *The Idea of Nature* (Oxford, 1945), pp. 51-53; Anaximenes displays a similar tendency in his doctrine of condensation and rarefaction; he is more concerned with arrangement than with substance, more concerned to account for behavior of matter than its underlying nature. See ibid., pp. 39-40.

¹⁶ Quoted in Frankfort, p. 260; this assumption, that one cannot think of something which does not exist, is, of course, the basis of the Platonic doctrine of the real universals; except that Plato has even more clearly reversed the terms: the thought of a general class of particulars, for example, at times appears to create the class.

¹⁷ Schuhl, p. 378.

¹⁸ Frazer, p. 1.

¹⁹ Schuhl, p. 147.

²⁰ Andrew Lang, *Myth, Ritual and Religion* (London, 1906), vol. I, 286 fn.

²¹ Gilbert Murray, *Five Stages of Greek Religion* (London, 1935), p. 75.

²² Schuhl, pp. 146-147.

²³ Ibid., pp. 352-353.

²⁴ Murray, p. 165; this is the period to which Murray applies his well-known phrase, 'The Failure of Nerve', and in a certain sense allegorical interpretation must be regarded as such a failure, a withdrawal from immediate acceptance of both the phenomenal world and the vivid imagism of the old stories.

²⁵ *Conv.* II. i.; *Ep.* xiii.

²⁶ Murray, Appendix, p. 202.

²⁷ Quoted by Murray, p. 168.

²⁸ Ibid., p. 168.

²⁹ Ibid., p. 167.

³⁰ Lewis, p. 56.

³¹ Ibid., pp. 48-56.

³² Murray, pp. 130-134.

³³ See *Aeneid*, I. 292-296.
³⁴ Lewis, pp. 57-58.
³⁵ Ibid., p. 62.
³⁶ Ibid., pp. 84-85.
³⁷ Anton C. Pegis, ed. *Introduction to Saint Thomas Aquinas* (Modern Library, 1948), introd., p. xviii.
³⁸ It is undoubtedly true, as Lewis maintains, that such figures as occur in the *Romance of the Rose* must have seemed very real to poet and audience alike, that they were not 'shadowy abstractions' at all; yet we cannot help feeling that this sense of reality was based upon an error both philosophical and theological, the error of supposing that God is limited in his Creation by the character of mental events, the nature of the human mind. This error would not have found ultimate favor in the Middle Ages, as we shall see in our discussion of Dante, nor, for different reasons, is it acceptable now. We believe, in short, that only in so far as the medieval allegories ventured beyond the preconceptive allegorical method, do they deserve to live as literature; that is, as cognitive instruments in a verbal mode capable of extending the range of man's perception of the truth of his world. We appear in this matter to be in agreement with Edwin Honig, in his interesting recent work on allegory, *Dark Conceit*: 'As a conceptual instrument allegory makes possible a cosmic view of the intrinsic relationships of all objects and beings, each of which, by attribute or action, discloses in respect to itself the typical likeness and unlikeness in every other object and being. Thus as concept allegory serves to define or devise states of separateness and togetherness, oppositions and unities. But in the practical completion of its design, the allegorical work dispenses with the concept of allegory, as something preconceived, in order to achieve the fullest fictional manifestation of life.'
In his work, Honig has thought fit to pass by the traditional distinction between symbolism, or sacramentalism, and allegory, as a distinction more productive of confusion than clarity. His choice to do so is perhaps unfortunate, since he often appears to defend allegory as a mode of creation identical with sacramentalism; and to damn it for the preconceptive, arbitrarily limiting, prescriptive characteristics that we have, in the present work, called allegory. Criticizing this latter and its polar opposite, programmatic realism, he says, 'Just as the concept of allegory, when taken prescriptively, leads to a limited personification allegory, so only the programmatic brand of realism and prescriptive allegory lack a foothold in reality; both deny the representative, confuse the universal with the particular, and neglect the moral qualifications that make experience meaningful.' Edwin Honig, *Dark Conceit: The Making of Allegory* (Cambridge, Mass., 1960), p. 180. We assume that once this difference of terminology is understood, Mr. Honig's and our comprehensions of the problem will be seen to be more or less coincident, except that his critique of the Coleridgean position on allegory *vs.* symbolism presents a highly distorted view of the importance of the Kantian Ego in Coleridge's formulation. Honig's attempt to relate Coleridge's bias with 'the typical inward regard of the later symbolists ... identifying the aim of art with the artist's conscientious expression of personality rather than with the mimetic principle of art as an imitation of nature and life' (p. 47) is very

24*

unfair to the comprehensiveness of Coleridge's conception, unless we intend to visit the sins of the sons upon the fathers. See Walter Jackson Bate, *Prefaces to Criticism* (Garden City, N. Y., 1959), pp. 155-161 and ff.

[39] Lewis, pp. 68-69.

[40] Pegis, p. xvi.

[41] Ibid., p. xvii.

[42] Ibid., pp. xviii-xix.

[43] *Confessions*, VII. 9.

[44] Charles S. Singleton, *Commedia: Elements of Structure* (Cambridge, Mass., 1954), p. 93; with the greatest admiration we attribute much of the substance of what follows to Professor Singleton's essay.

[45] Lewis, p. 48.

[46] Singleton, pp. 68-69.

[47] Ibid., p. 69.

[48] *Il Convivio*, II. i. 2-4.

[49] I. 10.

[50] Para. III.

[51] Singleton, p. 95.

[52] Ibid., pp. 92-93.

[53] Lewis, p. 82.

[54] Para. V.

[55] Para. VII.

[56] The central meaning of the word 'fictivus', which is used among several others in the letter to Can Grande (Para. IX) to describe the 'form of treatment' of his subject; he does not mean 'fictional'.

[57] *Summa*, I. 10.

[58] Para. VII.

[59] For a study of the early borderland between symbolism and allegory in the work of the third-century Hraban Maur, for whom language is dualistic—proper and figured senses—but for whom the figured sense is dependent upon an exploration of the physical realities of the object signified by the proper sense; see Edgar de Bruyne, Vol. I, Livre II, Chapitre V, p. 339. From formulations of this sort behind that of St. Thomas, it seems clear that his interpretation of scripture is not strictly allegorical at all, nor is it strictly symbolic, since in part Thomas, like Dante, looks upon Scripture and its proper sense as an 'allegory written by God' in Lewis's sense of the word. It is God's *expression* of his Meaning which we interpret symbolically only because God can write with things as well as words. Sensible substance is God's allegory but man's symbol, and since in his imitation Dante acts in both capacities, to create and interpret, the meaning of the *Commedia* is neither allegorical nor symbolic, and it is both.

[60] XV. 79-87; J. A. Carlyle and H. Oelsner, trans. *The Inferno* (London, (1954), p. 163. First ed. 1849; first pub. in Temple Classics, with revisions by Oelsner, 1900.

[61] *Confessions*, XIII. 7; quoted in Singleton, p. 7.

[62] Singleton, p. 69.

[63] J. J. Jusserand, *English Wayfaring Life in the Middle Ages*, trans. Lucy Toulmin Smith (London, 1905), p. 383. First pub. of trans. 1889.

[64] Quoted by Jusserand, p. 351. Second edition (1920), pp. 358-9.

[65] *General Prologue*, vv. 791-795.
[66] William Witherle Lawrence, *Chaucer and the Canterbury Tales* (New York, 1950), p. 6.
[67] Ibid., p. 148 fn.
[68] vv. 1-3, Robinson ed.
[69] Robert Dudley French, *A Chaucer Handbook* (New York, 1947), p. 333.
[70] vv. 48-51.
[71] vv. 69-73.
[72] French, pp. 335-336.
[73] Ibid., pp. 336-337.
[74] vv. 77-81.
[75] vv. 725-736.
[76] vv. 107-108.
[77] vv. 1090-1092.
[78] v. 1086.
[79] Lawrence, p. 164.
[80] Ibid., pp. 157-158.
[81] John Bunyan, *The Pilgrim's Progress from this World to That which is to Come* (New York, 1918), p. 1.
[82] Ibid., p. 168.
[83] Roger Sharrock, *John Bunyan* (London, 1954), pp. 17-18.
[84] *Summa*, I. 10.
[85] Henri A. Talon, *John Bunyan: L'Homme et l'Œuvre* (Moulins, 1948), p. 167.
[86] Bunyan, p. 38.
[87] Ibid., p. 39.
[88] Ibid., p. 43.
[89] Clifford Kent Wright, *Bunyan as a Man of Letters* (Oxford, 1916), pp. 6, 10.
[90] Samuel McChord Crothers, introd. to Bunyan, p. v.
[91] Ibid., p. 47.
[92] Ibid., p. 52.
[93] Ibid., p. 46.
[94] Ibid., p. 102.
[95] Ibid., p. 161.
[96] Quoted in Wright, p. 5.
[97] Bunyan, p. 91.
[98] Ibid., p. 92.

## NOTES — PART II

CHAPTER I

[1] See C. N. Coe, *Wordsworth and the Literature of Travel*, 1953.

[2] See *Early Letters*, p. 188, ed. by de Selincourt, 1935.

[3] *The Egotistical Sublime*, p. 14.

[4] The present study of *The Prelude* is based on the 1850 version, but in relevant places the 1805 text is referred to for comparison; both in de Selincourt's edition, 1928.

[5] De Selincourt agrees with Garrod that lines 1-54 were written in September 1795, 'on the way from Bristol to Racedown.' *The Prelude*, ed. E. de Selincourt, 1928, p. 500.

[6] Cf. Havens: 'The passage from 237 to 269 is a subtle analysis of the mood of dejection and morbid introspection which beset Wordsworth not only in the summer 1799 (the period here described) but much of the time from 1793 to 1796 and not infrequently thereafter.' *The Mind of a Poet*, II, p. 297.

[7] Cf. lines 255-60. See Havens, II, p. 330.

[8] Lines 63-68.

[9] Lines 45-50. Cf. also de Selincourt, *op. cit.* p. 514.

[10] Yet Wordsworth does not here identify Nature with God. Cf. 'I ... have lived / With God and Nature communing'. Lines 428-30.

[11] There is, it would seem, a contradiction between his claim here, 1.164, that his eye 'could find no surface where its power might sleep', and the passages where external nature fades from his eyes. Cf. II, lines 349-352, 408-09.

[12] The 1805 version has 'wanderings' l. 111, which suggests more of allegorical and epic pregnancy than the 1850 text: 'roving high and low', l. 110.

[13] De Selincourt has pointed out the connection between lines 150-51 and *Exodus*, xxxiv. 33-5 and 2 *Cor.* iii, 13-16. *Op. cit.*, p. 522.

[14] Lines 164-68. Apart from the usual omission of capital letters in the later version, as in 'Life', etc., the 1805 and 1850 texts are identical here.

[15] Cf. Book First, lines 69-85.

[16] Lines 201-203.

[17] De Selincourt states that in *The Prelude* as first planned by Wordsworth, in five books, the 'culminating episode was to be the consecration of his life to poetry upon the heights above Hawkshead (IV. 320-45). But though this was, perhaps, the great moment of his life, he realized that to stop there would not fulfil his purpose.' *Op. cit.* p. xxvi. Havens takes issue on the 'great moment of his life', *op. cit.* pp. 365-66.

[18] It is significant that even in this part of the poem, dealing with 'Books', the travel metaphor is recurrent, cf. lines 137, 148, 160, 172, 209, 235-241, 431, 587.

[19] For a more extensive comment on this passage and its educational implications, in particular with reference to Wordsworth's own childhood, and his disagreement with Rousseau, see de Selincourt, *op. cit.*, pp. 528-29. A general discussion of the educational ideas of Book Fifth is offered by Havens, *op. cit.* pp. 375-81, and 385-86.

[20] Later printed with *Poems of the Imagination*.

[21] Havens suggests that Wordsworth had two motives for his journey, i.e.

love of nature, and interest in man. Havens finds that the second is not strong. *Op. cit.* p. 419.

²² Cf. Havens, *op. cit.*, p. 420, for a discussion of the differences between the account of the journey given in *The Prelude* and *Descriptive Sketches*, and of relevant critical literature.

²³ Havens suggests that Wordsworth's picture of the valley may be partly inspired by Coleridge's poem, *Hymn before Sun-rise, in the Vale of Chamouni* (especially lines 39-53), written two years earlier. *Op. cit.*, p. 425.

²⁴ W. G. Fraser has noted that the passage breaks the narrative and that the experience recorded must have happened during the composition of the poem and not during the actual journey. See *The Times Literary Supplement*, April 4th, 1929. Havens, to whom we are indebted for this notice, agrees with this view and states that 'It is clear from A 525-6 and from the D and E versions of these lines that we are here dealing with an experience of 1804 and not of 1790.' *Op. cit.* p. 426.

²⁵ For a discussion of this mystical experience cf. de Selincourt, p. 541, and Havens, p. 427.

²⁶ Cf. *The Recluse* fragment, or 'Prospectus' of *The Excursion*, I, i, lines 63-68.

²⁷ Havens suggests that the sub-title 'is misleading since the book treats of the lofty conception of man, not with the love of him.' II, p. 452.

²⁸ De Selincourt, *op. cit.* p. 550; Barrow (1804) pp. 127-133.

²⁹ De Selincourt points out that the 'Domes of Pleasure' recall Coleridge's *Kubla Khan, op. cit.* p. 551. The expression 'standing forth / In no discordant opposition' (91-2) also suggests a Coleridgean influence.

³⁰ *The Egotistical Sublime*, p. 13.

³¹ The chronological progress in the account is not obvious or rapid enough to suggest a decisive change by the time he reached the age of 22. Cf. lines 348-9, 355, 485. De Selincourt accepts Wordsworth's account, and claims that 'the winter 1791-2 witnessed a shifting of his love from Nature to Man.' *Op. cit.* p. 562.

³² The other instances of travel imagery, in lines 477, 479, 563, are unimportant.

³³ Unimportant scattered phrases occur in lines 97-98, 290, 321, 371-2, 402; in the final apostrophe to Coleridge there is a more sustained imaginative excursion to the Mediterranean, 402-470.

³⁴ See *supra*, p. 117.

³⁵ Cf. 'intermeddling subtleties', 155.

³⁶ De Selincourt claims that lines 269-86 are 'A statement of the central point of Wordsworth's creed, that poetry is "emotion recollected in tranquillity", drawing its inspiration and its material from the great moments of the past, especially from the scenes of childhood and early youth, when feeling is strongest.' *Op. cit.* p. 595.

³⁷ Cf. De Selincourt, p. 598, who points out that Wordsworth planned and wrote part of *Guilt and Sorrow* on this walk. Havens draws attention to the Fenwick note to this poem where Wordsworth states that 'My ramble over many parts of Salisbury Plain ... left upon my mind imaginative impressions the force of which I have felt to this day.' Havens, II, pp. 599-600.

³⁸ For Wordsworth's use of 'Darkness' to describe a state of mystical insight or trance see V, 598, and Havens's comment, I, p. 162, II, p. 600.

³⁹ Cf. *Biographia Literaria*, ch. xiv.

[40] *Biographia Literaria*, Ch. xiii. On the points of difference between Coleridge and Wordsworth see de Selincourt, p. 599.

[41] De Selincourt comments on the change from the 1805 version, l. 183: 'the feeling of life endless, the great thought ...' to l. 204 here: 'It denotes a definite renunciation of that trust in the natural human feelings as the guide to truth which was characteristic of the earlier Wordsworth.' *Op. cit.* p. 607.

[42] *Op. cit.* p. lxi.

[43] Cf: 'A Traveller I am' (Book III, 195), 'While I was travelling back among those days' (Book V, 172), 'I too have been a wanderer' (Book VI, 252), the 'wandering on from day to day'; and 'in those wanderings deeply did I feel'; 'a youthful traveller' (Book XIII, 130, 206, 222) and the 'backward wanderings along thorny ways' (XIV, 138).

[44] Cf. MacNeice, *Modern Poetry*, N. Y. 1938, p. 113.

CHAPTER II

[1] *The Road to Xanadu*, p. 125.

[2] *Archetypal Patterns in Poetry*, pp. 26-89.

[3] *Samuel Taylor Coleridge*, p. 166.

[4] *Five Poems*, pp. 70-71.

[5] 'A Poem of Pure Imagination', *Kenyon Review*, VIII, 1946, p. 391 *et seq.* Strong objections to Warren's symbolist approach have been made by E. E. Stoll, *P.M.L.A.*, March 1948; and by E. Olson in *Modern Philology*, 1946-48, pp. 44-45.

[6] *Coleridge*, pp. 89, 101.

[7] *Op. cit.* pp. 132-33.

[8] *Op. cit.* pp. 70-71.

[9] Quite apart from the strictures of E. Olson and E. E. Stoll, there seems to be a general tendency among critics to think that the symbolic scheme set up by Warren is too rigid to accommodate the complexities of the poem, and that if the term symbol is used, it must be allowed 'a freer, wider, less exact reference'. H. House, *op. cit.* p. 108. See also J. B. Beer, *Coleridge the Visionary*, p. 168.

[10] *Poetic Process*, pp. 185-86. Similarly, Maud Bodkin stresses the need in Coleridge 'to find in natural objects an expression of his inner life'. *Op. cit.*, p. 34.

[11] According to Maud Bodkin such symbolism of wind and calm is archetypal. *Op. cit.* p. 35.

[12] *Op. cit.* p. 406.

[13] *Op. cit.* p. 407.

[14] R. Penn Warren, *op. cit.* p. 398; J. B. Beer, *op. cit.* p. 158; House, *op. cit.* pp. 96-98.

[15] *Op. cit.* p. 154.

[16] Warren also stresses the importance of the sudden change from moon to sun after the Mariner's crime: 'The crime, as it were, brings the sun. Ostensibly, the line ["The sun now rose upon the right"] simply describes a change in direction of the ship, but it suddenly and with dramatic violence, supplants moon with sun in association with the unexpected revelation of the crime, and with the fact indicates not only the change of the direction of the ship but the change of the direction of the Mariner's life.

The same device is repeated with the second murder of the Albatross — the acceptance of the crime by the fellow-mariners.' *Op. cit.* p. 408.

[17] *Op. cit.* p. 409.

[18] J. B. Beer traces Coleridge's symbolic use of the sun as an angry God to the speculations of Jacob Boehme: 'Boehme's insistence on the benevolence of God led him to the doctrine that if God at times seemed angry, this was no more than an appearance, engendered by the diseased imagination of fallen man. Cut off from the light of God, he could experience only the heat of his presence: and any exposure to his full glory would therefore be felt as nothing less than exposure to unendurable fire.' *Coleridge the Visionary*, p. 155.

[19] Cf. H. House: 'This is one of the places in which the parallel between the physical voyage and the spiritual experience is most perfectly realised. An experience you don't understand produces first a shock of new glorious delight and then turns out to be something else. It is the worst kind of ethical and spiritual mistake — accepting wrong values.' *Op. cit.* p. 99.

[20] *Op. cit.* p. 54.

[21] *Op. cit.* p. 160.

[22] *Op. cit.* p. 100.

[23] 131-134; 292-300; 397-429.

[24] Though Lowes *op. cit.* p. 189, has traced these flags to the Aurora Borealis in Hearne and Maupertuis, it is doubtful whether this significance is directly available or obvious to the reader in general, nor is it necessary to the actuality and precision of the image.

[25] *Op. cit.* p. 109.

[26] 'It would be difficult to find a better example of Coleridge's lifelong quest for harmonious unity in the universe than this attempt, both in poetry and speculation, to see light and sound as varying manifestations of a single identity.' *Op. cit.*, p. 164.

[27] *Ibid.* p. 161.

[28] *Op. cit.* p. 200.

[29] *Op. cit.* p. 165.

[30] J. B. Beer has pointed out the significance of the 'native country' in neoplatonic thought, and it would seem that Coleridge's vision of the perfectly ordered beauty and clarity of the harbour is influenced by, or related to, such ideas. *Op. cit.* p. 166.

[31] *Op. cit.* p. 285.

[32] Cf. G. Wilson Knight, *The Starlit Dome*, p. 87.

[33] Cf. Lowes, *op. cit.* Ch. xiv; Beer, *op. cit.* p. 145-148.

[34] Beer's claim that he is 'no longer at ease in the old dispensation' — after the 'angelic vision' (lines 354-57) has revealed to him the essential harmony of the universe, is not borne out strongly at any point in the poem. Cf. Beer, pp. 161, 164-65.

[35] Cf. also *Ode to the Departing Year*, st. VII.

CHAPTER III

[1] *Byron et le besoin de la Fatalité*, Paris 1929.

[2] *The Romantic Agony.*

[3] Addition to the Preface, 1813.

[4] Byron crossed Albuera in 1809, where the battle he refers to took place in 1811. The anachronism is resolved in the syntax of the stanza, and its underlying theme is the tragic unpredictability of Fate.

[5] *Byron and the Spoiler's Art*, p. 13.

[6] *Byron. The Years of Fame.* p. 304.

[7] Marchand notes that Byron felt his own downfall to be paralleled in the downfall of Napoleon: 'Now more than ever Byron felt a strong kinship with Napoleon in what he conceived to be the basic springs of his character.' II, p. 612.

[8] According to Medwin's *Journal*, Byron said that Shelley had 'dosed' him with Wordsworth 'even to nausea'. P. 237. Wordsworth's influence has been noted in particular in the contemporary poem *The Prisoner of Chillon*.

[9] *The Concept of Nature in Nineteenth Century English Poetry*, pp. 35-6.

[10] *Ibid.*, p. 34.

[11] *Ibid.*, p. 35.

[12] *Ibid.*, p. 36.

[13] Cf. Byron's solemn 'note' to these stanzas: 'It would be difficult to see Clarens ... without being forcibly struck with its peculiar adaptation to the persons and events with which it has been peopled. But this is not all; the feeling with which all around Clarens, and the opposite rocks of Meillerie, is invested, is of a still higher and more comprehensive order than the mere sympathy with individual passion; it is a sense of the existence of love in its most extended and sublime capacity, and of our own participation of its good and of its glory: it is the great principle of the universe, which is there more condensed, and of which, though knowing ourselves a part, we lose our individuality, and mingle in the beauty of the whole. —' In this statement Byron's kinship with the other romantics is strongly in evidence, and his claim that love is 'the great principle of the universe' shows that he is capable of a certain amount of philosophical detachment.

[14] *Journal*, p. 78.

[15] Robert Escarpit, *Lord Byron*, vol. 2. p. 69.

[16] See Kristian Smidt, *James Joyce and the Cultic Use of Fiction*.

[17] Cf. L. Marchand, III, p. 978. Shelley's letter, *ibid.* p. 977, is also of considerable interest to an understanding of Byron's religious attitude, and the 'delusions of Christianity, which, in spite of his reason, seem perpetually to recur, and to lie in ambush for the hours of sickness and distress.'

[18] John Wain, 'Byron: The Search for Identity', *The London Magazine*, July 1958.

[19] *Don Juan*, by Lord Byron. Ed. by L. A. Marchand 1958.

[20] *Op. cit.* p. 97.

[21] *Op. cit.* p. 21.

CHAPTER IV

[1] *The Well Wrought Urn*, 1947, p. 153.

[2] The 'antiquest' treatment in *The Lotos-Eaters* is, of course, ironical, and in most of the other poems it is stated by implication.

[3] *The Ulysses Theme*, 1954, p. 202.

[4] *The Enchafèd Flood*, 1950, p. 11.

[5] *Op. cit.* p. 202.

[6] Cf. Charles Tennyson, *Alfred Tennyson*, 1949, pp. 64-65.

[7] Sir James Knowles, 'Aspects of Tennyson,' *Nineteenth Century*, XXXIII, p. 182.

[8] Cf. Charles Tennyson: 'In after life he admitted that at the time the *Quarterly* article had almost crushed him.' *Alfred Tennyson*, p. 137.

[9] Cf. *Merlin and the Gleam*: 'The Master whisper'd "Follow The Gleam."' Hallam reviewed Tennyson's *Poems, Chiefly Lyrical* in *Englishman's Magazine*, 1831, ranging Tennyson with Shelley and Keats.

[10] *A Memoir*, I, p. 196.

[11] See also the death-wish in *Tithonus*: 'Release me, and restore me to the ground ...', which was probably written about the same time. Cf. Douglas Bush, *Mythology and the Romantic Tradition in English Poetry* (1957), p. 218, on a similar attitude in *Tiresias*: 'But for me, / I would that I were gather'd to my rest', dated by Tennyson's son to the same time as *Ulysses*.

[12] *A Memoir*, I, p. 124.

[13] On the Romantic conception of the hero as unhappy and neurotic, see W. H. Auden, *op. cit.*, pp. 107, 111.

[14] On the other hand, as Douglas Bush points out: 'The Greek world had no room for a mind and soul questing after the unknown'. *Op. cit.*, p. 209.

[15] Cf. Auden on the Romantic attitude: 'The sea is where the decisive events, the moments of eternal choice, of temptation, fall, and redemption occur. The shore life is always trivial.' *Op. cit.*, p. 14.

[16] *Op. cit.*, p. 203. The same view is taken by Friedrich Brie, 'Tennyson's *Ulysses*.' *Anglia*, LIX (1935) pp. 441-47.

[17] On the other hand, see Tennyson's ironical treatment of the indolence of the Lotos Eaters: 'Is there confusion in the little isle? Let what is broken so remain.'

[18] *Tennyson. An Introduction and Selection*, 1946, p. xix.

[19] Cf. G. R. Stange on *The Hesperides*, *P.M.L.A.*, 1952, p. 732: 'It strikes Tennyson's recurrent note of longing for a vanished or unattainable paradise and explores the persistent theme of the inhuman fascination of isolation and retreat.'

[20] *Op. cit.*, pp. 208-209.

[21] 'Tennyson's *In Memoriam*,' *Selected Prose* (Penguin), p. 181.

[22] There is a similarity in particular in their common scorn of the sensual pursuits of the 'savage race' and 'those dying generations', and in their sense of being neglected.

[23] Also in the unpublished *Youth* (1833), see *A Memoir*, I, pp. 112-15; and in the slighter piece *Sea Dreams*.

[24] Section ciii was written shortly after the Tennysons' removal from Somersby in 1837.

[25] Tennyson's sea is clearly not 'the symbol of primitive potential power ... of living barbarism ...' which Auden finds in the Romantic image. *The Enchafèd Flood*, p. 20.

[26] There is a different use of the sea-image in the ironical contemplation of the voyage in *The Lotos-Eaters*—'barren foam', and *The Voyage*—'waste waters'.

[27] The same symbol, in a different context, is used in *The Voyage*: 'New stars all night above the brim'.

[28] Cf. *The Two Voices, In Memoriam, Tithonus, Tiresias, The Ancient Sage, Faith*.

CHAPTER V

[1] Cf. De Vane, *A Browning Handbook*, p. 229, on the authority of Lillian Whiting, *The Brownings*, p. 261.

[2] Harold Golder, 'Browning's Childe Roland', *P.M.L.A.*, 1924, p. 963 ff.; Lionel Stevenson, 'The Pertinacious Victorian Poets', *University of Toronto Quarterly*, 21, p. 239; R. L. Lowe, 'Browning and Donne', *Notes and Queries*, Nov. 1953, p. 491.

[3] De Vane, 'The Landscape of Browning's *Childe Roland*', *P.M.L.A.*, 1925, p. 426 ff.

[4] See J. M. Cohen, 'The Young Robert Browning', *Cornhill Magazine*, 163: 245; and Betty Miller, *Robert Browning*, Penguin p. 178.

[5] Cf. Harold Golder, *op. cit.*

[6] Cf. W. L. Phelps, *Robert Browning*, pp. 232-7, and De Vane, *A Browning Handbook*, p. 231.

[7] J. M. Cohen, 'The Young Robert Browning', *Cornhill Magazine*, 163:245.

[8] W. Jackson Knight thinks that the ending may represent an initiation pattern, *Cumæan Gates*, p. 180.

CHAPTER VI

[1] Trilling, *Matthew Arnold*, p. 112.

[2] *Revaluation*, pp. 190-91; *The Common Pursuit*, p. 30.

[3] Wilson Knight, 'The Scholar-Gipsy, An Interpretation', *Review of English Studies*, 1955, pp. 53-62. A. E. Dyson, 'The Last Enchantments', *ibid.*, 1957, pp. 257-265.

[4] 'Behind his thought in *The Scholar Gipsy* there was, I fancy, a *Weltanschauung* not dissimilar to that of Comte. He saw the world as an evolving organism which, like a human being, had progressed through childhood and youth to maturity.' Dyson, *op. cit.* p. 259.

[5] Tinker and Lowry have shown that Arnold reduced the 'supernatural element', the mesmerism, which is so predominant in Glanvil. *The Poetry of Matthew Arnold*, p. 207.

[6] *Letters to Clough*, p. 146.

[7] There is a fair amount of agreement among scholars that Arnold's attitude to Nature was one of indecision and ambiguity. See Joseph Warren Beach, *The Concept of Nature in Nineteenth-Century English Poetry*, p. 397; Lionel Trilling, *op. cit.* p. 94; Hoxie Fairchild, *Religious Trends in English Poetry*, vol. iv, p. 486. Arnold's indecision as to the possibility of attributing moral qualities to Nature may best be seen in the sonnets *Quiet Work* and *In Harmony with Nature*; further in *The Youth of Nature* and *The Youth of Man*.

[8] Preface to Keats in Ward's *English Poets*, 1880. Arnold's early dislike of Keats was due to the fact that Keats 'passionately gave himself up to a sensuous genius', so that although he 'left admirable works; far more solid and complete works than those which Byron and Shelley have left', yet Keats's works had 'this defect,—they do not belong to that which is the main current of the literature of modern epochs, they do not apply modern ideas to life; they constitute, therefore, minor currents'. 'Heinrich Heine', *Essays in Criticism, First Series*.

[9] Even if Arnold had not told us that he had Goethe in mind, one divines here the literary prophet whose 'sad lucidity of soul' interprets the pre-

dicament of modern man. For the Goethe reference, see Chilson Leonard, *Modern Language Notes*, xlvi, 1931, p. 119. Other critics have argued that Arnold had Tennyson in mind; cf. Tinker and Lowry, *op. cit.*, pp. 209-211.

## CHAPTER VII

[1] *A Vision*, Macmillan Paperbacks Edition, 1961, pp. 279-280.

[2] 'The Byzantine Poems of W. B. Yeats', *The Review of English Studies*, vol. 22, 1946.

[3] The careful arrangement for the purpose of contrast is due to Yeats's radical revision of the first stanzas in order to bring them into line with the two final ones. See N. Jeffares, *op. cit.* pp. 44-46.

[4] A different view of the aptness of this image is taken by A. Alvarez, *The Shaping Spirit*, p. 33, and by A. Mizener, 'The Romanticism of W. B. Yeats.' *The Southern Review*, 1942, p. 616.

[5] For a thorough discussion of the gyre and perne images see T. R. Henn, *The Lonely Tower*, pp. 182 ff. and 214.

[6] Quoted from Cleanth Brooks, *Modern Poetry and the Tradition*, 1939, p. 191.

[7] Cf. Frank Kermode, *Romantic Image*, pp. 87-88, who attributes some importance to Moore's objection, though he rightly calls it a 'quibble'.

[8] N. Jeffares, *op. cit.*

[9] Cf. Richard Ellmann, *The Identity of Yeats*, p. 260. Since this chapter was written, my attention has been drawn to a similar view of the Golden Bough in Yeats's poem outlined by G. S. Fraser in an article, 'Yeats's Byzantium', *The Critical Quarterly*, 1960.

[10] *Archetypal Patterns in Poetry*, pp. 130, 135.

[11] *Op. cit.*, p. 220.

[12] 'The whole poetic effect, the purgation which will gather him "out of nature" into "the artifice of eternity", is made solely that he may celebrate better the world of love and creation and fecundity he has left behind.' A. Alvarez, *The Shaping Spirit*, p. 34.

[13] Cf. Peter Ure, *Towards a Mythology*.

[14] *The Trembling of the Veil*. 1922, p. 144. Cf. also T. R. Henn's comment: '*Shade*, then appears to be incorporeal spirit, but with certain properties of communication. *Image* would seem to be the shade in a more or less materialized condition.' *Op. cit.* p. 219.

[15] *Mediums and the Desolate Places*, by W. B. Yeats, in Lady Gregory: *Visions and Beliefs*, vol. ii, p. 330.

[16] For various useful comments on 'Hades' bobbin' see Cleanth Brooks, *op. cit.* p. 196; A. N. Jeffares, *op. cit.* p. 50; T. R. Henn, *op. cit.* p. 219, and R. Ellmann, *op. cit.* p. 220.

[17] *Op. cit.* pp. 166, 220.

[18] Cleanth Brooks has an enlightening gloss on the phrase 'flames begotten of flames'; this, he suggests, 'requires reference to Yeats's statement that 'the spirits do not get from it [the vehicle] the material from which their forms are made, but their forms take light from it as one candle takes light from another.' 'Anima Mundi', Brooks, *op. cit.* p. 179.

INDEX